JONATHAN SWIFT

Selected Prose and Poetry

JONATHAN
SWIFT

Selected Prose and Poetry

EDITED WITH INTRODUCTION BY EDWARD ROSENHEIM, JR.

Holt, Rinehart and Winston

NEW YORK · CHICAGO · SAN FRANCISCO
LONDON · TORONTO

Fourth Printing, December, 1964

27578-0119

Introduction copyright © 1959 by Edward Rosenheim, Jr.

Typography by Stefan Salter

Printed in the United States of America

All Rights Reserved

Library of Congress Catalog Card Number: 59-6209

Table of Contents

Introduction

One way of defining the satirist's mission is by saying that it is to make fun of things. The simple phrase suggests why a work of satire can still delight us centuries after the topics to which it is addressed have been forgotten. Swift, the greatest English satirist, makes superb fun, fun which remains almost entirely accessible to the reader of today.

There is, to be sure, much about Swift which must be taken very seriously. The historic figure of the man calls as much for compassion as for admiration. During the first forty years of Swift's life we see him as an undistinguished student, as the dependent of an eminent man who possiby undervalued and certainly overshadowed him, and as an essentially unknown Anglo-Irish clergyman. The last thirty years were spent in the relative isolation of Dublin. Here, though he contrived his own small world of associates and correspondents, the Dean of St. Patrick's, frustrated in spirit and suffering increasingly from ill health, remained hopelessly remote from the livelier world of men and affairs which, despite his protestations to the contrary, probably had the power to delight him almost as much as he delighted it. Only the brief, brilliant period of Swift's activity as the most effective pamphleteer that an English political faction has ever employed brought him truly into that world; and even here his glory fell far short of his power, while the power itself collapsed abruptly, without reward or permanent effect.

Again, we cannot dismiss the hundreds of pages which Swift wrote soberly and literally as a preacher, historian, critic, and political tractarian. They merit careful, respectful study, for, though they show few traces of Swift's humor, they bear the firm stamp of a vigorous and agile intellect. Above all, it is impossible to deny that within Swift's satiric works there are passages which are far more disturbing than they are amusing. They are probably his most memorable passages—Gulliver's shocking discovery of his resemblance to the Yahoos, for example, or the complex, astonishing paragraphs on delusion in the ninth chapter of *A Tale of a Tub*—but they are rare. They represent, indeed, the exceptional moments when the spectacle of human vice and folly appears to penetrate the layers of Swift's cool humor and awaken the "savage indignation" for which, in his epitaph, he asks to be remembered.

Precisely because it is so difficult to set aside what is strange, terrible, and tragic about Swift, there is considerable danger of our neglecting his great comic gift. It is a mistake to think of the laughter which Swift can provoke as inevitably a special, wry kind. A collection like the present one should reveal the extent of his power to amuse, to elicit laughter which is as unaffected and complete as that provided by traditional masters of the comic art. To note this power is not to make a case for Swift as a good-natured, innocently jocular writer by any means; but then one suspects that very little of the greatest comedy rests upon a foundation of benignity.

It is important to recognize in the most satiric of Swift's works the moments when the author is interested in laughter for its own sake. We should not, that is, confuse the purely comic with the satiric, let alone the philosophic. In both *A Tale of a Tub* and *The Battle of the Books* there is much that is clearly satiric—topical, particularized, designed to discredit and ridicule men, institutions, and ideas. At the same time, there is much that is designed for amusement—the reader's and, one often suspects, the author's. *A Tale of a Tub* is written by a fictional author, whose attitudes, posturings, and pronouncements are manifestly not Swift's own but, on the contrary, carefully designed to appear ridiculous. The character of this *persona,* as critics have come to call such a putative author, has bewildered all scholars who have tried to establish for him a consistent sustained personality and to find satiric significance in all that he writes. The problem, however, is not nearly so difficult as it seems, if we read with an awareness of Swift's capacity for caprice, his love of foolery. The *persona* is obviously used for vital satiric purposes—he displays, for example, the most egregious literary vices which Swift wishes to attack—but just as obviously he is at other times a grotesquely contradictory, irresponsible figure of fun. In *The Battle of the Books* we must be equally alert to the purely comic. The controversy over ancient and modern learning was, in its most important aspects, pretty well over by the time the *Battle* was written. Swift, by no means deeply involved in the real intellectual issues at stake, delivers a number of transient thrusts upon some relatively trivial side issues and clearly reveals his adherence to the Ancient cause. The chief appeal of the *Battle,* however, lies not in its rhetorical or satiric force, but in the ingenuity of the basic comic fiction, in the treatment of books and authors as combatants in epic warfare.

To read Swift with an awareness of the many passages whose appeal is almost entirely comic is to heighten one's consciousness of the satiric as well. One senses the point at which the comic art is turned to the uses of ridicule, at which the objects of laughter cease to be mere fictions or general prototypes and become instead historically genuine men, institutions, and ideas. Satire is at all times some sort of attack. It is attack which can be distinguished from ordinary polemic rhetoric by the satirist's weapons, which are obliquity, understatement, allegory, sheer artificial myth—indeed, any device which plainly removes his statements from the class of forthright, literal assertion. Like much comedy, satire is essentially derisive; like all comedy, it involves the creative imagination, for the satirist's office is to reveal the truth by distorting and posing and fabricating. At the same time, we can distinguish the satiric from the purely comic by recognizing the historic particulars which are the object of the satirist's attack.

The moments of satire in Gulliver's trip to Lilliput occur at precisely the points where the agreeable fiction of the Lilliputian court becomes secondary and we are aware that Swift is assaulting the English court. The *persona* of *A Tale of a Tub* becomes a satiric agent whenever he drops the amusing guise of a nameless and preposterous scribbler and assumes the unmistakable identity of Dryden or L'Estrange.

Swift the satirist is not necessarily less playful than Swift the jester, but the satirist's fun is clearly conducted at the expense of real men and ideas, of whose identity we must be aware.

Because we are not always aware of these identities, the satire of the past is difficult to appreciate at times. The particulars of history have a trick of slipping away from us and, though they may be recovered, it is often impossible to recapture the passions which prompted the satirist's assault and which he invited his original audience to share. Indeed, perhaps more than any other kind of serious literary artist, the satirist courts speedy oblivion. Within our own century, certain satiric writings have enjoyed tremendous brief popularity, only to fade forever from the public memory within a few years. Issues evaporate, villains grow old and die or reform, the foibles of one season yield to a new and different crop—and the wit and anger and laughter which they have elicited disappear with them.

Yet great satire survives, and Swift today is read, admired, and generally understood. Some of Swift's lasting popularity is due to the element we have already noted, to the purely comic pleasure which so much of his writing affords. Some of it is due, as well, to those passages of strange, unforgettable insight, to the unique intellectual power, for example, of the fourth book of *Gulliver's Travels*, which, far more than it is satire or comedy, is a philosophic myth, comparable in everything save its tragic vision to the myths which Plato devised. But, though it is vitally important to take into account these nonsatiric qualities of Swift's mind and art, the satiric works live to challenge and delight us.

There are, I think, several reasons why we can feel at home with Swift's satiric writing. In the first place, though the issues which concern him are necessarily particularized and often ephemeral, he has an extraordinary capacity for reviving them, documenting them, placing them before us in a rich, lively fashion which is sufficient unto itself. One needs, for example, to know very little about the Puritanism of the seventeenth century to understand the vigorous anti-Puritan satire of *A*

Tale of a Tub. Swift's hostile caricature may offend the advocates of fair play and historical accuracy, but we are left in no doubt about the grounds on which he found the Puritans offensive or the common charges which, true or false, were leveled against them. *A Modest Proposal* and the *Argument against Abolishing Christianity* may be puzzling documents, but we cannot clarify them by reference to history books; they make abundantly clear what Swift feels to be wrong with the economy of Ireland and the religion of England. We may wonder about the motivation for Swift's attacks on such men as Dryden or Wotton or the Earl of Wharton or Walpole, but our ignorance of the lives of these men is no impediment to our understanding of the satire itself. Swift's topicality, unlike that found in too much of the humor of our own day, is not of the species that merely exploits the allusions which, at the moment, are "good for a laugh." He doubtless could have counted upon an audience willing to chuckle at a mere reference to the allegedly prominent ears of the close-cropped Puritans, but in *A Tale of a Tub* he rises above this sort of thing. The common jest is used, instead, as the point of departure for a complete, extravagant humorous fabrication of his own.

Nevertheless, many passages in Swift acquire new meaning and force by the scholarly recovery of lost information. Recent researches, for example, reveal that several passages in *A Tale of a Tub* can be read as close parody of certain articles which appeared in the *Philosophical Transactions of the Royal Society*. Other recent scholarship makes it clear that, to a degree hitherto unrecognized, the *Tale* satirizes current literary practice by mimicking the style and substance of particular authors. These discoveries supply new particularity, new point to much of the satire in the *Tale,* and it is likely that continued scholarly exploration among possible objects of Swift's satire, in this and other works, will provide additional dimensions to Swift's satiric achievement.

Such inquiries are indispensable to the scholarly reader of Swift, who can be satisfied, professionally at least, only with an understanding of the text which is as nearly exhaustive as possible. But other readers—and they have always been the huge majority—who chiefly seek the pleasure and fascination which Swift affords can proceed with a minimal dependence upon information which lies beyond the works themselves. True, Swift has been misread, both by scholars and by common readers. His trick of assuming false positions, for example, has misled more than one critic into assuming that the *Argument against Abolishing Christianity* is actually an expediential plea that mere nominal religion be preserved. Errors of this sort, however, are not set straight by historical demonstration but by thoughtful scrutiny of the text itself. If almost any of Swift's satire is read attentively, there is little reason to wonder about the grounds or the direction of the satiric attack. And for the careful reader, Swift himself generally provides all the necessary "background." His own pages convey the tension and acrimony between the Church of England and the dissenting Puritan sects, the fear and anger which, for all his derision, a clergyman like Swift felt toward religious skepticism, the issues debated between Whig and Tory, and the whole kaleidoscope of vogue, habit, gossip, and opinion which go to make up the so-called "social milieu."

In this connection, it must be remembered that, like most other satirists, Swift was, in the most important sense of the term, a very worldly writer. As a satirist and pamphleteer, he saw clearly that his mission was to be read, understood, and respected by as hardheaded, sophisticated an audience as any author has ever appealed to. His contempt for his enemies and for many of the prevailing values of the day made itself felt because it was based on a shrewd and thorough knowledge of what he was attacking. No social reformer has ever been more willing to fight fire with fire, to combat complacency with violent shock treatment, to subordinate affirmative advocacy of the good to unabashed hatred of the bad. To argue effectively before the polite world in the reign of Queen Anne, a writer had to establish himself as the peer of his audience in sophistication. Neither this audience nor Swift himself seems to have been interested in his writing as "great literature" but rather as the stimulating, diverting, or infuriating observations of a man who wrote about the topics and issues of the moment.

It does not seem too farfetched to suggest that much of Swift's writing had for its original readers the kind of appeal which American readers of today find in magazines like the *New Yorker*. The worldly audience of the early eighteenth century expected urbanity and, where relevant, evidences of learning and of original reflection. At the same time, this audience could be most pleased by what was lively, intelligible, and directed, however critically, to the passions and preoccupations of the day. The issues which most concerned Swift and his readers resemble those which most concern the informed, inquiring people of our own time: foreign and domestic politics, the state of public conduct and morality, social justice, literary criticism, praise or blame of public figures. And even if we find something archaic in the precise terms of the religious controversy of Swift's period, we must certainly admit the survival into our own time of the basic problem of individual liberty which, then as now, lay at the heart of most discussions of toleration, loyalty, and conformity.

Swift's treatment of these questions is appropriately vigorous and concrete. He shuns abstractions, speculation, equivocation, dispassionate neutrality. He is generally ready to provide robust particulars, to name names, cite concrete examples, exploit true or fictional anecdote for his purposes. His ultimate effect is often vexation or astonishment, but he approaches his readers, in most instances, with the air of a candid, practical, informed observer of the contemporary scene.

It is a mistake to regard Swift's satire as the eccentric expression of a recluse—just as it is wrong to urge, as some have done, that his sentiments should be viewed as typical of his period. Strange, unpredictable, and solitary, he wrote nonetheless to be read, to move, and to convince. The satirist rarely strives for literary immortality; he carries out his attack in the arena of contemporary opinion. Swift's satire was addressed to an informed, influential, thoroughly human audience of readers, and we are not so different from that audience that we cannot join it.

Beyond the worldliness of the historical moment, however, the great satirists possess a special kind of knowledge, a higher worldliness which throws into proper perspective the fugitive concerns which dominate the ordinary mind. Here quite probably is our greatest source of sympathy with Swift the satirist. His is the kind of wisdom which penetrates and destroys whatever is banal, parochial, or half true. It can distinguish the permanent and important from the fleeting and trivial. It reflects a chronic incapacity to put up with foolishness. It is the wisdom which, in many places and ages, drives the satirist to explode superstition, expose unreason, and laugh out of countenance the bore and the charlatan and the autocrat.

Many people are honestly repelled by Swift's writing. They are dismayed by his coarseness. They lament the absence from his works of warmth and graciousness and the conventional qualities of lyricism. They are shocked at what they purport to find in his fundamental views about the human condition. But it is hard to see how even such detractors can fail to sympathize with Swift in his most important aversions. There is nothing trifling in his attacks on literary contemporaries; what emerges is an unqualified hatred of pretentiousness, servility, and mediocrity. He is inordinately sensitive to jargon; with the fierce glee of a twentieth-century sophisticate reporting on a Boosters' Club luncheon, he reproduces and derides the banalities of contemporary speech. From our own perspective he may fail to distinguish properly between pedantry and genuine learning, between irrational "projecting" and important scientific inquiry, but what he assails in scholars and scientists is invariably what strikes him as the folly of their labors and the arrogance of their claims. Austere as his religious views may seem, he is neither a witch-hunter nor a quibbler over doctrine. In Puritanism he finds hysteria, hypocrisy, and ugliness; in deism, malice and unreason. As a political writer he reveals, even in his most violently partisan moments, a sense of honest outrage at whatever is inept, inconsistent, or unprincipled.

Swift has never appealed to the softhearted or softheaded; neither for that matter has Rabelais or Voltaire or either of the Samuel Butlers or Bernard Shaw. The perennial "fool among knaves" does indeed cherish the happiness of being well deceived; to point out knavery to him only destroys his peace of mind. Nor, on the other hand, are the zealous, single-minded moralists often pleased by great satire. The satirist is no more moral than the next man; he is only more perceptive. He is not anxious to do battle with the Father of Evil but contents himself with the demidevils—with vanity, deviousness, obtuseness, and complacency. His temporal victims are the stuffed shirt, the charlatan, the fool, the fop, and all their dull, unlovely brethren. Such enemies are not fought with mirthless dogmatism but with imagination and wit. Perhaps this is why, for all of his wisdom and worldly insight, Swift appeals to us most with his sheer literary artistry.

It would be possible to dwell at length on many aspects of his artistry. In this brief introduction only two points will be made. The first has to do with Swift's imagination. We have already argued that the satirist's art involves, in some measure, the creation of fiction, that the satirist is obliged, by the nature of his task, to depart in some way from direct, literal exposition. The fiction can take simple and familiar forms: simple sarcasm is one of these, and so too is the use of the *faux ingénu*. But Swift is never content with conventional, well-worn devices. If he sarcastically adopts a position diametrically opposed to his own, if he produces a pat analogy, if he understates or exaggerates, he will use such devices only so long as they remain maximally lively and effective. His allegories, as we have suggested, become original, vigorous comic fictions. We cannot be lulled into false security by assuming that his true meaning can be found for any length of time merely by inverting his professed views. When he adopts a false character, it is complex, challenging, and usually a unique, independent fabrication. What is, after all, the most striking thing about

A Modest Proposal is not its "irony," however we define this shopworn term, but the *notion* of the cannibalistic salvation of Ireland—the notion which is a product of pure artistic inventiveness. If the allegory of the three brothers in *A Tale of a Tub* is not original with Swift, the details of the story, with their astonishing amalgam of aptness and droll fun, are the important ingredient, and again products of rare literary imagination. Swift's playfulness, that quality which struck us initially, is far more than caprice or unconventionality. It is the reflection of extraordinary talent and zest for the arts of storytelling, play acting, and illusion—the great literary arts of the imagination.

Secondly, and inevitably, something must be said about Swift's style of writing. There are those who hold that it is the single most important source of his timeless appeal and who agree with the noted English scholar, John Hayward, that "even now his style can knit together the dry bones of forgotten controversies and make them seem to live again." We have sought to show that far more than style survives to bridge the gap between Swift's concerns and our own, yet his brilliance gleams nowhere more brightly than in his mastery of prose technique. And to call it "mastery" is to do more than praise Swift with a hollow formula; never in the widely diversified literary tasks he undertakes do we sense the slightest wavering in the sureness and agility with which he controls his medium.

The perennial difficulty of isolating manner from matter, of assessing style without respect to substance, is particularly acute when we attempt to explain Swift. His style alone is curiously difficult to characterize in a satisfactory way. One obvious quality is, to be sure, its clarity. All of Swift's strictures against the language of his day reveal that he regards pretentiousness, jargon, superfluity—whatever, in short, detracts from maximum intelligibility with a minimum of language— as the enemy of sound expression. His attitude is put succinctly in his *Letter to a Young Gentleman Lately Entered into Holy Orders:*

When a Man's Thoughts are clear, the properest Words will generally offer themselves first; and his own Judgment will direct him
in what Order to place them, so that they may be best understood.
Where Men err against this Method, it is usually on Purpose, and to
shew their Learning, their Oratory, their Politeness, or their Knowledge of the World. In short, that Simplicity, without which no
human Performance can arrive to any great Perfection, is nowhere
more eminently useful than in this.

Yet in considering Swift's prose, we should not oversimplify
this very notion of simplicity. Within a single text, Swift can
be rigorously spare and incisive, playfully discursive, disarm-
ingly meek, shockingly coarse. He can endow a common term
like "happiness" with meanings so special and so crucial that
the entire text of a work the size of *A Tale of a Tub* receives
from the word a whole new dimension of meaning. His assumption of disguises depends basically upon his gift as a
parodist, upon the power of his words to ape and distort the
words of his victims. The whole dazzling diversity of moods
and attitudes and topics which emerges from his writing
makes itself felt by the language which he can produce to
meet the demands of the task.

The truth of the matter is that Swift's style is always the
faithful, infinitely flexible servant of his substance, of the
brilliant, unpredictable operation of his intellect. His language
is not designed to be fatuously rolled upon the tongue; its
rhythms are unobtrusive; its images are called into being by
the harsh demands of satiric utility. The teacher of composition who urges upon his pupils the examples of Addison or
Johnson would be ill-advised to do the same for Swift. One
cannot write like Swift unless one thinks like Swift. The searching, supple strength of his prose and of his mind are identical
—and inimitable.

The selection of Swift's works offered in this volume is
intended primarily for the reader or student whose acquaintance with Swift has hitherto been chiefly limited to *Gulliver's*

Travels. The works chosen are, in general, among those writings of Swift which are best known—if only by name.

As suggested by some of the foregoing remarks, it is the present editor's conviction that Swift's satiric writing presents the most important aspect of his genius, and it therefore follows that even a relatively modest compilation of his work should be heavily weighted in the direction of satire. Moreover, the problems of satire as a species of literature are at last receiving serious attention, not only from critics but in many college and even high school classrooms. The editor would be gratified to learn that these selections from the work of our language's greatest satirist are being used in courses concerned with the generic questions raised by all satiric writing as well as those directly devoted to Swift or his period.

At the same time, the diversity of Swift's art and the fascination of his career are such that even the most superficial introductory collection would be inadequate if it failed to include documents other than those which are essentially satiric. Accordingly, the present volume contains two or three nonsatiric essays, some of Swift's best-known poems, and selections both from *The Journal to Stella* and Swift's *Correspondence,* which have been chosen for their biographical significance as well as for their intrinsic intellectual interest.

Quite properly, *A Tale of a Tub* occupies the initial and focal position in this collection. Scholars have long recognized both its importance and its charm, but public opinion has tended to subordinate it to *Gulliver's Travels*—a view which several editors have done much to confirm by placing the *Tale,* when they include it at all, in a secondary position behind the *Travels.* Unlike the *Travels,* the *Tale* has little to offer the completely idle reader, but moderately thoughtful study should reveal why such men as Dr. Johnson and, in fact, Swift himself place it at the very pinnacle of the author's achievement. In its first edition, in 1704, the *Tale* was accompanied by *The Battle of the Books* and the *Discourse concerning the Mechanical Operation of the Spirit,* and, more often than not, they have continued to be reprinted as its neighbors up to the present day. While the issues and attitudes they reflect are also to be found in the *Tale,* there is no discernible structural relation between the three works, and each can be read as an independent literary production.

In the selection and arrangement of additional works, chronological order has been sacrificed in order to emphasize the diversity of Swift's satiric achievements and to contrast these, in turn, with his writing in modes other than satire. The immense spectrum of seriousness and intensity within which the satirist works is suggested, at one extreme, by *The Partridge-Bickerstaff* papers and, at the other, by the *Modest Proposal* and the *Argument against Abolishing Christianity.* The first of these is a sheer hoax, frivolous in tone and intent, but it is worth noting that these ludicrous papers did in fact succeed in discountenancing and infuriating the humbug Partridge. The *Modest Proposal* and the *Argument,* on the other hand, obviously spring from profound religious and social convictions, yet in both, satiric invention is the vehicle for preaching reform.

The *Drapier's Letters* should have some representation in any collection of Swift's work, if for no other reason than that, despite easy generalizations about the power of rhetoric, here is one of the very rare works which have demonstrably accomplished dramatic political effects. Though the *Drapier's Letters* display Swift's style at its vigorous best and though, notably in the fourth letter, they contain strongly satiric passages, their power is not primarily that of satire but of direct, compelling exhortation. Only the fourth letter is included here, but it is generally regarded as the most brilliant of the documents which Swift produced in his campaign against Wood's patent. *A Meditation upon a Broomstick,* in marked contrast, is an instance—alas, a rare one—of Swift's playfulness given free rein, unchecked by the need to make satiric points.

Swift's stature as a poet is a matter of debate. For many years his poems suffered the neglect of critics and the shabby mishandling of editors. In our own day they command a renewed interest, owing chiefly, perhaps, to the superb edition of Sir

Harold Williams, but reflecting as well a climate of opinion in which it is at last respectable to confer the name poet on both Swift and Swinburne. Whether even the best of Swift's verses can provide the singular delight and excitement of his prose is a question best left to the individual reader. It is obvious, however, that the poems contain some of the most striking technical and intellectual characteristics of the prose. The casual or occasional circumstances under which much of the poetry was written invited the full exercise of Swift's playful inclinations. These emerge not only in jocular posturings and narrative, in uninhibited derision and coarseness, but in whimsical manipulations of language itself. As in the prose, his poetic technique adjusts happily to the whole wide range of his moods and ideas. Within a single poem, the *Verses on the Death of Dr. Swift,* he shifts freely from jaunty witticisms to lines which are strangely moving in their wistful sincerity. Triteness, cant, and artificiality are discredited by both the substance of the poems and the cool, unaffected simplicity of the language. And for those whose chief concern is Swift's state of mind, there are recurrent manifestations in the poetry of his hatred of man's complacent self-deception, of vanity, pretension, lust, and self-seeking. The selection of poems offered in this volume is somewhat larger than is customary in editions of this sort, yet it represents only a very small part of the hundreds of verses Swift wrote. An attempt, however, has been made to suggest the rich diversity which is itself not the least striking feature of Swift's achievement as a poet.

The selections from *The Journal to Stella* have been made with traditional editorial misgivings. The reproduction of fragments is always an uneasy task, and it is almost impossible to establish firm principles of selection in excerpting from the *Journal.* The specimens chosen here will, it is hoped, convey some of the intimate, informal, yet extraordinarily eloquent, flavor of the *Journal* and, at the same time, yield insights into a few of the moments of Swift's proximity to the central current of English politics. In an analogous manner, the samples from Swift's *Correspondence* have been chosen to reveal characteristics of his epistolary style and to present, in context, some of his most important statements.

Inevitably, various omissions from this collection will be noted and deplored; the editor can only profess in return his own unhappiness at the need for excluding several much-loved works. Considerations of space and an editorial distaste for fragments have prompted the omission of the lengthy but delightful *Directions to Servants.* The omission of the *Memoirs of Martinus Scriblerus,* again too lengthy for inclusion in its entirety, can be further justified on the grounds that it is the work of several authors beside Swift and, unlike the majority of Swift's writings, demands from the reader considerable acquaintance with the works which it attacks satirically. Swift's sermons are not represented, nor are the rhetorically colored historical tracts, of which the best specimen is the *History of the Four Last Years of the Queen.* The variety and profusion of Swift's works, which a single volume can only suggest, are themselves another great reason for his towering literary stature. For of the insights and problems and pleasures to be found in reading Swift there is virtually no end. This selection is offered as a beginning.

Edward Rosenheim, Jr.

Chicago, Illinois
September, 1958

Chronology

Jonathan Swift born in Dublin, son of Abigaile Erick Swift and, posthumously, of Jonathan Swift, November 30, 1667.

Attended Kilkenny Grammar School from about 1673 to 1681.

Entered Trinity College, Dublin, April, 1682; completed undistinguished student career by being unflatteringly awarded his degree, *speciali gratia,* February, 1686.

Following residence with his mother at Leicester, entered the household of Sir William Temple, June, 1689. Here he probably first met Esther Johnson ("Stella") whom he tutored during his service as secretary to Temple.

Returned from England to Ireland, May, 1690.

Rejoined Temple household at Moor Park and remained there from August, 1691, to May, 1694; during this period received M.A. degree at Oxford, July, 1692; first appeared in print with *Ode to the Athenian Society,* published early in 1692.

In Ireland, May, 1694, to May, 1696. Ordained in the Anglican Church, October, 1694.

Returned to Sir William Temple at Moor Park, May, 1696. While in Temple's service between 1696 and 1699 probably composed major portion of *A Tale of a Tub.*

Following death of Temple, returned to Ireland as chaplain to Lord Berkeley, 1699.

Summer of 1699 to April, 1701, remained in Ireland; presented with livings, chief of which was Laracor, February, 1700; D.D. of Dublin, February, 1701.

Continued pursuit of Irish clerical career, 1701 to 1707. Early in this period, Swift was joined in Ireland by Stella and her older companion, Rebecca Dingley, who thereafter made Ireland their permanent residence. Swift resided in England during the summers of 1701 and 1702 and through the winter of 1703-1704.

A Tale of a Tub and companion pieces published, May, 1704.

Protracted stay in England, November, 1707, to June, 1709, as emissary of the Irish clergy, seeking remission of "first fruits," essentially a tax on Irish clerical incomes. Period of *The Partridge-Bickerstaff* papers (1708) and of the composition of important religious tracts, including *Argument against Abolishing Christianity*, most of which were not published until a somewhat later date.

Returned to parish at Laracor, remaining there from June, 1709 to September, 1710.

Returned to London, September, 1710, nominally to renew mission of "first fruits," actually to begin, whether consciously or not, four-year period of greatest political activity.

The Journal to Stella begun on September 2, 1710, and continued to June 6, 1713.

Renounced former Whig sympathies, committing himself to Tories in 1710 and contributing to the Tory *Examiner* from November, 1710, to June, 1711.

Publication of *Miscellanies in Prose and Verse,* February, 1711.

Political writings, including *The Conduct of the Allies,* published in 1711, contributed to Tory victory in December of that year.

Made Dean of St. Patrick's Cathedral, Dublin, June 13, 1713; following absence over the summer, returned to London in September, 1713.

Joined with Tory politicians and wits in formation of the Scriblerus Club, February, 1714.

Retired to Letcombe, Berkshire, June, 1714; following fall of Tory ministry and death of Queen Anne, returned to Ireland to take up permanent residence in Dublin, September, 1714.

Began writing *Gulliver's Travels,* probably in 1720.

First four *Drapier's Letters,* August to December, 1724.

Visit to England, including stay with Alexander Pope, March to August, 1726.

Publication of *Gulliver's Travels,* October 28, 1726.

Final trip to England, April to October, 1727.

Pope-Swift *Miscellanies,* Vols. I and II, published June, 1727.

Death of Stella, January 28, 1728.

Third (self-styled "last") volume of Pope-Swift *Miscellanies* published, March, 1728.

A Modest Proposal published October, 1729.

Verses on the Death of Doctor Swift composed in winter of 1731-
1732 (not published until 1739).

Fourth (self-styled "third") volume of *Miscellanies* published, October, 1732.

First collected edition of Swift's *Works* published in Dublin by
George Faulkner, 4 vols., 1735.

Fifth and last volume of *Miscellanies* published in 1736.

Perceptible decline in Swift's physical health and mental powers
began about 1738 or 1739; Guardians in Chancery appointed to
care for his affairs, March, 1742.

Swift died in the Deanery of St. Patricks, October 19, 1745.

Textual Comment

Largely within our own century, the labors of several brilliant editors have provided extremely authoritative texts for virtually all of Swift's most important works. In the present volume an attempt is made to reproduce, in each instance, a text which scholars most generally regard as the closest representation of Swift's final intention. The practices of the several editors thus relied upon vary somewhat with respect to such details as the regularization or modernization of punctuation or the preservation of typographical characteristics (such as italics) from early editions. It has seemed wisest to sacrifice complete uniformity within this volume with respect to these matters and to strive instead to adhere to the texts which have been produced by editors of great distinction.

The outstanding edition of *A Tale of a Tub, The Battle of the Books,* and the *Mechanical Operation of the Spirit* is that of A. C. Guthkelch and D. Nichol Smith (Oxford, 1920). Their text is that of the fifth edition of the *Tale* (1710), which, in addition to including the Apology and many playful notes for the first time, shows evidence of some textual alterations by Swift himself. As in the Guthkelch–Nichol Smith edition, the present volume indicates, by brackets within the text, variant readings from earlier editions which seem clearly to have been omitted or altered in the fifth edition through inadvertence. The notes in the present edition are those which appear in Swift's fifth edition (1710). These include Swift's original notes to the text (inserted marginally in the fifth edition but here placed above the rule) as well as the notes which, largely in facetious response to Wotton and other critics, Swift added to the fifth edition (here placed below the rule).

Most of the volumes of *The Prose Works of Jonathan Swift* (Oxford, 1939———), of which Herbert Davis is the general editor, are now in print and supersede the Temple Scott edition of the *Prose Works* (London, 1897-1908) as the standard, scholarly edition. Except where acknowledgment to other editions is made, the text employed for prose selections in this volume is that provided by the Davis edition. It is worth noting that Professor Davis's text of the *Drapier's Letters,* in addition to appearing in a uniform volume of the *Prose Works,* is available in a separate edition (Oxford, 1935) with extended and valuable comment and annotation.

Sir Harold Williams's remarkable contributions to Swift scholarship include his admirable editions of the *Poems* (3 vols., Oxford, 1937) and *The Journal to Stella* (2 vols., Oxford, 1948). They have been drawn upon exclusively for the selections from these two bodies of Swift's writing which appear in the present volume. *The Correspondence of Jonathan Swift,* edited by F. Elrington Ball (6 vols., London, 1910-1914), is the standard edition, at this time, of Swift's letters, but is augmented by *The Letters of Jonathan Swift to Charles Ford,* edited by D. Nichol Smith (Oxford, 1935); between them, these volumes provide the texts of all letters herein reproduced.

In a few relatively trifling instances, errors in modern editions have been checked against reliable sources and silently corrected.

Bibliographical Comment

Swift's life and work have, from his day to our own, been the object of abundant scholarly and critical attention. The student who proposes to explore the immense body of secondary materials surrounding Swift will be well advised to acquaint himself with appropriate bibliographical aids. Of these, the listing in *The Cambridge Bibliography of English Literature,* II, 593-596, is, while selective and not entirely current, extremely useful for general purposes. The standard bibliography is H. Teerink, *A Bibliography of the Writings in Prose and Verse of Jonathan Swift, D.D.* (The Hague, 1937). Despite grave omissions and inaccuracies, Teerink provides the only attempt until now at a thorough listing of works by and about Swift. An older but relatively reliable listing of early editions of Swift's works is the bibliography by W. Spencer Jackson which appears in Volume XII of Temple Scott's edition of the *Prose Works* (London, 1908). Louis A. Landa and James E. Tobin, in *Jonathan Swift: A List of Critical Studies Published from 1895 to 1945* (New York, 1945), provide a comprehensive compilation of Swift scholarship for a recent fifty-year period. Those wishing to keep abreast of current scholarship directed to Swift and his entire period will find it important to consult "English Literature, 1660-1800: A Current Bibliography," which appears annually in the July issue of *Philological Quarterly.*

No single biography of Swift looms above the others as definitive or indispensable. Swift's own writing is unusually illuminating, for not only do the *Correspondence* and *The Journal to Stella* provide singularly intimate insights into Swift's career and personality, but the three volumes of the *Poems,* as edited by Williams, reflect in a surprisingly sustained fashion the author's public and personal preoccupations over the years.

The enigmatic and controversial aspects of Swift's life impressed themselves abundantly on his earliest biographers. The first of these, John Boyle, Earl of Cork and Orrery, produced the *Remarks on the Life and Writings of Jonathan Swift* (Dublin, 1752), which is still a valuable, if highly colored, record of the impressions of a man who knew Swift personally. As if to set the tone of controversy which has ever since quite regularly characterized the interpretations of Swift's personality, Orrery's assertions were vigorously criticized by Swift's friend Patrick Delaney in his *Observations upon Lord Orrery's Remarks* (London, 1754). Swift's own nephew, somewhat confusingly named Deane Swift, was the author of *An Essay upon the Life, Writings, and Character of Dr. Jonathan Swift* (London, 1755), likewise of value chiefly because of its author's relation to his subject, although notable as well as the first attempt to provide a biography in traditional form. Dr. Johnson, of course, includes Swift in his *Lives of the English Poets,* although, as is often true of Johnson's treatment of the more illustrious writers, the essay is of far more importance from the standpoint of criticism than as a source of biographical information.

The best of Swift's nineteenth-century biographers can still be relied upon for well-ordered, substantially accurate accounts of his life. They include Sir Walter Scott, who provided a life of Swift in his edition of the *Works* (London, 1814); John Forster, only one volume of whose *Life of Jonathan Swift* ever appeared (London, 1875), but whose account of its subject's career up to 1711 is unusually intelligent; Sir Henry Craik, who, in his *Life of Jonathan Swift* (London, 1882) has supplied perhaps the closest approach to an acceptable "standard" biography; Leslie Stephen, whose *Swift* in the "English Men of Letters" series (London, 1882) remains a very useful brief biography; and John Churton Collins who, in *Jonathan Swift: A Biographical and Critical Study* (London, 1893), attempts, in an interesting way, an assessment of Swift's achievements.

Within our own century, Swift's life has attracted not only scholarly specialists but playwrights, novelists, and writers of

popular biography. The bibliographical aids already mentioned
will reveal the rich assortment of these works, together with
studies directed to more specialized biographical problems,
including psychoanalytic investigations, detailed examinations
of Swift's alleged marriage, and considerations of his clerical
career. The reader is urged, as well, to consult these sources
for listings of articles in periodicals covering all aspects of
Swift scholarship. These have appeared in such profusion and
are addressed to such a variety of problems that it seems
injudicious, if not impossible, to attempt a selection of the
most important of them.

Among the volumes which have shed new light on Swift's
career must be included Émile Pons, *Swift: Les Années de
Jeunesse et "Le Conte du Tonneau"* (Strasbourg, 1925). Unfortunately not available in translation, this work is an extremely valuable source of insight into Swift's early years as
well as a provocative, though not infallible, guide to *A Tale
of a Tub*. In relatively recent years a number of studies of
Swift, primarily biographical in emphasis, have appeared, and
while few of them have added significantly to our factual
information, they provide a stimulating variety of interpretations. A very partial list of these works includes Shane Leslie,
The Skull of Swift (Indianapolis, 1928); Carl Van Doren,
Swift (New York, 1930); W. D. Taylor, *Jonathan Swift: A
Critical Essay* (London, 1933); Mario Rossi and Joseph Hone,
Swift: or, The Egotist (London and New York, 1934), and,
most recently, *Jonathan Swift: A Critical Biography* by the
well-known English literary figure, John Middleton Murry
(London, 1954). The student seeking a single modern study
which combines thoughtful analysis of Swift's work and per-
sonality with an accurate account of his life will, however, do
well to rely on the work of a distinguished Swift scholar,
Ricardo Quintana's *The Mind and Art of Jonathan Swift*
(London and New York, 1936).

The works of Swift—including many of those contained in
this volume—have recently received valuable illumination
from a number of scholarly analyses. The reader of *A Tale of*

a Tub, for example, will receive great assistance in his study of that work from Miriam K. Starkman's *Swift's Satire on Learning in "A Tale of a Tub"* (Princeton, 1950). Other scholarly books which have recently appeared and which provide useful insights into most of the works reprinted here include Martin Price, *Swift's Rhetorical Art* (New Haven, 1953); John M. Bullitt, *Jonathan Swift and the Anatomy of Satire* (Oxford, 1953); and William B. Ewald, Jr., *The Masks of Jonathan Swift* (Oxford, 1954). The mere listing of these recent studies indicates the challenge and excitement which Swift continues to provide for serious scholars. Any reader should be able to feel something of the challenge and a great deal of the excitement in the pages which follow.

A Note on Dates

The discussion of dates in Swift's period is complicated by the "old style" then in effect. The important difference between old-style and modern practice is in the day on which, for purposes of recording dates, the new year is assumed to begin. This, under old style, was March 25; accordingly, days prior to that date would be designated under what we would regard as the previous year. What we, for example, would call February 15, 1711, would, in Swift's time, be called February 15, 1710 (or occasionally February 15, 1710-1711).

Within Swift's texts, as they appear in the present volume, all dates appear precisely as Swift wrote them and can therefore be assumed to be old style. In all editorial discussion, however, including the introduction, chronology, and notes, the modern method of dating has been employed. Thus, for example, the third volume of the Pope-Swift *Miscellanies*, which, properly for the time, bore the date 1727, actually appeared in what we would call February of 1728 and is so described by the present editor.

JONATHAN SWIFT

Selected Prose and Poetry

A Tale of a Tub

A Tale of a Tub first appeared in 1704 in a single volume along with *The Battle of the Books* and *The Mechanical Operation of the Spirit*. Within a year or so, the book went through three further editions. In 1710 there appeared the fifth edition, the text of which is reprinted here, including for the first time the Apology and the footnotes (see explanation on p. xxv) in which Swift playfully reprints and occasionally comments upon the hostile criticisms of William Wotton.

The greater part of the *Tale* was probably written between the years 1695 and 1699 while Swift was a member of Sir William Temple's household. Certain passages, however, could not have been completed until very shortly before the date of publication, while, on the other hand, initial plans for the work may well have begun as early as the period of Swift's student career.

Swift's choice of a title is illuminated by his facetious account within the Preface; at the same time, the reader should recognize that in Swift's day "a tale of a tub" signified an idle narrative of the sort that we today might characterize as a "cock and bull story." Thus considered, the title is significant, for it serves to justify much of the apparent shapelessness and digression in the book.

Within the apparent framework of an idle tale, however, we find satire that is clearly conceived and vigorously executed. The initial key to this satire lies, of course, in Swift's own profession in the Apology. Asserting that the "numerous and gross corruptions in Religion and Learning" are the targets of his attack, he undertakes to deal with religious abuses in "the Allegory of the Coats, and the three Brothers," and with the corruptions in learning in the digressions. Though this assertion provides only the broadest outlines of the *Tale,* it makes clear that the digressions and prefatory materials are as important as the narrative in carrying out the author's satiric intentions.

The story of the three brothers is, indeed, the simplest element in the *Tale*. Between the text and Swift's own notes, the great majority of satiric references are made abundantly clear. The sketchy allegorical history of Christianity is directed throughout to the primary task of assaulting the Puritan dissenters. It is true that, by adhering to an essentially frivolous allegorical device, Swift is virtually forced to treat religious history and even the Church of England with a certain levity—and this fact has given rise, from the time of the *Tale*'s first appearance, to heated but inconclusive controversy about its author's personal piety. But the satire against the Puritans, by its fierceness, extravagance, and sheer volume, clearly dominates the religious element in the book.

The point of departure for much of Swift's anti-Puritan satire lies in the rather superficial characteristics popularly attributed to the dissenting sects. Whether justly or not, there had arisen a common stereotype of the dissenting preacher: standing in a bleak and uncovered pulpit, his ears made prominent by a close-cropped head, he allegedly preached, in strange, snuffling tones, a fierce and extravagant discourse which was held to be the product of divine inspiration. The words "enthusiasm" and "zeal" which the Puritans applied to their own religious attitudes were equated, by their enemies, with fanaticism and, as Swift indicates, madness. The austerity of Puritan conduct was widely derided, and it was further maintained, probably without foundation, that in their indulgence in sexual lust the Puritans more than compensated for their restraint in other matters.

Beneath these superficial jibes, however, there is in the *Tale*, as in most of the anti-Puritan literature of the time, a sense of deep urgency, born of a period in which religious and political controversy were often identical. In the half century which preceded the writing of the *Tale*, one English king had lost his head and another his throne in struggles which were largely religious. From Swift's point of view, the Puritans now seeking freedom of worship and the right to hold public office remained the murderers of Charles I, tireless in their designs against the sacred union of the State and its Established Church.

Compared with his wholesale derision of the Puritans, Swift's strictures against the Roman Catholics are mild, almost good-natured. For the orthodox Anglican, Catholic doctrine was far less alien than were the views of dissenters or religious skeptics, whose own fierce hatred of "priestcraft" often embraced Catholic and Anglican alike. In the *Tale*, therefore, the assaults upon Catholicism rest chiefly upon doctrinal grounds. In his jocular treatment of the abuses leading to the Reformation and the current differences between Anglican and Catholic, Swift implies that there is more to deplore in the fact of controversy itself than in the views of either Peter or Martin.

Swift's attack upon "abuses in learning" springs in part, at least, from the famous controversy over Ancient and Modern learning and represents Swift's attempt to aid his patron, Sir William Temple, in upholding the cause of the Ancients. Temple had taken his stand in his *Essay upon the Ancient and Modern Learning* (1690). His espousal of the Ancients was answered by William Wotton's *Reflections on Ancient and Modern Learning* in 1694. Among the works cited by Temple as evidence of the Ancients' superiority was the *Epistles* of Phalaris; and a young adherent of the Ancients, Charles Boyle, produced a new edition of the text in 1695. In the course of his editorial labors he borrowed a manuscript from St. James's Library, whose famous librarian, the scholar Richard Bentley, is supposed to have asked summarily for its return. In reprisal, Boyle spoke scathingly, in a preface to the second edition of the *Epistles,* of Bentley's "singular humanity." Bentley, in turn, added to a new edition of Wotton's *Reflections,* in 1697, a careful defense of his own conduct and, more important, an irrefutable demonstration that the *Epistles* was the work of a later writer than Phalaris. It was at this point that Swift, among others, joined the ranks of the Ancients with both the *Tale* and *The Battle of the Books.*

To the main current of this quarrel, in itself only a belated skirmish in a war which had been long fought out on the Continent, Swift added very little. The arguments of Temple and Boyle, though not without wit and evidences of learning, could not stand up beneath the scholarly rigor of Wotton and, in particular, of Bentley. In the *Tale,* therefore, Swift resorts to a broad and rather unjust caricature of the learned Moderns. In his claims to universal knowledge, his arrogant assumption of Modern superiority in every respect, the author of the *Tale* is parodying the comprehensive but moderate assessment of modern achievements in the major fields of intellectual activity which Wotton provides in the *Reflections.* In his feigned zeal for scholarly minutiae, learned references, and solemn exposition, as well as in his slighting remarks about learning acquired through indexes and prefaces, he is dismissing Bentley as an unscrupulous pedant. And in his uncritical admiration of the most grotesquely useless pseudoscience, occultism, and materialism, he displays a fatuous approval of precisely those modern preoccupations which are most open to question.

Beyond the religious satire and the assaults upon Bentley and Wotton as Moderns, the *Tale* invades a third great area which, whether or not it can be lumped under the "abuses in learning," demands independent attention. This is the attack upon contemporary literary practice, particularly as reflected in the writings of certain clearly identified men. The most important structural aspects of the *Tale* and a number of individual passages can be explained as parody. Thus the plethora of introductory writings, the two dedications, the voluminous digressions, the alternating but equally self-conscious passages of apology and arrogance, together with various extravagant flights of language, are all distortions of prevailing literary practices which Swift finds objectionable. The *Tale,* in fact, takes its outward form chiefly from the literary habits most in vogue in Swift's day. It purports to be "in the modern kind," and from it we draw a very shabby picture of literary creation, publication, and reception, as Swift viewed them. The successful book, Swift implies, is truly a shapeless "tale of a tub," produced from dubious motives, concealing by formal adherence to convention a poverty of content, published by venal opportunists, and fleetingly enjoyed by a shallow, capricious public.

In this satire on literary customs, Swift is characteristically explicit about naming those whom he considers the worst offenders. Chief among these is John Dryden, whose death, in 1700, occurred after most of the *Tale* was composed. This illustrious author, a distant cousin of Swift's, is supposed to have incurred his animosity by discouraging his youthful efforts at poetry. Whatever the source of Swift's hostility, the *Tale* makes abundantly clear the grounds of Swift's distaste for Dryden's literary accomplishments. These include Dryden's addiction to lengthy prefaces and fulsome dedications, his public self-pity, his copious digressions, his activities as a translator and composer of fables, and his views on, among other things, the nature of satire and the creative role of the imagination. Swift's bill of particulars is sometimes advanced by devastating parody, at other times by heavily sarcastic praise, and at still others by associating Dryden with such inferior groups as Grub Street hacks and compilers of fables.

Other literary figures of the late seventeenth century serve as specific targets for Swift's satire. Notable among these is the questionable figure of Sir Roger L'Estrange, sometime politician, journalist, and editor, and an inveterate writer of prefaces, among them several "to Posterity." To L'Estrange's name should be added those of the dramatist Nahum Tate, the physician-poet Richard Blackmore, the controversial critic and playwright, John Dennis, and the prolific scribbler, Tom Durfey. While all of these men enjoyed considerable popular attention, the essential mediocrity of most of them was clear to the discerning reader of the *Tale*. In being lumped with this dreary list as an object of Swift's derision, Dryden —and Bentley and Wotton as well—suffered further from a kind of satiric guilt-by-association.

The great majority of Swift's satiric assaults in the *Tale* can be accounted for by his concern with abuses in religion, science and learning, or literature. The loose form of the Tale, however, permits various minor thrusts in other directions. Of these the most memorable are the reflections upon fashionable customs, particularly those embodied in the development of the "clothes philosophy," which, it should be noted, is introduced in the midst of the allegorical history of Christianity. In addition, there are incidental attacks upon individuals, of no great import in the total impact of the work, but significant in suggesting that the *Tale* contains covert, fleeting expressions of personal rancor, all of which have not yet been identified.

The deliberate formlessness of the *Tale,* as well as the rich diversity of its satiric objects, do not invite a quest for traditional kinds of artistic unity. Yet its thoughtful readers inevitably seek within and behind its pages for some basic affirmation of principle, some statement of belief which will lend added authority and meaning to the hundreds of apparently independent assaults within the work. This search has almost invariably led to the brilliant central section of Chapter IX, the celebrated "Digression concerning Madness." No summary comment upon these passages is adequate, for after the most minute scrutiny of their extraordinary complexity, distinguished scholars have differed widely in their interpretations. Yet the section does firmly suggest a view of human knowledge and happiness which explains Swift's hatred of learned Moderns, fanatic Puritans, and pretentious men of letters. At the core of this view is the conception of true knowledge as an object rarely and painfully attained, totally remote from what men call happiness, of no demonstrable value in a world in which conquests are achieved by madmen and felicity by fools. The aspect of this belief which Swift most conspicuously stresses is that worldly happiness is entirely a matter of being "well deceived" by the surfaces of things. Less obvious, but probably more important in terms of the entire *Tale,* is the corollary that knowledge which is readily acquired, reassuring in its possession, and easily communicated to others is false knowledge. The three great classes of Swift's antagonists in the *Tale* are alike in professing to know the truth and in their eagerness to impose their knowledge upon others. Preachers, poets, and pedants all claim their special sources of truth: divine inspiration, wide-ranging imagination, scholarly inquiry. For Swift, the easy systematizing of Wotton, the index-learning of Bentley, the painless instruction of the fable makers, the babble of Enthusiasts, the idle poem, the toothless satire, the empty symbol are all fraudulent exploitations of man's urge to achieve the happiness of illusion. The ordinary, myopic mortal falls an easy prey to the claims of pedants and projectors, the inspired belchings of Enthusiasts, and the flabby products of the poetic fancy.

For all its playfulness and obliquity, the "Digression concerning Madness" reveals an arresting philosophic position. It strikes nearer perhaps than anything else Swift ever wrote to the deep sources of his dissatisfaction with the world about him. But the *Tale* is not a philosophic document; it is a wonderful amalgam of broad comedy and pointed satire. To recognize that its gaiety and malice and wit and invention proceed from this austere and terrible view of the human condition is only to find Swift's achievement the more astonishing.

A TALE OF A TUB.

Written for the Universal Improvement of Mankind.

Diu multumque desideratum.

To which is added,

An ACCOUNT of a BATTEL

BETWEEN THE

Antient and Modern BOOKS in St. *James*'s Library.

Basima eacabasa eanaa irrauriſta, diarba da caeotaba fobor camelanthi. *Iren. Lib.* 1. C. 18.

———— *Juvatque novos decerpere flores,*
Insignemque meo capiti petere inde coronam,
Unde prius nulli velarunt tempora Musæ. Lucret.

The Fifth EDITION: With the Author's Apology and Explanatory Notes. By *W. W--tt--n*, B. D. and others.

LONDON: Printed for *John Nutt,* near *Stationers-Halt.* MDCCX.

Treatises wrote by the same Author, most of them mentioned in the following Discourses; which will be speedily published.

A Character of the present Set of Wits *in this Island.*
A Panegyrical Essay upon the Number THREE.
A Dissertation upon the principal Productions of Grubstreet.
Lectures upon a Dissection of Human Nature.
A Panegyrick upon the World
An Analytical Discourse upon Zeal, Histori-theo-physilogi-cally *considered.*
A general History of Ears.
A modest Defence of the Proceedings of the Rabble *in all Ages.*
A Discription of the Kingdom of Absurdities.
A Voyage into England, *by a Person of Quality in* Terra Australis incognita, *translated from the Original.*
A Critical Essay upon the Art of Canting, *Philosophically, Physically, and Musically considered.*

A N

A P O L O G Y

For the, &c.

*I*F good and ill Nature equally operated upon Mankind, I
might have saved my self the Trouble of this Apology; for it
is manifest by the Reception the following Discourse hath
met with, that those who approve it, are a great Majority
among the Men of Tast; yet there have been two or three
Treatises written expressly against it, besides many others that
have flirted at it occasionally, without one Syllable having
been ever published in its Defence, or even Quotation to its
Advantage, that I can remember, except by the Polite Author
of a late Discourse between a Deist and a Socinian.

Therefore since the Book seems calculated to live at least
as long as our Language, and our Tast admit no great Alterations, I am content to convey some Apology along with it.

The greatest Part of that Book was finished above thirteen
Years since, 1696, which is eight Years before it was published. The Author was then young, his Invention at the
Height, and his Reading fresh in his Head. By the Assistance
of some Thinking, and much Conversation, he had endeav-
our'd to Strip himself of as many real Prejudices as he could;
I say real ones, because under the Notion of Prejudices, he
knew to what dangerous Heights some Men have proceeded.
Thus prepared, he thought the numerous and gross Corrup-
tions in Religion and Learning might furnish Matter for a
Satyr, that would be useful and diverting: He resolved to
proceed in a manner, that should be altogether new, the
World having been already too long nauseated with endless
Repetitions upon every Subject. The Abuses in Religion he

9

proposed to set forth in the Allegory of the Coats, and the three Brothers, which was to make up the Body of the Discourse. Those in Learning he chose to introduce by way of Digressions. He was then a young Gentleman much in the World, and wrote to the Tast of those who were like himself; therefore in order to allure them, he gave a Liberty to his Pen, which might not suit with maturer Years, or graver Characters, and which he could have easily corrected with a very few Blots, had he been Master of his Papers for a Year or two before their Publication.

Not that he would have governed his Judgment by the ill-placed Cavils of the Sour, the Envious, the Stupid, and the Tastless, which he mentions with disdain. He acknowledges there are several youthful Sallies, which from the Grave and the Wise may deserve a Rebuke. But he desires to be answerable no farther than he is guilty, and that his Faults may not be multiply'd by the ignorant, the unnatural, and uncharitable Applications of those who have neither Candor to suppose good Meanings, nor Palate to distinguish true Ones. After which, he will forfeit his Life, if any one Opinion can be fairly deduced from that Book, which is contrary to Religion or Morality.

Why should any Clergyman of our Church be angry to see the Follies of Fanaticism and Superstition exposed, tho' in the most ridiculous Manner? since that is perhaps the most probable way to cure them, or at least to hinder them from farther spreading. Besides, tho' it was not intended for their Perusal; it raillies nothing but what they preach against. It contains nothing to provoke them by the least Scurillity upon their Persons or their Functions. It Celebrates the Church of England as the most perfect of all others in Discipline and Doctrine, it advances no Opinion they reject, nor condemns any they receive. If the Clergy's Resentments lay upon their Hands, in my humble Opinion, they might have found more proper Objects to employ them on: Nondum tibi defuit Hostis; *I mean those heavy, illiterate Scriblers, prostitute in their Reputations, vicious in their Lives, and ruin'd in their Fortunes, who to the shame of good Sense as well as Piety, are greedily read, meerly upon the Strength of bold, false, impious Assertions, mixt with unmannerly Reflections upon the Priesthood, and openly intended against all Religion; in short, full of such Principles as are kindly received, because they are levell'd to remove those Terrors that Religion tells Men will be the Consequence of immoral Lives. Nothing like which is to be met with in this Discourse, tho' some of them are pleased so freely to censure it. And I wish, there were no other Instance of what I have too frequently observed, that many of that Reverend Body are not always very nice in distinguishing between their Enemies and their Friends.*

Had the Author's Intentions met with a more candid Interpretation from some whom out of Respect he forbears to name, he might have been encouraged to an Examination of Books written by some of those Authors above-described, whose Errors, Ignorance, Dullness and Villany, he thinks he could have detected and exposed in such a Manner, that the Persons who are most conceived to be infected by them, would soon lay them aside and be ashamed: But he has now given over those Thoughts, since the weightiest *Men in the* weightiest *Stations are pleased to think it a more dangerous Point to laugh at those Corruptions in Religion, which they themselves must disapprove, than to endeavour pulling up those very Foundations, wherein all Christians have agreed.*

He thinks it no fair Proceeding, that any Person should offer determinately to fix a name upon the Author of this Discourse, who hath all along concealed himself from most of his nearest Friends: Yet several have gone a farther Step, and pronounced another Book* to have been the Work of the same Hand with this; which the Author directly affirms to be a thorough mistake; he having yet never so much as read that

---

* Letter of Enthusiasm.

Discourse, a plain Instance how little Truth, there often is in general Surmises, or in Conjectures drawn from a Similitude of Style, or way of thinking.

Had the Author writ a Book to expose the Abuses in Law, or in Physick, he believes the Learned Professors in either Faculty, would have been so far from resenting it, as to have given him Thanks for his Pains, especially if he had made an honourable Reservation for the true Practice of either Science: But Religion they tell us ought not to be ridiculed, and they tell us Truth, yet surely the Corruption in it may; for we are taught by the tritest Maxim in the World, that Religion being the best of Things, its Corruptions are likely to be the worst.

There is one Thing which the judicious Reader cannot but have observed, that some of those Passages in this Discourse, which appear most liable to Objection are what they call Parodies, where the Author personates the Style and Manner of other Writers, whom he has a mind to expose. I shall produce one Instance, it is in the 51st *Page.*[1] *Dryden, L'Estrange, and some others I shall not name, are here levelled at, who having spent their Lives in Faction, and Apostacies, and all manner of Vice, pretended to be Sufferers for Loyalty and Religion. So* Dryden *tells us in one of his Prefaces of his Merits and Suffering, thanks God that he* possesses his Soul in Patience: *In other Places he talks at the same Rate, and* L'Estrange *often uses the like Style, and I believe the Reader may find more Persons to give that Passage an Application: But this is enough to direct those who may have over-look'd the Authors Intention.*

There are three or four other Passages which prejudiced or ignorant Readers have drawn by great Force to hint at ill Meanings, as if they glanced at some Tenets in Religion; in answer to all which, the Author solemnly protests he is entirely Innocent, and never had it once in his Thoughts that any thing he said would in the least be capable of such Interpreta-

---

[1] [Page 53 of this edition.]

tions, which he will engage to deduce full as fairly from the most innocent Book in the World. And it will be obvious to every Reader, that this was not any part of his Scheme or Design, the Abuses he notes being such as all Church of England Men agree in, nor was it proper for his Subject to meddle with other Points, than such as have been perpetually controverted since the Reformation.

To instance only in that Passage about the three wooden Machines mentioned in the Introduction: In the Original Manuscript there was a description of a Fourth, which those who had the Papers in their Power, blotted out, as having something in it of Satyr, that I suppose they thought was too particular, and therefore they were forced to change it to the Number Three, from whence some have endeavour'd to squeeze out a dangerous Meaning that was never thought on. And indeed the Conceit was half spoiled by changing the Numbers; that of Four being much more Cabalistick, and therefore better exposing the pretended Virtue of Numbers, a Superstition there intended to be ridicul'd.

Another Thing to be observed is, that there generally runs an Irony through the Thread of the whole Book, which the Men of Tast will observe and distinguish, and which will render some Objections that have been made, very weak and insignificant.

This Apology being chiefly intended for the Satisfaction of future Readers, it may be thought unnecessary to take any notice of such Treatises as have been writ against this ensuing Discourse, which are already sunk into waste Paper and Oblivion; after the usual Fate of common Answerers to Books, which are allowed to have any Merit: They are indeed like Annuals that grow about a young Tree, and seem to vye with it for a Summer, but fall and die with the Leaves in Autumn, and are never heard of any more. When Dr. Eachard writ his Book about the Contempt of the Clergy, numbers of those Answerers immediately started up, whose Memory if he had not kept alive by his Replies, it would now be utterly unknown that he were ever answered at all. There is indeed an

Exception, when any great Genius thinks it worth his while to expose a foolish Piece; so we still read Marvel's *Answer to* Parker *with Pleasure, tho' the Book it answers be sunk long ago; so the Earl of* Orrery's *Remarks will be read with Delight, when the Dissertation he exposes will neither be sought nor found; but these are no Enterprises for common Hands, nor to be hoped for above once or twice in an Age. Men would be more cautious of losing their Time in such an Undertaking, if they did but consider, that to answer a Book effectually, requires more Pains and Skill, more Wit, Learning, and Judgment than were employ'd in the Writing it. And the Author assures those Gentlemen who have given themselves that Trouble with him, that his Discourse is the Product of the Study, the Observation, and the Invention of several Years, that he often blotted out much more than he left, and if his Papers had not been a long time out of his Possession, they must have still undergone more severe Corrections; and do they think such a Building is to be battered with Dirt-Pellets however envenom'd the Mouths may be that discharge them. He hath seen the Productions but of two Answerers, One of which first appear'd as from an unknown hand, but since avowed by a Person, who upon some Occasions hath discover'd no ill Vein of Humor. 'Tis a Pity any Occasions should put him under a necessity of being so hasty in his Productions, which otherwise might often be entertaining. But there were other Reasons obvious enough for his Miscarriage in this; he writ against the Conviction of his Talent, and enter'd upon one of the wrongest Attempts in Nature, to turn into ridicule by a Weeks Labour, a Work which had cost so much time, and met with so much Success in ridiculing others, the manner how he has handled his* Subject, *I have now forgot, having just look'd it over when it first came out, as others did, meerly for the sake of the Title.*

The other Answer is from a Person of a graver Character, and is made up of half Invective, and half Annotation. In the latter of which he hath generally succeeded well enough.

And the Project at that time was not amiss, to draw in Readers to his Pamphlet, several having appear'd desirous that there might be some Explication of the more difficult Passages. Neither can he be altogether blamed for offering at the Invective Part, because it is agreed on all hands that the Author had given him sufficient Provocation. The great Objection is against his manner of treating it, very unsuitable to one of his Function. It was determined by a fair Majority, that this Answerer had in a way not to be pardon'd, drawn his Pen against a certain great Man then alive, and universally reverenced for every good Quality that could possibly enter into the Composition of the most accomplish'd Person; it was observed, how he was pleased and affected to have that noble Writer call'd his Adversary, and it was a Point of Satyr well directed, for I have been told, Sir W. T. *was sufficiently mortify'd at the Term. All the Men of Wit and Politeness were immediately up in Arms, through Indignation, which prevailed over their Contempt, by the Consequences they apprehended from such an Example, and it grew to be* Porsenna's Case; Idem trecenti juravimus. *In short, things were ripe for a general Insurrection, till my Lord* Orrery *had a little laid the Spirit, and settled the Ferment. But his Lordship being principally engaged with another Antagonist, it was thought necessary in order to quiet the Minds of Men, that this Opposer should receive a Reprimand, which partly occasioned that Discourse of the Battle of the Books, and the Author was farther at the Pains to insert one or two Remarks on him in the Body of the Book.*

This Answerer has been pleased to find Fault with about a dozen Passages, which the Author will not be at the Trouble of defending, farther than by assuring the Reader, that for the greater Part the Reflecter is entirely mistaken, and forces Interpretations which never once entered into the Writer's Head, nor will he is sure into that of any Reader of Tast and Candor; he allows two or three at most there produced to have been deliver'd unwarily, for which he desires

*to plead the Excuse offered already, of his Youth, and Franck-
ness of Speech, and his Papers being out of his Power at the
Time they were published.*

*But this Answerer insists, and says, what he chiefly dis-
likes, is the* Design; *what that was I have already told, and I
believe there is not a Person in* England *who can understand
that Book, that ever imagined it to have been any thing else,
but to expose the Abuses and Corruptions in Learning and
Religion.*

But it would be good to know what Design *this Reflecter
was serving, when he concludes his Pamphlet with a Caution
to Readers, to beware of thinking the Authors Wit was
entirely his own, surely this must have had some Allay of
Personal Animosity, at least mixt with the* Design *of serving
the Publick by so useful a Discovery; and it indeed touches the
Author in a very tender Point, who insists upon it, that
through the whole Book he has not borrowed one single Hint
from any Writer in the World; and he thought, of all Criticisms, that would never have been one. He conceived it was
never disputed to be an Original, whatever Faults it might
have. However this Answerer produces three Instances to prove
this Author's Wit is not his own in many Places. The first is,
that the Names of* Peter, Martin *and* Jack *are borrowed from
a Letter of the late Duke of* Buckingham. *Whatever Wit is
contained in those three Names, the Author is content to give
it up, and desires his Readers will substract as much as they
placed upon that Account; at the same time protesting solemnly that he never once heard of that Letter, except in this
Passage of the Answerer: So that the Names were not borrowed
as he affirms, tho' they should happen to be the same, which
however is odd enough, and what he hardly believes; that of*
Jack, *being not quite so obvious as the other two. The second
Instance to shew* the Author's Wit is not his own, *is* Peter's
Banter (*as he calls it in his* Alsatia *Phrase) upon Transubstantiation, which is taken from the same Duke's Conference with
an* Irish *Priest, where a Cork is turned into a Horse. This the*

Author confesses to have seen, about ten Years after his Book
was writ, and a Year or two after it was published. Nay, the
Answerer overthrows this himself; for he allows the Tale was
writ in 1697; *and I think that Pamphlet was not printed in*
many Years after. It was necessary, that Corruption should
have some Allegory as well as the rest; and the Author in-
vented the properest he could, without enquiring what other
People had writ, and the commonest Reader will find, there
is not the least Resemblance between the two Stories. The
third Instance is in these Words: I have been assured, that the
Battle in St. *James's* Library, is *mutatis mutandis,* taken out
of a *French* Book, entituled, *Combat des livres,* if I misremember not. *In which Passage there are two Clauses observable:* I
have been assured; *and,* if I misremember not. *I desire first*
to know, whether if that Conjecture proves an utter falshood,
those two Clauses will be a sufficient Excuse for this worthy
Critick. The Matter is a Trifle; but, would he venture to pro-
nounce at this Rate upon one of greater Moment? I know
nothing more contemptible in a Writer than the Character of
a Plagiary; which he here fixes at a venture, and this, not for a
Passage, but a whole Discourse, taken out from another Book
only mutatis mutandis. *The Author is as much in the dark*
about this as the Answerer; and will imitate him by an
Affirmation at Random; that if there be a word of Truth in
this Reflection, he is a paultry, imitating Pedant, and the
Answerer is a Person of Wit, Manners and Truth. He takes
his Boldness, from never having seen any such Treatise in his
Life nor heard of it before; and he is sure it is impossible for
two Writers of different Times and Countries to agree in their
Thoughts after such a Manner, that two continued Discourses
shall be the same only mutatis mutandis. *Neither will he*
insist upon the mistake of the Title, but let the Answerer and
his Friend produce any Book they please, he defies them to
shew one single Particular, where the judicious Reader will
affirm he has been obliged for the smallest Hint; giving only
Allowance for the accidental encountring of a single Thought,

which he knows may sometimes happen; tho' he has never yet found it in that Discourse, nor has heard it objected by any body else.

So that if ever any design was unfortunately executed, it must be that of this Answerer, who when he would have it observed that the Author's Wit is not his own, is able to produce but three Instances, two of them meer Trifles, and all three manifestly false. If this be the way these Gentlemen deal with the World in those Criticisms, where we have not Leisure to defeat them, their Readers had need be cautious how they rely upon their Credit; and whether this Proceeding can be reconciled to Humanity or Truth, let those who think it worth their while, determine.

It is agreed, this Answerer would have succeeded much better, if he had stuck wholly to his Business as a Commentator upon the Tale of a Tub, *wherein it cannot be deny'd that he hath been of some Service to the Publick, and has given very fair Conjectures towards clearing up some difficult Passages; but, it is the frequent Error of those Men (otherwise very commendable for their Labors) to make Excursions beyond their Talent and their Office, by pretending to point out the Beauties and the Faults; which is no part of their Trade, which they always fail in, which the World never expected from them, nor gave them any thanks for endeavouring at. The Part of* Min-ellius, *or* Farnaby *would have fallen in with his Genius, and might have been serviceable to many Readers who cannot enter into the abstruser Parts of that Discourse; but* Optat ephippia bos piger. *The dull, unwieldly, ill-shaped Ox would needs put on the Furniture of a Horse, not considering he was born to Labour, to plow the Ground for the Sake of superior Beings, and that he has neither the Shape, Mettle nor Speed of that nobler Animal he would affect to personate.*

It is another Pattern of this Answerer's fair dealing, to give us Hints that the Author is dead, and yet to lay the Suspicion upon somebody, I know not who, in the Country; to which can be only returned, that he is absolutely mistaken in all his Conjectures; and surely Conjectures are at best too light a

Pretence to allow a Man to assign a Name in Publick. He condemns a Book, and consequently the Author, of whom he is utterly ignorant, yet at the same time fixes in Print, what he thinks a disadvantageous Character upon those who never deserved it. A Man who receives a Buffet in the Dark may be allowed to be vexed; but it is an odd kind of Revenge to go to Cuffs in broad day with the first he meets with, and lay the last Nights Injury at his Door. And thus much for this discreet, candid, pious, *and* ingenious *Answerer.*

How the Author came to be without his Papers, is a Story not proper to be told, and of very little use, being a private Fact of which the Reader would believe as little or as much as he thought good. He had however a blotted Copy by him, which he intended to have writ over, with many Alterations, and this the Publishers were well aware of, having put it into the Booksellers Preface, that they apprehended a surreptitious Copy, which was to be altered, &c. *This though not regarded by Readers, was a real Truth, only the surreptitious Copy was rather that which was printed, and they made all hast they could, which indeed was needless; the Author not being at all prepared; but he has been told, the Bookseller was in much Pain, having given a good Sum of Money for the Copy.*

In the Authors Original Copy there were not so many Chasms as appear in the Book; and why some of them were left he knows not; had the Publication been trusted to him, he should have made several Corrections of Passages against which nothing hath been ever objected. He should likewise have altered a few of those that seem with any Reason to be excepted against, but to deal freely, the greatest Number he should have left untouch'd, as never suspecting it possible any wrong Interpretations could be made of them.

The Author observes, at the End of the Book there is a Discourse called A Fragment; *which he more wondered to see in Print than all the rest. Having been a most imperfect Sketch with the Addition of a few loose Hints, which he once lent a Gentleman who had designed a Discourse of somewhat the same Subject; he never thought of it afterwards, and it was a sufficient Surprize to see it pieced up together, wholly out of the Method and Scheme he had intended, for it was the Ground-work of a much larger Discourse, and he was sorry to observe the Materials so foolishly employ'd.*

There is one farther Objection made by those who have answered this Book, as well as by some others, that Peter *is frequently made to repeat Oaths and Curses. Every Reader observes it was necessary to know that* Peter *did Swear and Curse. The Oaths are not printed out, but only supposed, and the Idea of an Oath is not immoral, like the Idea of a Prophane or Immodest Speech. A Man may laugh at the Popish Folly of cursing People to Hell, and imagine them swearing, without any crime; but lewd Words, or dangerous Opinions though printed by halves, fill the Readers Mind with ill Idea's; and of these the Author cannot be accused. For the judicious Reader will find that the severest Stroaks of Satyr in his Book are levelled against the modern Custom of Employing Wit upon those Topicks, of which there is a remarkable Instance in the* 153d. *Page,[2] as well as in several others, tho' perhaps once or twice exprest in too free a manner, excusable only for the Reasons already alledged. Some Overtures have been made by a third Hand to the Bookseller for the Author's altering those Passages which he thought might require it. But it seems the Bookseller will not hear of any such Thing, being apprehensive it might spoil the Sale of the Book.*

The Author cannot conclude this Apology, without making this one Reflection; that, as Wit is the noblest and most useful Gift of humane Nature, so Humor is the most agreeable, and where these two enter far into the Composition of any Work, they will render it always acceptable to the World. Now, the great Part of those who have no Share or Tast of either, but by their Pride, Pedantry and Ill Manners, lay themselves bare to the Lashes of Both, think the Blow is weak, because they are insensible, and where Wit hath any mixture of Raillery; 'Tis but calling it Banter, *and the work is done. This*

---

[2] [Pages 104 and 105 in this edition.]

Polite Word of theirs was first borrowed from the Bullies in White-Fryars, *then fell among the Footmen, and at last retired to the Pedants, by whom it is applied as properly to the Productions of Wit, as if I should apply it to Sir* Isaac Newton's *Mathematicks, but, if this* Bantring *as they call it, be so despisable a Thing, whence comes it to pass they have such a perpetual Itch towards it themselves? To instance only in the Answerer already mentioned; it is grievous to see him in some of his Writings at every turn going out of his way to be waggish, to tell us of a* Cow that prickt up her Tail, *and in his answer to this Discourse, he says* it is all a Farce and a Ladle: *With other Passages equally shining. One may say of these* Impedimenta Literarum, *that Wit ows them a Shame; and they cannot take wiser Counsel than to keep out of harms way, or at least not to come till they are sure they are called.*

To conclude; with those Allowances above-required, this Book should be read, after which the Author conceives, few things will remain which may not be excused in a young Writer. He wrote only to the Men of Wit and Tast, and he thinks he is not mistaken in his Accounts, when he says they have been all of his side, enough to give him the vanity of telling his Name, wherein the World with all its wise Conjectures, is yet very much in the dark, which Circumstance is no disagreeable Amusement either to the Publick or himself.

The Author is informed, that the Bookseller has prevailed on several Gentlemen, to write some explanatory Notes, for the goodness of which he is not to answer, having never seen any of them, nor intends it, till they appear in Print, when it is not unlikely he may have the Pleasure to find twenty Meanings, which never enter'd into his Imagination.

June 3, 1709.

POSTSCRIPT

*S*INCE *the writing of this which was about a Year ago; a Prostitute Bookseller hath publish'd a foolish Paper, under the Name of Notes on the* Tale of a Tub, *with some Account of the Author, and with an Insolence which I suppose is punishable by Law, hath presumed to assign certain Names. It will be enough for the Author to assure the World, that the Writer of that Paper is utterly wrong in all his Conjectures upon that Affair. The Author farther asserts that the whole Work is entirely of one Hand, which every Reader of Judgment will easily discover. The Gentleman who gave the Copy to the Bookseller, being a Friend of the Author, and using no other Liberties besides that of expunging certain Passages where now the Chasms appear under the Name of* Desiderata. *But if any Person will prove his Claim to three Lines in the whole Book, let him step forth and tell his Name and Titles, upon which the Bookseller shall have Orders to prefix them to the next Edition, and the Claimant shall from henceforward be acknowledged the undisputed Author.*

T O

The Right Honourable,

JOHN

Lord SOMMERS.

My LORD,

THO' the Author has written a large Dedication, yet That being address'd to a Prince, whom I am never likely to have the Honor of being known to; A Person, besides, as far as I can observe, not at all regarded, or thought on by any of our present Writers; And, being wholly free from that Slavery, which Booksellers usually lie under, to the Caprices of Authors; I think it a wise Piece of Presumption, to inscribe these Papers to your Lordship, and to implore your Lordship's Protection of them. God and your Lordship know their Faults, and their Merits; for as to my own Particular, I am altogether a Stranger to the Matter; And, tho' every Body else should be equally ignorant, I do not fear the Sale of the Book, at all the worse, upon that Score. Your Lordship's Name on the Front, in Capital Letters, will at any time get off one Edition: Neither would I desire any other Help, to grow an Alderman, than a Patent for the sole Priviledge of Dedicating to your Lordship.

I should now, in right of a Dedicator, give your Lordship a List of your own Virtues, and at the same time, be very un-willing to offend your Modesty; But, chiefly, I should celebrate your Liberality towards Men of great Parts and small Fortunes, and give you broad Hints, that I mean my self. And, I was just going on in the usual Method, to peruse a hundred or two of Dedications, and transcribe an Abstract, to be applied to your Lordship; But, I was diverted by a certain Accident. For, upon the Covers of these Papers, I casually observed written in large Letters, the two following Words, *DETUR DIGNIS-SIMO;* which, for ought I knew, might contain some important Meaning. But, it unluckily fell out, that none of the Authors I employ, understood *Latin* (tho' I have them often in pay, to translate out of that Language) I was therefore compelled to have recourse to the Curate of our Parish, who Englished it thus, *Let it be given to the Worthiest;* And his Comment was, that the Author meant, his Work should be dedicated to the sublimest Genius of the Age, for Wit, Learning, Judgment, Eloquence and Wisdom. I call'd at a Poet's Chamber (who works for my Shop) in an Alley hard by, shewed him the Translation, and desired his Opinion, who it was that the Author could mean; He told me, after some Consideration, that Vanity was a Thing he abhorr'd; but by the Description, he thought Himself to be the Person aimed at; And, at the same time, he very kindly offer'd his own Assistance *gratis,* towards penning a Dedication to Himself. I desired him, however, to give a second Guess; Why then, said he, it must be I, or my Lord *Sommers.* From thence I went to several other Wits of my Acquaintance, with no small Hazard and Weariness to my Person, from a prodigious Number of dark, winding Stairs; But found them all in the same Story, both of your Lordship and themselves. Now, your Lordship is to understand, that this Proceeding was not of my own Invention; For, I have somewhere heard, it is a Maxim, that those, to whom every Body allows the second Place, have an undoubted Title to the First.

This infallibly convinced me, that your Lordship was the Person intended by the Author. But, being very unacquainted in the Style and Form of Dedications, I employ'd those Wits aforesaid, to furnish me with Hints and Materials, towards a Panegyrick upon your Lordship's Virtues.

In two Days, they brought me ten Sheets of Paper, fill'd up on every Side. They swore to me, that they had ransack'd whatever could be found in the Characters of *Socrates, Aristides, Epaminondas, Cato, Tully, Atticus,* and other hard Names, which I cannot now recollect. However, I have Reason to believe, they imposed upon my Ignorance, because, when I came to read over their Collections, there was not a Syllable there, but what I and every body else knew as well as themselves: Therefore, I grievously suspect a Cheat; and, that these Authors of mine, stole and transcribed every Word, from the universal Report of Mankind. So that I look upon my self, as fifty Shillings out of Pocket, to no manner of Purpose.

If, by altering the Title, I could make the same Materials serve for another Dedication (as my Betters have done) it would help to make up my Loss: But, I have made several Persons, dip here and there in those Papers, and before they read three Lines, they have all assured me, plainly, that they cannot possibly be applied to any Person besides your Lordship.

I expected, indeed, to have heard of your Lordship's Bravery, at the Head of an Army; Of your undaunted Courage, in mounting a Breach, or scaling a Wall; Or, to have had your Pedigree trac'd in a Lineal Descent from the House of *Austria;* Or, of your wonderful Talent at Dress and Dancing; Or, your Profound Knowledge in *Algebra, Metaphysicks,* and the Oriental Tongues. But to ply the World with an old beaten Story of your Wit, and Eloquence, and Learning, and Wisdom, and Justice, and Politeness, and Candor, and Evenness of Temper in all Scenes of Life; Of that great Discernment in Discovering, and Readiness in Favouring deserving Men; with forty other common Topicks: I confess, I have neither Conscience, nor Countenance to do it. Because there is no Virtue, either of a Publick or Private Life, which some Circumstances of your own, have not often produced upon the Stage of the World; And those few, which for want of Occasions to exert them, might otherwise have pass'd unseen or unobserved by your *Friends,* your *Enemies* have at length brought to Light.

'Tis true, I should be very loth, the Bright Example of your Lordship's Virtues should be lost to After-Ages, both for their sake and your own; but chiefly, because they will be so very necessary to adorn the History of a *late Reign;* And That is another Reason, why I would forbear to make a Recital of them here; Because, I have been told by Wise Men, that as Dedications have run for some Years past, a good Historian will not be apt to have Recourse thither, in search of Characters.

There is one Point, wherein I think we Dedicators would do well to change our Measures; I mean, instead of running on so far, upon the Praise of our Patron's *Liberality,* to spend a Word or two, in admiring their *Patience.* I can put no greater Compliment on your Lordship's, than by giving you so ample an Occasion to exercise it at present. Tho', perhaps, I shall not be apt to reckon much Merit to your Lordship upon that Score, who having been formerly used to tedious Harangues, and sometimes to as little Purpose, will be the readier to pardon this, especially, when it is offered by one, who is with all Respect and Veneration,

> *My* Lord,
>
> > *Your Lordship's most Obedient,*
> >
> > > *and most Faithful Servant,*
> > >
> > > > The Bookseller.

The Bookseller

T O T H E

R E A D E R

IT is now Six Years since these Papers came first to my Hand, which seems to have been about a Twelvemonth after they were writ: For, the Author tells us in his Preface to the First Treatise, that he hath calculated it for the Year 1697, and in several Passages of that Discourse, as well as the second, it appears, they were written about that Time.

As to the Author, I can give no manner of Satisfaction; However, I am credibly informed that this Publication is without his Knowledge; for he concludes the Copy is lost, having lent it to a Person, since dead, and being never in Possession of it after: So that, whether the Work received his last Hand, or, whether he intended to fill up the defective Places, is like to remain a Secret.

If I should go about to tell the Reader, by what Accident, I became Master of these Papers, it would, in this unbelieving Age, pass for little more than the Cant, or Jargon of the Trade. I, therefore, gladly spare both him and my self so unnecessary a Trouble. There yet remains a difficult Question, why I publish'd them no sooner. I forbore upon two Accounts: First, because I thought I had better Work upon my Hands; and Secondly, because, I was not without some Hope of hearing from the Author, and receiving his Directions. But, I have been lately alarm'd with Intelligence of a surreptitious Copy, which a certain great Wit had new polish'd and refin'd, or as our present Writers express themselves, fitted to the Humor of the Age; as they have already done, with great Felicity, to Don Quixot, Boccalini, la Bruyere and other Authors. However, I though it fairer Dealing, to offer the whole Work in its Naturals. If any Gentleman will please to furnish me with a Key, in order to explain the more difficult Parts, I shall very gratefully acknowledge the Favour, and print it by it self.

THE

Epistle Dedicatory,

TO

His Royal Highness

PRINCE POSTERITY.

SIR,

I HERE present *Your Highness* with the Fruits of a very few leisure Hours, stollen from the short Intervals of a World of Business, and of an Employment quite alien from such Amusements as this: The poor Production of that Refuse of Time which has lain heavy upon my Hands, during a long Prorogation of Parliament, a great Dearth of Forein News, and a tedious Fit of rainy Weather: For which, and other Reasons, it cannot chuse extreamly to deserve such a Patronage as that of *Your Highness,* whose numberless Virtues in so few Years, make the World look upon You as the future Example to all Princes: For altho' *Your Highness* is hardly got clear of Infancy, yet has the universal learned World already resolv'd upon appealing to Your future Dictates with the lowest and most resigned Submission: Fate having decreed You sole Arbiter of the Productions of human Wit, in this polite and

---

The Citation out of Irenæus *in the* Title-Page, *which seems to be all* Gibberish, *is a Form of Initiation used antiently by the* Marcosian Hereticks. W. Wotton.

It is the usual Style of decry'd Writers to appeal to Posterity, *who is here represented as a Prince in his Nonage, and* Time *as his Governour, and the Author begins in a way very frequent with him, by personating other Writers, who sometimes offer such Reasons and Excuses for publishing their Works as they ought chiefly to conceal and be asham'd of.*

most accomplish'd Age. Methinks, the Number of Appellants were enough to shock and startle any Judge of a Genius less unlimited than Yours: But in order to prevent such glorious Tryals, the *Person* (it seems) to whose Care the Education of *Your Highness* is committed, has resolved (as I am told) to keep you in almost an universal Ignorance of our Studies, which it is Your inherent Birth-right to inspect.

It is amazing to me, that this *Person* should have Assurance in the face of the Sun, to go about persuading *Your Highness,* that our Age is almost wholly illiterate, and has hardly produc'd one Writer upon any Subject. I know very well, that when *Your Highness* shall come to riper Years, and have gone through the Learning of Antiquity, you will be too curious to neglect inquiring into the Authors of the very age before You: And to think that this *Insolent,* in the Account he is preparing for Your View, designs to reduce them to a Number so insignificant as I am asham'd to mention; it moves my Zeal and my Spleen for the Honor and Interest of our vast flourishing Body, as well as of my self, for whom I know by long Experience, he has profess'd, and still continues a peculiar Malice.

'Tis not unlikely, that when *Your Highness* will one day peruse what I am now writing, You may be ready to expostulate with Your *Governour* upon the Credit of what I here affirm, and command Him to shew You some of our Productions. To which he will answer, (for I am well informed of his Designs) by asking *Your Highness,* where they are? and what is become of them? and pretend it a Demonstration that there never were any, because they are not then to be found: Not to be found! Who has mislaid them? Are they sunk in the Abyss of Things? 'Tis certain, that in their own Nature they were *light* enough to swim upon the Surface for all Eternity. Therefore the Fault is in Him, who tied Weights so heavy to their Heels, as to depress them to the Center. Is their very Essence destroyed? Who has annihilated them? Were they drowned by *Purges* or martyred by *Pipes?* Who administred them to the Posteriors of ———? But that it may no longer be a Doubt with *Your Highness,* who is to be the Author of this universal Ruin; I beseech You to observe that large and terrible *Scythe* which your *Governour* affects to bear continually about him. Be pleased to remark the Length and Strength, the Sharpness and Hardness of his *Nails* and *Teeth;* Consider his baneful abominable *Breath,* Enemy to Life and Matter, infectious and corrupting: And then reflect whether it be possible for any mortal Ink and Paper of this Generation to make a suitable Resistance. Oh, that *Your Highness* would one day resolve to disarm this Usurping* *Maitre du Palais,* of his furious Engins, and bring your Empire† *hors de Page.*

It were endless to recount the several Methods of Tyranny and Destruction, which Your *Governour* is pleased to practise upon this Occasion. His inveterate Malice is such to the Writings of our Age, that of several Thousands produced yearly from this renowned City, before the next Revolution of the Sun, there is not one to be heard of: Unhappy Infants, many of them barbarously destroyed, before they have so much as learnt their *Mother-Tongue* to beg for Pity. Some he stifles in their Cradles, others he frights into Convulsions, whereof they suddenly die; Some he flays alive, others he tears Limb from Limb. Great Numbers are offered to *Moloch,* and the rest tainted by his Breath, die of a languishing Consumption.

But the Concern I have most at Heart, is for our Corporation of *Poets,* from whom I am preparing a Petition to *Your Highness,* to be subscribed with the Names of one hundred thirty six of the first Rate, but whose immortal Productions are never likely to reach your Eyes, tho' each of them is now an humble and an earnest Appellant for the Laurel, and has large comely Volumes ready to shew for a Support to his Pretensions. The *never-dying* Works of these illustrious Persons, Your *Governour,* Sir, has devoted to unavoidable Death, and *Your Highness* is to be made believe, that our Age has never arrived at the Honor to produce one single Poet.

---

* *Comptroller.*
† *Out of Guardianship.*

We confess *Immortality* to be a great and powerful Goddess, but in vain we offer up to her our Devotions and our Sacrifices, if *Your Highness's Governour,* who has usurped the *Priest-hood,* must by an unparallel'd Ambition and Avarice, wholly intercept and devour them.

To affirm that our Age is altogether Unlearned, and devoid of Writers in any kind, seems to be an Assertion so bold and so false, that I have been sometime thinking, the contrary may almost be proved by uncontroulable Demonstration. 'Tis true indeed, that altho' their Numbers be vast, and their Productions numerous in proportion, yet are they hurryed so hastily off the Scene, that they escape our Memory, and delude our Sight. When I first thought of this Address, I had pre-pared a copious List of *Titles* to present *Your Highness* as an undisputed Argument for what I affirm. The Originals were posted fresh upon all Gates and Corners of Streets; but returning in a very few Hours to take a Review, they were all torn down, and fresh ones in their Places: I enquired after them among Readers and Booksellers, but I enquired in vain, the *Memorial of them was lost among Men, their Place was no more to be found:* and I was laughed to scorn, for a *Clown* and a *Pedant,* without all Taste and Refinement, little versed in the Course of *present* Affairs, and that knew nothing of what had pass'd in the best Companies of Court and Town. So that I can only avow in general to *Your Highness,* that we do abound in Learning and Wit; but to fix upon Particulars, is a Task too slippery for my slender Abilities. If I should venture in a windy Day, to affirm to *Your Highness,* that there is a large Cloud near the *Horizon* in the Form of a *Bear,* another in the *Zenith* with the Head of an *Ass,* a third to the Westward with Claws like a *Dragon;* and *Your Highness* should in a few Minutes think fit to examine the Truth, 'tis certain, they would all be changed in Figure and Position, new ones would arise, and all we could agree upon would be, that Clouds there were, but that I was grossly mistaken in the *Zoography* and *Topography* of them.

But Your *Governour,* perhaps, may still insist, and put

the Question: What is then become of those immense Bales of Paper, which must needs have been employ'd in such Numbers of Books? Can these also be wholly annihilate, and so of a sudden as I pretend? What shall I say in return of so invidious an Objection? It ill befits the Distance between *Your Highness* and Me, to send You for ocular Conviction to a *Jakes,* or an *Oven;* to the Windows of a *Bawdy-house,* or to a sordid *Lanthorn.* Books, like Men their Authors, have no more than one Way of coming into the World, but there are ten Thousand to go out of it, and return no more.

I profess to *Your Highness,* in the Integrity of my Heart, that what I am going to say is literally true this Minute I am writing: What Revolutions may happen before it shall be ready for your Perusal, I can by no means warrant: However I beg You to accept it as a Specimen of our Learning, our Politeness and our Wit. I do therefore affirm upon the Word of a sincere Man, that there is now actually in being, a certain Poet called *John Dryden,* whose Translation of *Virgil* was lately printed in a large Folio, well bound, and if diligent search were made, for ought I know, is yet to be seen. There is another call'd *Nahum Tate,* who is ready to make Oath that he has caused many Rheams of Verse to be published, whereof both himself and his Bookseller (if lawfully required) can still produce authentick Copies, and therefore wonders why the World is pleased to make such a Secret of it. There is a Third, known by the Name of *Tom Durfey,* a Poet of a vast Comprehension, an universal Genius, and most profound Learning. There are also one Mr. *Rymer,* and one Mr. *Dennis,* most profound Criticks. There is a Person styl'd Dr. *B——tl——y,* who has written near a thousand Pages of immense Erudition, *giving a full and true Account* of a certain *Squable* of wonderful Importance between himself and a Bookseller: He is a Writer of infinite Wit and Humour; no Man raillyes with a better Grace, and in more sprightly Turns. Farther, I avow to *Your Highness,* that with these Eyes I have beheld the Person of *William W——tt——n,* B.D. who has written a good sizeable volume against a *Friend of Your Governor,* (from whom, alas! he must therefore look for little Favour) in a most gentlemanly Style, adorned with utmost Politeness and Civility; replete with Discoveries equally valuable for their Novelty and Use: and embellish'd with *Traits* of Wit so poignant and so apposite, that he is a worthy Yokemate to his foremention'd *Friend*.

Why should I go upon farther Particulars, which might fill a Volume with the just Elogies of my cotemporary Brethren? I shall bequeath this Piece of Justice to a larger Work: wherein I intend to write a Character of the present Set of *Wits* in our Nation: Their Persons I shall describe particularly, and at Length, their Genius and Understandings in *Mignature*.

In the mean time, I do here make bold to present *Your Highness* with a faithful Abstract drawn from the Universal Body of all Arts and Sciences, intended wholly for your Service and Instruction: Nor do I doubt in the least, but *Your Highness* will peruse it as carefully, and make as considerable Improvements, as *other* young *Princes* have already done by the many Volumes of late Years written for a Help to their Studies.

That *Your Highness* may advance in Wisdom and Virtue, as well as Years, and at last out-shine all Your Royal Ancestors, shall be the daily Prayer of,

SIR,

Decemb.
1697.

Your Highness's

Most devoted, &c.

THE

PREFACE

THE Wits of the present Age being so very numerous and penetrating, it seems, the Grandees of *Church* and *State* begin to fall under horrible Apprehensions, lest these Gentlemen, during the intervals of a long Peace, should find leisure to pick Holes in the weak sides of Religion and Government. To prevent which, there has been much Thought employ'd of late upon certain Projects for taking off the Force, and Edge of those formidable Enquirers, from canvasing and reasoning upon such delicate Points. They have at length fixed upon one, which will require some Time as well as Cost, to perfect. Mean while the Danger hourly increasing, by new Levies of Wits all appointed (as there is Reason to fear) with Pen, Ink, and Paper which may at an hours Warning be drawn out into Pamphlets, and other Offensive Weapons, ready for immediate Execution: It was judged of absolute necessity, that some present Expedient be thought on, till the main Design can be brought to Maturity. To this End, at a Grand Committee, some Days ago, this important Discovery was made by a certain curious and refined Observer; That Sea-men have a Custom when they meet a *Whale,* to fling him out an empty *Tub,* by way of Amusement, to divert him from laying violent Hands upon the Ship. This Parable was immediately mythologiz'd: The *Whale* was interpreted to be *Hobs's Leviathan,* which tosses and plays with all other Schemes of Religion and Government, whereof a great many are hollow, and dry, and empty, and noisy, and wooden, and given to Rotation. This is the *Leviathan* from whence the terrible Wits of our Age are said to borrow their Weapons. The *Ship* in danger, is easily understood to be its old Antitype the *Commonwealth*. But, how to analyze the *Tub,* was a Matter of difficulty; when after long Enquiry and Debate, the literal Meaning was preserved: And it was decreed, that in order to prevent these *Leviathans* from tossing and sporting with the *Commonwealth,* (which of it self is too apt to *fluctuate*) they should be diverted from that Game by a *Tale of a Tub.* And my Genius being conceived to lye not unhappily that way, I had the Honor done me to be engaged in the Performance.

This is the sole Design in publishing the following Treatise, which I hope will serve for an *Interim* of some Months to employ those unquiet Spirits, till the perfecting of that great Work: into the Secret of which, it is reasonable the courteous Reader should have some little Light.

It is intended that a large Academy be erected, capable of containing nine thousand seven hundred forty and three Persons; which by modest Computation is reckoned to be pretty near the current Number of *Wits* in this Island. These are to be disposed into the several Schools of this Academy, and there pursue those Studies to which their Genius most inclines them. The Undertaker himself will publish his Proposals with all convenient speed, to which I shall refer the curious Reader for a more particular Account, mentioning at present only a few of the Principal Schools. There is first, a large *Pederastick* School, with *French* and *Italian* Masters. There is also, the *Spelling* School, *a very spacious Building*: the School of *Looking Glasses*: The School of *Swearing*: the School of *Criticks*: the School of *Salivation*: The School of *Hobby-Horses*: The School of *Poetry*:* The School of *Tops*: The School of *Spleen*: The School of *Gaming*: with many others too tedious to recount. No Person to be admitted Member into any of these Schools, without an Attestation under two sufficient Persons Hands, certifying him to be a *Wit*.

---

* *This I think the Author should have omitted, it being of the very same Nature with the* School of Hobby-Horses, *if one may venture to censure one who is so severe a Censurer of others, perhaps with too little Distinction.*

But, to return. I am sufficiently instructed in the Principal Duty of a Preface, if my Genius were capable of arriving at it. Thrice have I forced my Imagination to make the *Tour* of my Invention, and thrice it has returned empty; the latter having been wholly drained by the following Treatise. Not so, my more successful Brethren the *Moderns,* who will by no means let slip a Preface or Dedication, without some notable distinguishing Stroke, to surprize the Reader at the Entry and kindle a Wonderful Expectation of what is to ensue. Such was that of a most ingenious Poet, who solliciting his Brain for something new, compared himself to the *Hangman,* and his Patron to the *Patient*: This was *Insigne, recens, indictum ore alio.* When I went thro' That necessary and noble †Course of Study, I had the happiness to observe many such egregious Touches, which I shall not injure the Authors by transplanting: Because I have remarked, that nothing is so very tender as a *Modern* Piece of Wit, and which is apt to suffer so much in the Carriage. Some things are extreamly witty *to day,* or *fasting,* or *in this place,* or *at eight a clock,* or *over a Bottle,* or *spoke by Mr.* What d'y'call'm, or *in a Summer's Morning*: Any of which, by the smallest Transposal or Misapplication, is utterly annihilate. Thus, *Wit* has its Walks and Purlieus, out of which it may not stray the breadth of an Hair, upon peril of being lost. The *Moderns* have artfully fixed this *Mercury,* and reduced it to the Circumstances of Time, Place and Person. Such a Jest there is, that will not pass out of *Covent-Garden;* and such a one, that is no where intelligible but at *Hide-Park* Corner. Now, tho' it sometimes tenderly affects me to consider, that all the towardly Passages I shall deliver in the following Treatise, will grow quite out of date and relish with the first shifting of the present Scene: yet I must need subscribe to the Justice of this Proceeding: because, I cannot imagine why we should be at Expence to furnish Wit for succeeding Ages,

* *Hor.*
† *Reading Prefaces,* &c.

---

* *Something extraordinary, new and never hit upon before.*

when the former have made no sort of Provision for ours; wherein I speak the Sentiment of the very newest, and consequently the most Orthodox Refiners, as well as my own. However, being extreamly sollicitous, that every accomplished Person who has got into the Taste of Wit, calculated for this present Month of *August,* 1697, should descend to the very *bottom* of all the *Sublime* throughout this Treatise; I hold fit to lay down this general Maxim. Whatever Reader desires to have a thorow Comprehension of an Author's Thoughts, cannot take a better Method, than by putting himself into the Circumstances and Postures of Life, that the Writer was in, upon every important Passage as it flow'd from his Pen; For this will introduce a Parity and strict Correspondence of Idea's between the Reader and the Author. Now, to assist the diligent Reader in so delicate an Affair, as far as brevity will permit, I have recollected, that the shrewdest Pieces of this Treatise, were conceived in Bed, in a Garret: At other times (for a Reason best known to my self) I though fit to sharpen my Invention with Hunger; and in general, the whole Work was begun, continued, and ended, under a long Course of Physick, and a great want of Money. Now, I do affirm, it will be absolutely impossible for the candid Peruser to go along with me in a great many bright Passages, unless upon the several Difficulties emergent, he will please to capacitate and prepare himself by these Directions. And this I lay down as my principal *Postulatum.*

Because I have profess'd to be a most devoted Servant of all *Modern* Forms: I apprehend some curious *Wit* may object against me, for proceeding thus far in a Preface, without declaiming, according to the Custom, against the Multitude of Writers whereof the whole Multitude of Writers most reasonably complains. I am just come from perusing some hundreds of Prefaces, wherein the Authors do at the very beginning address the gentle Reader concerning this enormous Grievance. Of these I have preserved a few Examples, and shall set them down as near as my Memory has been able to retain them.

One begins thus;

For a Man to set up for a Writer, when the Press swarms with, &c.

Another;

The Tax upon Paper does not lessen the Number of Scriblers, who daily pester, &c.

Another;

When every little Would-be-wit takes Pen in hand, 'tis in vain to enter the Lists, &c.

Another;

To observe what Trash the Press swarms with, &c.

Another;

SIR, It is merely in Obedience to your Commands that I venture into the Publick; for who upon a less Consideration would be of a Party with such a Rabble of Scriblers, &c.

Now, I have two Words in my own Defence, against this Objection. First: I am far from granting the Number of Writers, a Nuisance to our Nation, having strenuously maintained the contrary in several Parts of the following Discourse. Secondly: I do not well understand the Justice of this Proceeding, because I observe many of these polite Prefaces, to be not only from the same Hand, but from those who are most voluminous in their several Productions. Upon which I shall tell the Reader a short Tale.

A Mountebank in Leicester-Fields, *had drawn a huge Assembly about him. Among the rest, a fat unweildy Fellow, half stifled in the Press, would be every fit crying out, Lord! what a filthy Crowd is here; Pray, good People, give way a little, Bless me! what a Devil has rak'd this Rabble together: Z——ds, what squeezing is this! Honest Friend, remove your Elbow. At last, a* Weaver *that stood next him could hold no longer: A Plague confound you (said he) for an over-grown Sloven; and who (in the Devil's Name) I wonder, helps to make up the Crowd half so much as your self? Don't you consider (with a Pox) that you take up more room with that Carkass than any five here? Is not the Place as free for us as for you? Bring your own Guts to a reasonable Compass (and*

*be d——n'd) and then I'll engage we shall have room enough
for us all.*

There are certain common Privileges of a Writer, the
Benefit whereof, I hope, there will be no Reason to doubt;
Particularly, that where I am not understood, it shall be concluded, that something very useful and profound is coucht
underneath: And again, that whatever word or Sentence is
Printed in a different Character, shall be judged to contain
something extraordinary either of *Wit* or *Sublime.*

As for the Liberty I have though fit to take of praising my
self, upon some Occasions or none; I am sure it will need no
Excuse, if a Multitude of great Examples be allowed sufficient
Authority: For it is here to be noted, that *Praise* was originally
a Pension paid by the World: but the *Moderns* finding the
Trouble and Charge too great in collecting it, have lately
bought out the *Fee-Simple;* since which time, the Right of
Presentation is wholly in our selves. For this Reason it is, that
when an Author makes his own Elogy, he uses a certain form
to declare and insist upon his Title, which is commonly in
these or the like words, *I speak without Vanity;* which I think
plainly shews it to be a Matter of Right and Justice. Now, I do
here once for all declare, that in every Encounter of this
Nature, thro' the following Treatise, the Form aforesaid is
imply'd; which I mention, to save the Trouble of repeating it
on so many Occasions.

'Tis a great Ease to my Conscience that I have writ so
elaborate and useful a Discourse without one grain of Satyr
intermixt; which is the sole point wherein I have taken leave
to dissent from the famous Originals of our Age and Country.
I have observ'd some Satyrists to use the Publick much at the
Rate that Pedants do a naughty Boy ready Hors'd for Discipline: First expostulate the Case, then plead the Necessity
of the Rod, from great Provocations, and conclude every
Period with a Lash. Now, if I know any thing of Mankind,
these Gentlemen might very well spare their Reproof and
Correction: For there is not, through all Nature, another so

callous and insensible a Member as the *World's Posteriers,*
whether you apply to it the *Toe* or the *Birch.* Besides, most
of our late Satyrists seem to lye under a sort of Mistake, that
because Nettles have the Prerogative to Sting, therefore all
other Weeds must do so too. I make not this Comparison out
of the least Design to detract from these worthy Writers: For
it is well known among *Mythologists,* that *Weeds* have the
Preeminence over all other Vegetables; and therefore the first
Monarch of this Island, whose Taste and Judgment were so
acute and refined, did very wisely root out the *Roses* from the
Collar of the *Order,* and plant the *Thistles* in their stead as
the nobler Flower of the two. For which Reason it is conjectured by profounder Antiquaries, that the Satyrical Itch, so
prevalent in this part of our Island, was first brought among
us from beyond the *Tweed.* Here may it long flourish and
abound; May it survive and neglect the Scorn of the World,
with as much Ease and Contempt as the World is insensible
to the Lashes of it. May their own Dullness, or that of their
Party, be no Discouragement for the Authors to proceed;
but let them remember, it is with *Wits* as with *Razors,* which
are never so apt to *cut* those they are employ'd on, as when
they have *lost their Edge.* Besides, those whose Teeth are too
rotten to bite, are best of all others, qualified to revenge that
Defect with their Breath.

I am not like other Men, to envy or undervalue the Talents
I cannot reach; for which Reason I must needs bear a true
Honour to this large eminent Sect of our *British* Writers. And
I hope, this little Panegyrick will not be offensive to their
Ears, since it has the Advantage of being only designed for
themselves. Indeed, Nature her self has taken order, that
Fame and Honour should be purchased at a better Penny-
worth by Satyr, than by any other Productions of the Brain;
the World being soonest provoked to *Praise* by *Lashes,* as Men
are to *Love.* There is a Problem in an ancient Author, why
Dedications, and other Bundles of Flattery run all upon stale
musty Topicks, without the smallest Tincture of any thing
New; not only to the torment and nauseating of the *Christian*

Reader, but (if not suddenly prevented) to the universal spreading of that pestilent Disease, the Lethargy, in this Island: whereas, there is very little Satyr which has not some-thing in it untouch'd before. The Defects of the former are usually imputed to the want of Invention among those who are Dealers in that kind: But, I think, with a great deal of In-justice; the Solution being easy and natural. For, the Materials of Panegyrick being very few in Number, have been long since exhausted: For, as Health is but one Thing, and has been always the same, whereas Diseases are by thousands, besides new and daily Additions; So, all the Virtues that have been ever in Mankind, are to be counted upon a few Fingers, but his Follies and Vices are innumerable, and Time adds hourly to the Heap. Now, the utmost a poor Poet can do, is to get by heart a List of the Cardinal Virtues, and deal them with his utmost Liberality to his Hero or his Patron: He may ring the Changes as far as it will go, and vary his Phrase till he has talk'd round; but the Reader quickly finds, it is all *Pork, with a little variety of Sawce: For there is no inventing Terms of Art beyond our Idea's; and when Idea's are exhausted, Terms of Art must be so too.

But, tho' the Matter for Panegyrick were as fruitful as the Topicks of Satyr, yet would it not be hard to find out a sufficient Reason, why the latter will be always better received than the first. For, this being bestowed only upon one or a few Persons at a time, is sure to raise Envy, and consequently ill words from the rest, who have no share in the Blessing: But Satyr being levelled at all, is never resented for an offence by any, since every individual Person makes bold to understand it of others, and very wisely removes his particular Part of the Burthen upon the shoulders of the World, which are broad enough, and able to bear it. To this purpose, I have sometimes reflected upon the Difference between *Athens* and *England,* with respect to the Point before us. In the *Attick*† Common-

* *Plutarch.*
† *Vid. Xenoph.*

wealth, it was the Privilege and Birth-right of every Citizen and Poet, to rail aloud and in publick, or to expose upon the Stage by Name, any Person they pleased, tho' of the greatest Figure, whether a *Creon,* an *Hyperbolus,* an *Alcibiades,* or a *Demosthenes:* But on the other side, the least reflecting word let fall against the *People* in general, was immediately caught up, and revenged upon the Authors, however considerable for their Quality or their Merits. Whereas, in *England* it is just the Reverse of all this. Here, you may securely display your utmost *Rhetorick* against Mankind, in the Face of the World; tell them, *"That all are gone astray; That there is none that* *"doth good, no not one; That we live in the very Dregs of* *"Time; That Knavery and Atheism are Epidemick as the Pox;* *"That Honesty is fled with Astræa;* with any other Common places *equally* new and eloquent, which are furnished by the **Splendida bilis.* And when you have done, the whole Audience, far from being offended, shall return you thanks as a Deliverer of precious and useful Truths. Nay farther; It is but to venture your Lungs, and you may preach in *Convent-Garden* against Foppery and Fornication, and *something else:* Against Pride, and Dissimulation, and Bribery, at *White Hall:* You may expose Rapine and Injustice in the *Inns* of *Court* Chappel: And in a *City* Pulpit be as fierce as you please, against Avarice, Hypocrisie and Extortion. 'Tis but a *Ball* bandied to and fro, and every Man carries a *Racket* about Him to strike it from himself among the rest of the Company. But on the other side, whoever should mistake the Nature of things so far, as to drop but a single Hint in publick, How *such a one,* starved half the Fleet, and half-poison'd the rest: How *such a one,* from a true Principle of *Love* and *Honour,* pays no Debts but for *Wenches* and *Play:* How *such a one* has got a Clap and runs out of his Estate: †How *Paris* bribed by *Juno* and

* *Hor.*

---

* *Spleen.*

† Juno *and* Venus *are Money and a Mistress, very powerful Bribes to a Judge, if Scandal says true. I remember such Reflexions were cast about that time, but I cannot fix the Person intended here.*

Venus, loath to offend either Party, slept out the whole Cause on the Bench: Or, how *such an Orator* makes long Speeches in the Senate with much Thought, little Sense, and to no Purpose; whoever, I say, should venture to be thus particular, must expect to be imprisoned for *Scandalum Magnatum:* to have *Challenges* sent him; to be sued for *Defamation;* and to be *brought before the Bar of the House.*

But I forget that I am expatiating on a Subject, wherein I have no concern, having neither a Talent nor an Inclination for Satyr; On the other side, I am so entirely satisfied with the whole present Procedure of human Things, that I have been for some Years preparing Materials towards *A Panegyrick upon the World;* to which I intended to add a Second Part, entituled, *A Modest Defence of the Proceedings of the Rabble in all Ages.* Both these I had Thoughts to publish by way of Appendix to the following Treatise; but finding my Common-Place-Book fill much slower than I had reason to expect, I have chosen to defer them to another Occasion. Besides, I have been unhappily prevented in that Design, by a certain Domestick Misfortune, in the Particulars whereof, tho' it would be very seasonable, and much in the *Modern* way, to inform the *gentle Reader,* and would also be of great Assistance towards extending this Preface into the Size now in Vogue, which by Rule ought to be *large* in proportion as the subsequent Volume is *small;* Yet I shall now dismiss our impatient Reader from any farther Attendance at the *Porch;* and having duly prepared his Mind by a preliminary Discourse, shall gladly introduce him to the sublime Mysteries that ensue.

A

T A L E

O F   A

TUB, &c.

S E C T I O N   I.

The INTRODUCTION

WHOEVER hath an Ambition to be heard in a Crowd, must press, and squeeze, and thrust, and climb with indefatigable Pains, till he has exalted himself to a certain Degree of Altitude above them. Now, in all Assemblies, tho' you wedge them ever so close, we may observe this peculiar Property; that, over their Heads there is Room enough; but how to reach it, is the difficult Point; It being as hard to get quit of *Number* as of *Hell;*

> **———— Evadere ad auras,*
> *Hoc opus, hic labor est.*

To this End, the Philosopher's Way in all Ages has been by erecting certain *Edifices in the Air;* But, whatever Practice and Reputation these kind of Structures have formerly possessed, or may still continue in, not excepting even that of *Socrates,* when he was suspended in a Basket to help Contemplation; I think, with due Submission, they seem to labour

---

* *But to return, and view the cheerful Skies;*
In this the Task and mighty Labour lies.

under two Inconveniences. *First,* That the Foundations being laid too high, they have been often out of *Sight,* and ever out of *Hearing. Secondly,* That the Materials, being very transitory, have suffer'd much from Inclemencies of Air, especially in these North-West Regions.

Therefore, towards the just Performance of this great Work, there remain but three Methods that I can think on; Whereof the Wisdom of our Ancestors being highly sensible, has, to encourage all aspiring Adventurers, thought fit to erect three wooden Machines, for the Use of those Orators who desire to talk much without Interruption. These are, the *Pulpit,* the *Ladder,* and the *Stage-Itinerant.* For, as to the *Bar,* tho' it be compounded of the same Matter, and designed for the same Use, it cannot however be well allowed the Honor of a fourth, by reason of its level or inferior Situation, exposing it to perpetual Interruption from Collaterals. Neither can the *Bench* it self, tho raised to a proper Eminency, put in a better Claim, whatever its Advocates insist on. For if they please to look into the original Design of its Erection, and the Circumstances or Adjuncts subservient to that Design, they will soon acknowledge the present Practice exactly correspondent to the Primitive Institution, and both to answer the Etymology of the Name, which in the *Phœnician* Tongue is a Word of great Signification, importing, if literally interpreted, *The Place of Sleep;* but in common Acceptation, *A Seat well bolster'd and cushion'd, for the Repose of old and gouty Limbs: Senes ut in otia tuta recedant.* Fortune being indebted to them this Part of Retaliation, that, as formerly, they have long *Talkt,* whilst others *Slept,* so now they may *Sleep* as long whilst others *Talk.*

But if no other Argument could occur to exclude the *Bench* and the *Bar* from the List of Oratorial Machines, it were sufficient, that the Admission of them would overthrow a Number which I was resolved to establish, whatever Argument it might cost me; in imitation of that prudent Method observed by many other Philosophers and great Clerks, whose chief Art in Division has been, to grow fond of some proper

mystical Number, which their Imaginations have rendred
Sacred, to a Degree, that they force common Reason to find
room for it in every part of Nature; reducing, including, and
adjusting every *Genus* and *Species* within that Compass, by
coupling some against their Wills, and banishing others at any
Rate. Now among all the rest, the profound number THREE
is that which hath most employ'd my sublimest Speculations,
nor ever without wonderful Delight. There is now in the
Press, (and will be publish'd next Term) a Panegyrical Essay
of mine upon this Number, wherein I have by most convincing
Proofs, not only reduced the *Senses* and the *Elements* under
its Banner, but brought over several Deserters from its two
great Rivals *SEVEN* and *NINE*.

Now, the first of these Oratorial Machines in Place as well
as Dignity, is the *Pulpit*. Of *Pulpits* there are in this Island
several sorts; but I esteem only That made of Timber from the
Sylva Caledonia, which agrees very well with our Climate. If
it be upon its Decay, 'tis the better, both for Conveyance of
Sound, and for other Reasons to be mentioned by and by. The
Degree of Perfection in Shape and Size, I take to consist, in
being extreamly narrow, with little Ornament, and best of all
without a Cover; (for by antient Rule, it ought to be the only
uncover'd *Vessel* in every Assembly where it is rightfully used)
by which means, from its near Resemblance to a Pillory, it will
ever have a mighty Influence on human Ears.

Of *Ladders* I need say nothing: 'Tis observed by Foreigners
themselves, to the Honor of our Country, that we excel all
Nations in our Practice and Understanding of this Machine.
The ascending Orators do not only oblige their Audience in
the agreeable Delivery, but the whole World in their *early*
Publication of these Speeches; which I look upon as the
choicest Treasury of our *British* Eloquence, and whereof I
am informed, that worthy Citizen and Bookseller, Mr. *John
Dunton,* hath made a faithful and a painful Collection, which
he shortly designs to publish in Twelve Volumes in Folio,
illustrated with Copper-Plates. A Work highly useful and
curious, and altogether worthy of such a Hand.

The last Engine of Orators, is the *_Stage Itinerant_, erected with much Sagacity, †_sub Jove pluvio, in triviis & quadriviis_. It is the great Seminary of the two former, and its Orators are sometime[s] preferred to the One, and sometimes to the Other, in proportion to their Deservings, there being a strict and perpetual Intercourse between all three.

From this accurate Deduction it is manifest, that for obtaining Attention in Publick, there is of necessity required a _superiour Position of Place_. But, altho' this Point be generally granted, yet the Cause is little agreed in; and it seems to me, that very few Philosophers have fallen into a true, natural Solution of this _Phænomenon_. The deepest Account, and the most fairly digested of any I have yet met with, is this, That Air being a heavy Body, and therefore (according to the System of ‡_Epicurus_) continually descending, must needs be more so, when loaden and press'd down by Words; which are also Bodies of much Weight and Gravity, as it is manifest from those deep _Impressions_ they make and leave upon us; and therefore must be delivered from a due Altitude, or else they will neither carry a good Aim, nor fall down with a sufficient Force.

§_Corpoream quoque enim vocem constare fatendum est,_
   Et sonitum, quoniam possunt impellere Sensus.

Lucr. _Lib._ 4.

And I am the readier to favour this Conjecture, from a common Observation; that in the several Assemblies of these Orators, Nature it self hath instructed the Hearers, to stand with their Mouths open, and erected parallel to the Horizon, so as they may be intersected by a perpendicular Line from the Zenith to the Center of the Earth. In which position, if the

‡ _Lucret._ Lib. 2.

---

* _Is the_ Mountebank's Stage, _whose Orators the Author determines either to the_ Gallows _or a_ Conventicle.

† _In the open Air, and in Streets where the greatest Resort is._

§ _'Tis certain then, that_ Voice _that thus can wound_
Is all Material; Body _every_ Sound.

Audience be well compact, every one carries home a Share, and little or nothing is lost.

I confess, there is something yet more refined in the Contrivance and Structure of our Modern Theatres. For, First; the Pit is sunk below the Stage with due regard to the Institution above-deduced; that whatever *weighty* Matter shall be delivered thence (whether it be *Lead* or *Gold*) may fall plum into the Jaws of certain *Criticks* (as I think they are called) which stand ready open to devour them. Then, the Boxes are built round, and raised to a Level with the Scene, in deference to the Ladies, because, That large Portion of Wit laid out in raising Pruriences and Protuberances, is observ'd to run much upon a Line, and ever in a Circle. The whining Passions, and little starved Conceits, are gently wafted up by their own extreme Levity, to the middle Region, and there fix and are frozen by the frigid Understandings of the Inhabitants. Bombastry and Buffoonry, by Nature lofty and light, soar highest of all, and would be lost in the Roof, if the prudent Architect had not with much Foresight contrived for them a fourth Place, called *the Twelve-Peny Gallery,* and there planted a suitable Colony, who greedily intercept them in their Passage.

Now this Physico-logical Scheme of Oratorial Receptacles or Machines, contains a great Mystery, being a Type, a Sign, an Emblem, a Shadow, a Symbol, bearing Analogy to the spacious Commonwealth of Writers, and to those Methods by which they must exalt themselves to a certain Eminency above the inferiour World. By the *Pulpit* are adumbrated the Writings of our *Modern Saints* in *Great Britain,* as they have spiritualized and refined them from the Dross and Grossness of *Sense* and *Human Reason.* The Matter, as we have said, is of rotten Wood, and that upon two Considerations; Because it is the Quality of rotten Wood to give *Light* in the Dark: And secondly, Because its Cavities are full of Worms: which is a *Type with a Pair of Handles, having a Respect to the

---

* *The Two Principal Qualifications of a Phanatick Preacher are, his Inward Light, and his Head full of Maggots, and the Two different Fates of his Writings are, to be burnt or Worm eaten.*

two principal Qualifications of the Orator, and the two different Fates attending upon his works.

The *Ladder* is an adequate Symbol of *Faction* and of *Poetry*, to both of which so noble a Number of Authors are indebted for their Fame. *Of *Faction,* because *   *   *   *   *
*   *   *   *   *   *   *   *

Hiatus in   *   *   *   *   *   *   *   *
MS.   *   *   *   *   *   *   *   *

*   *   *   *   Of *Poetry,* because its Orators do *perorare* with a Song; and because climbing up by slow Degrees, Fate is sure to turn them off before they can reach within many Steps of the Top: And because it is a Preferment attained by transferring of Propriety, and a confounding of *Meum* and *Tuum.*

Under the *Stage-Itinerant* are couched those Productions designed for the Pleasure and Delight of Mortal Man; such as *Six-peny-worth of Wit,* Westminster *Drolleries, Delightful Tales, Compleat Jesters,* and the like; by which the Writers of and for *GRUB-STREET,* have in these latter Ages so nobly triumph'd over *Time;* have clipt his Wings, pared his Nails, filed his Teeth, turn'd back his Hour-Glass, blunted his Scythe, and drawn the Hob-Nails out of his Shoes. It is under this Classis, I have presumed to list my present Treatise, being just come from having the Honor conferred upon me, to be adopted a Member of that illustrious Fraternity.

Now, I am not unaware, how the Productions of the *Grubstreet* Brotherhood, have of late Years fallen under many Prejudices, nor how it has been the perpetual Employment of two *Junior* start-up Societies, to ridicule them and their Authors, as unworthy their established Post in the Commonwealth of Wit and Learning. Their own Consciences will easily inform them, whom I mean; Nor has the World been so negli-

---

* *Here is pretended a Defect in the Manuscript, and this is very frequent with our Author, either when he thinks he cannot say any thing worth Reading, or when he has no mind to enter on the Subject, or when it is a Matter of little Moment, or perhaps to amuse his Reader (whereof he is frequently very fond) or lastly, with some Satyrical Intention.*

gent a Looker on, as not to observe the continual Efforts made by the Societies of *Gresham* and of *Will's to edify a Name and Reputation upon the Ruin of OURS. And this is yet a more feeling Grief to Us upon the Regards of Tenderness as well as of Justice, when we reflect on their Proceedings, not only as unjust, but as ungrateful, undutiful, and unnatural. For, how can it be forgot by the World or themselves, (to say nothing of our own Records, which are full and clear in the Point) that they both are Seminaries, not only of our *Planting,* but our *Watering* too? I am informed, Our two *Rivals* have lately made an Offer to enter into the Lists with united Forces, and Challenge us to a Comparison of Books, both as to *Weight* and *Number.* In Return to which, (with Licence from our *President*) I humbly offer two Answers: First, We say, the proposal is like that which *Archimedes* made upon a †*smaller* Affair, including an impossibility in the Practice; For, where can they find Scales of *Capacity* enough for the first, or an Arithmetician of *Capacity* enough for the Second. Secondly, We are ready to accept the Challenge, but with this Condition, that a third indifferent Person be assigned, to whose impartial Judgment it shall be left to decide, which Society each Book, Treatise or Pamphlet do most properly belong to. This Point, God knows, is very far from being fixed at present; For, We are ready to produce a Catalogue of some Thousands, which in all common Justice ought to be entitled to Our Fraternity, but by the revolted and new-fangled Writers, most perfidiously ascribed to the others. Upon all which, we think it very unbecoming our Prudence, that the Determination should be remitted to the Authors themselves; when our Adversaries by Briguing and Caballing, have caused so universal a Defection from us, that the greatest Part of our Society hath already deserted to them, and our nearest Friends begin to stand aloof, as if they were half-ashamed to own Us.

† Viz. *About moving the Earth.*

---

* Will's Coffee-House, *was formerly the Place where the Poets usually met, which tho it be yet fresh in memory, yet in some Years may be forgot, and want this Explanation.*

This is the utmost I am authorized to say upon so ungrateful and melancholy a Subject; because We are extreme unwilling to inflame a Controversy, whose Continuance may be so fatal to the Interests of Us All, desiring much rather that Things be amicably composed; and We shall so far advance on our Side, as to be ready to receive the two *Prodigals* with open Arms, whenever they shall think fit to return from their *Husks* and their *Harlots;* which I think from the *present Course of their Studies they most properly may be said to be engaged in; and like an indulgent Parent, continue to them our Affection and our Blessing.

But the greatest Maim given to that general Reception, which the Writings of our Society have formerly received, (next to the transitory State of all sublunary Things,) hath been a superficial Vein among many Readers of the present Age, who will by no means be persuaded to inspect beyond the Surface and the Rind of Things; whereas, *Wisdom* is a *Fox,* who after long hunting, will at last cost you the Pains to dig out: 'Tis a *Cheese,* which by how much the richer, has the thicker, the homelier, and the courser Coat; and whereof to a judicious Pa[la]te, the *Maggots* are the best. 'Tis a *Sack-Posset,* wherein the deeper you go, you will find it the sweeter. *Wisdom* is a *Hen,* whose *Cackling* we must value and consider, because it is attended with an *Egg;* But then, lastly, 'tis a *Nut,* which unless you chuse with Judgment, may cost you a Tooth, and pay you with nothing but a *Worm.* In consequence of these momentous Truths, the *Grubæan* Sages have always chosen to convey their Precepts and their Arts, shut up within the Vehicles of Types and Fables, which having been perhaps more careful and curious in adorning, than was altogether necessary, it has fared with these Vehicles after the usual Fate of Coaches over-finely painted and gilt; that the transitory Gazers have so dazzled their Eyes, and fill'd their Imaginations with the outward Lustre, as neither to regard or consider, the Person or the Parts of the Owner within. A Misfortune we

* *Virtuoso Experiments, and Modern Comedies.*

undergo with somewhat less Reluctancy, because it has been common to us with *Pythagoras, Æsop, Socrates,* and other of our Predecessors.

However, that neither the World nor our selves may any longer suffer by such misunderstandings, I have been prevailed on, after much importunity from my Friends, to travel in a compleat and laborious Dissertation upon the prime Productions of our Society, which besides their beautiful Externals for the Gratification of superficial Readers, have darkly and deeply couched under them, the most finished and refined Systems of all Sciences and Arts; as I do not doubt to lay open by Untwisting or Unwinding, and either to draw up by Exantlation, or display by Incision.

This great Work was entred upon some Years ago, by one of our most eminent Members: He began with the History of *Reynard the Fox,* but neither lived to publish his Essay, nor to proceed farther in so useful an Attempt which is very much to be lamented, because the Discovery he made, and communicated with his Friends, is now universally received; nor, do I think, any of the Learned will dispute, that famous Treatise to be a compleat Body of Civil Knowledge, and the *Revelation,* or rather the *Apocalyps* of all State-*Arcana.* But the Progress I have made is much greater, having already finished my Annotations upon several Dozens; From some of which, I shall impart a few Hints to the candid Reader, as far as will be necessary to the Conclusion at which I aim.

The first Piece I have handled is that of *Tom Thumb,* whose Author was a *Pythagorean* Philosopher. This dark Treatise contains the whole Scheme of the *Metempsychosis,* deducing the Progress of the Soul thro' all her Stages.

The next is Dr. *Faustus,* penn'd by *Artephius,* an Author *bonæ notæ,* and an *Adeptus;* He published it in the †nine

† *He lived a thousand.*

---

* *The Author seems here to be mistaken, for I have seen a Latin Edition of* Reynard *the Fox, above an hundred Years old, which I take to be the Original; for the rest it has been thought by many People to contain some Satyrical Design in it.*

hundred eighty fourth Year of his Age; this Writer proceeds wholly by *Reincrudation,* or in the *via humida:* And the Marriage between *Faustus* and *Helen,* does most conspicuously dilucidate the fermenting of the *Male* and *Female Dragon.*

Whittington and his Cat, is the Work of that Mysterious *Rabbi, Jehuda Hannasi,* containing a Defence of the *Gemara* of the *Jerusalem Misna,* and its just preference to that of *Babylon,* contrary to the vulgar Opinion.

The Hind and Panther. This is the Master-piece of a famous Writer *now living, intended for a compleat Abstract of sixteen thousand Schoolmen from *Scotus* to *Bellarmin.*

Tommy Potts. Another Piece supposed by the same Hand, by way of Supplement to the former.

The Wise Men of Goatham, *cum Appendice.* This is a Treatise of immense Erudition, being the great Original and Fountain of those Arguments, bandied about both in *France* and *England,* for a just Defence of the *Moderns* Learning and Wit, against the Presumption, the Pride, and the Ignorance of the *Antients.* This unknown Author hath so exhausted the Subject, that a penetrating Reader will easily discover, whatever hath been written since upon that Dispute, to be little more than Repetition. † An Abstract of this Treatise hath been lately published by a *worthy Member* of our Society.

These Notices may serve to give the Learned Reader an Idea as well as a Taste of what the whole Work is likely to produce: wherein I have now altogether circumscribed my Thoughts and my Studies; and if I can bring it to a Perfection before I die, shall reckon I have well employ'd the ‡poor Remains of an unfortunate Life. This indeed is more than I can justly expect from a Quill worn to the Pith in the Service

* *Viz in the Year* 1698.

---

† *This I suppose to be understood of Mr.* W—tt—ns *Discourse of Antient and Modern Learning.*

‡ *Here the Author seems to personate* L'estrange, Dryden, *and some others, who after having past their Lives in Vices, Faction and Falsehood, have the Impudence to talk of Merit and Innocence and Sufferings.*

of the State, in *Pro's* and *Con's* upon *Popish Plots,* and *Meal-
Tubs, and *Exclusion Bills,* and *Passive Obedience,* and
Addresses of Lives and Fortunes; and *Prerogative,* and *Prop-
erty,* and *Liberty of Conscience,* and *Letters to a Friend:* From
an Understanding and a Conscience, thread-bare and ragged
with perpetual turning; From a Head broken in a hundred
places, by the Malignants of the opposite Factions, and from
a Body spent with Poxes ill cured, by trusting to Bawds and
Surgeons, who, (as it afterwards appeared) were profess'd
Enemies to Me and the Government, and revenged their
Party's Quarrel upon my Nose and Shins. Fourscore and eleven
Pamphlets have I written under three Reigns, and for the
Service of six and thirty Factions. But finding the State has no
farther Occasion for Me and my Ink, I retire willingly to draw
it out into Speculations more becoming a Philosopher, having,
to my unspeakable Comfort, passed a long Life, with a Con-
science void of Offence.

But to return. I am assured from the Reader's Candor, that
the brief Specimen I have given, will easily clear all the rest
of our Society's Productions from an Aspersion grown, as it is
manifest, out of Envy and Ignorance: That they are of little
farther Use or Value to Mankind, beyond the common Entertainments of their Wit and their Style: For these I am sure have
never yet been disputed by our keenest Adversaries: In both
which, as well as the more profound and mystical Part, I have
throughout this Treatise closely followed the most applauded
Originals. And to render all compleat, I have with much
Thought and Application of Mind, so ordered, that the chief
Title prefixed to it, (I mean, That under which I design it
shall pass in the common Conversations of Court and Town)
is modelled exactly after the Manner peculiar to *Our* Society.

I confess to have been somewhat liberal in the Business
of †Titles, having observed the Humor of multiplying them,

† *The Title Page in the Original was so torn, that it was not possible
to recover several Titles which the Author here speaks of.*

* *In King* Charles *the* II. *Time, there was an Account of a* Presbyterian
Plot, found in a Tub, which then made much Noise.

to bear great Vogue among certain Writers, whom I exceedingly Reverence. And indeed, it seems not unreasonable, that Books, the Children of the Brain, should have the Honor to be Christned with variety of Names, as well as other Infants of Quality. Our famous *Dryden* has ventured to proceed a Point farther, endeavouring to introduce also a Multiplicity of *God-fathers;* which is an Improvement of much more Advantage, upon a very obvious Account. 'Tis a Pity this admirable Invention has not been better cultivated, so as to grow by this time into general Imitation, when such an Authority serves it for a Precedent. Nor have my Endeavours been wanting to second so useful an Example: But it seems, there is an unhappy Expence usually annexed to the Calling of a God-Father, which was clearly out of my Head, as it is very reasonable to believe. Where the Pinch lay, I cannot certainly affirm; but having employ'd a World of Thoughts and Pains, to split my Treatise into forty Sections, and having entreated forty Lords of my Acquaintance, that they would do me the Honor to stand, they all made it a Matter of Conscience, and sent me their Excuses.

SECTION II.

ONCE upon a Time, there was a Man who had Three †Sons by one Wife, and all at a Birth, neither could the Mid-Wife tell certainly which was the Eldest. Their Father died while they were young, and upon his Death-Bed, calling the Lads to him, spoke thus,

SONS; because I have purchased no Estate, nor was born to any, I have long considered of some good Legacies to bequeath You; And at last, with much Care as well as Expence,

* *See* Virgil *translated,* &c.

---

† *By these three Sons,* Peter, Martyn *and* Jack; Popery, *the* Church *of* England, *and our* Protestant Dissenters *are designed.* W. Wotton.

have provided each of you (here they are) *a new *Coat. Now, you are to understand, that these Coats have two Virtues contained in them: One is, that with good wearing, they will last you fresh and sound as long as you live: The other is, that they will grow in the same proportion with your Bodies, lengthning and widening of themselves, so as to be always fit. Here, let me see them on you before I die. So, very well, Pray Children, wear them clean, and brush them often. You will find in my †Will* (here it is) *full Instructions in every particular concerning the Wearing and Management of your Coats; wherein you must be very exact, to avoid the Penalties I have appointed for every Transgression or Neglect, upon which your future Fortunes will entirely depend. I have also commanded in my Will, that you should live together in one House like Brethren and Friends, for then you will be sure to thrive, and not otherwise.*

Here the Story says, this good Father died, and the three Sons went all together to seek their Fortunes.

I shall not trouble you with recounting what Adventures they met for the first seven Years, any farther than by taking notice, that they carefully observed their Father's Will, and kept their Coats in very good Order; That they travelled thro' several Countries, encountred a reasonable Quantity of Gyants, and slew certain Dragons.

Being now arrived at the proper Age for producing themselves, they came up to Town, and fell in love with the Ladies, but especially three, who about that time were in chief Reputation; The ‡Dutchess *d'Argent, Madame de Grands*

---

* *By his Coats which he gave his Sons, the Garments of the* Israelites. W. Wotton.

An Error (with Submission) of the learned Commentator; for by the Coats are meant the Doctrine and Faith of Christianity, *by the Wisdom of the Divine Founder fitted to all Times, Places and Circumstances.* Lambin.

† *The New Testament.*

‡ *Their Mistresses are the* Dutchess d'Argent, Madamoiselle de Grands Titres, *and the* Countess d'Orgueil, *i.e.* Covetousness, Ambition *and* Pride, *which were the three great Vices that the ancient Fathers inveighed against as the first Corruptions of Christianity.* W. Wotton.

Titres, and the Countess *d'Orgueil.* On their first Appearance, our three Adventurers met with a very bad Reception; and soon with great Sagacity guessing out the Reason, they quickly began to improve in the good Qualities of the Town: They Writ, and Raillyed, and Rhymed, and Sung, and Said, and said Nothing; They Drank, and Fought, and Whor'd, and Slept, and Swore, and took Snuff: They went to new Plays on the first Night, haunted the *Chocolate*-Houses, beat the Watch, lay on Bulks, and got Claps: They bilkt Hackney-Coachmen, ran in Debt with Shop-keepers, and lay with their Wives: They kill'd Bayliffs, kick'd Fidlers down Stairs, eat at *Locket's,* loytered at *Will's:* They talk'd of the Drawing-Room and never came there, Dined with Lords they never saw; Whisper'd a Dutchess, and spoke never a Word; exposed the Scrawls of their Laundress for Billetdoux of Quality: came ever just from Court and were never seen in it; attended the Levee *sub dio;* Got a list of Peers by heart in one Company, and with great Familiarity retailed them in another. Above all, they constantly attended those Committees of Senators who are silent in the *House,* and loud in the *Coffee-House,* where they nightly adjourn to chew the Cud of Politicks, and are encompass'd with a Ring of Disciples, who lye in wait to catch up their Droppings. The three Brothers had acquired forty other Qualifications of the like Stamp, too tedious to recount, and by consequence, were justly reckoned the most accomplish'd Persons in the Town: But all would not suffice, and the Ladies aforesaid continued still inflexible: To clear up which Difficulty, I must with the Reader's good Leave and Patience, have recourse to some Points of Weight, which the Authors of that Age have not sufficiently illustrated.

For, *about this Time it happened a Sect arose, whose Tenents obtained and spread very far, especially in the *Grand Monde,* and among every Body of good Fashion. They worshipped a sort of *Idol,* who, as their Doctrine delivered, did daily create Men, by a kind of Manufactory Operation. This

---

* *This is an Occasional Satyr upon Dress and Fashion, in order to introduce what follows.*

Idol they placed in the highest Parts of the House, on an Altar erected about three Foot: He was shewn in the Posture of a *Persian* Emperor, sitting on a *Superficies,* with his Legs interwoven under him. This God had a *Goose* for his Ensign; whence it is, that some Learned Men pretend to deduce his Original from *Jupiter Capitolinus.* At his left Hand, beneath the Altar, *Hell* seemed to open, and catch at the Animals the *Idol* was creating; to prevent which, certain of his Priests hourly flung in Pieces of the uninformed Mass, or Substance, and sometimes whole Limbs already enlivened, which that horrid Gulph insatiably swallowed, terrible to behold. The *Goose* was also held a subaltern Divinity, or *Deus minorum Gentium,* before whose Shrine was sacrificed that Creature, whose hourly Food is humane Gore, and who is in so great Renown abroad, for being the Delight and Favourite of the †*Ægyptian Cercopithecus.* Millions of these Animals were cruelly slaughtered every Day, to appease the Hunger of that consuming Deity. The chief *Idol* was also worshipped as the Inventor of the *Yard* and the *Needle,* whether as the God of Seamen, or on Account of certain other mystical Attributes, hath not been sufficiently cleared.

The Worshippers of this Deity had also a System of their Belief, which seemed to turn upon the following Fundamental. They held the Universe to be a large *Suit of Cloaths,* which *invests* every Thing: That the Earth is *invested* by the Air; The Air is *invested* by the Stars; and the Stars are *invested* by the *Primum Mobile.* Look on this Globe of Earth, you will find it to be a very compleat and fashionable *Dress.* What is that which some call *Land,* but a fine Coat faced with Green? or the Sea, but a Wastcoat of Water-Tabby? Proceed to the particular Works of the Creation, you will find how curious *Journey-man* Nature hath been, to trim up the *vegetable* Beaux: Observe how sparkish a Perewig adorns the Head of a *Beech,* and what a fine Doublet of white Satin is worn by the

---

* *By this* Idol *is meant a Taylor.*

† *The Ægyptians* worship'd *a Monkey, which Animal is very fond of* eating Lice, *styled here Creatures that feed on Human Gore.*

Birch. To conclude from all, what is Man himself but a * *Micro-Coat,* or rather a compleat Suit of Cloaths with all its Trimmings? As to his Body, there can be no dispute; but examine even the Acquirements of his Mind, you will find them all contribute in their Order, towards furnishing out an exact Dress: To instance no more; Is not Religion a *Cloak,* Honesty a *Pair of Shoes,* worn out in Dirt, Self-love a *Surtout,* Vanity a *Shirt,* and Conscience a *Pair of Breeches,* which, tho' a Cover for Lewdness as well as Nastiness, is easily slipt down for the Services of both.

These *Postulata* being admitted, it will follow in due Course of Reasoning, that those Beings which the World calls improperly *Suits of Cloaths,* are in Reality the most refined Species of Animals, or to proceed higher, that they are Rational Creatures, or Men. For, is it not manifest, that They live, and move, and talk, and perform all other Offices of Human Life? Are not Beauty, and Wit, and Mien, and Breeding, their inseparable Proprieties? In short, we see nothing but them, hear nothing but them. Is it not they who walk the Streets, fill up *Parliament——, Coffee——, Play——, Bawdy-Houses?* 'Tis true indeed, that these Animals, which are vulgarly called *Suits of Cloaths,* or *Dresses,* do according to certain Compositions receive different Appellations. If one of them be trimm'd up with a Gold Chain, and a red Gown, and a white Rod, and a great Horse, it is called a *Lord-Mayor;* If certain Ermins and Furs be placed in a certain Position, we stile them a *Judge,* and so, an apt Conjunction of Lawn and black Sattin, we intitle a *Bishop.*

Others of these Professors, though agreeing in the main System, were yet more refined upon certain Branches of it; and held that Man was an Animal compounded of two *Dresses,* the *Natural* and the *Celestial Suit,* which were the Body and the Soul: That the Soul was the outward, and the Body the inward Cloathing; that the latter was *ex traduce;* but the

---

* *Alluding to the Word* Microcosm, *or a little World, as Man hath been called by Philosophers.*

former of daily Creation and Circumfusion. This last they proved by *Scripture*, because, *in Them we Live, and Move, and have our Being:* As likewise by Philosophy, because they are *All in All, and All in every Part.* Besides, said they, separate these two, and you will find the Body to be only a sensless unsavory Carcass. By all which it is manifest, that the outward Dress must needs be the Soul.

To this System of Religion were tagged several subaltern Doctrines, which were entertained with great Vogue: as particularly, the Faculties of the Mind were deduced by the Learned among them in this manner: *Embroidery*, was *Sheer wit; Gold Fringe* was *agreeable Conversation, Gold Lace* was *Repartee,* a huge long *Periwig* was *Humor*, and a *Coat full of Powder* was very good *Raillery:* All which required abundance of *Finesse* and *Delicatesse* to manage with Advantage, as well as a strict Observance after Times and Fashions.

I have with much Pains and Reading, collected out of antient Authors, this short Summary of a Body of Philosophy and Divinity, which seems to have been composed by a Vein and Race of Thinking, very different from any other Systems, either *Antient* or *Modern*. And it was not meerly to entertain or satisfy the Reader's Curiosity, but rather to give him Light into several Circumstances of the following Story: that knowing the State of Dispositions and Opinions in an Age so remote, he may better comprehend those great Events which were the issue of them. I advise therefore the courteous Reader, to peruse with a world of Application, again and again, whatever I have written upon this Matter. And [so] leaving these broken Ends, I carefully gather up the chief Thread of my Story, and proceed.

The first part of the Tale *is the History of* Peter; *thereby* Popery *is exposed, every Body knows the* Papists *have made great Additions to Christianity, that indeed is the great Exception which the* Church of England *makes against them, accordingly* Peter *begins his Pranks, with adding a* Shoulder-knot *to his Coat.* W. Wotton.

His Description of the Cloth of which the Coat was made, has a farther meaning than the Words may seen to import, "The Coats their Father had left them, were of very good Cloth, and besides so neatly

These Opinions therefore were so universal, as well as the Practices of them, among the refined Part of Court and Town, that our three Brother-Adventurers, as their Circumstances then stood, were strangely at a loss. For, on the one side, the three Ladies they address'd themselves to, (whom we have named already) were ever at the very Top of the Fashion, and abhorred all that were below it, but the breadth of a Hair. On the other side, their Father's Will was very precise, and it was the main Precept in it, with the greatest Penalties annexed, not to add to, or diminish from their Coats, one Thread, without a positive Command in the Will. Now, the Coats their Father had left them were, 'tis true, of very good Cloth, and besides, so neatly sown, you would swear they were all of a Piece, but at the same time, very plain, and with little or no Ornament; And it happened, that before they were a Month in Town, great * *Shoulder-knots* came up; Strait, all the World was *Shoulder-knots;* no approaching the Ladies *Ruelles* without the *Quota* of *Shoulder-knots: That Fellow,* cries one, *has no Soul; where is his Shoulder-knot?* Our three Brethren soon discovered their Want by sad Experience, meeting their Walks with forty Mortifications and Indignities. If they went to the *Play-house,* the Door-keeper shewed them into the Twelve-peny Gallery. If they called a Boat, says a Waterman, *I am first Sculler:* If they stept to the *Rose* to take a Bottle, the Drawer would cry, *Friend, we sell no Ale.* If they went to visit a Lady, a Footman met them at the Door with, *Pray send up your Message.* In this unhappy Case, they went immediately to consult their Father's Will, read it

---

Sown, you would swear it had been all of a Piece, but at the same time very plain with little or no Ornament." *This is the distinguishing Character of the Christian Religion.* Christiana Religio absoluta & simplex, *was* Ammianus Marcellinus's *Description of it, who was himself a Heathen.* W. Wotton.

* *By this is understood the first introducing of Pageantry, and unnecessary Ornaments in the Church, such as were neither for convenience nor Edification, as a* Shoulder-knot, *in which there is neither Symmetry nor Use.*

over and over, but not a Word of the *Shoulder-knot*. What should they do? What Temper should they find? Obedience was absolutely necessary, and yet *Shoulder-knots* appeared extreamly requisite. After much Thought, one of the Brothers who happened to be more *Book-learned* than the other two, said he had found an Expedient. *'Tis true,* said he, *there is nothing here in this Will,* *totidem verbis, *making mention of* Shoulder-knots, *but I dare conjecture, we may find them* inclusivè, *or* totidem syllabis. This Distinction was immediately approved by all; and so they fell again to examine the Will. But their evil Star had so directed the Matter, that the first Syllable was not to be found in the whole Writing. Upon which Disappointment, he, who found the former Evasion, took heart and said, *Brothers, there is yet Hopes; for tho' we cannot find them* totidem verbis, *nor* totidem syllabis, *I dare engage we shall make them out* tertio modo, *or* totidem literis. This Discovery was also highly commended, upon which they fell once more to the Scrutiny, and [soon] picked out *S, H, O, U, L, D, E, R;* when the same Planet, Enemy to their Repose, had wonderfully contrived, that a *K* was not to be found. Here was a weighty Difficulty! But the distinguishing Brother (for whom we shall hereafter find a Name) now his Hand was in, proved by a very good Argument, that *K* was a modern illegitimate Letter, unknown to the Learned Ages, nor any where to be found in antient Manuscripts. ['Tis true, said he, the Word] *Calendæ* hath in † *Q.V.C.* been sometimes writ with a *K,* but erroneously, for in the best Copies it is ever spelt with a *C.* And by consequence it was a gross Mistake in our Language to spell *Knot* with a *K,* but that from henceforward he would take care it should be writ with a *C.* Upon this, all

† *Quibusdam Veteribus Codicibus.*

* *When the Papists cannot find any thing which they want in Scripture, they go to* Oral Tradition: *Thus* Peter *is introduced satisfy'd with the Tedious way of looking for all the Letters of any Word, which he has occasion for in the* Will, *when neither the constituent Syllables, nor much less the whole Word, were there* in Terminis. W. Wotton.

† *Some antient Manuscripts.*

farther Difficulty vanished; *Shoulder-Knots* were made clearly out, to be *Jure Paterno*, and our three Gentlemen swaggered with as large and as flanting ones as the best.

But, as human Happiness is of a very short Duration, so in those Days were human Fashions, upon which it entirely depends. *Shoulder-Knots* had their Time, and we must now imagine them in their Decline; for a certain Lord came just from *Paris*, with fifty Yards of *Gold Lace* upon his Coat, exactly trimm'd after the Court-Fashion of that *Month*. In two Days, all Mankind appear'd closed up in Bars of * *Gold Lace*: whoever durst peep abroad without his Complement of *Gold Lace*, was as scandalous as a———, and as ill received among the Women. What should our three Knights do in this momentous Affair? They had sufficiently strained a Point already, in the Affair of *Shoulder-Knots:* Upon Recourse to the Will, nothing appeared there but *altum silentium*. That of the *Shoulder-Knots* was a loose, flying, circumstantial Point; but this of *Gold Lace*, seemed too considerable an Alteration without better Warrant; it did *aliquo modo essentiæ adhærere*, and therefore required a positive Precept. But about this time it fell out, that the Learned Brother aforesaid, had read *Aristotelis Dialectica*, and especially that wonderful Piece *de Interpretatione*, which has the Faculty of teaching its Readers to find out a Meaning in every Thing but it self; like Commentators on the *Revelations*, who proceed Prophets without understanding a Syllable of the Text. *Brothers*, said he, † *You are to be informed, that, of Wills*, duo sunt genera, ‡ *Nuncupatory and scriptory: that in the Scriptory Will here before us, there is no Precept or Mention about Gold Lace*, conceditur:

---

* *I cannot tell whether the Author means any new Innovation by this Word, or whether it be only to introduce the new Methods of forcing and perverting Scripture.*

† *The next Subject of our Author's Wit, is the Glosses and Interpretations of Scripture, very many absurd ones of which are allow'd in the most Authentick Books of the* Church of Rome. W. Wotton.

‡ *By this is meant* Tradition, *allowed to have equal Authority with the* Scripture, *or rather greater.*

But, si idem affirmetur de nuncupatorio, negatur, *For Brothers, if you remember, we heard a Fellow say when we were Boys, that he heard my Father's Man say, that he heard my Father say, that he would advise his Sons to get* Gold Lace *on their Coats, as soon as ever they could procure Money to buy it. By G——— that is very true,* cries the other; *I remember it perfectly well,* said the third. And so without more ado they got the largest *Gold Lace* in the Parish, and walk'd about as fine as Lords.

A while after, there came up *all in Fashion,* a pretty sort of * *flame Coloured Sattin* for Linings, and the *Mercer* brought a Pattern of it immediately to our three Gentlemen, *An please your Worships* (said he) † *My Lord* C———, *and Sir* J. W. *had Linings out of this very Piece last Night; it takes wonderfully, and I shall not have a Remnant left, enough to make my Wife a Pin-cushion by to morrow Morning at ten a Clock.* Upon this, they fell again to romage the Will, because the present Case also required a positive Precept, the Lining being held by Orthodox Writers to be of the Essence of the Coat. After long search, they could fix upon nothing to the Matter in hand, except a short Advice of their Fathers in the Will, ‡to take care of *Fire,* and put out their *Candles* before they went to Sleep. This tho' a good deal for the Purpose, and helping

---

* *This is Purgatory, whereof he speaks more particularly hereafter, but here only to shew how Scripture was perverted to prove it, which was done by giving equal Authority with the* Canon to Apocrypha, *called here a* Codicil annex'd.

It is likely the Author, in every one of these Changes in the Brother's Dresses, refers to some particular Error in the Church of Rome; *tho' it is not easy I think to apply them all, but by this of* Flame Colour'd Satin *is manifestly intended* Purgatory; *by Gold Lace may perhaps be understood, the lofty Ornaments and Plate in the Churches. The* Shoulder-Knots *and* Silver Fringe, *are not so obvious, at least to me; but the* Indian Figures *of Men, Women and Children plainly relate to the Pictures in the* Romish *Churches, of God like an old Man, of the Virgin* Mary *and our Saviour as a Child.*

† *This shews the Time the Author writ, it being about fourteen Years since those two Persons were reckoned the fine Gentlemen of the Town.*

‡ *That is, to take care of Hell, and, in order to do that, to subdue and extinguish their Lusts.*

very far towards Self-Conviction, yet not seeming wholly of
Force to establish a Command; and being resolved to avoid
farther Scruple, as well as future Occasion for Scandal, says He
that was the Scholar; *I remember to have read in Wills, of a
Codicil annexed, which is indeed a Part of the Will, and what
it contains hath equal authority with the rest. Now, I have
been considering of this same Will here before us, and I cannot
reckon it to be compleat for want of such a Codicil. I will
therefore fasten one in its proper Place very dexterously; I
have had it by me some Time, it was written by a * Dog-
keeper of my Grand-father's, and talks a great deal (as good
Luck would have it) of this very flame-colour'd Sattin.* The
Project was immediately approved by the other two; an old
Parchment Scrowl was tagged on according to Art, in the
Form of a *Codicil annext,* and the *Sattin* bought and worn.

Next Winter, a *Player,* hired for the Purpose by the Corporation of *Fringe-makers,* acted his Part in a new Comedy, all
covered with † *Silver Fringe,* and according to the laudable
Custom gave Rise to that Fashion. Upon which, the Brothers
consulting their Father's Will, to their great Astonishment
found these Words; Item, *I charge and command my said three
Sons, to wear no sort of* Silver Fringe *upon or about their said
Coats,* &c. with a Penalty in case of Disobedience, too long
here to insert. However, after some Pause the Brother so often
mentioned for his Erudition, who was well Skill'd in Criticisms,
had found in a certain Author, which he said should be nameless, that the same Word which in the Will is called *Fringe,*
does also signifie a *Broom-stick;* and doubtless ought to have
the same Interpretation in this Paragraph. This, another of the
Brothers disliked, because of that Epithet, *Silver,* which could
not, he humbly conceived, in Propriety of Speech be reasonably
applied to a *Broom-stick:* but it was replied upon him, that
this Epithet was understood in a *Mythological,* and *Allegorical*

---

* *I believe this refers to that part of the* Apocrypha *where mention is
made of* Tobit *and his* Dog.

† *This is certainly the farther introducing the Pomps of Habit and
Ornament.*

Sense. However, he objected again, why their Father should
forbid them to wear a *Broom-stick* on their Coats, a Caution
that seemed unnatural and impertinent; upon which he was
taken up short, as one that spoke irreverently of a *Mystery,*
which doubtless was very useful and significant, but ought not
to be over-curiously pryed into, or nicely reasoned upon. And
in short, their Father's Authority being now considerably sunk,
this Expedient was allowed to serve as a lawful Dispensation,
for wearing their full Proportion of *Silver Fringe.*

A while after, was revived an old Fashion, long antiquated,
of *Embroidery* with * *Indian Figures* of Men, Women and
Children. Here they [had no Occasion to examine the Will.
They] remembered but too well, how their Father had always
abhorred this Fashion; that he made several Paragraphs on
purpose, importing his utter Detestation of it, and bestowing
his everlasting Curse to his Sons whenever they should wear it.
For all this, in a few Days, they appeared higher in the Fashion
than any Body else in the Town. But they solved the Matter
by saying, that these Figures were not at all the *same* with
those that were formerly worn, and were meant in the Will.
Besides, they did not wear them in that Sense, as forbidden by
their Father, but as they were a commendable Custom, and of
great Use to the Publick. That these rigorous Clauses in the
Will did therefore require some *Allowance,* and a favourable
Interpretation, and ought to be understood *cum grano Salis.*

But, Fashions perpetually altering in that Age, the Scholastick Brother grew weary of searching farther Evasions, and
solving everlasting Contradictions. Resolved therefore at all
Hazards, to comply with the Modes of the World, they concerted Matters together, and agreed unanimously, to † lock up

---

* *The Images of Saints, the Blessed Virgin, and our Saviour an Infant.*
Ibid. *Images in the* Church of Rome *give him but too fair a Handle.*
The Brothers remembered, &c. *The Allegory here is direct.* W. Wotton.

† *The Papists formerly forbad the People the Use of Scripture in a
Vulgar Tongue,* Peter *therefore* locks up his Father's Will in a Strong
Box, brought out of *Greece* or *Italy. Those Countries are named because
the* New Testament *is written in* Greek; *and the* Vulgar Latin, *which is
the Authentick Edition of the* Bible *in the Church of* Rome, *is in the
Language of old* Italy. W. Wotton.

their Father's Will in a *Strong-Box,* brought out of *Greece* or *Italy,* (I have forgot which) and trouble themselves no farther to examine it, but only refer to its Authority whenever they thought fit. In consequence whereof, a while after, it grew a general Mode to wear an infinite Number of *Points,* most of them *tagg'd with Silver:* Upon which the Scholar pronounced *ex Cathedra,* that *Points* were absolutely *Jure Paterno,* as they might very well remember. 'Tis true indeed, the Fashion prescribed somewhat more than were directly named in the Will; However, that they, as Heirs general of their Father, had power to make and add certain Clauses for publick Emolument, though not deducible, *totidem verbis,* from the Letter of the Will, or else, *Multa absurda sequerentur.* This was understood for *Canonical,* and therefore on the following *Sunday* they came to Church all covered with *Points.*

The Learned Brother so often mentioned, was reckon'd the best Scholar in all that or the next Street to it; insomuch, as having run something behind-hand with the World; he obtained the Favour from a †*certain* Lord, to receive him into his House, and to teach his Children. A while after, the *Lord* died, and he by long Practice of his Father's Will, found the way of contriving a *Deed of Conveyance* of that House to Himself and his Heirs: Upon which he took Possession, turned the young Squires out, and received his Brothers in their stead.

---

* *The* Popes *in their Decretals and Bulls, have given their Sanction to very many gainful Doctrines which are now received in the* Church of Rome *that are not mention'd in Scriptures, and are unknown to the Primitive Church.* Peter *accordingly pronounces* ex Cathedra, *That* Points *tagged with Silver were absolutely* Jure Paterno, *and so they wore them in great Numbers.* W. Wotton.

† *This was* Constantine the Great, *from whom the* Popes *pretend a Donation of St.* Peter's *Patrimony, which they have been never able to produce.*

Ibid. *The Bishops of* Rome *enjoyed their Priviledges in* Rome *at first by the favour of Emperors, whom at last they shut out of their own Capital City, and then forged a Donation from* Constantine the Great, *the better to justifie what they did. In Imitation of this,* Peter *having run something behind hand in the World, obtained Leave of a certain Lord, &c.* W. Wotton.

SECTION III.

A Digression concerning Criticks.

THO' I have been hitherto as cautious as I could, upon
all Occasions, most nicely to follow the Rules and Methods of
Writing, laid down by the Example of our illustrious *Moderns;*
yet has the unhappy shortness of my Memory led me into an
Error, from which I must immediately extricate my self, before
I can decently pursue my Principal Subject. I confess with
Shame, it was an unpardonable Omission to proceed so far as
I have already done, before I had performed the due Discourses, Expostulatory, Supplicatory, or Deprecatory with my
good Lords the *Criticks.* Towards some Atonement for this
grievous Neglect, I do here make humbly bold to present them
with a short Account of themselves and their *Art,* by looking
into the Original and Pedigree of the Word, as it is generally
understood among us, and very briefly considering the antient
and present State thereof.

By the Word, *Critick,* at this Day so frequent in all Conversations, there have sometimes been distinguished three
very different Species of Mortal Men, according as I have read
in *Antient Books and Pamphlets.* For first, by this Term was
understood such Persons as invented or drew up Rules for
themselves and the World, by observing which, a careful
Reader might be able to pronounce upon the productions of
the *Learned,* form his Taste to a true Relish of the *Sublime*
and the *Admirable,* and divide every Beauty of Matter or of
Style from the Corruption that Apes it: In their common
perusal of Books, singling out the Errors and Defects, the
Nauseous, the Fulsome, the Dull, and the Impertinent, with
the Caution of a Man that walks thro' *Edenborough* Streets
in a Morning, who is indeed as careful as he can, to watch
diligently, and spy out the Filth in his Way, not that he is

curious to observe the Colour and Complexion of the Ordure, or take its Dimensions, much less to be padling in, or tasting it: but only with a Design to come out as cleanly as he may. These men seem, tho' very erroneously, to have understood the Appellation of *Critick* in a literal Sence; That one principal part of his Office was to Praise and Acquit; and, that a *Critick,* who sets up to Read, only for an Occasion of Censure and Reproof, is a Creature as barbarous as a *Judge,* who should take up a Resolution to hang all Men that came before him upon a Tryal.

Again; by the Word *Critick,* have been meant, the Restorers of Antient Learning from the Worms, and Graves, and Dust of Manuscripts.

Now, the Races of these two have been for some Ages utterly extinct; and besides, to discourse any farther of them would not be at all to my purpose.

The Third, and Noblest Sort, is that of the *TRUE CRITICK,* whose Original is the most Antient of all. Every *True Critick* is a Hero born, descending in a direct Line from a Celestial Stem, by *Momus* and *Hybris,* who begat *Zoilus,* who begat *Tigellius,* who begat *Etcætera* the Elder, who begat *B——tly,* and *Rym——r,* and *W——tton,* and *Perrault,* and *Dennis,* who begat *Etcætera* the Younger.

And these are the *Criticks* from whom the Commonwealth of Learning has in all Ages received such immense benefits, that the Gratitude of their Admirers placed their Origine in Heaven, among those of *Hercules, Theseus, Perseus,* and other great Deservers of Mankind. But Heroick Virtue it self hath not been exempt from the Obloquy of Evil Tongues. For it hath been objected, that those Antient Heroes, famous for their Combating so many Giants, and Dragons, and Robbers, were in their own Persons a greater Nuisance to Mankind, than any of those Monsters they subdued; and therefore, to render their Obligations more Compleat, when all *other* Vermin were destroy'd, should in Conscience have concluded with the same Justice upon themselves: [as] *Hercules* most generously did, and hath upon that Score, procured to himself more Temples and Votaries than the best of his Fellows. For these Reasons, I suppose, it is why some have conceived, it would be very expedient for the Publick Good of Learning, that every *True Critick,* as soon as he had finished his Task assigned, should immediately deliver himself up to Ratsbane, or Hemp, or from some convenient *Altitude,* and that no Man's Pretensions to so illustrious a Character, should by any means be received, before That Operation were performed.

Now, from this Heavenly Descent of *Criticism,* and the close Analogy it bears to *Heroick Virtue,* 'tis easie to Assign the proper Employment of a *True Antient Genuine Critick;* which is, to travel thro' this vast World of Writings: to pursue and hunt those Monstrous Faults bred within them: to drag out the lurking Errors like *Cacus* from his Den; to multiply them like *Hydra*'s Heads; and rake them together like *Augeas*'s Dung. Or else drive away a sort of *Dangerous Fowl,* who have a perverse Inclination to plunder the best Branches of the *Tree of Knowledge,* like those *Stimphalian* Birds that eat up the Fruit.

These Reasonings will furnish us with an adequate Definition of a *True Critick;* that, He is *a Discoverer and Collector of Writers Faults.* Which may be farther put beyond Dispute by the following Demonstration: That whoever will examine the Writings in all kinds, wherewith this antient Sect has honour'd the World, shall immediately find, from the whole Thread and Tenour of them, that the Idea's of the Authors have been altogether conversant, and taken up with the Faults and Blemishes, and Oversights, and Mistakes of other Writers; and let the Subject treated on be whatever it will, their Imaginations are so entirely possess'd and replete with the Defects of other Pens, that the very Quintessence of what is bad, does of necessity distill into their own: by which means the Whole appears to be nothing else but an *Abstract* of the *Criticisms* themselves have made.

Having thus briefly consider'd the Original and Office of a *Critick,* as the Word is understood in its most noble and universal Acceptation, I proceed to refute the Objections of those who argue from the Silence and Pretermission of Authors; by which they pretend to prove, that the very Art of *Criticism*, as now exercised, and by me explained, is wholly *Modern;* and consequently, that the *Criticks* of *Great Britain* and *France,* have no Title to an Original so Antient and Illustrious as I have deduced. Now, if I can clearly make out on the contrary, that the most Antient Writers have particularly described, both the Person and the Office of a *True Critick,* agreeable to the Definition laid down by me; their Grand Objection, from the Silence of Authors, will fall to the Ground.

I confess to have for a long time born a part in this general Error; from which I should never have acquitted my self, but thro' the Assistance of our Noble *Moderns;* whose most edifying Volumes I turn indefatigably over Night and Day, for the Improvement of my Mind, and the good of my Country: These have with unwearied Pains made many useful Searches into the weak sides of the *Antients,* and given us a comprehensive List of them. * Besides, they have proved beyond contradiction, that the very finest Things delivered of old, have been long since invented, and brought to Light by much later Pens, and that the noblest Discoveries those *Antients* ever made, of Art or of Nature, have all been produced by the transcending Genius of the present Age. Which clearly shews, how little Merit those *Ancients* can justly pretend to; and takes off that blind Admiration paid them by Men in a Corner, who have the Unhappiness of conversing too little with *present Things.* Reflecting maturely upon all this, and taking in the whole Compass of Human Nature, I easily concluded, that these *Antients,* highly sensible of their many Imperfections, must needs have endeavoured from some Passages in their Works, to obviate, soften, or divert the Censorious Reader, by *Satyr,* or *Panegyrick* upon the *True Criticks,* in Imitation of their *Masters* the *Moderns.* Now, in the *Common-Places* of † both these, I was plentifully instructed, by a long Course of

* *See* Wotton *of Antient and Modern Learning.*
† *Satyr, and Panegyrick upon Criticks.*

useful Study in *Prefaces* and *Prologues;* and therefore immediately resolved to try what I could discover of either, by
a diligent Perusal of the most Antient Writers, and especially
those who treated of the earliest Times. Here I found to my
great Surprize, that although they all entred, upon Occasion,
into particular Descriptions of the *True Critick,* according as
they were governed by their Fears or their Hopes: yet whatever
they touch'd of that kind, was with abundance of Caution,
adventuring no farther than *Mythology* and *Hieroglyphick.*
This, I suppose, gave ground to superficial Readers, for urging
the Silence of Authors, against the Antiquity of the *True
Critick;* tho' the *Types* are so apposite, and the Applications
so necessary and natural, that it is not easy to conceive, how
any Reader of a *Modern Eye* and *Taste* could over-look them.
I shall venture from a great Number to produce a few, which
I am very confident, will put this Question beyond Dispute.

It well deserves considering, that these *Antient Writers* in
treating Enigmatically upon the Subject, have generally fixed
upon the very *same Hieroglyph,* varying only the Story according to their Affections or their Wit. For first; *Pausanias* is of
Opinion, that the Perfection of Writing correct was entirely
owing to the Institution of *Criticks;* and, that he can possibly
mean no other than the *True Critick,* is, I think, manifest
enough from the following Description. He says, *They were a
Race of Men, who delighted to nibble at the Superfluities,
and Excrescencies of Books; which the Learned at length
observing, took Warning of their own Accord, to lop* the
Luxuriant, the *Rotten,* the *Dead,* the *Sapless,* and the *Over-
grown Branches from their Works.* But now, all this he cun-
ningly shades under the following Allegory; *that the* * Nau-
plians in* Argia, *learned the Art of pruning their Vines, by
observing, that when an* ASS *had browsed upon one of them,
it thrived the better, and bore fairer Fruit.* But † *Herodotus*
holding the very same *Hieroglyph,* speaks much plainer, and
almost *in terminis.* He hath been so bold as to tax the *True*

* *Lib——*
† *Lib.* 4.

Criticks, of Ignorance and Malice; telling us openly, for I think nothing can be plainer, that *in the Western Part of* Libya, *there were* ASSES *with* HORNS: Upon which Relation * *Ctesias* yet refines, mentioning the very same Animal about *India,* adding, *That whereas all other* ASSES *wanted a* Gall, *these horned ones were so redundant in that Part, that their Flesh was not to be eaten because of its extream* Bitterness.

Now, the Reason why those Antient Writers treated this Subject only by Types and Figures, was, because they durst not make open Attacks against a Party so Potent and so Terrible, as the *Criticks* of those Ages were: whose very Voice was so Dreadful, that a Legion of Authors would tremble, and drop their Pens at the Sound; For so † *Herodotus* tells us expressly in another Place, how *a vast Army of* Scythians *was put to flight in a Panick Terror, by the Braying of an* ASS. From hence it is conjectured by certain profound *Philologers,* that the great Awe and Reverence paid to a *True Critick,* by the Writers of *Britain,* have been derived to Us, from those our *Scythian* Ancestors. In short, this Dread was so universal, that in process of Time, those Authors who had a mind to publish their Sentiments more freely, in describing the *True Criticks* of their several Ages, were forced to leave off the use of the former *Hieroglyph,* as too nearly approaching the *Prototype,* and invented other Terms instead thereof that were more cautious and mystical; so ‡ *Diodorus* speaking to the same purpose, ventures no farther than to say, That *in the Mountains of* Helicon *there grows a certain* Weed, *which bears a Flower of so damned a Scent, as to poison those who offer to smell it.* Lucretius gives exactly the Same Relation,

§ *Est etiam in magnis Heliconis montibus arbos,*
   Floris odore hominem retro consueta necare. Lib. 6.

* Vide *excerpta ex eo apud* Photium.
† *Lib.* 4.
‡ *Lib.*

---

§ *Near* Helicon, *and round the Learned Hill, Grow Trees, whose Blossoms with their Odour kill.*

But *Ctesias,* whom we lately quoted, hath been a great deal bolder; He had been used with much severity by the *True Criticks* of his own Age, and therefore could not forbear to leave behind him, at least one deep Mark of his Vengeance against the whole Tribe. His Meaning is so near the Surface, that I wonder how it possibly came to be overlook'd by those who deny the Antiquity of [the] *True Criticks.* For pretending to make a Description of many strange Animals about *India,* he hath set down these remarkable Words. *Amongst the rest,* says he, *there is a* Serpent *that wants* Teeth, *and consequently cannot bite, but if its* Vomit *(to which it is much addicted) happens to fall upon any Thing, a certain Rotenness or Corruption ensues: These* Serpents *are generally found among the Mountains where* Jewels *grow, and they frequently emit a* poisonous Juice *whereof, whoever drinks, that Person's* Brains *flie out of his Nostrils.*

There was also among the *Antients* a sort of *Critick,* not distinguisht in *Specie* from the Former, but in Growth or Degree, who seem to have been only the *Tyro's* or *junior* Scholars; yet, because of their differing Employments, they are frequently mentioned as a Sect by themselves. The usual exercise of these younger Students, was to attend constantly at Theatres, and learn to Spy out the *worst Parts* of the Play, whereof they were obliged carefully to take Note, and render a rational Account, to their Tutors. Flesht at these smaller Sports, like young Wolves, they grew up in Time, to be nimble and strong enough for hunting down large Game. For it hath been observed both among Antients and Moderns, that a *True Critick* hath one Quality in common with a *Whore* and an *Alderman,* never to change his Title or his Nature; that a *Grey Critick* has been certainly a *Green* one, the Perfections and Acquirements of his Age being only the improved Talents of his Youth; like *Hemp,* which some Naturalists inform us, is bad for *Suffocations,* tho' taken but in the Seed. I esteem the Invention, or at least the Refinement of Prologues, to have been owing to these younger Proficients, of whom *Terence* makes frequent and honourable mention, under the Name of *Malevoli.*

Now, 'tis certain, the Institution of the *True Criticks,* was of absolute Necessity to the Commonwealth of Learning. For all Human Actions seem to be divided like *Themistocles* and his Company; One Man can *Fiddle,* and another can make *a small Town a great City,* and he that cannot do either one or the other, deserves to be kick'd out of the Creation. The avoiding of which Penalty, has doubtless given the first Birth to the Nation of *Criticks,* and withal, an Occasion for their secret Detractors to report; that a *True Critick* is a sort of Mechanick, set up with a Stock and Tools for his Trade, at as little Expence as a *Taylor;* and that there is much Analogy between the Utensils and Abilities of both: That the *Taylor's Hell* is the Type of a Critick's *Common-Place-Book,* and his Wit and Learning held forth by the *Goose:* That it requires at least as many of these, to the making up of one Scholar, as of the others to the Composition of a Man: That the Valour of both is equal, and their *Weapons* near of a Size. Much may be said in answer to those invidious Reflections; and I can positively affirm the first to be a Falshood: For, on the contrary, nothing is more certain, than that it requires greater Layings out, to be free of the *Critick's* Company, than of any other you can name. For, as to be a *true Beggar,* it will cost the richest Candidate every Groat he is worth; so, before one can commence a *True Critick,* it will cost a man all the good Qualities of his Mind; which, perhaps, for a less Purchase, would be thought but an indifferent Bargain.

Having thus amply proved the Antiquity of *Criticism,* and described the Primitive State of it; I shall now examine the present Condition of this Empire, and shew how well it agrees with its antient self. * A certain Author, whose Works have many Ages since been entirely lost, does in his fifth Book and eighth Chapter, say of *Criticks,* that *their Writings are the*

---

* *A Quotation after the manner of a great Author. Vide* Bently's *Dissertation, &c.*

Mirrors of Learning. This I understand in a literal Sense, and suppose our Author must mean, that whoever designs to be a perfect Writer, must inspect into the Books of *Criticks,* and correct his Invention there as in a Mirror. Now, whoever considers, that the *Mirrors* of the Antients were made of *Brass,* and *sine Mercurio,* may presently apply the two Principal Qualifications of a *True Modern Critick,* and consequently, must needs conclude, that these have always been, and must be for ever the same. For, *Brass* is an Emblem of Duration, and when it is skilfully burnished, will cast *Reflections* from its own *Superficies,* without any Assistance of *Mercury* from behind. All the other Talents of a *Critick* will not require a particular Mention, being included, or easily deducible to these. However, I shall conclude with three Maxims, which may serve both as Characteristicks to distinguish a *True Modern Critick* from a Pretender, and will be also of admirable Use to those worthy Spirits, who engage in so useful and honourable an Art.

The first is, That *Criticism,* contrary to all other Faculties of the Intellect, is ever held the truest and best, when it is the very *first* Result of the *Critick*'s Mind: As Fowlers reckon the first aim for the surest, and seldom fail of missing the Mark, if they stay not for a Second.

Secondly: The *True Criticks* are known by their Talent of swarming about the noblest Writers, to which they are carried meerly by Instinct, as a Rat to the best Cheese, or a Wasp to the fairest Fruit. So, when the *King* is a Horse-back, he is sure to be the *dirtiest* Person of the Company, and they that make their Court best, are such as *bespatter* him most.

Lastly; A *True Critick,* in the Perusal of a Book, is like a *Dog* at a Feast, whose Thoughts and Stomach are wholly set upon what the Guests *fling away,* and consequently, is apt to *Snarl* most, when there are the fewest *Bones.*

Thus much, I think, is sufficient to serve by way of Address to my Patrons, the *True Modern Criticks,* and may very well atone for my past Silence, as well as That which I am like to observe for the future. I hope I have deserved so well of their whole *Body,* as to meet with generous and tender Usage at their *Hands.* Supported by which Expectation, I go on boldly to pursue those Adventures already so happily begun.

SECTION IV.

A TALE of a TUB

I HAVE now with much Pains and Study, conducted the Reader to a Period, where he must expect to hear of great Revolutions. For no sooner had Our *Learned Brother,* so often mentioned, got a warm House of his own over his Head, than he began to look big, and to take mightily upon him; insomuch, that unless the Gentle Reader out of his great Candour, will please a little to exalt his Idea, I am afraid he will henceforth hardly know the *Hero* of the Play, when he happens to meet Him; his part, his Dress, and his Mien being so much altered.

He told his Brothers, he would have them to know, that he was their Elder, and consequently his Father's sole Heir; Nay, a while after, he would not allow them to call Him, Brother, but Mr. *PETER;* and then he must be styl'd *Father PETER;* and sometimes, *My Lord PETER.* To support this Grandeur, which he soon began to consider, could not be maintained without a Better *Fonde* than what he was born to; After much Thought, he cast about at last, to turn *Projector* and *Virtuoso,* wherein he so well succeeded, that many famous Discoveries, Projects and Machines, which bear great Vogue and Practice at present in the World, are owing entirely to *Lord Peter's* Invention. I will deduce the best Account I have been able to collect of the Chief amongst them, without considering much the Order they came out in; because, I think, Authors are not well agreed as to that Point.

I hope, when this Treatise of mine shall be translated into Foreign Languages, (as I may without Vanity affirm, That the

Labour of collecting, the Faithfulness in recounting, and the great Usefulness of the Matter to the Publick, will amply deserve that Justice) that the worthy Members of the several *Academies* abroad, especially those of *France* and *Italy,* will favourably accept these humble Offers, for the Advancement of Universal Knowledge. I do also advertise the most Reverend Fathers the *Eastern* Missionaries, that I have purely for their Sakes, made use of such Words and Phrases, as will best admit an easie Turn into any of the *Oriental* Languages, especially the *Chinese.* And so I proceed with great Content of Mind, upon reflecting, how much Emolument this whole Globe of Earth is like to reap by my labours.

The first Undertaking of Lord *Peter,* was to purchase a * Large Continent, lately said to have been discovered in *Terra Australis incognita.* This Tract of Land he bought at a very great Penny-worth from the Discoverers themselves, (tho' some pretended to doubt whether they had ever been there) and then retailed it into several Cantons to certain Dealers, who carried over Colonies, but were all Shipwreckt in the Voyage. Upon which, *Lord Peter* sold the said Continent to other Customers *again,* and *again,* and *again,* and *again,* with the same Success.

The second Project I shall mention, was his † Sovereign Remedy for the *Worms,* especially those in the *Spleen.* ‡ The Patient was to eat nothing after Supper for three Nights: as soon as he went to Bed, he was carefully to lye on one Side, and when he grew weary, to turn upon the other: He must also duly confine his two Eyes to the same object; and by no means break Wind at both Ends together, without manifest Occasion. These Prescriptions diligently observed, the *Worms*

---

* *That is Purgatory.*

† Penance *and* Absolution *are plaid upon under the Notion of a* Sovereign Remedy for the Worms, *especially in the Spleen, which by observing* Peters *Prescription would void sensibly by Perspiration ascending thro' the Brain,* &c. W. Wotton.

‡ *Here the Author ridicules the Penances of the Church of* Rome, *which may be made as easy to the Sinner as he pleases, provided he will pay for them accordingly.*

would void insensibly by Perspiration, ascending thro' the *Brain*.

A third Invention, was the Erecting of a *Whispering-Office,* for the Publick Good and Ease of all such as are Hypochondriacal, or troubled with the Cholick; as [likewise of all Eves-droppers, Physicians,] Midwives, small Politicians, Friends fallen out, Repeating Poets, Lovers Happy or in Despair, Bawds, Privy-Counsellours, Pages, Parasites and Buffoons; In short, of all such as are in Danger of bursting with too much *Wind*. An *Asse*'s Head was placed so conveniently, that the Party affected might easily with his Mouth accost either of the Animal's Ears; which he was to apply close for a certain Space, and by a fugitive Faculty, peculiar to the Ears of that Animal, receive immediate Benefit, either by Eructation, or Expiration, or Evomition.

Another very beneficial Propect of *Lord Peter*'s was an † *Office of Ensurance,* for Tobacco-Pipes, Martyrs of the Modern Zeal; Volumes of Poetry, Shadows, ———— ———— ———— ———— and Rivers: That these, nor any of these shall receive Damage by *Fire*. From whence our *Friendly Societies* may plainly find themselves, to be only Transcribers from this Original; tho' the one and the other have been of *great* Benefit to the Undertakers, as well as of *equal* to the Publick.

Lord Peter was also held the Original Author of ‡ *Puppets* and *Raree-Shows;* the great Usefulness whereof being so generally known, I shall not enlarge farther upon this Particular.

But, another Discovery for which he was much renowned, was his famous Universal § *Pickle*. For having remark'd how

---

* *By his* Whispering-Office, *for the Relief of Eves-droppers, Physitians, Bawds, and Privy-counsellours, he ridicules Auricular Confession, and the Priest who takes it, is described by the Asses Head.* W. Wotton.

† *This I take to be the Office of* Indulgences, *the gross Abuses whereof first gave Occasion for the Reformation.*

‡ *I believe are the Monkeries and ridiculous Processions,* &c. *among the Papists.*

§ *Holy Water, he calls an* Universal Pickle *to preserve Houses, Gardens, Towns, Men, Women, Children and Cattle, wherein he could preserve them as sound as Insects in Amber.* W. Wotton.

your * Common *Pickle* in use among Huswives, was of no
farther Benefit than to preserve dead Flesh, and certain kinds
of Vegetables; *Peter,* with great Cost as well as Art, had contrived a *Pickle* proper for Houses, Gardens, Towns, Men,
Women, Children, and Cattle; wherein he could preserve
them as Sound as Insects in Amber. Now, this *Pickle* to the
Taste, the Smell, and the Sight, appeared exactly the same,
with what is in common Service for Beef, and Butter, and
Herrings, (and has been often that way applied with great
Success) but for its many Sovereign Virtues was a quite
different Thing. For *Peter* would put in a certain Quantity
of his † *Powder Pimperlim pimp,* after which it never failed
of Success. The Operation was performed by *Spargefaction* in
a proper Time of the Moon. The Patient who was to be
pickled, if it were a House, would infallibly be preserved from
all Spiders, Rats, and Weazels; if the Party affected were a
Dog, he should be exempt from Mange, and Madness, and
Hunger. It also infallibly took away all Scabs and Lice, and
scall'd Heads from Children, never hindring the Patient from
any Duty, either at Bed or Board.

But of all *Peter*'s Rarieties, he most valued a certain set of
‡ *Bulls,* whose Race was by great Fortune preserved in a lineal
Descent from those that guarded the *Golden Fleece.* Tho'
some who pretended to observe them curiously, doubted the
Breed had not been kept entirely chast; because they had

---

* *This is easily understood to be Holy Water, composed of the same
Ingredients with many other Pickles.*

† *And because Holy Water differs only in Consecration from common
Water, therefore he tells us that his Pickle by the Powder of* Pimperlim-
pimp *receives new Virtues though it differs not in Sight nor Smell from
the common Pickle, which preserves Beef, and Butter, and Herrings.*
W. Wotton.

‡ *The Papal* Bulls *are ridicul'd by Name, So that here we are at no
loss for the Authors Meaning.* W. Wotton.

Ibid. *Here the Author has kept the Name, and means the* Popes Bulls,
*or rather his Fulminations and Excommunications, of Heretical Princes,
all sign'd with Lead and the Seal of the Fisherman.*

degenerated from their Ancestors in some Qualities, and had acquired others very extraordinary, but a Forein Mixture. The *Bulls* of *Colchos* are recorded to have *brazen Feet;* But whether it happen'd by ill Pasture and Running, by an Allay from intervention of other Parents, from stolen Intrigues; Whether a Weakness in their Progenitors had impaired the seminal Virtue; Or by a Decline necessary thro' a long Course of Time, the Originals of Nature being depraved in these latter sinful Ages of the World; Whatever was the Cause, 'tis certain that *Lord Peter*'s *Bulls* were extreamely vitiated by the Rust of Time in the Mettal of their Feet, which was now sunk into common *Lead.* However the terrible *roaring* peculiar to their Lineage, was preserved; as likewise that Faculty of breathing out *Fire* from their Nostrils; which notwithstanding many of their Detractors took to be a Feat of Art, [and] to be nothing so terrible as it appeared; proceeding only from their usual Course of Dyet, which was of * *Squibs* and *Crackers.* However, they had two peculiar Marks which extreamly distinguished them from the *Bulls of Jason,* and which I have not met together in the Description of any other Monster, beside that in *Horace*;

> *Varias inducere plumas,*
> and
> *Atrum desinit in piscem.*

For, these had *Fishes Tails,* yet upon Occasion, could *out-fly* any Bird in the Air. *Peter* put these *Bulls* upon several Employs. Sometimes he would set them a *roaring* to fright † *Naughty Boys,* and make them quiet. Sometimes he would send them out upon Errands of great Importance; where it is wonderful to recount, and perhaps the cautious Reader may think much to believe it; An *Appetitus sensibilis,* deriving itself thro' the whole Family, from their Noble Ancestors,

---

* *These are the Fulminations of the Pope threatning Hell and Damnation to those Princes who offend him.*

† *That is Kings who incurr his Displeasure.*

Guardians of the *Golden-Fleece;* they continued so extremely fond of *Gold,* that if *Peter* sent them abroad, though it were only upon a Complement; they would *Roar,* and *Spit,* and *Belch,* and *Piss,* and *Fart,* and *Snivel* out *Fire,* and keep a perpetual Coyl, till you flung them a Bit of *Gold;* but then, *Pulveris exigui jactu,* they would grow calm and quiet as Lambs. In short, whether by secret Connivance, or Encouragement from their Master, or out of their own Liquorish Affection to Gold, or both; it is certain they were no better than a sort of sturdy, swaggering Beggars; and where they could not prevail to get an Alms, would make Women miscarry, and Children fall into Fits; who, to this very Day, usually call Sprites and Hobgoblins by the Name of *Bull-Beggars.* They grew at last so very troublesome to the Neighbourhood, that some Gentlemen of the *North-West,* got a Parcel of right *English Bull-Dogs,* and baited them so terribly, that they felt it ever after.

I must needs mention one more of *Lord Peter*'s Projects, which was very extraordinary, and discovered him to be Master of a high Reach, and profound Invention. Whenever it happened that any Rogue of *Newgate* was condemned to be hang'd, *Peter* would offer him a Pardon for a certain Sum of Money, which when the poor Caitiff had made all Shifts to scrape up and send; *His Lordship* would return a * Piece of Paper in this Form.

T O *all Mayors, Sheriffs, Jaylors, Constables, Bayliffs, Hangmen,* &c. *Whereas we are informed that* A. B. *remains in the Hands of you, or any of you, under the Sentence of Death. We will and command you upon Sight hereof, to let the said Prisoner depart to his own Habitation, whether he stands condemned for Murder, Sodomy, Rape, Sacrilege, Incest, Treason, Blasphemy,* &c. *for which this shall be your sufficient Warrant:*

---

* *This is a Copy of a General Pardon sign'd* Servus Servorum.

Ibid. *Absolution in* Articulo Mortis, *and the Tax* Cameræ Apostolicæ *are jested upon in Emperor* Peter's *Letter.* W. Wotton.

And if you fail hereof, G——— d——mn You and Yours to all Eternity. And so we bid you heartily Farewel.

Your most Humble
Man's Man,
EMPEROR PETER.

The Wretches trusting to this, lost their Lives and Money too.

I desire of those whom the *Learned* among Posterity will appoint for Commentators upon this elaborate Treatise; that they will proceed with great Caution upon certain dark points, wherein all who are not *Verè adepti,* may be in Danger to form rash and hasty Conclusions, especially in some mysterious Paragraphs, where certain *Arcana* are joyned for brevity sake, which in the Operation must be divided. And, I am certain, that future Sons of Art, will return large Thanks to my Memory, for so grateful, so useful an *Innuendo.*

It will be no difficult Part to persuade the Reader, that so many worthy Discoveries met with great Success in the World; tho' I may justly assure him that I have related much the smallest Number; My Design having been only to single out such, as will be of most Benefit for Publick Imitation, or which best served to give some Idea of the Reach and Wit of the Inventor. And therefore it need not be wondred, if by this Time, *Lord Peter* was become exce[e]ding Rich. But alas, he had kept his Brain so long, and so violently upon the Rack, that at last it *shook* it self, and began to *turn round* for a little Ease. In short, what with Pride, Projects, and Knavery, poor *Peter* was grown distracted, and conceived the strangest Imaginations in the World. In the Height of his Fits (as it is usual with those who run mad out of Pride) He would call Himself * *God Almighty,* and sometimes *Monarch of the Universe.* I have seen him, (says my Author) take three old †*high-crown'd Hats,* and clap them all on his Head, three Story high,

---

* *The Pope is not only allow'd to be the Vicar of* Christ, *but by several Divines is call'd God upon Earth, and other blasphemous Titles.*

† *The Triple Crown.*

with a huge Bunch of * *Keys* at his Girdle, and an *Angling Rod* in his Hand. In which Guise, whoever went to take him by the Hand in the way of Salutation, *Peter* with much Grace, like a well educated Spaniel, would present them with his † *Foot,* and if they refused his Civility, then he would raise it as high as their Chops, and give them a damn'd Kick on the Mouth, which hath ever since been call'd [a] *Salute.* Whoever walkt by, without paying him their Complements, having a wonderful strong Breath, he would blow their Hats off into the Dirt. Mean time, his Affairs at home went upside down; and his two Brothers had a wretched Time; Where his first ‡ *Boutade* was, to kick both their § *Wives* one Morning out of Doors, and his own too, and in their stead, gave Orders to pick up the first three Strolers could be met with in the Streets. A while after, he nail'd up the Cellar-Door: and would not allow his Brothers a || Drop of *Drink* to their Victuals. Dining one Day at an Alderman's in the City, *Peter* observed him expatiating after the Manner of his Brethren, in the Praises of his Surloyn of Beef. *Beef,* said the sage Magistrate, *is the King of Meat; Beef comprehends in it the Quintessence of Partridge, and Quail, and Venison, and Pheasant, and Plum-pudding, and Custard.* When *Peter* came home, he would needs take the Fancy of cooking up this Doctrine into Use, and apply the Precept in default of a Surloyn, to his brown loaf: *Bread,* says he, *Dear Brothers, is the Staff of Life; in which Bread is contained,* inclusivé, *the Quintessence of Beef,*

---

* *The Keys of the Church.*

Ibid. *The Pope's Universal Monarchy, and his Triple Crown, and Fisher's Ring.* W. Wotton.

† *Neither does his arrogant way of requiring men to kiss his Slipper, escape Reflexion.* Wotton.

‡ *This Word properly signifies a sudden Jerk, or Lash of an Horse, when you do not expect it.*

§ *The* Celibacy *of the* Romish Clergy *is struck at in* Peter's *beating his own and Brothers Wives out of Doors.* W. Wotton.

|| *The Pope's refusing the Cup to the Laity, persuading them that the Blood is contain'd in the Bread, and that the Bread is the real and entire Body of* Christ.

*Mutton, Veal, Venison, Partridge, Plum-pudding, and Custard:
And to render all compleat, there is intermingled a due
Quantity of Water, whose Crudities are also corrected by
Yeast or Barm, thro' which means it becomes a wholesome
fermented Liquor, diffused thro' the* Mass *of the* Bread. Upon
the Strength of these Conclusions, next Day at Dinner was
the brown Loaf served up in all the Formality of a City Feast.
Come Brothers, said *Peter, fall to, and spare not; here is excellent good* * *Mutton; or hold, now my Hand is in, I'll help
you.* At which word, in much Ceremony, with Fork and Knife,
he carves out two good Slices of a Loaf, and presents each on
a Plate to his Brothers. The Elder of the two not suddenly
entring into *Lord Peter's* Conceit, began with very civil
Language to examine the Mystery. *My Lord,* said he, *I doubt,
with great Submission, there may be some Mistake. What,* says
*Peter, you are pleasant; Come then, let us hear this Jest, your
Head is so big with. None in the world, my Lord; but unless
I am very much deceived, your Lordship was pleased a while
ago, to let fall a Word about Mutton, and I would be glad to
see it with all my Heart. How,* said *Peter,* appearing in great
Surprise, *I do not comprehend this at all*———Upon which,
the younger interposing, to set the Business right; *My Lord,*
said he *My Brother, I suppose is hungry, and longs for the
Mutton, your Lordship hath promised us to Dinner. Pray,* said
*Peter, take me along with you, either you are both mad, or
disposed to be merrier than I approve of; If You there, do not
like your Piece, I will carve you another, tho' I should take that
to be the choice Bit of the whole Shoulder. What then, my
Lord,* replied the first, *it seems this is a shoulder of Mutton
all this while. Pray Sir,* says *Peter, eat your Vittles and leave
off your Impertinence, if you please, for I am not disposed to
relish it at present:* But the other could not forbear, being
over-provoked at the affected Seriousness of *Peter's* Counte-

---

* Transubstantiation. Peter *turns his Bread into Mutton, and according to the Popish Doctrine of Concomitants, his Wine too, which in his
way he calls,* Pauming his damn'd Crusts upon the Brothers for Mutton.
W. Wotton.

nance. *By G——, My Lord,* said he, *I can only say, that to my Eyes, and Fingers, and Teeth, and Nose, it seems to be nothing but a Crust of Bread.* Upon which, the second put in his Word: *I never saw a Piece of Mutton in my Life, so nearly resembling a Slice from a Twelve-peny Loaf. Look ye, Gentlemen,* cries *Peter* in a Rage, *to convince you, what a couple of blind, positive, ignorant, wilful Puppies you are, I will use but this plain Argument; By G——, it is true, good, natural Mutton as any in* Leaden-Hall *Market; and G—— confound you both eternally, if you offer to believe otherwise.* Such a thundring Proof as this, left no farther Room for Objection: The two Unbelievers began to gather and pocket up their Mistake as hastily as they could. *Why, truly,* said the first, *upon more mature Consideration———-Ay,* says the other, interrupting him, *now I have thought better on the Thing, your Lordship seems to have a great deal of Reason. Very well,* said *Peter, Here Boy, fill me a Beer-Glass of Claret. Here's to you both with all my Heart.* The two Brethren much delighted to see him so readily appeas'd returned their most humble Thanks, and said, they would be glad to pledge His Lordship. *That you shall,* said Peter, *I am not a Person to refuse you any Thing that is reasonable; Wine moderately taken, is a Cordial; Here is a Glass apiece for you; 'Tis true natural Juice from the Grape; none of your damn'd* Vintners *Brewings.* Having spoke thus, he presented to each of them another large dry Crust, bidding them drink it off, and not be bashful, for it would do them no Hurt. The two Brothers, after having performed the usual Office in such delicate Conjunctures, of staring a sufficient Period at *Lord Peter,* and each other; and finding how Matters were like to go, resolved not to enter on a new Dispute, but let him carry the Point as he pleased; for he was now got into one of his mad Fits, and to Argue or Expostulate further, would only serve to render him a hundred times more untractable.

I have chosen to relate this worthy Matter in all its Circumstances, because it gave a principal Occasion to that great and famous * *Rupture,* which happened about the same time among these Brethren, and was never afterwards made up. But, of That, I shall treat at large in another Section.

However, it is certain, that *Lord Peter,* even in his lucid Intervals, was very lewdly given in his common Conversation, extream wilful and positive, and would at any time rather argue to the Death, than allow himself to be once in an Error. Besides, he had an abominable Faculty of telling huge palpable *Lies* upon all Occasions; and swearing, not only to the Truth, but cursing the whole Company to Hell, if they pretended to make the least Scruple of believing Him. One time, he swore, he had a † *Cow* at home, which gave as much Milk at a Meal, as would fill three thousand Churches; and what was yet more extraordinary, would never turn Sower. Another time, he was telling of an old ‡ *Sign-Post* that belonged to his *Father,* with Nails and Timber enough on it, to build sixteen large Men of War. Talking one Day of *Chinese* Waggons, which were made so light as to sail over Mountains: *Z——nds,* said *Peter, where's the Wonder of that? By G——, I saw a § Large House of Lime and Stone travel over Sea and Land (granting that it stopt sometimes to bait) above two thousand* German *Leagues.* And that which was the good of it, he would swear desperately all the while, that he never told a Lye in his Life; And at every Word; *By G——, Gentle-*

---

* *By this* Rupture *is meant the* Reformation.

† *The ridiculous Multiplying of the Virgin* Mary's Milk *among the* Papists, *under the Allegory of a* Cow, *which gave as much Milk at a Meal, as would fill three thousand Churches.* W. Wotton.

‡ *By this* Sign-Post *is meant the* Cross *of our Blessed Saviour.*

§ *The Chappel of* Loretto. *He falls here only upon the ridiculous Inventions of Popery: The Church of* Rome *intended by these Things, to gull silly, superstitious People, and rook them of their Money; that the World had been too long in Slavery, our Ancestors gloriously redeem'd us from that Yoke. The Church of* Rome *therefore ought to be expos'd, and he deserves well of Mankind that does expose it.* W. Wotton.

Ibid. *The Chappel of* Loretto, *which travell'd from the* Holy Land *to* Italy.

*men, I tell you nothing but the Truth; And the D——l broil
them eternally that will not believe me.*

In short, *Peter* grew so scandalous, that all the Neighbourhood began in plain Words to say, he was no better than a
Knave. And his two Brothers long wary of his ill Usage, resolved at last to leave him; but first, they humbly desired a
Copy of their Father's *Will,* which had now lain by neglected,
time out of Mind. Instead of granting this Request, he called
them *dam'd Sons of Whores, Rogues, Traytors,* and the rest
of the vile Names he could muster up. However, while he
was abroad one Day upon his Projects, the two Youngsters
watcht their Opportunity, made a Shift to come at the *Will,*
* and took a *Copia vera,* by which they presently saw how
grosly they had been abused; Their Father having left them
equal Heirs, and strictly commanded, that whatever they got,
should lye in common among them all. Pursuant to which,
their next Enterprise was to break open the Cellar-Door, and
get a little good † *Drink* to spirit and comfort their Hearts.
In copying the *Will,* they had met another Precept against
Whoring, Divorce, and separate Maintenance; Upon which,
their next ‡ Work was to discard their Concubines, and send
for their Wives. Whilst all this was in agitation, there enters
a Sollicitor from *Newgate,* desiring *Lord Peter* would please to
procure a *Pardon* for a *Thief* that was to be *hanged to morrow.*
But the two Brothers told him, he was a Coxcomb to seek
Pardons from a Fellow, who deserv'd to be hang'd much
better than his Client; and discovered all the Method of that
Imposture, in the same Form I delivered it a while ago, advising the Sollicitor to put his Friend upon obtaining § *a
Pardon from the King.* In the midst of all this Clutter and

---

* *Translated the Scriptures into the vulgar Tongues.*
† *Administered the Cup to the Laity at the Communion.*
‡ *Allowed the Marriages of Priests.*
§ *Directed Penitents not to trust to Pardons and Absolutions procur'd
for Money, but sent them to implore the Mercy of God, from whence
alone Remission is to be obtain'd.*

Revolution, in comes *Peter* with a File of * Dragoons at his Heels, and gathering from all Hands what was in the Wind, He and his Gang, after several Millions of Scurrilities and Curses, not very important here to repeat, by main Force, very fairly † kicks them both out of Doors, and would never let them come under his Roof from that Day to this.

S E C T I O N V.

A Digression in the Modern Kind.

WE whom the World is pleased to honor with the Title of *Modern Authors,* should never have been able to compass our great Design of an everlasting Remembrance, and never-dying Fame, if our Endeavours had not been so highly serviceable to the general Good of Mankind. This, *O Universe,* is the Adventurous Attempt of me thy Secretary;

> ——— *Quemvis perferre laborem*
> *Suadet, & inducit noctes vigilare serenas.*

To this End, I have some Time since, with a World of Pains and Art, dissected the Carcass of *Humane Nature,* and read many useful Lectures upon the several Parts, both *Containing* and *Contained;* till at last it *smelt* so strong, I could preserve it no longer. Upon which, I have been at a great Expence to fit up all the Bones with exact Contexture, and in due Symmetry; so that I am ready to shew a very compleat Anatomy thereof to all curious *Gentlemen and others.* But not to Digress farther in the midst of a Digression, as I have known some Authors inclose Digressions in one another, like a Nest of Boxes; I do affirm, that having carefully cut up

---

* *By Peter's Dragoons, is meant the Civil Power which those Princes, who were bigotted to the Romish Superstition, employ'd against the Reformers.*

† *The Pope shuts all who dissent from him out of the Church.*

Humane Nature, I have found a very strange, new, and important Discovery; That the Publick Good of Mankind is performed by two Ways, *Instruction,* and *Diversion.* And I have farther proved in my said several Readings, (which, perhaps, the World may one day see, if I can prevail on any Friend to steal a Copy, or on certain Gentlemen of my Admirers, to be very Importunate) that, as Mankind is now disposed, he receives much greater Advantage by being *Diverted* than *Instructed;* His Epidemical Diseases being *Fastidiosity, Amorphy,* and *Oscitation;* whereas in the present universal Empire of Wit and Learning, there seems but little Matter left for *Instruction.* However, in Compliance with a Lesson of Great Age and Authority, I have attempted carrying the Point in all its Heights; and accordingly throughout this Divine Treatise, have skilfully kneaded up both together with a *Layer* of *Utile* and a *Layer* of *Dulce.*

When I consider how exceedingly our Illustrious *Moderns* have eclipsed the weak glimmering Lights of the *Antients,* and turned them out of the Road of all fashionable Commerce, to a degree, that our choice * Town-Wits of most refined Accomplishments, are in grave Dispute, whether there have been ever any *Antients* or no: In which Point we are like to receive wonderful Satisfaction from the most useful Labours and Lucubrations of that Worthy *Modern,* Dr. *B——tly:* I say, when I consider all this, I cannot but bewail, that no famous *Modern* hath ever yet attempted an universal System in a small portable Volume, of all Things that are to be Known, or Believed, or Imagined, or Practised in Life. I am, however, forced to acknowledge, that such an enterprise was thought on some Time ago by a great Philosopher of † *O. Brazile.* The Method he proposed, was by a certain

---

* *The Learned Person here meant by our Author, hath been endeavouring to annihilate so many Antient Writers, that until he is pleas'd to stop his hand it will be dangerous to affirm, whether there have been any Antients in the World.*

† *This is an imaginary Island, of Kin to that which is call'd the* Painters Wives Island, *placed in some unknown part of the Ocean, meerly at the Fancy of the Map-maker.*

curious *Receipt,* a *Nostrum,* which after his untimely Death, I found among his Papers; and do here out of my great Affection to the *Modern Learned,* present them with it, not doubting, it may one Day encourage some worthy Undertaker.

You take fair correct Copies, well bound in Calfs Skin, and Lettered at the Back, of all Modern Bodies of Arts and Sciences whatsoever, and in what Language you please. These you distil in balneo Mariæ, *infusing* Quintessence of Poppy Q. S. *together with three Pints of* Lethe, *to be had from the Apothecaries. You cleanse away carefully the* Sordes *and* Caput mortuum, *letting all that is volatile evaporate. You preserve only the first Running, which is again to be distilled seventeen times, till what remains will amount to about two Drams. This you keep in a Glass Viol* Hermetically *sealed, for one and twenty Days. Then you begin your Catholick Treatise, taking every Morning fasting, (first shaking the Viol) three Drops of this* Elixir, *snuffing it strongly up your Nose. It will dilate it self about the Brain (where there is any) in fourteen Minutes, and you immediately perceive in your Head an infinite Number of* Abstracts, Summaries, Compendiums, Extracts, Collections, Medulla's, Excerpta quædam's, Florilegia's *and the like, all disposed into great Order, and reducible upon Paper.*

I must needs own, it was by the Assistance of this *Arcanum,* that I, tho' otherwise *impar,* have adventured upon so daring an Attempt; never atchieved or undertaken before, but by a certain Author called *Homer,* in whom, tho' otherwise a Person not without some Abilities, and *for an Ancient,* of a tolerable Genius; I have discovered many gross Errors, which are not to be forgiven his very Ashes, if by chance any of them are left. For whereas, we are assured, he design'd his Work for a * compleat Body of all Knowledge Human, Divine, Political, and Mechanick; it is manifest, he hath wholly neglected some, and been very imperfect in the rest. For, first of all, as eminent a *Cabbalist* as his Disciples would represent Him, his

---

* *Homerus omnes res humanas Poematis complexus est.* Xenoph, in conviv.

Account of the *Opus magnum* is extreamly poor and deficient; he seems to have read but very superficially, either *Sendivog[i]us, Behmen,* or * *Anthroposophia Theomagica.* He is also quite mistaken about the *Sphæra Pyroplastica,* a neglect not to be attoned for; and (if the Reader will admit so severe a Censure) *Vix crederem Autorem hunc, unquam audivisse ignis vocem.* His Failings are not less prominent in several Parts of the *Mechanicks.* For, having read his Writings with the utmost Application usual among *Modern Wits,* I could never yet discover the least Direction about the Structure of that useful Instrument a *Save-all.* For want of which, if the *Moderns* had not lent their Assistance, we might yet have wandred *in the Dark.* But I have still behind, a Fault far more notorious to tax this Author with; I mean, † his gross Ignorance in the *Common Laws of this Realm,* and in the Doctrine as well as Discipline of the Church of *England.* A Defect indeed, for which both he and all the Ancients stand most justly censured by my worthy and ingenious Friend Mr. *W——tt——on,* Batchelor of Divinity, in his incomparable Treatise of *Ancient and Modern Learning*; A Book never to be sufficiently valued, whether we consider the happy Turns and Flowings of the Author's Wit, the great Usefulness of his sublime Discoveries upon the Subject of *Flies* and *Spittle,* or the laborious Eloquence of his Stile. And I cannot forbear doing that Author the Justice of my publick Acknowledgments, for the great *Helps* and *Liftings* I had out of his incomparable Piece, while I was penning this Treatise.

But, besides these Omissions in *Homer* already mentioned, the curious reader will also observe several Defects in that Author's Writings, for which he is not altogether so account-

---

* *A Treatise written fifty Years ago, by a* Welsh *Gentleman of* Cambridge, *his Name, as I remember, was* Vaughan, *as appears by the Answer to it, writ by the Learned Dr.* Henry Moor, *it is a Piece of the most unintelligible Fustian, that, perhaps, was ever publish'd in any Language.*

† *Mr.* W—tt—n *(to whom our Author never gives any Quarter) in his Comparison of Antient and Modern Learning, Numbers Divinity, Law,* &c. *among those Parts of Knowledge wherein we excel the Antients.*

able. For whereas every Branch of Knowledge has received such wonderful Acquirements since his Age, especially within these last three Years, or thereabouts; it is almost impossible, he could be so very perfect in Modern Discoveries, as his Advocates pretend. We freely acknowledge Him to be the Inventor of the *Compass,* of *Gun-Powder,* and the *Circulation of the Blood:* But, I challenge any of his Admirers to shew me in all his Writings, a compleat Account of the *Spleen;* Does he not also leave us wholly to seek in the Art of *Political Wagering?* What can be more defective and unsatisfactory than his long Dissertation upon *Tea?* and as to his Method of *Salivation without Mercury,* so much celebrated of late, it is to my own Knowledge and Experience, a Thing very little to be relied on.

It was to supply such momentous Defects, that I have been prevailed on after long Sollicitation, to take Pen in Hand; and I dare venture to Promise, the Judicious Reader shall find nothing neglected here, that can be of Use upon any Emergency of Life. I am confident to have included and exhausted all that Human Imagination can *Rise* or *Fall* to. Particularly, I recommend to the Perusal of the Learned, certain Discoveries that are wholly untoucht by others; whereof I shall only mention among a great many more; *My New help of Smatterers, or the Art of being Deep-learned, and Shallow-read. A curious Invention about Mouse-Traps. An Universal Rule of Reason, or Every Man his own Carver;* Together with a most useful Engine for *catching of Owls.* All which the judicious Reader will find largely treated on, in the several Parts of this Discourse.

I hold my self obliged to give as much Light as is possible, into the beauties and Excellencies of what I am writing, because it is become the Fashion and Humor most applauded among the first Authors of this Polite and Learned Age, when they would correct the ill Nature of Critical, or inform the Ignorance of Courteous Readers. Besides, there have been several famous Pieces lately published both in Verse and Prose; wherein, if the Writers had not been pleas'd, out of

their great Humanity and Affection to the Publick, to give us
a nice Detail of the *Sublime,* and the *Admirable* they contain; it is a thousand to one, whether we should ever have
discovered one Grain of either. For my own particular, I cannot deny, that whatever I have said upon this Occasion, had
been more proper in a Preface, and more agreeable to the
Mode, which usually directs it there. But I here think fit to lay
hold on that great and honourable Privilege of being the *Last
Writer;* I claim an absolute Authority in Right, as the
freshest Modern, which gives me a Despotick Power over all
Authors before me. In the Strength of which Title, I do
utterly disapprove and declare against that pernicious Custom,
of making the Preface a Bill of Fare to the Book. For I have
always lookt upon it as a high Point of Indiscretion in
Monster-mongers and other *Retailers of strange Sights;* to hang
out a fair large Picture over the Door, drawn after the Life,
with a most eloquent Description underneath: This hath saved
me many a Threepence, for my Curiosity was fully satisfied,
and I never offered to go in, tho' often invited by the urging
and attending Orator, with his last *moving* and *standing* Piece
of Rhetorick; *Sir, Upon my Word, we are just going to begin.*
Such is exactly the Fate, at this Time, of *Prefaces, Epistles,
Advertisements, Introductions, Prolegomena's, Apparatus's,
To-the-Reader's.* This Expedient was admirable at first; Our
Great *Dryden* has long carried it as far as it would go, and
with incredible Success. He has often said to me in Confidence,
that the World would have never suspected him to be so great
a Poet, if he had not assured them so frequently in his
Prefaces, that it was impossible they could either doubt or
forget it. Perhaps it may be so; However, I much fear, his
Instructions have edify'd out of their Place, and taught Men
to grow Wiser in certain Points, where he never intended they
should; For it is lamentable to behold, with what a lazy Scorn,
many of the yawning Readers in our Age, do now a-days
twirl over forty or fifty Pages of *Preface* and *Dedication,*
(which is the usual *Modern* Stint) as if it were so much *Latin.*
Tho' it must be also allowed on the other Hand that a very

considerable Number is known to proceed *Criticks* and *Wits,* by reading nothing else. Into which two Factions, I think, all present Readers may justly be divided. Now, for my self, I profess to be of the former Sort; and therefore having the *Modern* Inclination to expatiate upon the Beauty of my own Productions, and display the bright Parts of my Discourse; I thought best to do it in the body of the Work, where, as it now lies, it makes a very considerable Addition to the Bulk of the Volume, *a Circumstance by no means to be neglected by a skilful Writer.*

Having thus paid my due Deference and Acknowledgment to an establish'd Custom of our newest Authors, by *a long Digression unsought for,* and *an universal Censure unprovoked;* By forcing into the Light, with much Pains and Dexterity, my own Excellencies and other Mens Defaults, with great Justice to my self and Candor to them; I now happily resume my Subject, to the Infinite Satisfaction both of the Reader and the Author.

S E C T I O N   V I .

A TALE of a TUB

WE left *Lord Peter* in open Rupture with his two Brethren; both for ever discarded from his House, and resigned to the wide World, with little or nothing to trust to. Which are Circumstances that render them proper Subjects for the Charity of a Writer's Pen to work on; Scenes of Misery, ever affording the fairest Harvest for great Adventures. And in this, the World may perceive the Difference between the Integrity of a generous Author, and that of a common Friend. The latter is observed to adhere close in Prosperity, but on the Decline of Fortune, to drop suddenly off. Whereas, the generous Author, just on the contrary, finds his Hero on the Dunghil, from thence by gradual Steps, raises Him to a Throne, and then immediately withdraws, expecting not so much as Thanks for his Pains: in imitation of which Example, I have placed *Lord Peter* in a Noble House, given Him a Title to wear, and money to spend. There I shall leave Him for some Time; returning where common Charity directs me, to the Assistance of his two Brothers, at their lowest Ebb. However, I shall by no means forget my Character of an Historian, to follow the Truth, step by step, whatever happens, or where-ever it may lead me.

The two Exiles so nearly united in Fortune and Interest, took a Lodging together; where, at their first Leisure, they began to reflect on the numberless Misfortunes and Vexations of their Life past, and could not tell, on the sudden, to what Failure in their Conduct they ought to impute them; When, after some Recollection, they called to Mind the Copy of their Father's *Will,* which they had so happily recovered. This was immediately produced, and a firm Resolution taken between them, to alter whatever was already amiss, and reduce all their future Measures to the strictest Obedience prescribed therein. The main Body of the *Will* (as the Reader cannot easily have forgot) consisted in certain admirable Rules about the wearing of their Coats; in the Perusal whereof, the two Brothers at every Period duly comparing the Doctrine with the Practice, there was never seen a wider Difference between two Things; horrible down-right Transgressions of every Point. Upon which, they both resolved without further Delay, to fall immediately upon reducing the Whole, exactly after their Father's Model.

But, here it is good to stop the hasty Reader, ever impatient to see the End of an Adventure, before We Writers can duly prepare him for it. I am to record, that these two Brothers began to be distinguished at this Time, by certain Names. One of them desired to be called * *MARTIN,* and the other took the Appellation of † *JACK.* These two had lived in much Friendship and Agreement under the Tyranny of their Brother

---

* *Martin Luther.*

† *John Calvin.*

Peter, as it is the Talent of Fellow-Sufferers to do; Men in Misfortune, being like Men in the Dark, to whom all Colours are the same: But when they came forward into the World, and began to display themselves to each other, and to the Light, their Complexions appear'd extreamly different; which the present Posture of their Affairs gave them sudden Opportunity to discover.

But, here the severe Reader may justly tax me as a Writer of short Memory, a Deficiency to which a true *Modern* cannot but of Necessity be a little subject: Because, *Memory* being an Employment of the Mind upon things past, is a Faculty, for which the Learned, in our Illustrious Age, have no manner of Occasion, who deal entirely with *Invention,* and strike all Things out of themselves, or at least, by Collision, from each other: Upon which Account we think it highly Reasonable to produce our great Forgetfulness, as an Argument unanswerable for our great Wit. I ought in Method, to have informed the Reader about fifty Pages ago, of a Fancy *Lord Peter* took, and infused into his Brothers, to wear on their Coats whatever Trimmings came up in Fashion; never pulling off any, as they went out of the Mode, but keeping on all together; which amounted in time to a Medley, the most Antick you can possibly conceive; and this to a Degree, that upon the Time of their falling out there was hardly a Thread of the Original Coat to be seen, but an infinite Quantity of *Lace,* and *Ribbands,* and *Fringe,* and *Embroidery,* and *Points;* (I mean, only those * *tagg'd with Silver,* for the rest fell off.) Now, this material Circumstance, having been forgot in due Place; as good Fortune hath ordered, comes in very properly here, when the two Brothers are just going to reform their Vestures into the Primitive State, prescribed by their Father's *Will.*

They both unanimously entred upon this great Work, looking sometimes on their Coats, and sometimes on the *Will.* *Martin* laid the first Hand; at one twitch brought off a large

---

* *Points tagg'd with Silver, are those Doctrines that promote the Greatness and Wealth of the Church, which have been therefore woven deepest in the Body of Popery.*

Handful of *Points,* and with a second pull, stript away ten dozen Yards of *Fringe.* But when He had gone thus far, he demurred a while: He knew very well, there yet remained a great deal more to be done; however, the first Heat being over, his Violence began to cool, and he resolved to proceed more moderately in the rest of the Work; having already very narrowly scap'd a swinging Rent in pulling off the *Points,* which being *tagged with Silver* (as we have observed before) the judicious Workman had with much Sagacity, double sown, to preserve them from *falling.* Resolving therefore to rid his Coat of a huge Quantity of *Gold Lace;* he pickt up the Stitches with much Caution, and diligently gleaned out all the loose Threads as he went, which proved to be a Work of Time. Then he fell about the embroidered *Indian* Figures of Men, Women and Children; against which, as you have heard in its due Place, their Father's Testament was extreamly exact and severe: These, with much Dexterity and Application, were after a while, quite eradicated, or utterly defaced. For the rest, where he observed the Embroidery to be workt so close, as not to be got away without damaging the Cloth, or where it served to hide or strengthen any Flaw in the Body of the Coat, contracted by the perpetual tampering of Workmen upon it; he concluded the wisest Course was to let it remain, resolving in no Case whatsoever, that the Substance of the Stuff should suffer Injury; which he thought the best Method for serving the true Intent and Meaning of his Father's *Will.* And this is the nearest Account I have been able to collect, of *Martin*'s Proceedings upon this great Revolution.

But his Brother *Jack,* whose Adventures will be so extraordinary, as to furnish a great Part in the Remainder of this Discourse; entred upon the Matter with other Thoughts, and a quite different Spirit. For, the Memory of *Lord Peter*'s Injuries, produced a Degree of Hatred and Spight, which had a much greater Share of inciting Him, than any Regards after his Father's Commands, since these appeared at best, only Secondary and Subservient to the other. However, for this Meddly of Humor, he made a Shift to find a very plausible

Name, honoring it with the Title of *Zeal;* which is, perhaps, the most significant Word that hath been ever yet produced in any Language; As, I think, I have fully proved in my excellent *Analytical* Discourse upon that Subject; wherein I have deduced a *Histori-theo-physi-logical* Account of *Zeal,* shewing how it first proceeded from a *Notion* into a *Word,* and from thence in a hot Summer, ripned into a *tangible Substance.* This Work containing three large Volumes in Folio, I design very shortly to publish by the *Modern* way of *Subscription,* not doubting but the Nobility and Gentry of the Land will give me all possible Encouragement, having already had such a Taste of what I am able to perform.

I record therefore, that Brother *Jack,* brimful of this miraculous Compound, reflecting with Indignation upon *PETER*'s Tyranny, and farther provoked by the Despondency of *Martin;* prefaced his Resolutions to this purpose. *What;* said he; *A Rogue that lock'd up his Drink, turned away our Wives, cheated us of our Fortunes; paumed his damned Crusts upon us for Mutton; and at last kickt us out of Doors; must we be in His Fashions with a Pox? A Rascal, besides, that all the Street cries out against.* Having thus kindled and enflamed himself as high as possible, and by Consequence, in a delicate Temper for beginning a Reformation, he set about the Work immediately, and in three Minutes, made more Dispatch than *Martin* had done in as many Hours. For, (Courteous Reader) you are given to understand, that *Zeal* is never so highly obliged, as when you set it a *Tearing:* and *Jack,* who doated on that Quality in himself, allowed it at this Time its full Swinge. Thus it happened, that stripping down a Parcel of *Gold Lace,* a little too hastily, he rent the *main Body* of his *Coat* from Top to Bottom; and whereas his Talent was not of the happiest in *taking up a Stitch,* he knew no better way, than to dern it again with *Packthred* and a *Scewer.* But the Matter was yet infinitely worse (I record it with Tears) when he proceeded to the *Embroidery:* For, being Clumsy by Nature, and of Temper, Impatient; withal, beholding Millions of Stitches, that required the nicest Hand, and sedatest Constitution, to extricate, in a great Rage, he tore off the whole Piece, Cloth and all, and flung it into the Kennel, and furiously thus continuing his Career; *Ah, Good Brother* Martin, said he, *do as I do, for the Love of God; Strip, Tear, Pull, Rent, Flay off all, that we may appear as unlike the Rogue* Peter, *as it is possible: I would not for a hundred Pounds carry the least Mark about me, that might give Occasion to the Neighbours, of suspecting I was related to such a Rascal.* But *Martin,* who at this Time happened to be extremely flegmatick and sedate, *begged his Brother of all Love, not to damage his Coat by any Means; for he never would get such another:* Desired him *to consider, that it was not their Business to form their Actions by any Reflection upon* Peter, *but by observing the Rules prescribed in their Father's* Will. That *he should remember,* Peter *was still their Brother, whatever Faults or Injuries he had committed; and therefore they should by all means avoid such a Thought, as that of taking Measures for Good and Evil, from no other Rule, than of Opposition to him.* That *it was true, the Testament of their good Father was very exact in what related to the wearing of their* Coats; *yet was it no less penal and strict in prescribing Agreement, and Friendship, and Affection between them. And therefore, if straining a Point were at all dispensable, it would certainly be so, rather to the Advance of Unity, than Increase of Contradiction.*

Martin had still proceeded as gravely as he began; and doubtless, would have delivered an admirable Lecture of Morality, which might have exceedingly contributed to my Reader's *Repose, both of Body and Mind:* (the true ultimate End of *Ethicks;*) but *Jack* was already gone a Flight-shot beyond his Patience. And as in Scholastick Disputes, nothing serves to rouze the Spleen of him that *Opposes,* so much as a kind of Pedantick affected Calmness in the *Respondent;* Disputants being for the most part like unequal Scales, where the *Gravity* of one Side advances the *Lightness* of the Other, and causes it to fly up and kick the Beam; So it happened here, that the *Weight* of *Martin's* Argument exalted *Jack's Levity,* and made him fly out and spurn against his Brother's Moderation. In short, *Martin*'s *Patience* put *Jack* in a *Rage;* but that which most afflicted him was, to observe his Brother's Coat so well reduced into the State of Innocence; while his own was either wholly rent to his Shirt; or those Places which had scaped his cruel Clutches, were still in *Peter*'s Livery. So that he looked like a drunken *Beau,* half rifled by *Bullies;* Or like a fresh Tenant of *Newgate,* when he has refused the Payment of *Garnish;* Or like a discovered *Shoplifter,* left to the Mercy of *Exchange-Women;* Or like a *Bawd* in her old Velvet-Petti-coat, resign'd into the secular Hands of the *Mobile.* Like any, or like all of these, a Meddley of *Rags,* and *Lace,* and *Rents,* and *Fringes,* unfortunate *Jack* did now appear: He would have been extremely glad to see his Coat in the Condition of *Martin*'s but infinitely gladder to find that of *Martin*'s in the same Predicament with his. However, since neither of these was likely to come to pass, he thought fit to lend the whole Business another Turn, and to dress up Necessity into a Virtue. Therefore, after as many of the *Fox*'s Arguments, as he could muster up, for bringing *Martin* to *Reason,* as he called it; or, as he meant it, into his own ragged, bobtail'd Condition; and observing he said all to little purpose; what, alas, was left for the forlorn *Jack* to do, but after a Million of Scurrilities against his Brother, to run mad with Spleen, and Spight, and Contradiction. To be short, here began a mortal Breach between these two. *Jack* went immediately to *New Lodgings,* and in a few Days it was for certain reported, that he had run out of his Wits. In a short time after, he appeared abroad, and confirmed the Report, by falling into the oddest Whimsies that ever a sick Brain conceived.

And now the little Boys in the Streets began to salute him with several Names. Sometimes they would call Him, * *Jack the Bald;* sometimes, † *Jack with a Lanthorn;* sometimes, ‡ *Dutch Jack;* sometimes, § *French Hugh;* sometimes, ‖ *Tom*

---

* *That is* Calvin, *from* Calvus, *Bald.*

† *All those who pretend to Inward Light.*

‡ Jack *of* Leyden, *who gave Rise to the* Anabaptists.

§ *The* Hugonots.

‖ *The* Gueuses, *by which Name some Protestants in* Flanders *were call'd.*

the Beggar; and sometimes, * *Knocking Jack of the North.* And it was under one, or some, or all of these Appellations (which I leave the Learned Reader to determine) that he hath given Rise to the most Illustrious and Epidemick Sect of *Æolists,* who with honourable Commemoration, do still acknowledge the Renowned *JACK* for their Author and Founder. Of whose Original, as well as Principles, I am now advancing to gratify the World with a very particular Account.

———*Mellæo contingens cuncta Lepore.*

SECTION VII.

A Digression in Praise of Digressions.

I HAVE sometimes *heard* of an *Iliad* in a *Nut-shell;* but it hath been my Fortune to have much oftner *seen* a *Nut-shell* in a[n] *Iliad.* There is no doubt, that Human Life has received most wonderful Advantages from both; but to which of the two the World is chiefly indebted, I shall leave among the Curious, as a Problem worthy of their utmost Enquiry. For the Invention of the latter, I think the Commonwealth of Learning is chiefly obliged to the great *Modern* Improvement of *Digressions:* The late Refinements in Knowledge, running parallel to those of Dyet in our Nation, which among Men of a judicious Taste, are drest up in various Compounds, consisting in *Soups* and *Ollio's, Fricassées* and *Ragousts.*

'Tis true, there is a sort of morose, detracting, ill-bred People, who pretend utterly to disrelish these polite Innovations: And as to the Similitude from Dyet, they allow the Parallel, but are so bold to pronounce the Example it self, a Corruption and Degeneracy of Taste. They tell us, that the Fashion of jumbling fifty Things together in a Dish, was at first introduced in Compliance to a depraved and *debauched*

---

* John Knox, *the Reformer of* Scotland.

Appetite, as well as to a *crazy Constitution;* And to see a Man hunting thro' an *Ollio,* after the *Head* and *Brains* of a *Goose,* a *Wigeon,* or a *Woodcock,* is a Sign, he wants a Stomach and Digestion for more substantial Victuals. Farther, they affirm, that *Digressions* in a Book, are like *Forein Troops* in a *State,* which argue the Nation to want a *Heart* and *Hands* of its own, and often, either *subdue* the *Natives,* or drive them into the most *unfruitful Corners.*

But, after all that can be objected by these supercilious Censors; 'tis manifest, the Society of Writers would quickly be reduced to a very inconsiderable Number, if Men were put upon making Books, with the fatal Confinement of delivering nothing beyond what is to the Purpose. 'Tis acknowledged, that were the Case the same among Us, as with the *Greeks* and *Romans,* when Learning was in its *Cradle,* to be reared and fed, and cloathed by *Invention;* it would be an easy Task to fill up Volumes upon particular Occasions, without farther exspatiating from the Subject, than by moderate Excursions, helping to advance or clear the main Design. But with *Knowledge,* it has fared as with a numerous Army, encamped in a fruitful Country; which for a few Days maintains it self by the Product of the Soyl it is on; Till Provisions being spent, they send to forrage many a Mile, among Friends or Enemies it matters not. Mean while, the neighbouring Fields trampled and beaten down, become barren and dry, affording no Sustenance but Clouds of Dust.

The whole Course of Things being thus entirely changed between *Us* and the *Antients;* and the *Moderns* wisely sensible of it, we of this Age have discovered a shorter, and more prudent Method, to become *Scholars* and *Wits,* without the Fatigue of *Reading* or of *Thinking.* The most accomplisht Way of using Books at present, is twofold: Either first, to serve them as some Men do *Lords,* learn their *Titles* exactly, and then brag of their Acquaintance. Or Secondly, which is indeed the choicer, the profounder, and politer Method, to get a thorough Insight into the *Index,* by which the whole Book is governed and turned, like *Fishes* by the *Tail.* For, to enter

the Palace of Learning at the *great Gate,* requires an Expence
of Time and Forms; therefore Men of much Haste and little
Ceremony, are content to get in by the *Back-Door.* For, the
Arts are all in a *flying* March, and therefore more easily
subdued by attacking them in the *Rear.* Thus Physicians discover the State of the whole Body, by consulting only what
comes from *Behind.* Thus Men catch Knowledge by throwing
their *Wit* on the *Posteriors* of a Book, as Boys do Sparrows
with flinging *Salt* upon their *Tails.* Thus Human Life is best
understood by the wise man's Rule of *Regarding the End.*
Thus are the Sciences found like *Hercules*'s Oxen, by *tracing
them Backwards.* Thus are *old Sciences* unravelled like *old
Stockings,* by beginning at the *Foot.*

Besides all this, the Army of the Sciences hath been of late,
with a world of Martial Discipline, drawn into its *close Order,*
so that a View, or a Muster may be taken of it with abundance
of Expedition. For this great Blessing we are wholly indebted
to *Systems* and *Abstracts,* in which the *Modern* Fathers of
Learning, like prudent Usurers, spent their Sweat for the Ease
of Us their Children. For *Labor* is the Seed of *Idleness,* and
it is the peculiar Happiness of our Noble Age to gather the
Fruit.

Now the Method of growing Wise, Learned, and *Sublime,*
having become so regular an Affair, and so established in all
its Forms; the Numbers of Writers must needs have encreased
accordingly, and to a Pitch that has made it of absolute
Necessity for them to interfere continually with each other.
Besides, it is reckoned, that there is not at this present, a
sufficient Quantity of new Matter left in Nature, to furnish and
adorn any one particular Subject to the Extent of a Volume.
This I am told by a very skillful *Computer,* who hath given
a full Demonstration of it from Rules of *Arithmetick.*

This, perhaps, may be objected against, by those, who
maintain the Infinity of Matter, and therefore, will not allow
that any *Species* of it can be exhausted. For Answer to which,
let us examine the noblest Branch of *Modern* Wit or Invention,
planted and cultivated by the present Age, and, which of all

others, hath born the most, and the fairest Fruit. For tho'
some Remains of it were left us by the *Antients*, yet have not
any of those, as I remember, been translated or compiled into
Systems for *Modern* Use. Therefore We may affirm, to our own
Honor, that it has in some sort, been both invented, and
brought to a Perfection by the same Hands. What I mean, is
that highly celebrated Talent among the *Modern* Wits, of
deducing Similitudes, Allusions, and Applications, very Surprizing, Agreeable, and Apposite, from the *Pudenda* of either
Sex, together with *their proper Uses.* And truly, having
observed how little Invention bears any Vogue, besides what
is derived into these *Channels,* I have sometimes had a
Thought, That the happy Genius of our Age and Country,
was prophetically held forth by that antient *typical Description of the *Indian* Pygmies; *whose Stature did not exceed
above two Foot; Sed quorum pudenda crassa, & ad talos usque
pertingentia.* Now, I have been very curious to inspect the
late Productions, wherein the Beauties of this kind have most
prominently appeared. And altho' this *Vein* hath bled so
freely, and all Endeavours have been used in the Power of
Human Breath, to dilate, extend, and keep it open: Like the
Scythians, †*who had a Custom, and an Instrument, to blow
up the Privities of their Mares, that they might yield the more
Milk;* Yet I am under an Apprehension, it is near growing
dry, and past all Recovery; And that either some new *Fonde*
of Wit should, if possible, be provided, or else that we must
e'en be content with Repetition here, as well as upon all
other Occasions.

This will stand as an uncontestable Argument, that our
Modern Wits are not to reckon upon the Infinity of Matter,
for a constant Supply. What remains therefore, but that our
last Recourse must be had to large *Indexes,* and little *Compendiums; Quotations* must be plentifully gathered, and bookt
in Alphabet; To this End, tho' Authors need be little consulted, yet *Criticks,* and *Commentators,* and *Lexicon*s carefully

* *Ctesiæ fragm. apud Photium.*
† *Herodot.* L. 4.

must. But above all, those judicious Collectors of *bright Parts,* and *Flowers,* and *Observanda's,* are to be nicely dwelt on; by some called the *Sieves* and *Boulters* of Learning; tho' it is left undetermined, whether they dealt in *Pearls* or *Meal;* and consequently, whether we are more to value that which *passed thro',* or what *staid behind.*

By these Methods, in a few Weeks, there starts up many a Writer, capable of managing the profoundest, and most universal Subjects, For, what tho' his *Head* be empty, provided his *Common-place-Book* be full; And if you will bate him but the Circumstances of *Method,* and *Style,* and *Grammar,* and *Invention;* allow him but the common Priviledges of transcribing from others, and digressing from himself, as often as he shall see Occasion; He will desire no more Ingredients towards fitting up a Treatise, that shall make a very comely Figure on a Bookseller's Shelf, there to be preserved neat and clean, for a long Eternity, adorn'd with the Heraldry of its Title, fairly inscribed on a Label; never to be thumb'd or greas'd by Students, nor bound to everlasting Chains of Darkness in a Library: But when the Fulness of time is come, shall happily undergo the Tryal of Purgatory, in order *to ascend the Sky.*

Without these Allowances, how is it possible, we *Modern* Wits should ever have an Opportunity to introduce our Collections listed under so many thousand Heads of a different Nature? for want of which, the Learned World would be deprived of infinite Delight, as well as Instruction, and we our selves buried beyond Redress in an inglorious and undistinguisht Oblivion.

From such Elements as these, I am alive to behold the Day, wherein the Corporation of Authors can outvie all its Brethren in the *Field.* A Happiness derived to us with a great many others, from our *Scythian* Ancestors; among whom, the Number of *Pens* was so infinite, that the * *Grecian* Eloquence had no other way of expressing it, than by saying, *That in the Regions,*

* *Herodot.* L. 4.

far to the North, *it was hardly possible for a Man to travel, the very Air was so replete with* Feathers.

The Necessity of this Digression, will easily excuse the Length; and I have chosen for it as proper a Place as I could readily find. If the judicious Reader can assign a fitter, I do here empower him to remove it into any other Corner he pleases. And so I return with great Alacrity to pursue a more important Concern.

S E C T I O N   V I I I .

A TALE of a TUB

THE Learned **Æolists,* maintain the Original Cause of all Things to be *Wind,* from which Principle this whole Universe was at first produced, and into which it must at last be resolved; that the same Breath which had kindled, and blew *up* the Flame of Nature, should one Day blow it *out.*

> *Quod procul à nobis flectat Fortuna gubernans.*

This is what the *Adepti* understand by their *Anima Mundi;* that is to say, the *Spirit,* or *Breath,* or *Wind* of the World: for Examine the whole System by the Particulars of Nature, and you will find it not to be disputed. For, whether you please to call the *Forma informans* of Man, by the Name of *Spiritus, Animus, Afflatus,* or *Anima;* What are all these but several Appellations for *Wind?* which is the ruling *Element* in every Compound, and into which they all resolve upon their Corruption. Farther, what is Life itself, but as it is commonly call'd, the *Breath* of our Nostrils? Whence it is very justly observed by Naturalists, that *Wind* still continues of great Emolument in *certain Mysteries* not to be named, giving Occasion for those happy Epithets of *Turgidus,* and *Inflatus,* apply'd either to the *Emittent,* or *Recipient* Organs.

---

* *All Pretenders to Inspiration whatsoever.*

By what I have gathered out of antient Records, I find the *Compass* of their Doctrine took in two and thirty Points, wherein it would be tedious to be very particular. However, a few of their most important Precepts, deducible from it, are by no means to be omitted; among which the following Maxim was of much Weight; That since *Wind* had the Master-Share, as well as Operation in every Compound, by Consequence, those Beings must be of chief Excellence, wherein that *Primordium* appears most prominently to abound; and therefore, *Man* is in highest Perfection of all created Things, as having by the great Bounty of Philosophers, been endued with three distinct *Anima's* or *Winds,* to which the Sage *Æolists,* with much Liberality, have added a fourth of equal Necessity, as well as Ornament with the other three; by this *quartum Principium,* taking in the four Corners of the World; which gave Occasion to that Renowned *Cabbalist,* * *Bumbastus,* of placing the Body of Man, in due position to the four *Cardinal* Points.

In Consequence of this, their next Principle was, that *Man* brings with him into the World a peculiar Portion or Grain of *Wind,* which may be called a *Quinta essentia,* extracted from the other four. This *Quintessence* is of a Catholick Use upon all Emergencies of Life, is improvable into all Arts and Sciences, and may be wonderfully refined, as well as enlarged by certain Methods in Education. This, when *blown* up to its Perfection, ought not to be covetously hoarded up, stifled, or hid under a Bushel, but freely communicated to Mankind. Upon these Reasons, and others of equal Weight, the Wise *Æolists,* affirm the Gift of BELCHING, to be the noblest Act of a Rational Creature. To cultivate which Art, and render it more serviceable to Mankind, they made Use of several Methods. At certain Seasons of the Year, you might behold the Priests amongst them in vast Numbers, with their † *Mouths*

---

* *This is one of the Names of* Paracelsus; *He was call'd* Christophorus, Theophrastus, Paracelsus, Bumbastus.

† *This is meant of those Seditious Preachers; who blow up the Seeds of Rebellion,* &c.

gaping wide against a Storm. At other times were to be seen several Hundreds link'd together in a circular Chain, with every Man a Pair of Bellows applied to his Neighbour's Breech, by which they blew up each other to the Shape and Size of a *Tun;* and for that Reason, with great Propriety of Speech, did usually call their Bodies, their *Vessels.* When, by these and the like Performances, they were grown sufficiently replete, they would immediately depart, and disembogue for the Publick Good, a plentiful Share of their Acquirements into their Disciples Chaps. For we must here observe, that all Learning was esteemed among them to be compounded from the same Principle. Because, First, it is generally affirmed, or confess'd that Learning *puffeth Men up:* And Secondly, they proved it by the following Syllogism; *Words are but Wind; and Learning is nothing but Words;* Ergo, *Learning is nothing but Wind.* For this Reason, the Philosophers among them, did in their Schools, deliver to their Pupils, all their Doctrines and Opinions by *Eructation,* wherein they had acquired a wonderful Eloquence, and of incredible Variety. But the great Characteristick, by which their chief Sages were best distinguished, was a certain Position of Countenance, which gave undoubted Intelligence to what Degree or Proportion, the Spirit agitated the inward Mass. For, after certain Gripings, the *Wind* and Vapours issuing forth; having first by their Turbulence and Convulsions within, caused an Earthquake in Man's little World; distorted the Mouth, bloated the Cheeks, and gave the Eyes a terrible kind of *Relievo.* At which Junctures, all their *Belches* were received for Sacred, the Sourer the better, and swallowed with infinite Consolation by their meager Devotees. And to render these yet more compleat, because the Breath of Man's Life is in his Nostrils, therefore, the choicest, most edifying, and most enlivening *Belches,* were very wisely conveyed thro' that Vehicle, to give them a Tincture as they passed.

Their Gods were the four *Winds,* whom they worshipped, as the Spirits that pervade and enliven the Universe, and as those from whom alone all *Inspiration* can properly be said to proceed. However, the Chief of these, to whom they performed the Adoration of *Latria,* was the *Almighty-North.* An antient Deity, whom the Inhabitants of *Megalopolis* in *Greece,* had likewise in highest Reverence. * *Omnium Deorum Boream maxime celebrant.* This God, tho' endued with Ubiquity, was yet supposed by the profounder *Æolists,* to possess one peculiar Habitation, or (to speak in Form) a *Cœlum Empyræum,* wherein he was more intimately present. This was situated in a certain Region, well known to the Antient *Greeks,* by them called, Σκοτία, or the *Land of Darkness.* And altho' many Controversies have arisen upon that Matter; yet so much is undisputed, that from a Region of the *like Denomination,* the most refined *Æolists* have borrowed their Original, from whence, in every Age, the zealous among their Priesthood, have brought over their choicest *Inspiration,* fetching it with their own Hands, from the Fountain Head, in certain *Bladders,* and disploding it among the Sectaries in all Nations, who did, and do, and ever will, daily Gasp and Pant after it.

Now, their Mysteries and Rites were performed in this Manner. 'Tis well known among the Learned, that the Virtuoso's of former Ages, had a Contrivance for carrying and preserving *Winds* in Casks or Barrels, which was of great Assistance upon long Sea Voyages; and the Loss of so useful an Art at present, is very much to be lamented, tho' I know not how, with great Negligence omitted by † *Pancirollus.* It was an Invention ascribed to *Æolus* himself, from whom this Sect is denominated, and who in Honour of their Founder's Memory, have to this Day preserved great Numbers of those *Barrels,* whereof they fix one in each of their Temples, first beating out the Top; into this *Barrel,* upon Solemn Days, the Priest enters; where, having before duly prepared himself by the methods already described, a secret Funnel is also convey'd from his Posteriors, to the Bottom of the Barrel, which admits new Supplies of Inspiration from a *Northern* Chink or Crany.

---

* *Pausan.* L. 8.

† *An Author who writ* De Artibus Perditis, &c. *of Arts lost, and of Arts invented*

Whereupon, you behold him swell immediately to the Shape and Size of his *Vessel*. In this Posture he disembogues whole Tempests upon his Auditory, as the Spirit from beneath gives him Utterance; which issuing *ex adytis,* and *penetralibus,* is not performed without much Pain and Gripings. And the *Wind* in breaking forth, *deals with his Face, as it does with that of the Sea; first *blackning,* then *wrinkling,* and at last, *bursting it into a Foam*. It is in this Guise, the Sacred *Æolist* delivers his oracular *Belches* to his panting Disciples; Of whom, some are greedily gaping after the sanctified Breath; others are all the while hymning out the Praises of the *Winds;* and gently wafted to and fro by their own Humming, do thus represent the soft Breezes of their Deities appeased.

It is from this Custom of the Priests, that some Authors maintain these *Æolists,* to have been very antient in the World. Because, the Delivery of their Mysteries, which I have just now mention'd, appears exactly the same with that of other antient Oracles, whose Inspirations were owing to certain subterraneous *Effluviums* of *Wind,* delivered with the *same* Pain to the Priest, and much about the *same* Influence on the People. It is true indeed, that these were frequently managed and directed by *Female* Officers, whose Organs were understood to be better disposed for the Admission of those Oracular *Gusts,* as entring and passing up thro' a Receptacle of greater Capacity, and causing also a Pruriency by the Way, such as with due Management, hath been refined from [a] Carnal, into a Spiritual Extasie. And to strengthen this profound Conjecture, it is farther insisted, that this Custom of † *Female* Priests is kept up still in certain refined Colleges of our *Modern Æolists,* who are agreed to receive their Inspiration, derived thro' the Receptacle aforesaid, like their Ancestors, the *Sibyls*.

And, whereas the mind of Man, when he gives the Spur and Bridle to his Thoughts, doth never stop, but naturally

---

* *This is an exact Description of the Changes made in the Face by Enthusiastick Preachers.*

† *Quakers who suffer their Women to preach and pray.*

sallies out into both extreams of High and Low, of Good and Evil; His first Flight of Fancy, commonly transports Him to Idea's of what is most Perfect, finished, and exalted; till having soared out of his own Reach and Sight, not well perceiving how near the Frontiers of Height and Depth, border upon each other; With the same Course and Wing, he falls down plum into the lowest Bottom of Things; like one who travels the *East* into the *West;* or like a strait Line drawn by its own Length into a Circle. Whether a Tincture of Malice in our Natures, makes us fond of furnishing every bright Idea with its Reverse; Or, whether Reason reflecting upon the Sum of Things, can, like the Sun, serve only to enlighten one half of the Globe, leaving the other half, by Necessity, under Shade and Darkness: Or, whether Fancy, flying up to the imagination of what is Highest and Best, becomes over-short, and spent, and weary, and suddenly falls like a dead Bird of Paradise, to the Ground. Or, whether after all these *Metaphysical* Conjectures, I have not entirely missed the true Reason; The Proposition, however, which hath stood me in so much Circumstance, is altogether true; That, as the most unciviliz'd Parts of Mankind, have some way or other, climbed up into the Conception of a *God,* or Supream Power, so they have seldom forgot to provide their Fears with certain ghastly Notions, which instead of better, have served them pretty tolerably for a *Devil.* And this Proceeding seems to be natural enough; For it is with Men, whose Imaginations are lifted up very high, after the same Rate, as with those, whose Bodies are so; that, as they are delighted with the Advantage of a nearer Contemplation upwards, so they are equally terrified with the dismal Prospect of the Precipice below. Thus, in the Choice of a *Devil*, it hath been the usual Method of Mankind, to single out some Being, either in Act, or in Vision, which was in most Antipathy to the God they had framed. Thus also the Sect of *Æolists,* possessed themselves with a Dread, and Horror, and Hatred of two Malignant Natures, betwixt whom, and the Deities they adored, perpetual Enmity was established.

The first of these, was the * *Camelion,* swore Foe to *Inspiration,* who in Scorn, devoured large Influences of their God; without refunding the smallest Blast by *Eructation.* The other was a huge terrible Monster, called *Moulinavent,* who with four strong Arms, waged eternal Battel with all their Divinities, dextrously turning to avoid their Blows, and repay them with Interest.

Thus furnisht, and set out with *Gods,* as well as *Devils,* was the renowned Sect of *Æolists;* which makes at this Day so illustrious a Figure in the World, and whereof, that Polite Nation of *Laplanders,* are beyond all Doubt, a most Authentick Branch; Of whom, I therefore cannot, without Injustice, here omit to make honourable Mention; since they appear to be so closely allied in Point of Interest, as well as Inclinations, with their Brother *Æolists* among Us, as not only to buy their *Winds* by wholesale from the *same* Merchants, but also to retail them after the *same* Rate and Method, and to Customers much alike.

Now, whether the System here delivered, was wholly compiled by *Jack,* or, as some Writers believe, rather copied from the Original at *Delphos,* with certain Additions and Emendations suited to Times and Circumstances, I shall not absolutely determine. This I may affirm, that *Jack* gave it at least a new Turn, and formed it into the same Dress and Model, as it lies deduced by me.

I have long sought after this Opportunity, of doing Justice to a Society of Men, for whom I have a peculiar Honour, and whose Opinions, as well as Practices, have been extreamly misrepresented, and traduced by the Malice or Ignorance of their Adversaries. For, I think it one of the greatest, and best of humane Actions, to remove Prejudices, and place Things in their truest and fairest Light; which I therefore boldly undertake without any Regards of my own, beside the Conscience, the Honour, and the Thanks.

---

* *I do not well understand what the Author aims at here, any more than by the terrible Monster, mention'd in the following Lines, called* Moulinavent, *which is the* French *Word for a Windmill.*

A Digression concerning the Original,

the Use and Improvement of Madness

in a Commonwealth.

NOR shall it any ways detract from the just Reputation of this famous Sect, that its Rise and Institution are owing to such an Author as I have described *Jack* to be; A Person whose Intellectuals were overturned, and his Brain shaken out of its Natural Position; which we commonly suppose to be a Distemper, and call by the Name of *Madness* or *Phrenzy*. For, if we take a Survey of the greatest Actions that have been performed in the World, under the Influence of Single Men; which are, *The Establishment of New Empires by Conquest: The Advance and Progress of New Schemes in Philosophy; and the contriving, as well as the propagating of New Religions:* We shall find the Authors of them all, to have been Persons, whose natural Reason hath admitted great Revolutions from their Dyet, their Education, the Prevalency of some certain Temper, together with the particular Influence of Air and Climate. Besides, there is something Individual in human Minds, that easily kindles at the accidental Approach and Collision of certain Circumstances, which tho' of paltry and mean Appearance, do often flame out into the greatest Emergencies of Life. For great Turns are not always given by strong Hands, but by lucky Adaption, and at proper Seasons; and it is of no import, where the Fire was kindled, if the Vapor has once got up into the Brain. For the *upper Region* of Man, is furnished like the *middle Region* of the Air; The Materials are formed from Causes of the widest Difference, yet produce at last the same Substance and Effect. Mists arise from the Earth, Streams from Dunghils, Exhalations from the Sea, and Smoak from Fire; yet all Clouds are the same in Composition, as well as Consequences: and the Fumes issuing from a Jakes, will furnish as comely and useful a Vapor, as Incense from an Altar. Thus far, I suppose, will easily be granted me; and then it will follow, that as the Face of Nature never produces Rain, but when it is overcast and disturbed, so Human Understanding, seated in the Brain, must be troubled and overspread by Vapours, ascending from the lower Faculties, to water the Invention, and render it fruitful. Now, altho' these Vapours (as it hath been already said) are of as various Original, as those of the Skies, yet the Crop they produce, differ[s] both in Kind and Degree, meerly according to the Soil. I will produce two Instances to prove and Explain what I am now advancing.

*A certain Great Prince raised a mighty Army, filled his Coffers with infinite Treasures, provided an invincible Fleet, and all this, without giving the least Part of his Design to his greatest Ministers, or his nearest Favourites, Immediately the whole World was alarmed; the neighbouring Crowns, in trembling Expectation, towards what Point the Storm would burst; the small Politicians, every where forming profound Conjectures. Some believed he had laid a Scheme for Universal Monarchy: Others, after much Insight, determined the Matter to be a Project for pulling down the *Pope,* and setting up the *Reformed* Religion, which had once been his own. Some, again, of a deeper Sagacity, sent him into *Asia* to subdue the *Turk,* and recover *Palestine.* In the midst of all these Projects and Preparations; a certain † *State-Surgeon,* gathering the Nature of the Disease by these Symptoms, attempted the Cure, at one Blow performed the Operation, broke the Bag, and out flew the *Vapour;* nor did any thing want to render it a compleat Remedy, only, that the Prince unfortunately happened to Die in the Performance. Now, is the Reader ex-

---

* *This was* Harry *the Great of* France.
† Ravillac, *who stabb'd* Henry *the Great in his Coach.*

ceeding curious to learn, from whence this *Vapour* took its Rise, which had so long set the Nations at a Gaze? What secret Wheel, what hidden Spring could put into Motion so wonderful an Engine? It was afterwards discovered, that the Movement of this whole Machine had been directed by an absent *Female,* whose Eyes had raised a Protuberancy, and before Emission, she was removed into an Enemy's Country. What should an unhappy Prince do in such ticklish Circumstances as these? He tried in vain the Poet's never-failing Receipt of *Corpora quæque;* For,

> *Idque petit corpus mens unde est saucia amore;*
> *Unde feritur, eo tendit, gestitq; coire.*   Lucr.

Having to no purpose used all peaceable Endeavours, the collected part of the *Semen,* raised and enflamed, became adust, converted to Choler, turned head upon the spinal Duct, and ascended to the Brain. The very same Principle that influences a *Bully* to break the Windows of a Whore, who has jilted him, naturally stirs up a Great Prince to raise mighty Armies, and dream of nothing but Sieges, Battles, and Victories.

> ———*Teterrima belli*
> *Causa* ————————

The other * Instance is, what I have read somewhere, in a very antient Author, of a mighty King, who for the space of above thirty Years, amused himself to take and loose Towns; beat Armies, and be beaten; drive Princes out of their Dominions; fright Children from their Bread and Butter; burn, lay waste, plunder, dragoon, massacre Subject and Stranger, Friend and Foe, Male and Female. 'Tis recorded, that the Philosophers of each Country were in grave Dispute, upon Causes Natural, Moral, and Political, to find out where they should assign an original Solution of this *Phænomenon.* At last the *Vapour* or *Spirit,* which animated the Hero's Brain, being in perpetual Circulation, seized upon that Region of [the]

---

* *This is meant of the Present* French *King.*

Human Body, so renown'd for furnishing the * *Zibeta Oc-cidentalis,* and gathering there into a Tumor, left the rest of the World for that Time in Peace. Of such mighty Consequence it is, where those Exhalations fix; and of so little, from whence they proceed. The same Spirits which in their superior Progress would conquer a Kingdom, descending upon the *Anus,* conclude in a *Fistula.*

Let us next examine the great Introducers of new Schemes in Philosophy, and search till we can find, from what Faculty of the Soul the Disposition arises in mortal Man, of taking it into his Head, to advance new Systems with such an eager Zeal, in things agreed on all hands impossible to be known: from what Seeds this Disposition springs, and to what Quality of human Nature these Grand Innovators have been indebted for their Number of Disciples. Because, it is plain, that several of the chief among them, both *Antient* and *Modern,* were usually mistaken by their Adversaries, and indeed, by all, except their own Followers, to have been Persons Crazed, or out of their Wits, having generally proceeded in the common Course of their Words and Actions, by a Method very different from the vulgar Dictates of *unrefined* Reason: agreeing for the most Part in their several Models, with their present undoubted Successors in the *Academy* of *Modern Bedlam* (whose Merits and Principles I shall farther examine in due Place.) Of this Kind were *Epicurus, Diogenes, Apollonius, Lucretius, Paracelsus, Des Cartes,* and others; who, if they were now in the World, tied fast, and separate from their Followers, would in this our undistinguishing Age, incur manifest Danger of *Phlebotomy,* and *Whips,* and *Chains,* and *dark Chambers,* and *Straw.* For, what Man in the natural State, or Course of Thinking, did ever conceive it in his Power, to reduce the Notions of all Mankind, exactly to the same Length, and Breadth, and

---

* Paracelsus, *who was so famous for Chymistry, try'd an Experiment upon human Excrement, to make a Perfume of it, which when he had brought to Perfection, he called* Zibeta Occidentalis, *or* Western-Civet, *the back Parts of Man (according to his Division mention'd by the Author,* page [108],) *being the* West.

Heighth of his own? Yet this is the first humble and civil Design of all Innovators in the Empire of Reason. *Epicurus* modestly hoped, that one Time or other, a certain Fortuitous Concourse of all Mens Opinions, after perpetual Justlings, the Sharp with the Smooth, the Light and the Heavy, the Round and the Square, would by certain *Clinamina*, unite in the Notions of *Atoms* and *Void*, as these did in the Originals of all Things. *Cartesius* reckoned to see before he died, the Sentiments of all Philosophers, like so many lesser Stars in his *Romantick* System, rapt and drawn within his own *Vortex*. Now, I would gladly be informed, how it is possible to account for such Imaginations as these in particular Men, without Recourse to my *Phœnomenon* of *Vapours*, ascending from the lower Faculties to over-shadow the Brain, and there distilling into Conceptions, for which the Narrowness of our Mother-Tongue has not yet assigned any other Name, besides that of *Madness* or *Phrenzy*. Let us therefore now conjecture how it comes to pass, that none of these great Prescribers, do ever fail providing themselves and their Notions, with a Number of implicite Disciples. And, I think, the Reason is easie to be assigned: For, there is a peculiar *String* in the Harmony of Human Understanding, which in several individuals is exactly of the same Tuning. This, if you can dexterously screw up to its right Key, and then strike gently upon it; Whenever you have the Good Fortune to light among those of the same Pitch, they will by a secret necessary Sympathy, strike exactly at the same time. And in this one Circumstance, lies all the Skill or Luck of the Matter; for if you chance to jar the String among those who are either above or below your own Height, instead of subscribing to your Doctrine, they will tie you fast, call you Mad, and feed you with Bread and Water. It is therefore a Point of the nicest Conduct to distinguish and adapt this noble Talent, with respect to the Differences of Persons and of Times. *Cicero* understood this very well, when writing to a Friend in *England*, with a Caution, among other Matters, to beware of being cheated by our *Hackney-Coachmen* (who, it seems, in those days, were as arrant Rascals as they are now) has these remarkable Words. * *Est quod gaudeas te in ista loca venisse, ubi aliquid sapere viderere.* For, to speak a bold Truth, it is a fatal Miscarriage, so ill to order Affairs, as to pass for a *Fool* in one Company, when in another you might be treated as a *Philosopher.* Which I desire *some certain Gentlemen of my Acquaintance,* to lay up in their Hearts, as a very seasonable *Innuendo.*

This, indeed, was the Fatal Mistake of that worthy Gentleman, my most ingenious Friend, Mr. *W——tt——n:* A Person, in appearance ordain'd for great Designs, as well as Performances; whether you will consider his *Notions* or his *Looks.* Surely, no Man ever advanced into the Publick, with fitter Qualifications of Body and Mind, for the Propagation of a new Religion. Oh, had those happy Talents misapplied to vain Philosophy, been turned into their proper Channels of *Dreams* and *Visions,* where *Distortion* of Mind and Countenance, are of such Sovereign Use; the base detracting World would not then have dared to report, that something is amiss, that his Brain hath undergone an unlucky Shake; which even his Brother *Modernists* themselves, like Ungrates, do whisper so loud, that it reaches up to the very Garret I am now writing in.

Lastly, Whosoever pleases to look into the Fountains of *Enthusiasm,* from whence, in all Ages, have eternally proceeded such fatning Streams, will find the Spring Head to have been as *troubled* and *muddy* as the Current; Of such great Emolument, is a Tincture of this *Vapour,* which the World calls *Madness,* that without its Help, the World would not only be deprived of those two great Blessings, *Conquests* and *Systems,* but even all Mankind would [un]happily be reduced to the same Belief in Things Invisible. Now, the former *Postulatum* being held, that it is of no Import from what Originals this *Vapour* proceeds, but either in what *Angles* it strikes and spreads over the Understanding, or upon what *Species* of Brain it ascends; It will be a very delicate Point, to cut the Feather,

* *Epist. ad Fam. Trebatio.*

and divide the several Reasons to a Nice and Curious Reader, how this numerical Difference in the Brain, can produce Effects of so vast a Difference from the same *Vapour,* as to be the sole Point of Individuation between *Alexander the Great, Jack of Leyden,* and Monsieur *Des Cartes.* The present Argument is the most abstracted that ever I engaged in, it strains my Faculties to their highest Stretch; and I desire the Reader to attend with utmost Perpensity; For, I now proceed to unravel this knotty Point.

* There is in Mankind a certain * * * * *
* * * * * * * * * * * *
* * * * * * * * *

Hic multa
desiderantur. * * * * * * * * *

* * * * * * * * * * * *

* * * * And this I take to be a clear Solution of the Matter.

Having therefore so narrowly past thro' this intricate Difficulty, the Reader will, I am sure, agree with me in the Conclusion; that if the *Moderns* mean by *Madness,* only a Disturbance or Transposition of the Brain, by Force of certain *Vapours* issuing up from the lower Faculties; Then has this *Madness* been the Parent of all those mighty Revolutions, that have happened in *Empire,* in *Philosophy,* and in *Religion.* For, the Brain, in its natural Position and State of Serenity, disposeth its Owner to pass his Life in the common Forms, without any Thought of subduing Multitudes to his own *Power,* his *Reasons* or his *Visions;* and the more he shapes his Understanding by the Pattern of Human Learning, the less he is inclined to form Parties after his particular Notions; because that instructs him in his private Infirmities, as well as in the stubborn Ignorance of the People. But when a Man's Fancy gets *astride* on his Reason, when Imagination is at Cuffs with

---

* *Here is another Defect in the Manuscript, but I think the Author did wisely, and that the Matter which thus strained his Faculties, was not worth a Solution; and it were well if all Metaphysical Cobweb Problems were no otherwise answered.*

the Senses, and common Understanding, as well as common Sense, is Kickt out of Doors; the first Proselyte he makes, is Himself, and when that is once compass'd, the Difficulty is not so great in bringing over others; A strong Delusion always operating from *without,* as vigorously as from *within.* For, Cant and Vision are to the Ear and the Eye, the same that Tickling is to the Touch. Those Entertainments and Pleasures we most value in Life, are such as *Dupe* and play the Wag with the Senses. For, if we take an Examination of what is generally understood by *Happiness,* as it has Respect, either to the Understanding or the Senses, we shall find all its Properties and Adjuncts will herd under this short Definition: That, *it is a perpetual Possession of being well Deceived.* And first, with Relation to the Mind or Understanding; 'tis manifest, what mighty Advantages Fiction has over Truth; and the Reason is just at our Elbow; because Imagination can build nobler Scenes, and produce more wonderful Revolutions than Fortune or Nature will be at Expence to furnish. Nor is Mankind so much to blame in his Choice, thus determining him, if we consider that the Debate meerly lies between *Things past,* and *Things conceived;* and so the Question is only this; Whether Things that have Place in the *Imagination,* may not as properly be said to *Exist,* as those that are seated in the *Memory;* which may be justly held in the Affirmative, and very much to the Advantage of the former, since This is acknowledged to be the *Womb* of Things, and the other allowed to be no more than the *Grave.* Again, if we take this Definition of Happiness, and examine it with Reference to the Senses, it will be acknowledged wonderfully adapt. How fading and insipid do all Objects accost us that are not convey'd in the Vehicle of *Delusion?* How shrunk is every Thing, as it appears in the Glass of Nature? So, that if it were not for the Assistance of Artificial *Mediums,* false Lights, refracted Angles, Varnish, and Tinsel; there would be a mighty Level in the Felicity and Enjoyments of Mortal Men. If this were seriously considered by the World, as I have a certain Reason to suspect it hardly will; Men would no longer reckon among their high Points of Wisdom, the Art of exposing weak Sides, and publishing Infirmities; an Employment in my Opinion, neither better nor worse than that of *Unmasking,* which I think, has never been allowed fair Usage, either in the *World* or the *Play-House.*

In the Proportion that Credulity is a more peaceful Possession of the Mind, than Curiosity, so far preferable is that Wisdom, which converses about the Surface, to that pretended Philosophy which enters into the Depth of Things, and then comes gravely back with Informations and Discoveries, that in the inside they are good for nothing. The two Senses, to which all Objects first address themselves, are the Sight and the Touch; These never examine farther than the Colour, the Shape, the Size, and whatever other Qualities dwell, or are drawn by Art upon the Outward of Bodies; and then comes Reason officiously, with Tools for cutting, and opening, and mangling, and piercing, offering to demonstrate, that they are not of the same consistence quite thro'. Now, I take all this to be the last Degree of perverting Nature; one of whose Eternal Laws it is, to put her best Furniture forward. And therefore, in order to save the Charges of all such expensive Anatomy for the Time to come; I do here think fit to inform the Reader, that in such Conclusions as these, Reason is certainly in the Right; and that in most Corporeal Beings, which have fallen under my Cognizance, the *Outside* hath been infinitely preferable to the *In:* Whereof I have been farther convinced from some late Experiments. Last Week I saw a Woman *flay'd,* and you will hardly believe, how much it altered her Person for the worse. Yesterday I ordered the Carcass of a *Beau* to be stript in my Presence; when we were all amazed to find so many unsuspected Faults under one Suit of Cloaths: Then I laid open his *Brain, his Heart,* and his *Spleen;* But, I plainly perceived at every Operation, that the farther we proceeded, we found the Defects encrease upon us in Number and Bulk: from all which, I justly formed this Conclusion to my self; That whatever Philosopher or Projector can find out an Art to sodder and patch up the

Flaws and Imperfections of Nature, will deserve much better of Mankind, and teach us a more useful Science, than that so much in present Esteem, of widening and exposing them (like him who held *Anatomy* to be the ultimate End of *Physick*.) And he, whose Fortunes and Dispositions have placed him in a convenient Station to enjoy the Fruits of this noble Art; He that can with *Epicurus* content his Ideas with the *Films* and *Images* that fly off upon his Senses from the *Superficies* of Things; Such a Man truly wise, creams off Nature, leaving the Sower and the Dregs, for Philosophy and Reason to lap up. This is the sublime and refined Point of Felicity, called, *the Possession of being well deceived;* The Serene Peaceful State of being a Fool among Knaves.

But to return to *Madness.* It is certain, that according to the System I have above deduced; every *Species* thereof proceeds from a Redundancy of *Vapours;* therefore, as some Kinds of *Phrenzy* give double Strength to the Sinews, so there are of other *Species,* which add Vigor, and Life, and Spirit to the Brain: Now, it usually happens, that these active Spirits, getting Possession of the Brain, resemble those that haunt other waste and empty Dwellings, which for want of Business, either vanish, and carry away a Piece of the House, or else stay at home and fling it all out of the Windows. By which are mystically display'd the two principal Branches of *Madness,* and which some Philosophers not considering so well as I, have mistook to be different in their Causes, over-hastily assigning the first to Deficiency, and the other to Redundance.

I think it therefore manifest, from what I have here advanced, that the main Point of Skill and Address, is to furnish Employment for this Redundancy of *Vapour,* and prudently to adjust the Season of it; by which means it may certainly become of Cardinal and Catholick Emolument in a Commonwealth. Thus one Man chusing a proper Juncture, leaps into a Gulph, from whence proceeds a Hero, and is called the Saver of his Country; Another atchieves the same Enterprise, but unluckily timing it, has left the Brand of *Madness,* fixt as a Reproach upon his Memory; Upon so nice a Distinction are we taught to repeat the Name of *Curtius* with Reverence and Love; that of *Empedocles,* with Hatred and Contempt. Thus, also it is usually conceived, that the Elder *Brutus* only personated the *Fool* and *Madman,* for the Good of the Publick: but this was nothing else, than a Redundancy of the same *Vapor,* long misapplied, called by the *Latins,* * *Ingenium par negotiis:* Or, (to translate it as nearly as I can) a sort of *Phrenzy,* never in its right Element, till you take it up in Business of the State.

Upon all which, and many other Reasons of equal Weight, though not equally curious; I do here gladly embrace an Opportunity I have long sought for, of Recommending it as a very noble Undertaking, to Sir *E——d S——r,* Sir *C——r M——ve,* Sir *J——n B——ls, J——n H——w,* Esq; and other Patriots concerned, that they would move for Leave to bring in a Bill, for appointing Commissioners to Inspect into *Bedlam,* and the Parts adjacent; who shall be empowered to *send for Persons, Papers, and Records:* to examine into the Merits and Qualifications of every Student and Professor; to observe with utmost Exactness their several Dispositions and Behaviour; by which means, duly distinguishing and adapting their Talents, they might produce admirable Instruments for the several Offices in a State, * * * * * * * *Civil* and *Military;* proceeding in such Methods as I shall here humbly propose. And, I hope the Gentle Reader will give some Allowance to my great Solicitudes in this important Affair, upon Account of that high Esteem I have ever born that honourable Society, whereof I had some Time the Happiness to be an unworthy Member.

Is any Student tearing his Straw in piece-meal, Swearing and Blaspheming, biting his Grate, foaming at the Mouth, and emptying his Pispot in the Spectator's Faces? Let the Right Worshipful, the *Commissioners of Inspection,* give him a Regiment of Dragoons, and send him into *Flanders* among the *Rest.* Is another eternally talking, sputtering, gaping, bawling,

* *Tacit.*

in a Sound without Period or Article? What wonderful Talents are here mislaid! Let him be furnished immediately with a green Bag and Papers, and * *three Pence* in his Pocket, and away with Him to *Westminster-Hall*. You will find a Third, gravely taking the Dimensions of his Kennel; A Person of Foresight and Insight, tho' kept quite in the Dark; for why, like *Moses, Ecce* †*cornuta erat ejus facies*. He walks duly in one Pace, intreats your Penny with due Gravity and Ceremony; talks much of hard Times, and Taxes, and the *Whore of Babylon;* Bars up the woodden Window of his Cell constantly at eight a Clock: Dreams of *Fire,* and *Shop-lifters,* and *Court-Customers,* and *Priviledg'd Places.* Now, what a Figure would all these Acquirements amount to, if the Owner were sent into the *City* among his Brethren! Behold a Fourth, in much and deep Conversation with himself, biting his Thumbs at proper Junctures; His Countenance chequered with Business and Design; sometimes walking very fast, with his Eyes nailed to a Paper that he holds in his Hands: A great Saver of Time, somewhat thick of Hearing, very short of Sight, but more of Memory. A Man ever in Haste, a great Hatcher and Breeder of Business, and excellent at the Famous Art of *whispering Nothing.* A huge Idolater of Monosyllables and Procrastination; so ready to *Give* his Word to every Body, that he never *keeps* it. One that has forgot the common *Meaning* of Words, but an admirable Retainer of the *Sound.* Extreamly subject to the *Loosness,* for his *Occasions* are perpetually *calling him away.* If you approach his Grate in his familiar Intervals; *Sir,* says he, *Give me a Penny, and I'll sing you a Song: But give me the Penny first.* (Hence comes the common Saying, and commoner Practice of parting with Money for a *Song.*) What a compleat System of *Court-Skill* is here described in every Branch of it, and all utterly lost with wrong Application? Accost the Hole of another Kennel, first stopping your Nose,

---

* *A Lawyer's Coach-hire.*

---

† Cornutus, *is either Horned or Shining, and by this Term,* Moses *is described in the vulgar* Latin *of the Bible.*

you will behold a surley, gloomy, nasty, slovenly Mortal, raking in his own Dung, and dabling in his Urine. The best Part of his Diet, is the Reversion of his own Ordure, which exspiring into Steams, whirls perpetually about, and at last reinfunds. His Complexion is of a dirty Yellow, with a thin scattered Beard, exactly agreeable to that of his Dyet upon its first Declination; like other Insects, who having their Birth and Education in an Excrement, from thence borrow their Colour and their Smell. The Student of this Apartment is very sparing of his Words, but somewhat over-liberal of his Breath; He holds his Hand out ready to receive your Penny, and immediately upon Receipt, withdraws to his former Occupations. Now, is it not amazing to think, the Society of *Warwick-Lane,* should have no more Concern, for the Recovery of so useful a Member, who, if one may judge from these Appearances, would become the greatest Ornament to that Illustrious Body? Another Student struts up fiercely to your Teeth, puffing with his Lips, half squeezing out his Eyes, and very graciously holds you out his Hand to kiss. The *Keeper* desires you not to be afraid of this Professor, for he will do you no Hurt: To him alone is allowed the Liberty of the Anti-Chamber, and the *Orator* of the Place gives you to understand, that this solemn Person is a *Taylor* run mad with Pride. This considerable Student is adorned with many other Qualities, upon which, at present, I shall not farther enlarge. – – – – – * *Heark in your Ear* – – – – – I am strangely mistaken, if all his Address, his Motions, and his Airs, would not then be very natural, and in their proper Element.

I shall not descend so minutely, as to insist upon the vast Number of *Beaux, Fidlers, Poets,* and *Politicians,* that the World might recover by such a Reformation; But what is more material, besides the clear Gain redounding to the Commonwealth, by so large an Acquisition of Persons to em-

---

* *I cannot conjecture what the Author means here, or how this Chasm could be fill'd, tho' it is capable of more than one Interpretation.*

ploy, whose Talents and Acquirements, if I may be so bold to affirm it, are now buried, or at least misapplied: It would be a mighty Advantage accruing to the Publick from this Enquiry, that all these would very much excel, and arrive at great Perfection in their several Kinds; which, I think, is manifest from what I have already shewn; and shall inforce by this one plain Instance; That even, I my self, the Author of these momentous Truths, am a Person, whose Imaginations are hard-mouth'd, and exceedingly disposed to run away with his *Reason,* which I have observed from long Experience, to be a very light Rider, and easily shook off; upon which Account, my Friends will never trust me alone, without a solemn Promise, to vent my Speculations in this, or the like manner, for the universal Benefit of Human kind; which, perhaps, the gentle, courteous, and candid Reader, brimful of that *Modern* Charity and Tenderness, usually annexed to his *Office,* will be very hardly persuaded to believe.

S E C T I O N X .

A TALE of a TUB

IT is an unanswerable Argument of a very refined Age, the wonderful Civilities that have passed of late Years, between the Nation of *Authors,* and that of *Readers.* There can hardly *pop out a *Play,* a *Pamphlet,* or a *Poem,* without a Preface full of Acknowledgement to the World, for the general Reception and Applause they have given it, which the Lord knows where, or when, or how, or from whom it received. In due Deference to so laudable a Custom, I do here return my humble Thanks to *His Majesty,* and both Houses of *Parliament;* To the *Lords* of the King's most honourable Privy-Council, to the Reverend the *Judges:* To the *Clergy,* and

---

* *This is literally true, as we may observe in the Prefaces to most Plays, Poems,* &c.

~~Gentry,~~ and *Yeomantry* of this Land: But in a more especial manner, to my worthy Brethren and Friends at *Will's Coffee-House,* and *Gresham-College,* and *Warwick-Lane,* and *Moor-Fields,* and *Scotland-Yard,* and *Westminster-Hall,* and *Guild-Hall;* In short, to all Inhabitants and Retainers whatsoever, either in Court, or Church, or Camp, or City, or Country; for their generous and universal Acceptance of this Divine Treatise. I accept their Approbation, and good Opinion with extream Gratitude, and to the utmost of my poor Capacity, shall take hold of all Opportunities to return the Obligation.

I am also happy, that Fate has flung me into so blessed an Age for the mutual Felicity of *Booksellers* and *Authors,* whom I may safely affirm to be at this Day the two only satisfied Parties in *England.* Ask an *Author* how his last Piece hath succeeded; *Why, truly he thanks his Stars, the World has been very favourable, and he has not the least Reason to complain: And yet, By G——, He writ it in a Week at Bits and Starts, when he could steal an Hour from his urgent Affairs;* as it is a hundred to one, you may see farther in the Preface, to which he refers you; and for the rest, to the Bookseller. There you go as a Customer, and make the same Question: *He blesses his God, the* Thing *takes wonderfully, he is just Printing a Second Edition, and has but three left in his Shop. You beat down the* Price: *Sir, we shall not differ;* and in hopes of your Custom another Time, lets you have it as reasonable as you please; *And, pray send as many of your Acquaintance as you will, I shall upon your Account furnish them all at the same Rate.*

Now, it is not well enough consider'd, to what Accidents and Occasions the World is indebted for the greatest Part of those noble Writings, which hourly start up to entertain it. If it were not for a *rainy Day, a drunken Vigil, a Fit of the Spleen, a Course of Physick, a sleepy Sunday, an ill Run at Dice, a long Taylor's Bill, a Beggar's Purse, a factious Head, a hot Sun, costive Dyet, Want of Books, and a just Contempt of Learning.* But for these Events, I say, and some Others too long to recite,

(especially *a prudent Neglect of taking Brimstone inwardly,*)
I doubt, the Number of *Authors,* and of *Writings* would
dwindle away to a Degree most woful to behold. To confirm
this Opinion, hear the Words of the famous *Troglodyte*
Philosopher: *'Tis certain* (said he) *some Grains of Folly are of
course annexed, as Part of the Composition of Human Nature,
only the Choice is left us, whether we please to wear them*
Inlaid *or* Embossed; *And we need not go very far to seek how
that is usually determined, when we remember, it is with
Human Faculties as with Liquors, the lightest will be ever at
the Top.*

There is in this famous Island of *Britain* a certain paultry
Scribbler, very voluminous, whose Character the Reader cannot
wholly be a Stranger to. He deals in a pernicious Kind of
Writings, called *Second Parts,* and usually passes under the
Name of *The Author of the First.* I easily foresee, that as soon
as I lay down my Pen, this nimble *Operator* will have stole it,
and treat me as inhumanly as he hath already done Dr.
Bl——re, L——ge, and many others who shall here be nameless. I therefore fly for Justice and Relief, into the Hands of
that great *Rectifier of Saddles,* and *Lover of Mankind,* Dr.
B——tly, begging he will take this enormous Grievance into
his most *Modern* Consideration: And if it should so happen,
that the *Furniture of an Ass,* in the Shape of a *Second Part,*
must for my Sins be clapt, by a Mistake upon my Back, that
he will immediately please, in the Presence of the World,
to lighten me of the Burthen, and take it home to *his own
House,* till the *true Beast* thinks fit to call for it.

In the mean time I do here give this publick Notice, that
my Resolutions are, to circumscribe within this Discourse
the whole Stock of Matter I have been so many Years providing. Since my *Vein* is once opened, I am content to exhaust it
all at a Running, for the peculiar Advantage of my dear
Country, and for the universal Benefit of Mankind. Therefore
hospitably considering the Number of my Guests, they shall
have my whole Entertainment at a Meal; And I scorn to set

up the *Leavings* in the Cupboard. What the *Guests* cannot eat may be given to the *Poor,* and the * *Dogs* under the Table may gnaw the *Bones;* This I understand for a more generous Proceeding, than to turn the Company's Stomach, by inviting them again to morrow to a scurvy Meal of *Scraps.*

If the Reader fairly considers the Strength of what I have advanced in the foregoing Section, I am convinced it will produce a wonderful Revolution in his Notions and Opinions; And he will be abundantly better prepared to receive and to relish the concluding Part of this miraculous Treatise. Readers may be divided into three Classes, the *Superficial,* the *Ignorant,* and the *Learned:* And I have with much Felicity fitted my Pen to the Genius and Advantage of each. The *Superficial* Reader will be strangely provoked to *Laughter;* which clears the Breast and the Lungs, is Soverain against the *Spleen,* and the most innocent of all *Diureticks.* The *Ignorant* Reader (between whom and the former, the Distinction is extreamly nice) will find himself disposed to *Stare;* which is an admirable Remedy for ill Eyes, serves to raise and enliven the Spirits, and wonderfully helps *Perspiration.* But the Reader truly *Learned,* chiefly for whose Benefit I wake, when others sleep, and sleep when others wake, will here find sufficient Matter to employ his Speculations for the rest of his Life. It were much to be wisht, and I do here humbly propose for an Experiment, that every Prince in *Christendom* will take seven of the *deepest Scholars* in his Dominions, and shut them up close for *seven* Years, in *seven* Chambers, with a Command to write *seven* ample Commentaries on this comprehensive Discourse. I shall venture to affirm, that whatever Difference may be found in their several Conjectures, they will be all, without the least Distortion, manifestly deduceable from the Text. Mean time, it is my earnest Request, that so useful an Undertaking may be entered upon (if their Majesties please) with all convenient speed; because I have a strong Inclination,

---

* *By Dogs, the Author means common injudicious Criticks, as he explains it himself before in his* Digression upon Criticks, *page* [76].

before I leave the World, to taste a Blessing, which we *mysterious* Writers can seldom reach, till we have got into our Graves. Whether it is, that *Fame* being a Fruit grafted on the Body, can hardly grow, and much less ripen, till the *Stock* is in the Earth: Or, whether she be a Bird of Prey, and is lured among the rest, to pursue after the Scent of a *Carcass:* Or, whether she conceives, her Trumpet sounds best and farthest, when she stands on a *Tomb,* by the Advantage of a rising Ground, and the Echo of a hollow Vault.

'Tis true, indeed, the Republick of *dark* Authors, after they once found out this excellent Expedient of *Dying,* have been peculiarly happy in the Variety, as well as Extent of their Reputation. For, *Night* being the universal Mother of Things, wise Philosophers hold all Writings to be *fruitful* in the Proportion they are *dark;* And therefore, the * *true illuminated* (that is to say, the *Darkest* of all) have met with such numberless Commentators, whose *Scholiastick* Midwifry hath deliver'd them of Meanings, that the Authors themselves, perhaps, never conceived, and yet may very justly be allowed the Lawful Parents of them: † The Words of such Writers being like Seed, which, however scattered at random, when they light upon a fruitful Ground, will multiply far beyond either the Hopes or Imagination of the Sower.

And therefore in order to promote so useful a Work, I will here take Leave to glance a few *Innuendo's*, that may be of great Assistance to those sublime Spirits, who shall be appointed to labor in a universal Comment upon this wonderful Discourse. And First, ‡ I have couched a very profound Mystery in the Number of O's multiply'd by *Seven,* and divided by *Nine.* Also, if a devout Brother of the *Rosy Cross* will pray fervently for sixty three Mornings, with a lively Faith, and then transpose certain letters and Syllables accord-

* *A Name of the* Rosycrucians.

---

† *Nothing is more frequent than for Commentators to force Interpretation, which the Author never meant.*

‡ *This is what the* Cabbalists *among the* Jews *have done with the* Bible, *and pretend to find wonderful Mysteries by it.*

ing to Prescription, in the second and fifth Section; they will certainly reveal into a full Receit of the *Opus Magnum*. Lastly, Whoever will be at the Pains to calculate the whole Number of each Letter in this Treatise, and sum up the Difference exactly between the several Numbers, assigning the true natural Cause for every such Difference; the Discoveries in the Product, will plentifully reward his Labour. But then he must beware of * *Bythus* and *Sigè,* and be sure not to forget the Qualities of *Acamoth; A cujus lacrymis humecta prodit Substantia, à risu lucida, à tristitiâ solida, & à timore mobilis,* wherein † *Eugenius Philalethes* hath committed an unpardonable Mistake.

S E C T I O N   X I .

A TALE of a TUB

AFTER so wide a Compass as I have wandred, I do now gladly overtake, and close in with my Subject, and shall hence-

---

† *Vid. Anima magica abscondita.*

---

* *I was told by an Eminent Divine, whom I consulted on this Point, that these two Barbarous Words, with that of Acamoth and its Qualities, as here set down, are quoted from* Irenæus. *This he discover'd by searching that Antient Writer for another Quotation of our Author, which he has placed in the Title Page, and refers to the Book and Chapter; the Curious were very Inquisitive, whether those Barbarous Words,* Basima Eacabasa, &c. *are really in* Irenæus, *and upon enquiry 'twas found they were a sort of Cant or Jargon of certain Hereticks, and therefore very properly prefix'd to such a Book as this of our Author.*

† *To the abovementioned Treatise, called* Anthroposophia Theomagica, *there is another annexed, called* Anima Magica Abscondita, *written by the same Author* Vaughan, *under the Name of* Eugenius Philalethes, *but in neither of those Treatises is there any mention of Acamoth or its Qualities, so that this is nothing but Amusement, and a Ridicule of dark, unintelligible Writers; only the Words,* A cujus lacrymis, &c, *are as we have said, transcribed from* Irenæus, *tho' I know not from what part. I believe one of the Authors Designs was to set curious Men a hunting thro' Indexes, and enquiring for Books out of the common Road.*

forth hold on with it an even Pace to the End of my Journey, except some beautiful Prospect appears within sight of my Way; whereof, tho' at present I have neither Warning nor Expectation, yet upon such an Accident, come when it will, I shall beg my Readers Favour and Company, allowing me to conduct him thro' it along with my self. For in *Writing,* it is as in *Travelling:* If a Man is in haste to be at home, (which I acknowledge to be none of my Case, having never so little Business, as when I am there) if his *Horse* be tired with long Riding, and ill Ways, or be naturally a Jade, I advise him clearly to make the straitest and the commonest Road, be it ever so dirty; But, then surely, we must own such a Man to be a scurvy Companion at best; He *spatters* himself and his Fellow-Travellers at every Step: All their Thoughts, and Wishes, and Conversation turn entirely upon the Subject of their Journey's End; and at every Splash, and Plunge, and Stumble, they heartily wish one another at the Devil.

On the other side, when a Traveller and his *Horse* are in Heart and Plight, when his Purse is full, and the Day before him; he takes the Road only where it is clean or convenient; entertains his Company there as agreeably as he can; but upon the first Occasion, carries them along with him to every delightful Scene in View, whether of Art, of Nature, or of both; and if they chance to refuse out of Stupidity or Weariness; let them jog on by themselves, and be d——n'd; He'll overtake them at the next Town; at which arriving, he Rides furiously thro', the Men, Women, and Children run out to gaze, a hundred * *noisy Curs* run *barking* after him, of which, if he honors the boldest with a *Lash of his Whip,* it is rather out of Sport than Revenge: But should some *sourer Mungrel* dare too near an Approach, he receives a *Salute* on the Chaps by an accidental Stroak from the Courser's Heels, (nor is any Ground lost by the Blow) which sends him yelping and limping home.

I now proceed to sum up the singular Adventures of my

---

* *By these are meant what the Author calls, The* True Criticks, *page* [76].

renowned *Jack;* the State of whose Dispositions and Fortunes, the careful Reader does, no doubt, most exactly remember, as I last parted with them in the Conclusion of a former Section. Therefore, his next Care must be from two of the foregoing, to extract a Scheme of Notions, that may best fit his Understanding for a true Relish of what is to ensue.

Jack had not only calculated the first Revolution of his Brain so prudently, as to give Rise to that Epidemick Sect of *Æolists,* but succeeding also into a new and strange Variety of Conceptions, the Fruitfulness of his Imagination led him into certain Notions, which, altho' in Appearance very unaccountable, were not without their Mysteries and their Meanings, nor wanted Followers to countenance and improve them. I shall therefore be extreamly careful and exact in recounting such material Passages of this Nature, as I have been able to collect, either from undoubted Tradition, or indefatigable Reading; and shall describe them as graphically as it is possible, and as far as Notions of that Height and Latitude can be brought within the Compass of a Pen. Nor do I at all question, but they will furnish Plenty of noble Matter for such, whose converting Imaginations dispose them to reduce all Things into *Types;* who can make *Shadows,* no thanks to the Sun; and then mold them into Substances, no thanks to Philosophy; whose peculiar Talent lies in fixing Tropes and Allegories to the *Letter,* and refining what is Literal into Figure and Mystery.

Jack had provided a fair Copy of his Father's *Will,* engrossed in Form upon a large Skin of Parchment; and resolving to act the Part of a most dutiful Son, he became the fondest Creature of it imaginable. For, altho', as I have often told the Reader, it consisted wholly in certain plain, easy Directions about the management and wearing of their Coats, with Legacies and Penalties, in case of Obedience or Neglect; yet he began to entertain a Fancy, that the Matter was *deeper* and *darker,* and therefore must needs have a great deal more of Mystery at the Bottom. *Gentlemen,* said he, *I will prove this very*

*Skin of Parchment to be Meat, Drink, and Cloth, to be the Philosopher's Stone, and the Universal Medicine.** In consequence of which Raptures, he resolved to make use of it in the most necessary, as well as the most paltry Occasions of Life. He had a Way of working it into any Shape he pleased; so that it served him for a Night-cap when he went to Bed, and for an Umbrello in rainy Weather. He would lap a Piece of it about a sore Toe, or when he had Fits, burn two Inches under his Nose; or if any Thing lay heavy on his Stomach, scrape off, and swallow as much of the Powder as would lie on a silver Penny, they were all infallible Remedies. With Analogy to these Refinements, his common Talk and Conversation† ran wholly in the Phrase of his Will, and he circumscribed the utmost of his Eloquence within that Compass, not daring to let slip a Syllable without Authority from thence. Once at a strange House, he was suddenly taken short, upon an urgent Juncture, whereon it may not be allowed to particularly to dilate; and being not able to call to mind, with that Suddenness, the Occasion required, an Authentick Phrase for demanding the Way to the Backside; he chose rather as the more prudent Course, to incur the Penalty in such Cases usually annexed. Neither was it possible for the united Rhetorick of Mankind to prevail with him to make himself clean again: Because having consulted the Will upon this Emergency, he met with a ‡ Passage near the Bottom (whether foisted in by the Transcriber, is not known) which seemed to forbid it.

He made it a Part of his Religion, never to say § Grace to

---

* *The Author here lashes those Pretenders to Purity, who place so much Merit in using Scripture Phrase on all Occasions.*

† *The* Protestant Dissenters *use* Scripture Phrases *in their serious Discourses, and Composures more than the* Church of England-Men, *accordingly* Jack *is introduced making his common Talk and Conversation to run wholly in the Phrase of his WILL.* W. Wotton.

‡ *I cannot guess the Author's meaning here, which I would be very glad to know, because it seems to be of Importance.*

§ *The slovenly way of Receiving the Sacrament among the Fanaticks.*

his Meat, nor could all the World persuade him, as the common Phrase is to * eat his Victuals *like a Christian*.

He bore a strange kind of Appetite to † *Snap-Dragon*, and to the livid Snuffs of a burning Candle, which he would catch and swallow with an Agility, wonderful to conceive; and by this Procedure, maintained a perpetual Flame in his Belly, which issuing in a glowing Steam from both his Eyes, as well as his Nostrils, and his Mouth; made his Head appear in a dark Night, like the Scull of an Ass, wherein a roguish Boy hath conveyed a Farthing Candle, *to the Terror of His Majesty's Liege Subjects*. Therefore, he made use of no other Expedient to light himself home, but was wont to say, That *a Wise Man was his own Lanthorn*.

He would shut his Eyes as he walked along the Streets, and if he happened to bounce his Head against a Post, or fall into the Kennel (as he seldom missed either to do one or both) he would tell the gibing Prentices, who looked on, that *he submitted with entire Resignation, as to a Trip, or a Blow of Fate, with whom he found, by long Experience, how vain it was either to wrestle or to cuff; and whoever durst undertake to do either, would be sure to come off with a swinging Fall, or a bloody Nose. It was ordained*, said he, *some few Days before the Creation, that my Nose and this very Post should have a Rencounter; and therefore, Nature thought fit to send us both into the World in the same Age, and to make us Country-men and Fellow-Citizens. Now, had my Eyes been open, it is very likely, the Business might have been a great deal worse; For, how many a confounded Slip is daily got by Man, with all his Foresight about him? Besides, the Eyes of the Understanding see best, when those of the Senses are out of*

---

* *This is a common Phrase to express Eating cleanlily, and is meant for an Invective against that undecent Manner among some People in Receiving the Sacrament, so in the Lines before 'tis said, Jack would never* say Grace to his Meat, *which is to be understood of the Dissenters refusing to kneel at the Sacrament.*

† *I cannot well find the Author's meaning here, unless it be the hot, untimely, blind Zeal of Enthusiasts.*

the way; and therefore, blind Men are observed to tread their Steps with much more Caution, and Conduct, and Judgment, than those who rely with too much Confidence, upon the Virtue of the visual Nerve, which every little Accident shakes out of Order, and a Drop, or a Film, can wholly disconcert; like a Lanthorn among a Pack of warring Bullies, when they scower the Streets; exposing its Owner, and it self, to outward Kicks and Buffets, which both might have escaped, if the Vanity of Appearing would have suffered them to walk in the Dark. But, farther; if we examine the Conduct of these boasted Lights, it will prove yet a great deal worse than their Fortune: 'Tis true, I have broke my Nose against this Post, because Fortune either forgot, or did not think it convenient to twitch me by the Elbow, and give me notice to avoid it. But, let not this encourage either the present Age or Posterity, to trust their Noses into the keeping of their Eyes, which may prove the fairest Way of losing them for good and all. O ye Eyes, Ye blind Guides; miserable Guardians are Ye of our frail Noses; Ye, I say, who fasten upon the first Precipice in view, and then tow our wretched willing Bodies after You, to the very Brink of Destruction: But, alas, that Brink is rotten, our Feet slip, and we tumble down prone into a Gulph, without one hospitable Shrub in the Way to break the Fall; a Fall, to which not any Nose of mortal Make is equal, except that of the Giant * Laurcalco, who was Lord of the Silver Bridge. *Most properly, therefore, O Eyes, and with great Justice, may You be compared to those foolish Lights, which conduct Men thro' Dirt and Darkness, till they fall into a deep Pit, or a noisom Bog.*

This I have produced, as a Scantling of *Jack*'s great Eloquence, and the Force of his Reasoning upon such abstruse Matters.

He was besides, a Person of great Design and Improvement in Affairs of *Devotion,* having introduced a new Deity, who hath since met with a vast Number of Worshippers; by some

---

* *Vide* Don Quixot.

called *Babel,* by others, *Chaos;* who had an antient Temple of *Gothick* Structure upon *Salisbury*-Plain; famous for its Shrine, and Celebration by Pilgrims.

* When he had some Roguish Trick to play, he would come down with his Knees, up with his Eyes, and fall to Prayers, tho' in the midst of the Kennel. Then it was that those who understood his Pranks, would be sure to get far enough out of his Way; And whenever Curiosity attracted Strangers to Laugh, or to Listen; he would of a sudden, with one Hand out with his *Gear,* and piss full in their Eyes, and with the other, all to bespatter them with Mud.

† In Winter he went always loose and unbuttoned, and clad as thin as possible, to let *in* the ambient Heat; and in Summer, lapt himself close and thick to keep it *out.*

‡ In all Revolutions of Government, he would make his Court for the Office of *Hangman* General; and in the Exercise of that Dignity, wherein he was very dextrous, would make use of § no other *Vizard* than a long *Prayer.*

He had a Tongue so Musculous and Subtil, that he could twist it up into his Nose, and deliver a strange Kind of Speech from thence. He was also the first in these Kingdoms, who began to improve the *Spanish* Accomplishment of *Braying;* and having large Ears, perpetually exposed and arrected, he carried his Art to such a Perfection, that it was a Point of great Difficulty to distinguish either by the View or the Sound, between the *Original* and the *Copy.*

He was troubled with a Disease, reverse to that called the Stinging of the *Tarantula;* and would ‖ run Dog-mad, at the Noise of *Musick,* especially a *Pair of Bag-Pipes.* But he would

---

* *The Villanies and Cruelties committed by Enthusiasts and Phanaticks among us, were all performed under the Disguise of Religion and long Prayers.*

† *They affect Differences in Habit and Behaviour.*

‡ *They are severe Persecutors, and all in a Form of Cant and Devotion.*

§ Cromwell *and his Confederates went, as they called it,* to seek God, *when they resolved to murther the King.*

‖ *This is to expose our Dissenters Aversion to Instrumental Musick in Churches.* W. Wotton.

cure himself again, by taking two or three Turns in *Westminster-Hall,* or *Billingsgate,* or in a *Boarding-School,* or the *Royal-Exchange,* or a *State Coffee-House.*

He was a Person that * *feared no Colours,* but mortally *hated* all, and upon that Account, bore a cruel Aversion to *Painters,* insomuch, that in his Paroxysms, as he walked the Streets, he would have his Pockets loaden with Stones, to pelt at the *Signs.*

Having from this manner of Living, frequent Occasion to *wash* himself, he would often leap over Head and Ears into the Water, tho' it were in the midst of the Winter, but was always observed to come out again much *dirtier,* if possible, than he went in.

He was the first that ever found out the Secret of contriving a † *Soporiferous* Medicine to be convey'd in at the *Ears;* It was a Compound of *Sulphur* and *Balm of Gilead,* with a little *Pilgrim's Salve.*

He wore a large Plaister of artificial *Causticks* on his Stomach, with the Fervor of which, he could set himself a *groaning,* like the famous *Board* upon Application of a redhot Iron.

‡ He would stand in the Turning of a Street, and calling to those who passed by, would cry to One; *Worthy Sir, do me the Honour of a good Slap in the Chaps:* To another, *Honest Friend, pray, favour me with a handsom Kick on the Arse: Madam, shall I entreat a small Box on the Ear, from your Ladyship's fair Hands? Noble Captain, Lend a reasonable Thwack, for the Love of God, with that Cane of yours, over these poor Shoulders.* And when he had by such earnest Sollicitations, made a shift to procure a Basting sufficient to swell

---

* *They quarrel at the most Innocent Decency and Ornament, and defaced the Statues and Paintings on all the Churches in* England.

† *Fanatick Preaching, composed either of Hell and Damnation, or a fulsome Description of the Joys of Heaven, both in such a dirty, nauseous Style, as to be well resembled to Pilgrims Salve.*

‡ *The Fanaticks have always had a way of affecting to run into Persecution, and count vast Merit upon every little Hardship they suffer.*

up his Fancy and his Sides, He would return home extremely comforted, and full of terrible Accounts of what he had undergone for the *Publick Good*. *Observe this Stroak*, (said he, shewing his bare Shoulders) *a plaguy* Janisary *gave it me this very Morning at seven a Clock, as, with much ado, I was driving off the* Great Turk. *Neighbours mine, this broken Head deserves a Plaister; had poor* Jack *been tender of his Noddle, you would have seen the* Pope, *and the* French *King, long before this time of Day, among your Wives and your Warehouses. Dear* Christians, *the* Great Mogul *was come as far as* White-Chappel, *and you may thank these poor Sides that he hath not (God bless us) already swallowed up Man, Woman, and Child.*

   * It was highly worth observing, the singular Effects of that Aversion, or Antipathy, which *Jack* and his Brother *Peter* seemed, even to an Affectation, to bear toward each other. *Peter* had lately done *some Rogueries,* that forced him to abscond; and he seldom ventured to stir out before Night, for fear of Bayliffs. Their Lodgings were at the two most distant Parts of the Town, from each other; and whenever their Occasions, or Humors called them abroad, they would make Choice of the oddest unlikely Times, and most uncouth Rounds they could invent; that they might be sure to avoid one another: Yet after all this, it was their perpetual Fortune to meet. The Reason of which, is easy enough to apprehend: For, the Phrenzy and the Spleen of both, having the same Foundation, we may look upon them as two Pair of Compasses, equally extended, and the fixed Foot of each, remaining in the

---

   * *The Papists and Fanaticks, tho' they appear the most Averse to each other, yet bear a near Resemblance in many things, as has been observed by Learned Men.*

   Ibid. *The Agreement of our Dissenters and the Papists in that which* Bishop Stillingfleet *called,* The Fanaticism of the Church of *Rome, is ludicrously described for several Pages together by* Jack's *Likeness to* Peter, *and their being often mistaken for each other, and their frequent Meeting, when they least intended it.* W. Wotton.

same Center; which, tho' moving contrary Ways at first, will be sure to encounter somewhere or other in the Circumference. Besides, it was among the great Misfortunes of *Jack,* to bear a huge Personal Resemblance with his Brother *Peter.* Their Humour and Dispositions were not only the same, but there was a close Analogy in their Shape, and Size and their Mien. Insomuch, as nothing was more frequent than for a Bayliff to seize *Jack* by the Shoulders, and cry, *Mr.* Peter, *You are the King's Prisoner.* Or, at other Times, for one of *Peter's* nearest Friends, to accost *Jack* with open Arms, *Dear* Peter, *I am glad to see thee, pray send me one of your best Medicines for the Worms.* This we may suppose, was a mortifying Return of those Pains and Proceedings, *Jack* had laboured in so long; And finding, how directly opposite all his Endeavours had answered to the sole End and Intention, which he had proposed to himself; How could it avoid having terrible Effects upon a Head and Heart so furnished as his? However, the poor Remainders of his *Coat* bore all the Punishment; The orient Sun never entred upon his diurnal Progress, without missing a Piece of it. He hired a Taylor to stitch up the Collar so close, that it was ready to choak him, and squeezed out his Eyes at such a Rate, as one could see nothing but the White. What little was left of the main Substance of the Coat, he rubbed every day for two hours, against a rough-cast Wall, in order to grind away the Remnants of *Lace* and *Embroidery;* but at the same time went on with so much Violence, that he proceeded a *Heathen Philosopher.* Yet after all he could do of this kind, the Success continued still to disappoint his Expectation. For, as it is the Nature of Rags, to bear a kind of mock Resemblance to Finery; there being a sort of fluttering Appearance in both, which is not to be distinguished at a Distance, in the Dark, or by short-sighted Eyes: So, in those Junctures, it fared with *Jack* and his Tatters, that they offered to the first View a ridiculous Flanting, which assisting the Resemblance in Person and Air, thwarted all his Projects of Separation, and left so near a Similitude between them, as frequently deceived the very Disciples and Followers of both.

*   *   *   *   *   *   *   *   *   *   *   *
    *   *   *   *   *   *   *   *   *   *
Desunt   *   *   *   *   *   *   *   *   *   *
non-nulla.   *   *   *   *   *   *   *   *   *
*   *   *   *   *   *   *   *   *   *   *   *

The old *Sclavonian* Proverb said well, That *it is with* Men, *as with* Asses; *whoever would keep them fast, must find a very good Hold at their Ears.* Yet, I think, we may affirm, that it hath been verified by repeated Experience, that,

> *Effugiet tamen hæc sceleratus vincula Proteus.*

It is good therefore, to read the Maxims of our Ancestors, with great Allowances to Times and Persons: For, if we look into Primitive Records, we shall find, that no Revolutions have been so great, or so frequent, as those of human *Ears.* In former Days, there was a curious Invention to catch and keep them; which, I think, we may justly reckon among the *Artes Perditæ:* And how can it be otherwise, when in these latter Centuries, the very Species is not only diminished to a very lamentable Degree, but the poor Remainder is also degenerated so far, as to mock our skilfullest *Tenure?* For, if the only slitting of one *Ear* in a Stag, hath been found sufficient to propagate the Defect thro' a whole Forest; Why should we wonder at the greatest Consequences, from so many Loppings and Mutilations, to which the Ears of our Fathers and our own, have been of late so much exposed: 'Tis true, indeed, that while this *Island* of ours, was under the *Dominion of Grace,* many Endeavours were made to improve the Growth of *Ears* once more among us. The Proportion of Largeness, was not only lookt upon as an Ornament of the *Outward* Man, but as a Type of Grace in the *Inward.* Besides, it is held by Naturalists, that if there be a Protuberancy of Parts in the *Superiour* Region of the Body, as in the *Ears* and *Nose,* there must be a Parity also in the *Inferior:* And therefore in that truly pious Age, the *Males* in every Assembly, according as they were gifted, appeared very forward in exposing their

Ears to view, and the Regions about them; because * *Hippoc-rates* tells us, that *when the Vein behind the Ear happens to be cut, a Man becomes a Eunuch:* And the *Females* were nothing backwarder in beholding and edifying by them: Whereof those who had already *used the Means,* lookt about them with great Concern, in hopes of conceiving a suitable Offspring by such a Prospect: Others, who stood Candidates for *Benevolence,* found there a plentiful Choice, and were sure to fix upon such as discovered the largest *Ears,* that the Breed might not dwindle between them. Lastly, the devouter Sisters, who lookt upon all extraordinary Dilatations of that Member, as Protrusions of Zeal, or spiritual Excrescencies, were sure to honor every Head they sat upon, as if they had been *Marks of Grace;* but, especially, that of the Preacher, whose *Ears* were usually of the prime Magnitude; which upon that Account, he was very frequent and exact in exposing with all Advantages to the People: in his Rhetorical *Paroxysms,* turning sometimes to *hold forth* the one, and sometimes to *hold forth* the other: From which Custom, the whole Oper-ation of Preaching is to this very Day among their Professors, styled by the Phrase of *Holding forth.*

Such was the Progress of the *Saints,* for advancing the Size of that Member; And it is thought, the Success would have been every way answerable, if in Process of time, a † cruel King had not arose, who raised a bloody Persecution against all *Ears,* above a certain Standard: Upon which, some were glad to hide their flourishing Sprouts in a black Border, others crept wholly under a Perewig: some were slit, others cropt, and a great Number sliced of to the Stumps. But of this, more hereafter, in my *general History of Ears;* which I design very speedily to bestow upon the Publick.

From this brief Survey of the falling State of *Ears,* in the last Age, and the small Care had to advance their antient

---

* *Lib. de aëre locis & aquis.*

---

† *This was King* Charles *the Second, who at his Restauration, turned out all the Dissenting Teachers that would not conform.*

Growth in the present, it is manifest, how little Reason we can have to rely upon a Hold so short, so weak, and so slippery; and that, whoever desires to catch Mankind fast, must have Recourse to some other Methods. Now, he that will examine Human Nature with Circumspection enough, may discover several *Handles,* whereof the * *Six* Senses afford one apiece, beside a great Number that are screw'd to the Passions, and some few riveted to the Intellect. Among these last, *Curiosity* is one, and of all others, affords the firmest Grasp: *Curiosity,* that Spur in the side, that Bridle in the Mouth, that Ring in the Nose, of a lazy, an impatient, and a grunting Reader. By this *Handle* it is, that an Author should seize upon his Readers; which as soon as he hath once compast, all Resistance and struggling are in vain; and they become his Prisoners as close as he pleases, till Weariness or Dullness force him to let go his Gripe.

And therefore, I the Author of this miraculous Treatise, having hitherto, beyond Expectation, maintained by the aforesaid *Handle,* a firm Hold upon my gentle Readers; it is with great Reluctance, that I am at length compelled to remit my Grasp; leaving them in the Perusal of what remains, to that natural *Oscitancy* inherent in the Tribe. I can only assure thee, Courteous Reader, for both our Comforts, that my Concern is altogether equal to thine, for my Unhappiness in losing, or mislaying among my Papers the remaining Part of these Memoirs; which consisted of Accidents, Turns, and Adventures, both New, Agreeable, and Surprizing; and therefore, calculated in all due Points, to the delicate Taste of this our noble Age. But, alas, with my utmost Endeavours, I have been able only to retain a few of the Heads. Under which, there was a full Account, how *Peter* got a *Protection* out of the *King's-Bench;* And of a † Reconcilement between *Jack* and

---

* *Including* Scaliger's.

---

† *In the Reign of King* James *the Second, the Presbyterians by the King's Invitation, joined with the Papists, against the Church of England, and Addrest him for Repeal of the Penal-Laws and Test. The King by his Dispensing Power, gave Liberty of Conscience, which both Papists*

Him, upon a Design they had in a certain *rainy Night*, to trepan Brother *Martin* into a *Spunging-house*, and there strip him to the Skin. How *Martin*, with much ado, shew'd them both a fair pair of Heels. How a *new Warrant* came out against *Peter:* upon which, how *Jack* left him in the lurch, *stole his Protection, and made use of it himself.* How *Jack*'s Tatters came into Fashion in *Court* and *City;* how *he* * got *upon a great Horse, and eat* † *Custard.* But the Particulars of all these, with several others, which have now slid out of my Memory, are lost beyond all Hopes of Recovery. For which Misfortune, leaving my Readers to condole with each other, as far as they shall find it to agree with their several Constitutions; but conjuring them by all the Friendship that hath passed between Us, from the Title-Page to this, not to proceed so far as to injure their Healths, for an Accident past Remedy; I now go on to the Ceremonial Part of an accomplish'd Writer, and therefore, by a Courtly *Modern,* least of all others to be omitted.

THE

CONCLUSION

*G*OING *too long* is a Cause of Abortion as effectual, tho' not so frequent, as *Going too short;* and holds true especially in the *Labors* of the Brain. Well fare the Heart of that Noble

---

and Presbyterians made use of, but upon the Revolution, the Papists being down of Course, the Presbyterians freely continued their Assemblies, by Virtue of King James's Indulgence, before they had a Toleration by Law; this I believe the Author means by Jack's stealing Peter's Protection, and making use of it himself.

   * Sir Humphry Edwyn, a Presbyterian, was some Years ago Lord-Mayor of London, and had the Insolence to go in his Formalities to a Conventicle, with the Ensigns of his Office.

   † Custard is a famous Dish at a Lord-Mayors Feast.

* *Jesuit,* who first adventur'd to confess in Print, that Books must be suited to their several Seasons, like Dress, and Dyet, and Diversions; And better fare our noble Nation, for refining upon this, among other *French* Modes. I am living fast, to see the Time, when a *Book* that misses its Tide, shall be neglected, as the *Moon* by Day, or like *Mackarel* a Week after the Season. No Man hath more nicely observed our Climate, than the Bookseller who bought the Copy of this Work; He knows to a Tittle what Subjects will best go off in a *dry Year,* and which it is proper to expose foremost, when the Weather-glass is fallen to *much Rain.* When he had seen this Treatise, and consulted his *Almanack* upon it; he gave me to under-stand, that he had manifestly considered the two Principal Things, which were the *Bulk,* and the *Subject;* and found, it would never *take,* but after a long Vacation, and then only, in cast it should happen to be a hard Year for Turnips. Upon which I desired to know, *considering my urgent Necessities,* what he thought might be acceptable this Month. He lookt *Westward,* and said, *I doubt we shall have a Fit of bad Weather; However, if you could prepare some pretty little* Banter (but not in Verse) *or a small Treatise upon the* ——— *it would run like Wild-Fire. But,* if it hold up, *I have already hired an Author to write something against* Dr. B——tl——y, *which, I am sure, will turn to Account.*

At length we agreed upon this Expedient; That when a Customer comes for one of these, and desires in Confidence to know the Author; he will tell him very privately, as a Friend, naming which ever of the Wits shall happen to be that Week in the Vogue; and if *Durfy*'s last Play should be in Course, I had as lieve he may be the Person as *Congreve.* This I men-tion, because I am wonderfully well acquainted with the present Relish of Courteous Readers; and have often observed, with singular Pleasure, that a *Fly* driven from a *Honey-pot,* will immediately, with very good Appetite alight, and finish his Meal on an *Excrement.*

* *Pere d'Orleans.*

I have one Word to say upon the Subject of *Profound Writers,* who are grown very numerous of late; And, I know very well, the judicious World is resolved to list me in that Number. I conceive therefore, as to the Business of being *Profound,* that it is with *Writers,* as with *Wells;* A Person with good Eyes may see to the Bottom of the deepest, provided any *Water* be there; and, that often, when there is nothing in the World at the Bottom, besides *Dryness* and *Dirt,* tho' it be but a Yard and half under Ground, it shall pass, however, for wondrous *Deep,* upon no wiser a Reason than because it is wondrous *Dark.*

I am now trying an Experiment very frequent among Modern Authors; which is, to *write upon Nothing;* When the Subject is utterly exhausted, to let the Pen still move on; by some called, the Ghost of Wit, delighting to walk after the Death of its Body. And to say the Truth, there seems to be no Part of Knowledge in fewer Hands, than That of Discerning *when to have Done.* By the Time that an Author has writ out a Book, he and his Readers are become old Acquaintants, and grow very loth to part: So that I have sometimes known it to be in Writing, as in Visiting, where the Ceremony of taking Leave, has employ'd more Time than the whole Conversation before. The Conclusion of a Treatise, resembles the Conclusion of Human Life, which hath sometimes been compared to the End of a Feast; where few are satisfied to depart, *ut plenus vitæ conviva:* For Men will sit down after the fullest Meal, tho' it be only to *doze,* or to *sleep* out the rest of the Day. But, in this latter, I differ extreamly from other Writers; and shall be too proud, if by all my Labors, I can have any ways contributed to the *Repose* of Mankind in * Times so turbulent and unquiet as these. Neither do I think such an Employment so very alien from the Office of a *Wit,* as some would suppose. For among a very Polite Nation in † *Greece,* there were the *same* Temples built and consecrated to *Sleep*

† *Trezenii Pausan.* l. 2.

---

* *This was writ before the Peace of* Riswick.

and the *Muses,* between which two Deities, they believed the strictest Friendship was established.

I have one concluding Favour, to request of my Reader; that he will not expect to be equally diverted and informed by every Line, or every Page of this Discourse; but give some Allowance to the Author's Spleen, and short Fits or Intervals of Dullness, as well as his own; And lay it seriously to his Conscience, whether, if he were walking the Streets, in dirty Weather, or a rainy Day; he would allow it fair Dealing in Folks at their Ease from a Window, to Critick his Gate, and ridicule his Dress at such a Juncture.

In my Disposure of Employments of the Brain, I have thought fit to make *Invention* the *Master,* and give *Method* and *Reason,* the Office of its *Lacquays.* The Cause of this Distribution was, from observing it my peculiar Case, to be often under a Temptation of being *Witty,* upon Occasion, where I could be neither *Wise* nor *Sound,* nor any thing to the Matter in hand. And, I am too much a Servant of the *Modern* Way, to neglect any such Opportunities, whatever Pains or Improprieties I may be at, to introduce them. For, I have observed, that from a laborious Collection of Seven Hundred Thirty Eight *Flowers,* and *shining Hints* of the best *Modern* Authors, digested with great Reading, into my Book of *Common-places;* I have not been able after five Years to draw, hook, or force into common Conversation, any more than a Dozen. Of which Dozen, the one Moiety failed of Success, by being dropt among unsuitable Company; and the other cost me so many Strains, and Traps, and *Ambages* to introduce, that I at length resolved to give it over. No, this Disappointment, (to discover a Secret) I must own, gave me the first Hint of setting up for an *Author;* and, I have since found among some particular Friends, that it is become a very general Complaint, and has produced the same Effects upon many others. For, I have remarked many a *towardly Word,* to be wholly neglected or despised in *Discourse,* which hath passed very smoothly, with some Consideration and Esteem, after its Preferment and Sanction in *Print.* But now, since by the

Liberty and Encouragement of the Press, I am grown absolute Master of the Occasions and Opportunities, to expose the Talents I have acquired; I already discover, that the *Issues* of my *Observanda* begin to grow too large for the *Receipts*. Therefore, I shall here pause awhile, till I find, by feeling the World's Pulse, and my own, that it will be of absolute Necessity for us both, to resume my Pen.

F I N I S.

The Battle of the Books

The Battle of the Books presents few of the problems encountered in *A Tale of a Tub*. It adheres substantially to the single satiric device of a mock-epic allegorical narrative, and leaves no doubt as to the identity of its satiric victims. In its style, characters, and incident it often parodies the *Iliad,* and, less frequently, the *Aeneid,* but the satiric allegory proceeds straightforwardly, uncomplicated by posturings on the part of its author or other kinds of attack by indirection.

Although first published, with the *Tale* and *The Mechanical Operation of the Spirit,* in 1704, the *Battle* was probably written in 1697 and 1698, at a time when the exchanges over Ancient and Modern learning between Sir William Temple and William Wotton had tended to yield to controversy between Charles Boyle and Richard Bentley. There is, indeed, some reason to believe that publication of the *Battle* was delayed because of Temple's reluctance to involve himself in further quarreling with Bentley. As a matter of fact, by this stage of the contest, the original substantive issues had been pretty well exhausted. Bentley had rather thoroughly discredited the *Epistles* of Phalaris which Boyle, applauded by Temple, had recently edited; he had cast grave doubts, as well, upon the historical figure of Aesop, who had also appeared prominently in Temple's claims for the superiority of the Ancients. As both Swift's Preface and the *Battle* itself suggest, the Ancient tactic now consisted mainly in deploring the bad manners, arrogance, and pedantry of the scholarly Moderns.

Thus to the actual case for the superiority of Ancient learning, the *Battle,* even had it been promptly published, could not have contributed very weightily. Wotton himself, upon the ultimate publication of the work, did not appear to smart unduly beneath its strictures; though he throughly excoriated *A Tale of a Tub,* he was content with asserting, perhaps with some truth, that the *Battle* had been plagiarized from an earlier French work. In the history of the Ancients-Moderns quarrel, the *Battle,* though expressly designed to aid the cause of Temple and his allies, essentially contributed a highly colored and abusive summary of the controversy to date.

The relative simplicity of the *Battle*, however, displays to excellent advantage certain literary qualities of Swift which his more complicated works often obscure. The flexibility of his style is apparent in the ease with which he moves from lucid if facetious narration to the profane splutterings of the spider and cool response of the bee, only to shift again to a deft burlesque of the Homeric manner. His much-discussed penchant for indelicacy here serves (as, in fact, it usually does) the purposes of artful vituperation. The outlines of the bare, inconclusive plot are vastly enriched by a variety of ingenious incident, description, allusion, and, not least, an amalgam of words, syntax, and substance to produce a brilliant, headlong tempo.

Several passages in the *Battle*—the initial account of the two hills, the soliloquy of Momus, and most notably the incident of the spider and the bee—forcefully summarize the essence of the Ancients' attitude. Characteristically, Swift is at his best in epitomizing Modern vices. The figure of the bee, as the symbol of liberal and judicious learning, had in fact been suggested by Temple. It is Swift, however, who creates the spider to represent the obtuseness, arrogance, and shabby, ungracious eclecticism which for him are the stamp of Modern learning.

In his choice of warriors, particularly among the Ancients, Swift follows very closely the selections on which Temple had based his arguments in the *Essay* which precipitated the controversy. Swift's own personal animus, however, is revealed in his treatment of Dryden, who, in addition to other indignities, is lumped with such patently inferior writers as Wither, Blackmore, and Ogleby. In addition, Swift's particular dissatisfactions emerge clearly in passages, such as those involving Momus, which shift the attack from the area of learned controversy onto the pervasive moral and intellectual infirmities of the Modern age.

Although the *Battle* reveals few of the detailed intellectual grounds upon which the Ancients-Moderns quarrel proceeded, it remains of considerable historical value, for, like *A Tale of a Tub*, it eloquently expresses the basic attitude with which gentlemen-scholars of the breed of Temple, Boyle, and the young Swift viewed the complex of manifestations they called "Modern." The attitude is in part one of distaste—distaste for the crabbed researches of single-minded scholarship, for the eccentricity of scientific experiment, and for the affectations of popular literature. More fundamentally, it is an attitude of uneasiness, the perennial discomfort of the conservative in the face of the progressive who questions what has been and exults in what will be. For conservatives like Swift, the Modern spirit meant not only an indecorous violation of the canons of taste but an alarming skepticism toward the ancient rules and monuments. The Modern was likely to display an impious belief in man's continual improvement, a habit of asking and even answering improper questions, and a deplorable latitude towards the opinions of the ungodly, the unlettered, and the unwashed. For Swift, Modernity embodied more than intellectual error; it embodied grave moral danger. It is not surprising that the most memorable passages in *The Battle of the Books* bear the color of genuine moral indignation.

A

Full and True Account

OF THE

BATTEL

Fought laſt *FRIDAY*,

Between the

Antient and the *Modern*

BOOKS

IN

St. *JAMES*'s

LIBRARY.

LONDON:
Printed in the Year, MDCCX.

The Bookseller

T O T H E

READER

THE following Discourse, as it is unquestionably of the
same Author, so it seems to have been written about the same
time with the former, I mean, the Year 1697, when the famous
Dispute was on Foot, about *Antient and Modern Learning*. The
Controversy took its Rise from an Essay of Sir *William
Temple*'s, upon that Subject; which was answer'd by *W. Wotton,* B.D. with an Appendix by Dr. *Bently,* endeavouring to
destroy the Credit of *Æsop* and *Phalaris,* for Authors, whom
Sir *William Temple* had in the Essay before-mentioned, highly
commended. In that Appendix, the Doctor falls hard upon a
new Edition of *Phalaris,* put out by the Honourable *Charles
Boyle* (now *Earl* of *Orrery*) to which, Mr. *Boyle* replyed at
large, with great Learning and Wit; and the Doctor, voluminously, rejoyned. In this Dispute, the Town highly resented to
see a Person of Sir *William Temple*'s Character and Merits,
roughly used by the two Reverend Gentlemen aforesaid, and
without any manner of Provocation. At length, there appearing no End of the Quarrel, our Author tells us, that the
BOOKS in St. *James*'s Library, looking upon themselves as
Parties principally concerned, took up the Controversie, and
came to a decisive Battel; But, the Manuscript, by the Injury
of Fortune, or Weather, being in several Places imperfect, we
cannot learn to which side the Victory fell.

I must warn the Reader, to beware of applying to Persons
what is here meant, only of Books in the most literal Sense. So,
when *Virgil* is mentioned, we are not to understand the Person
of a famous Poet, call'd by that Name, but only certain Sheets
of Paper, bound up in Leather, containing in Print, the Works
of the said Poet, and so of the rest.

THE
PREFACE
OF THE
AUTHOR

*S*ATYR *is a sort of* Glass, *wherein Beholders do generally discover every body's Face but their Own; which is the chief Reason for that kind Reception it meets in the World, and that so very few are offended with it. But if it should happen otherwise, the Danger is not great; and, I have learned from long Experience, never to apprehend Mischief from those Understandings, I have been able to provoke; For, Anger and Fury, though they add Strength to the* Sinews *of the* Body, *yet are found to relax those of the* Mind, *and to render all its Efforts feeble and impotent.*

There is a Brain *that will endure but one* Scumming: *Let the Owner gather it with Discretion, and manage his little Stock with Husbandry; but of all things, let him beware of bringing it under the* Lash *of his* Betters; *because, That will make it all bubble up into Impertinence, and he will find no new Supply:* Wit, *without knowledge, being a Sort of* Cream, *which gathers in a Night to the Top, and by a skilful Hand, may be soon* whipt *into* Froth; *but once scumm'd away, what appears underneath will be fit for nothing, but to be thrown to the Hogs.*

A Full and True

ACCOUNT

OF THE

BATTEL

Fought last FRIDAY, &c.

WHOEVER examines with due Circumspection into the
* *Annual Records* of *Time,* will find it remarked, that *War
is the Child of Pride,* and *Pride the Daughter of Riches;* The
former of which Assertions may be soon granted; but one
cannot so easily subscribe to the latter: For *Pride* is nearly
related to Beggary and *Want,* either by Father or Mother, and
sometimes by both; And, to speak naturally, it very seldom
happens among Men to fall out, when all have enough: In-
vasions usually travelling from *North* to *South,* that is to say,
from Poverty upon Plenty. The most antient and natural
Grounds of Quarrels, are *Lust* and *Avarice;* which, tho' we
may allow to be Brethren or collateral Branches of *Pride,* are
certainly the Issues of *Want.* For, to speak in the Phrase of
Writers upon the Politicks, we may observe in the Republick
of *Dogs,* (which in its Original seems to be an Institution of
the *Many*) that the whole State is ever in the profoundest
Peace, after a full Meal; and, that Civil Broils arise among
them, when it happens for one great *Bone* to be seized on by
some *leading Dog,* who either divides it among the *Few,* and
then it falls to an *Oligarchy,* or keeps it to Himself, and then
it runs up to a *Tyranny.* The same Reasoning also, holds

---

* *Riches produceth Pride; Pride is War's Ground, &c.* Vid. Ephem.
de *Mary Clarke;* opt. Edit.

Place among them, in those Dissensions we behold upon a Turgescency in any of their Females. For, the Right of Possession lying in common (it being impossible to establish a Property in so delicate a Case) Jealousies and Suspicions do so abound, that the whole Commonwealth of that Street, is reduced to a manifest *State of War,* of every *Citizen* against every *Citizen;* till some One of more Courage, Conduct, or Fortune than the rest, seizes and enjoys the Prize; Upon which, naturally arises Plenty of Heartburning, and Envy, and Snarling against the *Happy Dog.* Again, if we look upon any of these Republicks engaged in a Forein War, either of Invasion or Defence, we shall find, the same Reasoning will serve, as to the Grounds and Occasions of each; and, that *Poverty,* or *Want,* in some Degree or other, (whether Real, or in Opinion, which makes no Alteration in the Case) has a great Share, as well as *Pride,* on the Part of the Aggressor.

Now, whoever will please to take this Scheme, and either reduce or adapt it to an Intellectual State, or Commonwealth of Learning, will soon discover the first Ground of Disagreement between the two great Parties at this Time in Arms; and may form just Conclusions upon the Merits of either Cause. But the Issue or Events of this War are not so easie to conjecture at: For, the present Quarrel is so enflamed by the warm Heads of either Faction, and the Pretensions *somewhere or other* so exorbitant, as not to admit the least Overtures of Accommodation: This Quarrel first began (as I have heard it affirmed by an old Dweller in the Neighbourhood) about a small Spot of Ground, *lying* and *being* upon one of the two Tops of the Hill *Parnassus;* the highest and largest of which, had it seems, been time out of Mind, in quiet Possession of certain Tenants, call'd the *Antients;* And the other was held by the *Moderns.* But, these disliking their present Station, sent certain Ambassadors to the *Antients,* complaining of a great Nuisance, how the Height of that Part of *Parnassus,* quite spoiled the Prospect of theirs, especially towards the *East;* and therefore, to avoid a War, offered them the Choice of this Alternative; either that the *Antients* would please to remove themselves and their Effects down to the lower Summity, which the *Moderns* would graciously surrender to them, and advance in their Place; or else, that the said *Antients* will give leave to the *Moderns* to come with Shovels and Mattocks, and level the said Hill, as low as they shall think it convenient. To which, the *Antients* made Answer: How little they expected such a Message as this, from a Colony, whom they had admitted out of their own Free Grace, to so near a Neighbourhood. That, as to their own Seat, they were *Aborigines* of it, and therefore, to talk with them of a Removal or Surrender, was a Language they did not understand. That, if the Height of the Hill, on their side, shortned the Prospect of the *Moderns,* it was a Disadvantage they could not help, but desired them to consider, whether that Injury (if it be any) were not largely recompenced by the *Shade* and *Shelter* it afforded them. That, as to the levelling or digging down, it was either Folly or Ignorance to propose it, if they did, or did not know, how that side of the Hill was an entire Rock, which would break their Tools and Hearts; without any Damage to itself. That they would therefore advise the *Moderns,* rather to raise their own side of the Hill, than dream of pulling down that of the *Antients,* to the former of which, they would not only give Licence, but also largely contribute. All this was rejected by the *Moderns,* with much Indignation, who still insisted upon one of the two Expedients; And so this Difference broke out into a long and obstinate War, maintain'd on the one Part, by Resolution, and by the Courage of certain Leaders and Allies; but, on the other, by the greatness of their Number, upon all Defeats, affording continual Recruits. In this Quarrel, whole Rivulets of *Ink* have been exhausted, and the Virulence of both Parties enormously augmented. Now, it must here be understood, that *Ink* is the great missive Weapon, in all Battels of the *Learned,* which, convey'd thro' a sort of Engine, call'd a *Quill,* infinite Numbers of these are darted at the Enemy, by the Valiant on each side, with equal Skill and Violence, as if it were an Engagement of *Porcupines.* This malignant Liquor was compounded by the Engineer, who invented it, of two

Ingredients, which are *Gall* and *Copperas,* by its Bitterness and Venom, to *Suit* in some Degree, as well as to *Foment* the Genius of the Combatants. And as the *Grecians,* after an Engagement, when they could not *agree* about the Victory, were wont to set up Trophies on both sides, the beaten Party being content to be at the same Expence, to keep it self in Countenance (A laudable and antient Custom, happily reviv'd of late, in the Art of War) so the *Learned,* after a sharp and bloody Dispute, do on both sides hang out their Trophies too, which-ever comes by the worst. These Trophies have largely inscribed on them the Merits of the Cause; a full impartial Account of such a Battel, and how the Victory fell clearly to the Party that set them up. They are known to the World under several Names; As, *Disputes, Arguments, Rejoynders, Brief Considerations, Answers, Replies, Remarks, Reflexions, Objections, Confutations.* For a very few Days they are fixed up in all Publick Places, either by themselves or their * Representatives, for Passengers to gaze at: From whence the chiefest and largest are removed to certain Magazines, they call, *Libraries,* there to remain in a Quarter purposely assign'd them, and from thenceforth, begin to be called, *Books of Controversie.*

In these Books, is wonderfully instilled and preserved, the Spirit of each Warrier, while he is alive; and after his Death, his Soul transmigrates there, to inform them. This, at least, is the more common Opinion; But, I believe, it is with Libraries, as with other Cœmeteries, where some Philosophers affirm, that a certain Spirit, which they call *Brutum hominis,* hovers over the Monument, till the Body is corrupted, and turns to *Dust,* or to *Worms,* but then vanishes or dissolves: So, we may say, a restless Spirit haunts over every *Book,* till *Dust* or *Worms* have seized upon it; which to some, may happen in a few Days, but to others, later; And therefore, *Books* of Controversy, being of all others, haunted by the most disorderly Spirits, have always been confined in a separate Lodge from

* *Their Title-Pages.*

the rest; and for fear of mutual violence against each other, it was thought Prudent by our Ancestors, to bind them to the Peace with strong Iron Chains. Of which Invention, the original Occasion was this: When the Works of *Scotus* first came out, they were carried to a certain great Library, and had Lodgings appointed them; But this Author was no sooner settled, than he went to visit his Master *Aristotle,* and there both concerted together to seize *Plato* by main Force, and turn him out from his antient Station among the *Divines,* where he had peaceably dwelt near Eight Hundred Years. The Attempt succeeded, and the two Usurpers have reigned ever since in his stead: But to maintain Quiet for the future, it was decreed, that all *Polemicks* of the larger Size, should be held fast with a Chain.

By this Expedient, the publick Peace of Libraries, might certainly have been preserved, if a new Species of controversial Books had not arose of late Years, instinct with a most malignant Spirit, from the War above-mentioned, between the *Learned,* about the higher Summity of *Parnassus.*

When these Books were first admitted into the Publick Libraries, I remember to have said upon Occasion, to several Persons concerned, how I was sure, they would create Broyls wherever they came, unless a World of Care were taken: And therefore, I advised, that the Champions of each side should be coupled together, or otherwise mixt, that like the blending of contrary Poysons, their Malignity might be employ'd among themselves. And it seems, I was neither an ill Prophet, nor an ill Counsellor; for it was nothing else but the Neglect of this Caution, which gave Occasion to the terrible Fight that happened on *Friday* last between the *Antient* and *Modern Books* in the *King's Library.* Now, because the Talk of this Battel is so fresh in every body's Mouth, and the Expectation of the Town so great to be informed in the Particulars; I, being possessed of all Qualifications requisite in an *Historian,* and retained by neither Party; have resolved to comply with the urgent *Importunity of my Friends,* by writing down a full impartial Account thereof.

The *Guardian* of the *Regal Library*, a Person of great Valor, but chiefly renowned for his * *Humanity*, had been a fierce Champion for the *Moderns*, and in an Engagement upon *Parnassus*, had vowed, with his own Hands, to knock down two of the *Antient* Chiefs, who guarded a small Pass on the superior Rock; but endeavouring to climb up, was cruelly obstructed by his own unhappy Weight, and tendency towards his Center; a Quality, to which, those of the *Modern* Party, are extreme subject; For, being lightheaded, they have in Speculation, a wonderful Agility, and conceive nothing too high for them to mount; but in reducing to Practice, discover a mighty Pressure about their Posteriors and their Heels. Having thus failed in his Design, the disappointed Champion bore a cruel Rancour to the *Antients*, which he resolved to gratifie, by shewing all Marks of his Favour to the *Books* of their Adversaries, and lodging them in the fairest Apartments; when at the same time, whatever *Book* had the boldness to own it self for an Advocate of the *Antients*, was buried alive in some obscure Corner, and threatned upon the least Displeasure, to be turned out of Doors. Besides, it so happened, that about this time, there was a strange Confusion of Place among all the *Books* in the Library; for which several Reasons were assigned. Some imputed it to a great heap of *learned Dust*, which a perverse Wind blew off from a Shelf of *Moderns* into the *Keeper*'s Eyes. Others affirmed, He had a Humour to pick the Worms out of the *Schoolmen*, and swallow them fresh and fasting; whereof some fell upon his *Spleen*, and some climbed up into his Head, to the great Perturbation of both. And lastly, others maintained, that by walking much in the dark about the Library, he had quite lost the Situation of it out of his Head; And therefore, in replacing his *Books*, he was apt to Mistake, and clap *DesCartes* next to *Aristotle*; Poor *Plato* had got between *Hobbes* and the *Seven Wise Masters*,

---

* *The Honourable Mr.* Boyle, *in the Preface to his Edition of* Phalaris, *says, he was refus'd a Manuscript by the Library-Keeper*, pro solita Humanitate suâ.

and *Virgil* was hemm'd in with *Dryden* on one side, and *Withers* on the other.

Mean while, those *Books* that were Advocates for the *Moderns,* chose out one from among them, to make a Progress thro' the whole Library, examine the Number and Strength of their Party, and concert their Affairs. This Messenger performed all things very industriously, and brought back with him a List of their Forces, in all Fifty Thousand, consisting chiefly of *light Horse, heavy-armed Foot,* and *Mercenaries;* Whereof the *Foot* were in general but sorrily armed, and worse clad; Their *Horses* large, but extremely out of Case and Heart; However, some few by trading among the *Antients,* had furnisht themselves tolerably enough.

While Things were in this Ferment; *Discord* grew extremely high, hot Words passed on both sides, and ill blood was plentifully bred. Here a solitary *Antient,* squeezed up among a whole Shelf of *Moderns,* offered fairly to dispute the Case, and to prove by manifest Reasons, that the Priority was due to them, from long Possession, and in regard of their Prudence, Antiquity, and above all, their great Merits towards the *Moderns.* But these denied the Premises, and seemed very much to wonder, how the *Antients* could pretend to insist upon their Antiquity, when it was so plain (if they went to that) the *Moderns* were much the more * *Antient* of the two. As for any Obligations they owed to the *Antients,* they renounced them all. *'Tis true,* said they, *we are informed, some few of our Party have been so mean to borrow their Subsistence from You; But the rest, infinitely the greater number (and especially, we* French *and* English) *were so far from stooping to so base an Example, that there never passed, till this very hour, six Words between us. For, our* Horses *are of our own breeding, our* Arms *of our own forging, and our* Cloaths *of our own cutting out and sowing.* Plato was by chance upon the next Shelf, and observing those that spoke to be in the ragged Plight, mentioned a while ago; their *Jades* lean and foundred,

---

* *According to the Modern Paradox.*

their *Weapons* of rotten Wood, their *Armour* rusty, and nothing but Raggs underneath; he laugh'd loud, and in his pleasant way, swore, *By G——, he believ'd them.*

Now, the *Moderns* had not proceeded in their late Negotiation, with Secrecy enough to escape the Notice of the Enemy. For, those Advocates, who had begun the Quarrel, by setting first on Foot the Dispute of Precedency, talkt so loud of coming to a Battel, that *Temple* happened to over-hear them, and gave immediate Intelligence to the *Antients;* who thereupon drew up their scattered Troops together, resolving to act upon the defensive; Upon which, several of the *Moderns* fled over to their Party, and among the rest, *Temple* himself. This *Temple* having been educated and long conversed among the *Antients,* was, of all the *Moderns,* their greatest Favorite, and became their greatest Champion.

Things were at this Crisis, when a material Accident fell out. For, upon the highest Corner of a large Window, there dwelt a certain *Spider,* swollen up to the first Magnitude, by the Destruction of infinite Numbers of *Flies,* whose Spoils lay scattered before the Gates of his Palace, like human Bones before the Cave of some Giant. The Avenues to his Castle were guarded with Turn-pikes, and Palissadoes, all after the *Modern* way of Fortification. After you had passed several Courts, you came to the Center, wherein you might behold the *Constable* himself in his own Lodgings, which had Windows fronting to each Avenue, and Ports to sally out upon all Occasions of Prey or Defence. In this Mansion he had for some Time dwelt in Peace and Plenty, without Danger to his *Person* by *Swallows* from above, or to his *Palace* by *Brooms* from below: When it was the Pleasure of Fortune to conduct thither a wandring *Bee,* to whose Curiosity a broken Pane in the Glass had discovered it self; and in he went, where expatiating a while, he at last happened to alight upon one of the outward Walls of the *Spider's* Cittadel; which yielding to the unequal Weight, sunk down to the very Foundation. Thrice he endeavoured to force his Passage, and Thrice the Center shook. The *Spider* within, feeling the terrible Con-

vulsion, supposed at first, that *Nature* was approaching to her
final Dissolution; or else, that *Beelzebub* with all his Legions,
was come to revenge the Death of many thousands of his
Subjects, whom his Enemy had slain and devoured. However,
he at length valiantly resolved to issue forth, and meet his
Fate. Mean while, the *Bee* had acquitted himself of his Toils,
and posted securely at some Distance, was employed in cleansing
his Wings, and disengaging them from the ragged Remnants
of the Cobweb. By this time the *Spider* was adventured out,
when beholding the Chasms, and Ruins, and Dilapidations of
his Fortress, he was very near at his Wit's end, he stormed and
swore like a Mad-man, and swelled till he was ready to burst.
At length, casting his Eye upon the *Bee,* and wisely gathering
Causes from Events, (for they knew each other by Sight) *A
Plague split you,* said he, *for a giddy Son of a Whore; Is it
you, with a Vengeance, that have made this Litter here? Could
not you look before you, and be d——n'd? Do you think I
have nothing else to do (in the Devil's Name) but to Mend
and Repair after your Arse? Good Words, Friend,* said the
Bee, (having now pruned himself, and being disposed to drole)
*I'll give you my Hand and Word to come near your Kennel
no more; I was never in such a confounded Pickle since I was
born. Sirrah,* replied the *Spider, if it were not for breaking an
old Custom in our Family, never to stir abroad against an
Enemy, I should come and teach you better Manners. I pray,
have Patience,* said the *Bee, or you will spend your Substance,
and for ought I see, you may stand in need of it all, towards
the Repair of your House. Rogue, Rogue,* replied the *Spider,
yet, methinks, you should have more Respect to a Person,
whom all the World allows to be so much your Betters. By my
Troth,* said the *Bee, the Comparison will amount to a very
good Jest, and you will do me a Favour, to let me know the
Reasons, that all the World is pleased to use in so hopeful a
Dispute.* At this, the *Spider* having swelled himself into the
Size and Posture of a Disputant, began his Argument in the
true Spirit of Controversy, with a Resolution to be heartily
scurrilous and angry, to urge *on* his own Reasons, without

the least Regard to the Answers or Objections of his Opposite; and fully predetermined in his Mind against all Conviction.

Not to disparage my self, said he, *by the Comparison with such a Rascal; What art thou but a Vagabond without House or Home, without Stock or Inheritance; Born to no Possession of your own, but a Pair of Wings, and a Drone-Pipe. Your Livelihood is an universal Plunder upon Nature; a Freebooter over Fields and Gardens; and for the sake of Stealing, will rob a Nettle as readily as a Violet. Whereas I am a domestick Animal, furnisht with a Native Stock within my self. This large Castle (to shew my Improvements in the Mathematicks) is all built with my own Hands, and the Materials extracted altogether out of my own Person.*

I am glad, answered the *Bee, to hear you grant at least, that I am come honestly by my Wings and my Voice, for then, it seems, I am obliged to Heaven alone for my Flights and my Musick; and Providence would never have bestowed on me two such Gifts, without designing them for the noblest Ends. I visit, indeed, all the Flowers and Blossoms of the Field and the Garden, but whatever I collect from thence, enriches my self, without the least Injury to their Beauty, their Smell, or their Taste. Now, for you and your Skill in Architecture, and other Mathematicks, I have little to say: In that Building of yours, there might, for ought I know, have been Labor and Method enough, but by woful Experience for us both, 'tis too plain, the Materials are nought, and I hope, you will henceforth take Warning, and consider Duration and matter, as well as method and Art. You, boast, indeed, of being obliged to no other Creature, but of drawing, and spinning out all from your self; That is to say, if we may judge of the Liquor in the Vessel by what issues out, You possess a good plentiful Store of Dirt and Poison in your Breast; and, tho' I would by no means, lessen or disparage your genuine Stock of either, yet, I doubt you are somewhat obliged for an Encrease of both, to a little foreign Assistance. Your inherent Portion of Dirt, does not fail of Acquisitions, by Sweepings exhaled from below: and one Insect furnishes you with a share of Poison to destroy another.*

So that in short, the Question comes all to this; Whether is the nobler Being of the two, That which by a lazy Contemplation of four Inches round; by an over-weening Pride, which feeding and engendering on it self, turns all into Excrement and Venom; producing nothing at all, but Fly-bane and a Cobweb: Or That, which, by an universal Range, with long Search, much Study, true Judgment, and Distinction of Things, brings home Honey and Wax.

This Dispute was managed with such Eagerness, Clamor, and Warmth, that the two Parties of *Books* in Arms below, stood Silent a while, waiting in Suspense what would be the Issue; which was not long undetermined: For the *Bee* grown impatient at so much loss of Time, fled strait away to a bed of Roses, without looking for a Reply; and left the *Spider* like an Orator, *collected* in himself, and just prepared to burst out.

It happened upon this Emergency, that *Æsop* broke silence first. He had been of late most barbarously treated by a strange Effect of the *Regent's Humanity,* who had tore off his Title-page, sorely defaced one half of his Leaves, and chained him fast among a Shelf of *Moderns.* Where soon discovering how high the Quarrel was like to proceed, He tried all his Arts, and turned himself to a thousand Forms: At length in the borrowed Shape of an *Ass,* the *Regent* mistook him for a *Modern;* by which means, he had Time and Opportunity to escape to the *Antients,* just when the *Spider* and the *Bee* were entring into their Contest; to which He gave His Attention with a world of Pleasure; and when it was ended, swore in the loudest Key, that in all his Life, he had never known two Cases so parallel and adapt to each other, as That in the Window, and this upon the Shelves. The *Disputants,* said he, *have admirably managed the Dispute between them, have taken in the full Strength of all that is to be said on both sides, and exhausted the Substance of every Argument* pro *and* con. *It is but to adjust the Reasonings of both to the present Quarrel, then to compare and apply the Labors and Fruits of each, as the* Bee *has learnedly deduced them; and we shall find the Conclusion fall plain and close upon the* Moderns *and* Us. *For, pray Gentlemen, was ever any thing so* Modern *as the* Spider *in his Air, his Turns, and his Paradoxes? He argues in the Behalf of* You *his Brethren, and Himself, with many Boastings of his native Stock, and great Genius; that he Spins and Spits wholly from himself, and scorns to own any Obligation or Assistance from without. Then he displays to you his great Skill in Architecture, and Improvement in the Mathematicks. To all this, the* Bee, *as an Advocate, retained by us the* Antients, *thinks fit to Answer; That if one may judge of the great Genius or Inventions of the* Moderns, *by what they have produced, you will hardly have Countenance to bear you out in boasting of either. Erect your Schemes with as much Method and Skill as you please; yet, if the materials be nothing but Dirt, spun out of your own Entrails (the Guts of* Modern *Brains) the Edifice will conclude at last in a* Cobweb: *The Duration of which, like that of other* Spiders *Webs, may be imputed to their being forgotten, or neglected, or hid in a Corner. For any Thing else of Genuine, that the* Moderns *may pretend to, I cannot recollect; unless it be a large Vein of Wrangling and Satyr, much of a Nature and Substance with the* Spider's *poison; which, however, they pretend to spit wholly out of themselves, is improved by the same Arts, by feeding upon the* Insects *and* Vermin *of the Age. As for* Us, *the* Antients, *We are content with the* Bee, *to pretend to Nothing of our own, beyond our* Wings *and our* Voice: *that is to say, our* Flights *and our* Language; *For the rest, whatever we have got, has been by infinite Labor, and search, and ranging thro' every Corner of Nature: The Difference is, that instead of* Dirt *and* Poison, *we have rather chose to fill our Hives with* Honey *and* Wax, *thus furnishing Mankind with the two Noblest of Things, which are* Sweetness *and* Light.

'Tis wonderful to conceive the Tumult arisen among the *Books,* upon the close of this long Descant of *Æsop;* Both Parties took the Hint, and heightened their Animosities so on a sudden, that they resolved it should come to a Battel. Immediately, the two main Bodies withdrew under their several Ensigns, to the farther Parts of the Library, and there entred into Cabals, and Consults upon the present Emergency. The *Moderns* were in very warm Debates upon the Choice of their *Leaders,* and nothing less than the Fear impending from their Enemies, could have kept them from Mutinies upon this Occasion. The Difference was greatest among the *Horse,* where every private *Trooper* pretended to the chief Command, from *Tasso* and *Milton,* to *Dryden* and *Withers.* The *Light-Horse* were Commanded by *Cowly* and *Despreaux.* There, came the *Bowmen* under their valiant Leaders, *Des-Cartes, Gassendi,* and *Hobbes,* whose Strength was such, that they could shoot their Arrows beyond the *Atmosphere,* never to fall down again, but turn like that of *Evander* into *Meteors,* or like the *Canonball* into *Stars. Paracelsus* brought a *Squadron* of *Stink-Pot-Flingers* from the snowy Mountains of *Rhœtia.* There, came a vast Body of *Dragoons,* of different Nations, under the leading of *Harvey,* their great *Aga:* Part armed with *Scythes,* the Weapons of Death; Part with *Launces* and long *Knives,* all steept in *Poison;* Part shot *Bullets* of a most malignant Nature, and used *white Powder* which infallibly killed without *Report.* There, came several Bodies of *heavy-armed Foot,* all *Mercenaries,* under the Ensigns of *Guiccardine, Davila, Polydore Virgil, Buchanan, Mariana, Cambden,* and others. The *Engineers* were commanded by *Regiomontanus* and *Wilkins.* The rest were a confused Multitude, led by *Scotus, Aquinas,* and *Bellarmine;* of mighty Bulk and Stature, but without either Arms, Courage, or Discipline. In the last Place, came infinite Swarms of * *Calones,* a disorderly Rout led by *Lestrange;* Rogues and Raggamuffins, that follow the Camp for nothing but the Plunder; All without *Coats* to cover them.

The Army of the *Antients* was much fewer in Number; *Homer* led the *Horse,* and *Pindar* the *Light-Horse; Euclid* was chief *Engineer: Plato* and *Aristotle* commanded the *Bow men, Herodotus* and *Livy* the *Foot, Hippocrates* the *Dragoons.* The *Allies,* led by *Vossius* and *Temple,* brought up the Rear.

---

* *These are Pamphlets, which are not bound or cover'd.*

All things violently tending to a decisive Battel; *Fame,* who much frequented, and had a large Apartment formerly assigned her in the *Regal Library,* fled up strait to *Jupiter,* to whom she delivered a faithful account of all that passed between the two Parties below. (For, among the Gods, she always tells Truth.) *Jove* in great concern, convokes a Council in the *Milky-Way.* The Senate assembled, he declares the Occasion of convening them; a bloody Battel just impendent between two mighty Armies of *Antient* and *Modern* Creatures, call'd *Books,* wherein the Celestial Interest was but too deeply concerned. *Momus,* the Patron of the *Moderns,* made an Excellent Speech in their Favor, which was answered by *Pallas* the Protectress of the *Antients.* The Assembly was divided in their affections; when *Jupiter* commanded the Book of Fate to be laid before Him. Immediately were brought by *Mercury,* three large Volumes in Folio, containing Memoirs of all Things past, present, and to come. The Clasps were of Silver, double Gilt; the Covers, of Celestial Turky-leather, and the Paper such as here on Earth might almost pass for Vellum. *Jupiter* having silently read the Decree, would communicate the Import to none, but presently shut up the Book.

Wihout the Doors of this Assembly, there attended a vast Number of light, nimble Gods, menial Servants to *Jupiter:* These are his ministring Instruments in all Affairs below. They travel in a Caravan, more or less together, and are fastened to each other like a Link of Gally-slaves, by a light Chain, which passes from them to *Jupiter*'s great Toe: And yet in receiving or delivering a Message, they may never approach above the lowest Step of his Throne, where he and they whisper to each other thro' a long hollow Trunk. These Deities are call'd by mortal Men, *Accidents,* or *Events;* but the Gods call them, *Second Causes. Jupiter* having delivered his Message to a certain Number of these Divinities, they flew immediately down to the Pinnacle of the Regal Library, and consulting a few Minutes, entered unseen, and disposed the Parties according to their Orders.

Mean while, *Momus* fearing the worst, and calling to mind

an antient Prophecy, which bore no very good Face to his
Children the *Moderns;* bent his Flight to the Region of a
malignant Deity, call'd *Criticism*. She dwelt on the Top of a
snowy Mountain in *Nova Zembla;* there *Momus* found her
extended in her Den, upon the Spoils of numberless Volumes
half devoured. At her right Hand sat *Ignorance,* her Father
and Husband, blind with Age; at her left, *Pride* her Mother,
dressing her up in the Scraps of Paper herself had torn. There,
was *Opinion* her Sister, light of Foot, hoodwinkt, and head-
strong, yet giddy and perpetually turning. About her play'd
her Children, *Noise* and *Impudence, Dullness* and *Vanity,
Positiveness, Pedantry,* and *Ill-Manners*. The Goddess herself
had Claws like a Cat: Her Head, and Ears, and Voice,
resembled those of an *Ass;* Her Teeth fallen out before; Her
Eyes turned inward, as if she lookt only upon herself: Her
Diet was the overflowing of her own *Gall:* Her *Spleen* was so
large, as to stand prominent like a Dug of the first Rate, nor
wanted Excrescencies in form of Teats, at which a Crew of
ugly Monsters were greedily sucking; and, what is wonderful
to conceive, the bulk of Spleen encreased faster than the
Sucking could diminish it. *Goddess,* said *Momus, can you sit
idly here, while our devout Worshippers, the* Moderns, *are
this Minute entring into a cruel Battel, and, perhaps, now
lying under the Swords of their Enemies; Who then hereafter,
will ever sacrifice, or build Altars to our Divinities? Haste
therefore to the* British Isle, *and, if possible, prevent their
Destruction, while I make Factions among the Gods, and gain
them over to our Party*.

Momus having thus delivered himself, staid not for an
answer, but left the Goddess to her own Resentment; Up she
rose in a Rage, and as it is the Form upon such Occasions,
began a Soliloquy. *'Tis I* (said she) *who give Wisdom to Infants
and Idiots; By Me, Children grow wiser than their Parents.
By Me,* Beaux *become Politicans; and* School-boys, *Judges of
Philosophy. By Me, Sophisters debate, and conclude upon
the Depths of Knowledge; and Coffee-house Wits instinct by
Me, can correct an Author's Style and display his minutest*

Errors, without understanding a Syllable of his Matter or his Language. By Me, Striplings spend their Judgment, as they do their Estate, before it comes into their Hands. 'Tis I, who have deposed Wit and Knowledge from their Empire over Poetry, *and advanced my self in their stead. And shall a few* upstart Antients *dare oppose me?*———*But, come, my aged Parents, and you, my Children dear, and thou my beauteous Sister; let us ascend my Chariot, and hast to assist our devout* Moderns, *who are now sacrificing to us a* Hecatomb, *as I perceive by that grateful Smell, which from thence reaches my Nostrils.*

The Goddess and her Train having mounted the Chariot, which was drawn by *tame Geese,* flew over infinite Regions, shedding her Influence in due Places, till at length, she arrived at her beloved Island of *Britain;* but in hovering over its *Metropolis,* what Blessings did she not let fall upon her Seminaries of *Gresham* and *Covent-Garden?* And now she reach'd the fatal Plain of St. *James*'s Library, at what time the two Armies were upon the Point to engage; where entring with all her Caravan, unseen, and landing upon a Case of Shelves, now desart, but once inhabited by a Colony of *Virtuoso's,* she staid a while to observe the Posture of both Armies.

But here, the tender Cares of a Mother began to fill her Thoughts, and move in her Breast. For, at the Head of a Troop of *Modern Bow-men,* she cast her Eyes upon her Son *W*——*tt*——*n;* to whom the Fates had assigned a very short Thread. *W*——*tt*——*n,* a young Hero, whom an unknown Father of mortal Race, begot by stollen Embraces with this Goddess. He was the Darling of his Mother, above all her Children, and she resolved to go and comfort Him. But first, according to the good old Custom of Deities, she cast about to change her Shape; for fear the Divinity of her Countenance might dazzle his Mortal Sight, and over-charge the rest of his Senses. She therefore gathered up her Person into an *Octavo* Compass: Her Body grew white and arid, and split in pieces with Driness; the thick turned into Pastboard, and the thin into Paper, upon which, her Parents and Children, artfully

strowed a Black Juice, or Decoction of Gall and Soot, in Form
of Letters; her Head, and Voice, and Spleen, kept their primitive Form, and that which before, was a Cover of Skin, did
still continue so. In which Guise, she march'd on towards the
Moderns, undistinguishable in Shape and Dress from the
Divine B——ntl——y, W——tt——n's dearest Friend. *Brave
W——tt——n,* said the Goddess, *Why do our Troops stand
idle here, to spend their present Vigour and Opportunity of
this Day? Away, let us haste to the Generals, and advise to give
the Onset immediately.* Having spoke thus, she took the
ugliest of her Monsters, full glutted from her Spleen, and
flung it invisibly into his Mouth; which flying strait up into
his Head, squeez'd out his Eye-Balls, gave him a distorted
Look, and half over-turned his Brain. Then she privately
ordered two of her beloved Children, *Dulness* and *Ill-Manners,*
closely to attend his Person in all Encounters. Having thus
accoutred him, she vanished in a Mist, and the *Hero*
perceived it was the Goddess, his Mother.

The destined Hour of Fate, being now arrived, the Fight
began; whereof, before I dare adventure to make a particular
Description, I must, after the Example of other Authors, petition for a hundred Tongues, and Mouths, and Hands, and
Pens; which would all be too little to perform so immense a
Work. Say, Goddess, that presidest over History; who it was
that first advanced in the Field of Battel. *Paracelsus,* at the
Head of his *Dragoons,* observing *Galen* in the adverse Wing,
darted his Javelin with a mighty Force, which the brave
Antient received upon his Shield, the Point breaking in the
second fold.   *   *   *   *   *   *   *   *   *

Hic pauca   *   *   *   *   *   *   *   *   *
desunt.   *   *   *   *   *   *   *   *   *

They bore the wounded *Aga,* on their Shields to his Chariot

Desunt non-   *   *   *   *   *   *   *   *   *
nulla.   *   *   *   *   *   *   *   *   *

*   *   *   *   *   *   *   *   *   *   *

*   *   *   *   *   *   *   *   *   *   *

*   *   *   *   *   *   *   *   *   *   *

Then *Aristotle* observing *Bacon* advance with a furious Mien, drew his Bow to the Head, and let fly his Arrows, which mist the valiant *Modern,* and went hizzing over his Head; but *Des-Cartes* it hit; The Steel Point quickly found a *Defect* in his *Head-piece;* it pierced the Leather and the Past-board, and went in at his Right Eye. The Torture of the Pain, whirled the valiant *Bow-man* round, till Death, like a Star of superior Influence, drew him into his own *Vortex.*   *   *   *   *

Ingens hia-   *   *   *   *   *   *   *   *   *
tus hic in MS.   *   *   *   *   *   *   *   *   *
*   *   *   *   *   *   *   *   *   *   *

when *Homer* appeared at the Head of the Cavalry, mounted on a furious Horse, with Difficulty managed by the Rider himself, but which no other Mortal durst approach; He rode among the Enemies Ranks, and bore down all before him. Say, Goddess, whom he slew first, and whom he slew last. First, *Gondibert* advanced against Him, clad in heavy Armour, and mounted on a staid sober Gelding, not so famed for his Speed as his Docility in kneeling, whenever his Rider would mount or alight. He had made a Vow to *Pallas,* that he would never leave the Field, till he had spoiled * *Homer* of his Armour; Madman, who had never once *seen* the Wearer, nor understood his Strength. Him *Homer* overthrew, Horse and Man to the Ground, there to be trampled and choak'd in the Dirt. Then, with a long Spear, he slew *Denham,* a stout *Modern,* who from his† Father's side, derived his Lineage from *Apollo,* but his Mother was of Mortal Race. He fell, and bit the Earth. The Celestial Part *Apollo* took, and made it a Star, but the Terrestrial lay wallowing upon the Ground. Then *Homer* slew *W——sl——y* with a kick of his Horse's heel; He took *Perrault* by mighty Force out of his Saddle, then hurl'd him at *Fontenelle,* with the same Blow dashing out both their Brains.

* *Vid. Homer.*

---

† *Sir* John Denham's *Poems are very Unequal, extremely Good, and very Indifferent, so that his Detractors said, he was not the real Author of* Coopers-Hill.

On the left Wing of the Horse, *Virgil* appeared in shining Armor, compleatly fitted to his Body; He was mounted on a dapple grey Steed, the slowness of whose Pace, was an Effect of the highest Mettle and Vigour. He cast his Eye on the adverse Wing, with a desire to find an Object worthy of his valour, when behold, upon a sorrel Gelding of a monstrous Size, appear'd a Foe, issuing from among the thickest of the Enemy's Squadrons; But his Speed was less than his Noise; for his Horse, old and lean, spent the Dregs of his Strength in a high Trot, which tho' it made slow advances, yet caused a loud Clashing of his Armor, terrible to hear. The two Cavaliers had now approached within the Throw of a Lance, when the Stranger desired a Parley, and lifting up the Vizard of his Helmet, a Face hardly appeared from within, which after a pause, was known for that of the renowned *Dryden*. The brave *Antient* suddenly started, as one possess'd with Surprize and Disappointment together: For, the Helmet was nine times too large for the Head, which appeared Situate far in the hinder Part, even like the Lady in a Lobster, or like a Mouse under a Canopy of State, or like a shriveld Beau from within the Penthouse of a modern Perewig: And the voice was suited to the Visage, sounding weak and remote. *Dryden* in a long Harangue soothed up the good *Antient,* called him *Father,* and by a large deduction of Genealogies, made it plainly appear, that they were nearly related. Then he humbly proposed an Exchange of Armor, as a lasting Mark of Hospitality between them. *Virgil* consented (for the Goddess *Diffidence* came unseen, and cast a Mist before his Eyes) tho' his was of Gold, and cost a hundred Beeves, the others but of rusty Iron.* However, this glittering Armor became the *Modern* yet worse than his Own. Then, they agreed to exchange Horses; but when it came to the Trial, *Dryden* was afraid, and utterly unable to mount.   *   *   *   *   *

Alter hiatus   *   *   *   *   *   *   *   *
in MS.   *   *   *   *   *   *   *   *

* *Vid. Homer.*

*   *   *   *   *   *   *   Lucan appeared upon a fiery Horse, of admirable Shape, but head-strong, bearing the Rider where he list, over the Field; he made a mighty Slaughter among the Enemy's Horse; which Destruction to stop, *Bl——ckm——re,* a famous *Modern* (but one of the *Mercenaries*) strenuously opposed himself; and darted a Javelin, with a strong Hand, which falling short of its Mark, struck deep in the Earth. Then *Lucan* threw a Lance; but *Æsculapius* came unseen, and turn'd off the Point. *Brave* Modern, *said* Lucan, *I perceive some God protects you, for never did my Arm so deceive me before; but, what Mortal can contend with a God? Therefore, let us Fight no longer, but present Gifts to each other. Lucan* then bestowed the *Modern* a Pair of Spurs, and *Bl——ckm——re* gave *Lucan* a *Bridle.* *Pauca desunt.*   *   *   *   *   *   *   *   *   *

*   *   *   *   *   *   *   *   *   *   *   *

Creech; But, the Goddess *Dulness* took a Cloud, formed into the Shape of *Horace,* armed and mounted, and placed it in a flying Posture before Him. Glad was the Cavalier, to begin a Combat with a flying Foe, and pursued the Image, threatning loud; till at last it led him to the peaceful Bower of his Father *Ogleby,* by whom he was disarmed, and assigned to his Repose.

Then *Pindar* slew ——, and ——, and *Oldham,* and —— and *Afra* the *Amazon* light of foot; Never advancing in a direct Line, but wheeling with incredible Agility and Force, he made a terrible Slaughter among the Enemies *Light-Horse.* Him, when *Cowley* observed, his generous Heart burnt within him, and he advanced against the fierce *Antient,* imitating his Address, and Pace, and Career, as well as the Vigour of his Horse, and his own Skill would allow. When the two Cavaliers had approach'd within the Length of three Javelins; first *Cowley* threw a Lance, which miss'd *Pindar,* and passing into the Enemy's Ranks, fell ineffectual to the Ground. Then *Pindar* darted a Javelin, so large and weighty, that scarce a dozen *Cavaliers,* as *Cavaliers* are in our degenerate Days, could raise it from the Ground: yet he threw it with Ease, and it went by an unerring Hand, singing through the Air; Nor could the *Modern* have avoided present Death, if he had not luckily opposed the Shield that had been given Him by *Venus*. And now both Hero's drew their Swords, but the *Modern* was so aghast and disordered, that he knew not where he was; his Shield dropt from his Hands; thrice he fled, and thrice he could not escape; at last he turned, and lifting up his Hands, in the Posture of a Suppliant, *God-like* Pindar, said he, *spare my Life, and possess my Horse with these Arms; besides the Ransom which my Friends will give, when they hear I am alive, and your Prisoner. Dog,* said Pindar, *Let your Ransom stay with your Friends; But your Carcass shall be left for the* Fowls of the Air, *and the* Beasts of the Field. With that, he raised his Sword, and with a mighty Stroak, cleft the wretched *Modern* in twain, the Sword pursuing the Blow; and one half lay panting on the Ground, to be trod in pieces by the Horses Feet, the other half was born by the frighted Steed thro' the Field. This * *Venus* took, and wash'd it seven times in *Ambrosia,* then struck it thrice with a Sprig of *Amarant;* upon which, the Leather grew round and soft, and the Leaves turned into Feathers, and being gilded before, continued gilded still; so it became a *Dove,* and She harness'd it to her Chariot.   *

Hiatus valdè * * * * * * * * *
deflendus in MS. * * * * * * * *
* * * * * * * * * * * *

Day being far spent, and the numerous Forces of the *Moderns* half inclining to a Retreat, there issued forth from a Squadron of their *heavy armed Foot,* a Captain, whose Name was *B——ntl——y;* †in Person, the most deformed of all the *Moderns;* Tall, but without Shape or Comeliness; Large, but without Strength or Proportion. His Armour was patch'd up of a thousand incoherent Pieces; and the Sound of it, as he march'd, was loud and dry, like that made by the Fall of a

---

† *The Episode of* B——ntl——y *and* W——tt—n.

---

* *I do not approve the Author's Judgment in this, for I think* Cowley's Pindaricks *are much preferable to his* Mistress.

Sheet of Lead, which an *Etesian Wind* blows suddenly down from the Roof of some Steeple. His Helmet was of old rusty Iron, but the Vizard was Brass, which tainted by his Breath, corrupted into Copperas, nor wanted Gall from the same Fountain; so, that whenever provoked by Anger or Labour, an atramentous Quality, of most malignant Nature, was seen to distil from his Lips. In his *right Hand he grasp'd a Flail, and (that he might never be unprovided of an *offensive* Weapon) a Vessel full of *Ordure* in his Left: Thus, compleatly arm'd, he advanc'd with a slow and heavy Pace, where the *Modern* Chiefs were holding a Consult upon the Sum of Things; who, as he came onwards, laugh'd to behold his crooked Leg, and hump Shoulder, which his Boot and Armour vainly endeavouring to hide were forced to comply with, and expose. The Generals made use of him for his Talent of Railing; which kept within Government, proved frequently of great Service to their Cause, but at other times did more Mischief than Good; For at the least Touch of Offence, and often without any at all, he would, like a wounded Elephant, convert it against his Leaders. Such, at this Juncture, was the Disposition of *B——ntl——y*, grieved to see the Enemy prevail, and dissatisfied with every Body's Conduct but his own. He humbly gave the *Modern* Generals to understand, that he conceived, with great Submission, they were all a Pack of *Rogues,* and *Fools,* and *Sons of Whores,* and *d——mn'd Cowards,* and *confounded Loggerheads,* and *illiterate Whelps,* and *nonsensical Scoundrels;* That if Himself had been constituted General, those *presumptuous Dogs,* the *Antients,* would long before this, have been beaten out of the Field. † *You,* said he, *sit here idle, but, when I, or any other valiant* Modern, *kill an Enemy, you are sure to seize the Spoil. But, I will not march one Foot against the Foe, till you all swear to me, that, whomever I take or kill, his Arms I shall quietly*

† *Vid. Homer de Thersite.*

---

* *The Person here spoken of, is famous for letting fly at every Body without Distinction, and using mean and foul Scurrilities.*

possess. B——ntl——y having spoke thus, *Scaliger* bestowing him a sower Look; *Miscreant* Prater, said he, *Eloquent only in thine own Eyes, Thou railest without Wit, or Truth, or Discretion, The Malignity of thy Temper perverteth Nature, Thy* Learning *makes thee more* Barbarous, *thy Study of* Humanity, *more* Inhuman; *Thy* Converse *amongst Poets more* groveling, miry, *and* dull. *All Arts of* civilizing *others, render thee* rude *and* untractable; Courts *have taught thee* ill Manners, *and* polite Conversation *has finished thee a* Pedant. *Besides, a greater Coward burtheneth not the Army. But never despond, I pass my Word, whatever Spoil thou takest, shall certainly be thy own; though, I hope, that vile Carcass will first become a prey to Kites and Worms.*

B——ntl——y durst not reply; but half choaked with Spleen and Rage, withdrew, in full Resolution of performing some great Achievment. With him, for his Aid and Companion, he took his beloved *W——tt——n;* resolving by Policy or Surprize, to attempt some neglected Quarter of the *Antients* Army. They began their March over Carcasses of their slaughtered Friends; then to the Right of their own Forces: then wheeled North-ward, till they came to *Aldrovandus*'s Tomb, which they pass'd on the side of the declining Sun. And now they arrived with Fear towards the Enemy's Out-guards; looking about, if haply, they might spy the Quarters of the Wounded, or some strag-gling Sleepers, unarm'd and remote from the rest. As when two *Mungrel-Curs,* whom *native Greediness,* and *domestick Want,* provoke, and join in Partnership, though fearful, nightly to invade the Folds of some rich Grazier; They, with Tails depress'd, and lolling Tongues, creep soft and slow; mean while, the conscious *Moon,* now in her *Zenith,* on their guilty Heads, darts perpendicular Rays; Nor dare they bark, though much provok'd at her refulgent Visage, whether seen in Puddle by Reflexion, or in Sphear direct; but one surveys the Region round, while t'other scouts the Plain, if haply, to discover at distance from the Flock, some *Carcass* half devoured, the Refuse of gorged Wolves, or ominous Ravens. So march'd this lovely, loving Pair of Friends, nor with less Fear and Circumspection; when, at distance, they might perceive two shining Suits of Armor, hanging upon an Oak, and the Owners not far off in a profound Sleep. The two Friends drew Lots, and the pursuing of this Adventure, fell to B——ntl——y; On he went, and in his Van *Confusion* and *Amaze;* while *Horror* and *Affright* brought up the Rear. As he came near; Behold two Hero's of the *Antients* Army, *Phalaris* and *Æsop,* lay fast asleep: B——ntl——y would fain have dispatch'd them both, and stealing close, aimed his Flail at *Phalaris*'s Breast. But, then, the Goddess *Affright* interposing, caught the *Modern* in her icy Arms, and dragg'd him from the Danger she foresaw; For both the dormant Hero's happened to turn at the same Instant, tho' soundly Sleeping, and busy in a Dream. * For *Phalaris* was just that Minute dreaming, how a most vile *Poetaster* had lampoon'd him, and how he had got him roaring in his *Bull.* And *Æsop* dream'd, that as he and the *Antient Chiefs* were lying on the Ground, a *Wild Ass* broke loose, ran about trampling and kicking, and dunging in their Faces. B——ntl——y leaving the two Hero's asleep, seized on both their Armors, and withdrew in quest of his Darling W——tt——n.

He, in the mean time, had wandred long in search of some *Enterprize,* till at length, he arrived at a small *Rivulet,* that issued from a Fountain hard by, call'd in the Language of mortal Men, *Helicon.* Here he stopt, and, parch'd with thirst, resolved to allay it in this limpid Stream. Thrice, with profane Hands, he essay'd to raise the Water to his Lips, and thrice it slipt all thro' his Fingers. Then he stoop'd prone on his Breast, but e'er his Mouth had kiss'd the liquid Crystal, *Apollo* came, and, in the Channel, held his *Shield* betwixt the *Modern* and the Fountain, so that he drew up nothing but *Mud.* For, altho' no Fountain on Earth can compare with the Clearness of *Helicon,* yet there lies at Bottom, a thick sediment of *Slime* and *Mud;* For, so *Apollo* begg'd of *Jupiter,* as a Punishment

---

* *This is according to* Homer, *who tells the Dreams of those who were kill'd in their Sleep.*

to those who durst attempt to taste it with unhallowed Lips, and for a Lesson to all, not to *draw too deep,* or *far from the Spring.*

At the Fountain Head, *W——tt——n* discerned two Hero's; The one he could not distinguish, but the other was soon known for *Temple,* General of the *Allies* to the *Antients.* His Back was turned, and he was employ'd in Drinking large Draughts in his Helmet, from the Fountain, where he had withdrawn himself to rest from the Toils of the War. *W——tt——n,* observing him, with quaking Knees, and trembling Hands, spoke thus to Himself: *Oh, that I could kill this Destroyer of our Army, what Renown should I purchase among the Chiefs! But to issue out against Him, Man for Man, Shield against Shield, and Launce against Launce;* *what Modern *of us dare? For, he fights like a God, and* Pallas *or* Apollo *are ever at his Elbow. But, Oh,* Mother! *if what Fame reports, be true, that I am the Son of so great a Goddess, grant me to Hit* Temple *with this Launce, that the Strøak may send Him to Hell, and that I may return in Safety and Triumph, laden with his Spoils.* The first Part of his Prayer, the Gods granted, at the Intercession of His *Mother* and of *Momus;* but the rest, by a perverse Wind sent from *Fate,* was scattered in the Air. Then *W——tt——n* grasp'd his Launce, and brandishing it thrice over his head, darted it with all his Might, the *Goddess,* his *Mother,* at the same time, adding Strength to his Arm. Away the Launce went hizzing, and reach'd even to the Belt of the averted *Antient,* upon which, lightly grazing, it fell to the Ground. *Temple* neither felt the Weapon touch him, nor heard it fall; And *W——tt——n,* might have escaped to his Army, with the Honor of having remitted his Launce against so great a Leader, unrevenged; But, *Apollo* enraged, that a Javelin, flung by the Assistance of so foul a *Goddess,* should pollute his Fountain, put on the shape of ——, and softly came to young *Boyle,* who then accompanied *Temple:* He pointed, first to the Launce, then

* Vid. Homer.

to the distant *Modern* that flung it, and commanded the young Hero to take immediate Revenge. *Boyle,* clad in a suit of Armor which had been *given him by all the Gods,* immediately advanced against the trembling Foe, who now fled before him. As a young Lion, in the *Libyan Plains,* or *Araby Desart,* sent by his aged Sire to hunt for Prey, or Health, or Exercise; He scours along, wishing to meet some Tiger from the Mountains, or a furious Boar; If Chance, a *Wild Ass,* with Brayings importune, affronts his Ear, the generous Beast, though loathing to distain his Claws with Blood so vile, yet much provok'd at the offensive Noise; which *Echo,* foolish Nymph, like her *ill judging Sex,* repeats much louder, and with more Delight than *Philomela*'s Song: He vindicates the Honor of the Forest, and hunts the noisy, long-ear'd Animal. So *W——tt——n* fled, so *Boyle* pursued. But *W——tt——n* heavy-arm'd, and slow of foot, began to slack his Course; when his Lover *B——ntl——y* appeared, returning laden with the Spoils of the two sleeping *Antients. Boyle* observed him well, and soon discovering the Helmet and Shield of *Phalaris,* his Friend, both which he had lately with his own Hands, new polish'd and gilded; Rage sparkled in His Eyes, and leaving his Pursuit after *W——tt——n,* he furiously rush'd on against this new Approacher. Fain would he be revenged on both; but now both fled different Ways: *And as a Woman in a little House, that gets a painful Livelihood by Spinning; if chance her *Geese* be scattered o'er the Common, she courses round the Plain from side to side, compelling here and there, the Stragglers to the Flock; They cackle loud, and flutter o'er the Champain. So *Boyle* pursued, so fled this Pair of Friends: finding at length, their Flight was vain, they bravely joyn'd, and drew themselves in *Phalanx.* First, *B——ntl——y* threw a Spear with all his Force, hoping to pierce the Enemy's Breast; But *Pallas* came unseen, and in the

* *Vid. Homer.*

---

* *This is also, after the manner of* Homer; *the Woman's getting a painful Livelihood by Spinning, has nothing to do with the Similitude, nor would be excusable without such an Authority.*

Air took off the Point, and clap'd on one of *Lead*, which after a dead Bang against the Enemy's Shield, fell blunted to the Ground. Then *Boyle* observing well his Time, took a Launce of wondrous Length and sharpness; and as this Pair of Friends compacted stood close Side to Side, he wheel'd him to the right, and with unusual Force, darted the Weapon. *B——ntl——y* saw his Fate approach, and flanking down his Arms, close to his Ribs, hoping to save his Body; in went the Point, passing through Arm and Side, nor stopt, or spent its Force, till it had also pierc'd the valiant *W——tt——n*, who going to sustain his dying Friend, shared his Fate. As, when a skilful Cook has truss'd a Brace of *Woodcocks*, He, with Iron Skewer, pierces the tender Sides of both, their Legs and Wings close pinion'd to their Ribs; So was this pair of Friends transfix'd, till down they fell, joyn'd in their Lives, joyn'd in their Deaths; so closely joyn'd, that *Charon* would mistake them both for one, and waft them over *Styx* for half his Fare. Farewel, beloved, loving Pair; Few Equals have you left behind: And happy and immortal shall you be, if all my Wit and Eloquence can make you.

And, now   *   *   *   *   *   *   *   *   *
*   *   *   *   *   *   *   *   *   *   *   *
*   *   *   *   *   *   *
*   *   *   *   *   *Desunt cætera.*

F   I   N   I   S.

A Discourse Concerning the Mechanical

Operation of the Spirit

There is no way of knowing precisely when Swift wrote this "fragment" of *A Discourse Concerning the Mechanical Operation of the
Spirit*. It shared the first appearance of *A Tale of a Tub* and *The
Battle of the Books* in 1704 and is probably, like them, chiefly a
product of the period Swift spent in the household of Sir William
Temple. In his Apology to the fifth edition of the *Tale* (1710),
Swift disavows the printed version of the *Mechanical Operation* and
adds a derogatory footnote to the text, but neither these additions
nor the assertions in the Bookseller's Advertisement (undoubtedly
by Swift) concerning the fragmentary nature of the work are to be
taken any more seriously than are most of Swift's attempts to obscure
the facts of composition or publication.

The principal target of the *Mechanical Operation* is the religious
Enthusiasm which was most flamboyantly displayed by some of the
more eccentric Dissenting splinter groups in the seventeenth century but which Swift tends to attribute in some degree to all Puritans. Various indelicate allegations were not uncommon in the
polemical writing of the period, including a good deal of the anti-
Puritan satire, and, however diverting one finds this work, it cannot
be denied that there is much venomous coarseness in Swift's attack.
Where Swift's singular artistry emerges is in his choice of a method
which permits a concurrent satiric assault in quite another direction.
The author of this letter is clearly a caricature of the intellectually
curious Modern, with his faith in science, his international correspondence, his gratuitous display of erudition, and, above all, his
strongly materialistic orientation. The "mechanical" approach which
Swift apes here was in part a matter of philosophic materialism,
with its sources in such influential works as those of Lucretius or
Descartes. More immediately, however, it was manifested in the
scientists' attempts to increase man's empirical knowledge, to reveal
the material components in much that had hitherto been reserved for
metaphysical speculation. In its very title, the *Discourse Concerning*

the Mechanical Operation of the Spirit facetiously implies that man's mechanistic prying will lead him to the arrogant exploration of that realm which is, of all others, the least material. Swift's "little animals" are a distorted reflection of reports on microscopic experiments which had appeared in the *Philosophical Transactions of the Royal Society*. His fanatic branches of learning mock the inquiries which were being soberly pursued by men of science and learning. His accounts of foreign customs derisively echo the carefully compiled and eagerly attended reports of foreign travelers. The writer of this letter is, in short, Swift's caricature of a learned Modern, solemnly dedicated to projects which are either false, futile, or impious. It is characteristic of Swift, though of few other satirists, that in the execution of this reduction to absurdity, he is able simultaneously to achieve a scathing attack upon his religious enemies.

There are a number of obvious similarities between the *Mechanical Operation* and elements of *A Tale of a Tub*. The "author" of this fragment, in his posturing and projecting, his digressions, his epistolary habits, and his claims to universal wisdom, might well be the self-conscious Modern who frequently emerges as the writer of the *Tale*. Elements in the *Mechanical Operation* are adumbrated in the titles of "An Analytical Discourse upon Zeal, Histori-theo-physi-logically considered" and "A Critical Essay upon the Art of Canting, Philosophically, Physically, and Musically considered" which the author of the *Tale* claims to have written. The substance of the discourse has a good deal in common with chapters eight and nine of the *Tale* and, in particular, with the description of the Aeolists. And it is apparent that, in his major assaults upon Puritan Enthusiasm and scientific materialism, as well as in his passing sallies against various forms of pedantry, Swift is upon ground abundantly familiar to readers of the Tale.

These resemblances have prompted various attempts to establish a structural relation between the *Mechanical Operation* and the *Tale*. A curious pirated edition of the *Tale*, published in 1720, moved the *Mechanical Operation* from its accustomed place following *The Battle of the Books* to a position directly behind the *Tale* and referred to it as a fragment of that work. Very recently, too, there have been scholarly arguments that the *Tale*, the *Battle*, and the *Mechanical Operation* should be viewed, at the very least, as components of a unified satiric project. But the similarities between the *Mechanical Operation* and the *Tale* are no more than we might expect from products of the same pen, written at approximately the same period upon the same general topics. There is not the slightest external evidence to show that Swift regarded them as parts of a single work. Nor does any internal principle of structure seem to be served by such a unification. In fact, the degree to which the shorter work echoes portions of the *Tale* discourages such attempts. To include the *Mechanical Operation* within the same framework as the Aeolist myth or the "Digression concerning Madness" would be to make a redundant and relatively thin addition. Whatever is missing from the *Mechanical Operation* cannot be supplied by searching in other works. Clearly founded upon a single lewd conceit, deliberately rambling and fragmentary, the document is self-contained and must stand upon its own merits.

THE

BOOKSELLER'S

Advertisement

TH E following Discourse came into my Hands perfect and entire. But there being several Things in it, which the present Age would not very well bear, I kept it by me some Years, resolving it should never see the Light. At length, by the Advice and Assistance of a judicious Friend, I retrench'd those Parts that might give most Offence, and have now ventured to publish the Remainder; Concerning the Author, I am wholly ignorant; neither can I conjecture, whether it be the same with That of the two foregoing Pieces, the Original having been sent me at a different Time, and in a different Hand. The Learned Reader will better determine; to whose Judgment I entirely submit it.

A
DISCOURSE
Concerning the
Mechanical Operation
OF THE
SPIRIT.
IN A
LETTER
To a FRIEND.
A
FRAGMENT.

LONDON:
Printed in the Year, MDCCX.

A DISCOURSE

Concerning the

MECHANICAL OPERATION

OF THE

SPIRIT, &c.

For T. H. *Esquire, at his Chambers in the Academy of the* Beaux Esprits *in* New-Holland.

SIR,

IT is now a good while since I have had in my Head something, not only very material, but absolutely necessary to my Health, that the World should be informed in. For, to tell you a Secret, I am able to *contain* it no longer. However, I have been perplexed for some time, to resolve what would be the most proper Form to send it abroad in. To which End, I have three Days been coursing thro' *Westminster-Hall,* and St. *Paul's Church yard,* and *Fleet-street,* to peruse *Titles;* and, I do not find any which holds so general a Vogue, as that of *A Letter to a Friend:* Nothing is more common than to meet with long Epistles address'd to Persons and Places, where, at first think-

---

This Discourse is not altogether equal to the two Former, the best Parts of it being omitted; whether the Bookseller's Account be true, that he durst not print the rest, I know not, nor indeed is it easie to determine whether he may be rely'd on, in any thing he says of this, or the former Treatises, only as to the Time they were writ in, which, however, appears more from the Discourses themselves than his Relation.

ing, one would be apt to imagine it not altogether so necessary or Convenient; Such as, *a Neighbour at next Door, a mortal Enemy, a perfect Stranger,* or *a Person of Quality in the Clouds;* and these upon Subjects, in appearance, the least proper for Conveyance by the Post; as, *long Schemes in Philosophy; dark and Wonderful Mysteries of State; Laborious Dissertations in Criticism and Philosophy, Advice to Parliaments,* and the like.

Now, Sir, to proceed after the Method in present Wear. (For, let me say what I will to the contrary, I am afraid you will publish this *Letter,* as soon as ever it comes to your Hands;) I desire you will be my Witness to the World, how careless and sudden a Scribble it has been; That it was but Yesterday, when You and I began accidentally to fall into Discourse on this Matter: That I was not very well, when we parted; That the Post is in such haste, I have had no manner of Time to digest it into Order, or correct the Style; And if any other Modern Excuses, for Haste and Negligence, shall occur to you in Reading, I beg you to insert them, faithfully promising they shall be thankfully acknowledged.

Pray, Sir, in your next Letter to the *Iroquois Virtuosi,* do me the Favour to present my humble Service to that illustrious Body, and assure them, I shall send an Account of those *Phenomena,* as soon as we can determine them at *Gresham.*

I have not had a Line from the *Literati* of *Tobinambou,* these three last Ordinaries.

And now, Sir, having dispatch'd what I had to say of Forms, or of Business, let me intreat, you will suffer me to proceed upon my Subject; and to pardon me, if I make no farther Use of the Epistolary Stile, till I come to conclude.

S E C T I O N   I .

'TIS recorded of *Mahomet,* that upon a Visit he was going to pay in *Paradise,* he had an Offer of several Vehicles to conduct him upwards; as fiery Chariots, wing'd Horses, and celestial Sedans; but he refused them all, and would be born to Heaven upon nothing but his *Ass*. Now, this Inclination of *Mahomet,* as singular as it seems, hath been since taken up by a great Number of devout *Christians;* and doubtless, with very good Reason. For, since That *Arabian* is known to have borrowed a Moiety of his Religious System from the *Christian* Faith; it is but just he should pay Reprisals to such as would Challenge them; wherein the good People of *England,* to do them all Right, have not been backward. For, tho' there is not any other Nation in the World, so plentifully provided with Carriages for that Journey, either as to Safety or Ease; yet there are abundance of us, who will not be satisfied with any other Machine, beside this of *Mahomet*.

For my own part, I must confess to bear a very singular Respect to this Animal, by whom I take human Nature to be most admirably held forth in all its Qualities as well as Operations: And therefore, whatever in my small Reading, occurs, concerning this our Fellow-Creature, I do never fail to set it down, by way of Common-place; and when I have occasion to write upon Human Reason, Politicks, Eloquence, or Knowledge; I lay my *Memorandums* before me, and insert them with a wonderful Facility of Application. However, among all the Qualifications, ascribed to this distinguish'd Brute, by Antient or Modern Authors; I cannot remember this Talent, of bearing his Rider to Heaven, has been recorded for a Part of his Character, except in the two Examples mentioned already; Therefore, I conceive the Methods of this Art, to be a Point of useful Knowledge in very few Hands, and which the Learned World would gladly be better informed in. This is what I have undertaken to perform in the following Discourse. For, towards the Operation already mentioned, many peculiar Properties are required, both in the *Rider* and the *Ass;* which I shall endeavour to set in as clear a Light as I can.

But, because I am resolved, by all means, to avoid giving Offence to any Party whatever; I will leave off discoursing so closely to the *Letter* as I have hitherto done, and go on for the future by way of Allegory, tho' in such a manner, that the judicious Reader, may without much straining, make his Applications as often as he shall think fit. Therefore, if you please from hence forward, instead of the Term, *Ass,* we shall make use of *Gifted,* or *enlightened Teacher;* And the Word *Rider,* we will exchange for that of *Fanatick Auditory,* or any other Denomination of the like Import. Having settled this weighty Point; the great Subject of Enquiry before us, is to examine, by what Methods this *Teacher* arrives at his *Gifts* or *Spirit,* or *Light;* and by what Intercourse between him and his Assembly, it is cultivated and supported.

In all my Writings, I have had constant Regard to this great End, not to suit and apply them to particular Occasions and Circumstances of Time, of Place, or of Person; but to calculate them for universal Nature, and Mankind in General. And of such Catholick use, I esteem this present Disquisition: For I do not remember any other Temper of Body, or Quality of Mind, wherein all Nations and Ages of the World have so unanimously agreed, as That of a *Fanatick* Strain, or Tincture of *Enthusiasm;* which improved by certain Persons or Societies of Men, and by them practised upon the rest, has been able to produce Revolutions of the greatest Figure in History; as will soon appear to those who know any thing of *Arabia, Persia, India,* or *China,* of *Morocco* and *Peru:* Farther, it has possessed as great a Power in the Kingdom of Knowledge, where it is hard to assign one Art or Science, which has not annexed to it some *Fanatick* Branch: Such are the *Philosopher's Stone;* * *The Grand Elixir; The Planetary Worlds; The Squaring of the Circle; The Summum bonum;* Utopian *Commonwealths;* with some others of less or subordinate Note; which all serve for nothing else, but to employ or amuse this Grain of *Enthusiasm,* dealt into every Composition.

But, if this Plant has found a Root in the Fields of *Empire,* and of *Knowledge,* it has fixt deeper, and spread yet farther upon *Holy Ground.* Wherein, though it hath pass'd under the

* Some Writers hold them for the same, others not.

general Name of *Enthusiasm*, and perhaps arisen from the same Original, yet hath it produced certain Branches of a very different Nature, however often mistaken for each other. The Word in its universal Acceptation, may be defined, *A lifting up of the Soul or its Faculties above Matter*. This Description will hold good in general; but I am only to understand it, as applied to *Religion; wherein there are three general Ways of ejaculating the Soul, or transporting it beyond the Sphere of Matter. The first, is the immediate Act of God, and is called, *Prophecy* or *Inspiration*. The second, is the immediate Act of the Devil, and is termed *Possession*. The third, is the Product of natural Causes, the effect of strong Imagination, Spleen, violent Anger, Fear, Grief, Pain, and the like. These three have been abundantly treated on by Authors and therefore shall not employ my Enquiry. But, the fourth Method of *Religious Enthusiasm*, or launching out of the Soul, as it is purely an Effect of Artifice and *Mechanick Operation*, has been sparingly handled, or not at all, by any Writer; because tho' it is an Art of great Antiquity, yet having been confined to few Persons, it long wanted these Advancements and Refinements, which it afterwards met with, since it has grown so Epidemick, and fallen into so many cultivating Hands.

It is therefore upon this *Mechanical Operation of the Spirit*, that I mean to treat, as it is at present performed by our *British Workmen*. I shall deliver to the Reader the Result of many judicious Observations upon the Matter; tracing, as near as I can, the whole Course and Method of this *Trade*, producing parallel Instances, and relating certain Discoveries that have luckily fallen in my way.

I have said, that there is one Branch of *Religious Enthusiasm*, which is purely an Effect of Nature; whereas, the Part I mean to handle, is wholly an Effect of Art, which, however, is inclined to work upon certain Natures and Constitutions, more than others. Besides, there is many an Operation, which in its Original, was purely an Artifice, but through a long Succession of Ages, hath grown to be natural. *Hippocrates* tells us, that among our Ancestors, the *Scythians*, there was a

Nation call'd * *Longheads,* which at first began by a Custom among Midwives and Nurses, of molding, and squeezing, and bracing up the Heads of Infants; by which means, Nature shut out at one Passage, was forc'd to seek another, and finding room above, shot upwards, in the Form of a Sugar-Loaf; and being diverted that way, for some Generations, at last found it out of her self, needing no Assistance from the Nurse's Hand. This was the Original of the *Scythian Long-heads,* and thus did Custom, from being a second Nature proceed to be a first. To all which, there is something very analogous among Us of this Nation, who are the undoubted Posterity of that refined People. For, in the Age of our Fathers, there arose a Generation of Men in this Island, call'd *Round-heads,* whose Race is now spread over three Kingdoms, yet in its Beginning, was meerly an Operation of Art, produced by a pair of Cizars, a Squeeze of the Face, and a black Cap. These Heads, thus formed into a perfect Sphere in all Assemblies, were most exposed to the view of the Female Sort, which did influence their Conceptions so effectually, that Nature, at last, took the Hint, and did it of her self; so that a *Round-head* has been ever since as familiar a Sight among Us, as a *Long-head* among the *Scythians.*

Upon these Examples, and others easy to produce, I desire the curious Reader to distinguish, First between an Effect grown from *Art* into *Nature,* and one that is natural from its Beginning; Secondly, between an Effect wholly natural, and one which has only a natural Foundation, but where the Superstructure is entirely Artificial. For, the first and the last of these, I understand to come within the Districts of my Subject. And having obtained these allowances, they will serve to remove any objections that may be raised hereafter against what I shall advance.

The Practitioners of this famous Art, proceed in general upon the following Fundamental; That, *the Corruption of the Senses is the Generation of the Spirit:* Because the *Senses* in

* *Macrocephali.*

Men are so many Avenues to the Fort of *Reason*, which in this Operation is wholly block'd up. All Endeavours must be therefore used, either to divert, bind up, stupify, fluster, and amuse the *Senses,* or else to justle them out of their Stations; and while they are either absent, or otherwise employ'd or engaged in a Civil War against each other, the *Spirit* enters and performs its Part.

Now, the usual Methods of managing the Senses upon such Conjunctures, are what I shall be very particular in delivering, as far as it is lawful for me to do; but having had the Honour to be Initiated into the Mysteries of every Society, I desire to be excused from divulging any Rites, wherein the *Profane* must have no Part.

But here, before I can proceed farther, a very dangerous Objection must, if possible, be removed: For, it is positively denied by certain Criticks, that the *Spirit* can by any means be introduced into an Assembly of Modern Saints, the Disparity being so great in many material Circumstances, between the Primitive Way of Inspiration, and that which is practised in the present Age. This they pretend to prove from the second Chapter of the *Acts,* where comparing both, it appears; First, that *the Apostles were gathered together with one accord in one place;* by which is meant, an universal Agreement in Opinion, and Form of Worship; a Harmony (say they) so far from being found between any two Conventicles among Us, that it is in vain to expect it between any two Heads in the same. Secondly, the *Spirit* instructed the Apostles in the Gift of speaking several Languages; a Knowledge so remote from our Dealers in this Art, that they neither understand Propriety of Words, or Phrases in their own. Lastly, (say these Objectors) The Modern Artists do utterly exclude all Approaches of the *Spirit,* and bar up its antient Way of entring, by covering themselves so close, and so industriously a top. For, they will needs have it as a Point clearly gained, that the *Cloven Tongues* never sat upon the Apostles Heads, while their Hats were on.

Now, the Force of these Objections, seems to consist in the different Acceptation of the Word, *Spirit:* which if it be understood for a supernatural Assistance, approaching from without, the Objectors have Reason, and their Assertions may be allowed; But the *Spirit* we treat of here, proceeding entirely from within, the Argument of these Adversaries is wholly eluded. And upon the same Account, our Modern Artificers, find it an Expedient of absolute Necessity, to cover their Heads as close as they can, in order to prevent Perspiration, than which nothing is observed to be a greater Spender of Mechanick Light, as we may, perhaps, farther shew in convenient Place.

To proceed therefore upon the *Phænomenon* of *Spiritual Mechanism,* It is here to be noted, than in forming and working up the *Spirit,* the Assembly has a considerable Share, as well as the Preacher; The Method of this *Arcanum,* is as follows. They violently strain their Eye balls inward, half closing the Lids; Then, as they sit, they are in a perpetual Motion of *See-saw,* making long Hums at proper Periods, and continuing the Sound at equal Height, chusing their Time in those Intermissions, while the Preacher is at Ebb. Neither is this Practice, in any part of it, so singular or improbable, as not to be traced in distant Regions, from Reading and Observation. For, first, the * *Jauguis,* or enlightened Saints of *India,* see all their Visions, by help of an acquired straining and pressure of the Eyes. Secondly, the Art of *See-saw* on a Beam, and swinging by Session upon a Cord, in order to raise artificial Extasies, hath been derived to Us, from our † *Scythian* Ancestors, where it is practised at this Day, among the Women. Lastly, the whole Proceeding, as I have here related it, is performed by the Natives of *Ireland,* with a considerable Improvement; And it is granted, that this noble Nation, hath of all others, admitted fewer Corruptions, and degenerated

* *Bernier, Mem. de Mogol.*
† *Guagnini Hist. Sarmat.*

least from the Purity of the Old *Tartars*. Now it is usual for a Knot of *Irish*, Men and Women, to abstract themselves from Matter, bind up all their Senses, grow visionary and spiritual, by Influence of a short Pipe of Tobacco, handed round the Company; each preserving the Smoak in his Mouth, till it comes again to his Turn to take in fresh: At the same Time, there is a Consort of a continued gentle Hum, repeated and renewed by Instinct, as Occasion requires, and they move their Bodies up and down, to a Degree, that sometimes their Heads and Points lie parallel to the Horison. Mean while, you may observe their Eyes turn'd up in the Posture of one, who endeavours to keep himself awake; by which, and many other Symptoms among them, it manifestly appears, that the Reasoning Faculties are all suspended and superseded, that Imagination hath usurped the Seat, scattering a thousand Deliriums over the Brain. Returning from this Digression, I shall describe the Methods, by which the *Spirit* approaches. The Eyes being disposed according to Art, at first, you can see nothing, but after a short pause, a small glimmering Light begins to appear, and dance before you. Then, by frequently moving your Body up and down, you perceive the Vapors to ascend very fast, till you are perfectly dosed and flustred like one who drinks too much in a Morning. Mean while, the Preacher is also at work; He begins a loud Hum, which pierces you quite thro'; This is immediately returned by the Audience, and you find your self prompted to imitate them, by a meer spontaneous Impulse, without knowing what you do. The *Interstitia* are duly filled up by the Preacher, to prevent too long a Pause, under which the *Spirit* would soon faint and grow languid.

This is all I am allowed to discover about the Progress of the *Spirit*, with relation to that part, which is born by the *Assembly;* But in the Methods of the Preacher, to which I now proceed, I shall be more large and particular.

SECTION II.

YOU will read it very gravely remarked in the Books of those illustrious and right eloquent Pen-men, the Modern Travellers; that the fundamental Difference in Point of Religion, between the wild *Indians* and Us, lies in this; that We Worship *God*, and they worship the *Devil*. But, there are certain Criticks, who will by no means admit of this Distinction; rather believing, that all Nations whatsoever, adore the *true God*, because, they seem to intend their Devotions to some invisible Power, of greatest *Goodness* and *Ability* to help them, which perhaps will take in the brightest Attributes ascribed to the Divinity. Others, again, inform us, that those Idolaters adore two *Principles;* the *Principle* of *Good*, and That of *Evil:* Which indeed, I am apt to look upon as the most Universal Notion, that Mankind, by the meer Light of Nature, ever entertained of Things Invisible. How this Idea hath been managed by the *Indians* and Us, and with what Advantage to the Understanding of either, may well deserve to be examined. To me, the difference appears little more than this, That They are put oftener upon their Knees by their *Fears*, and We by our *Desires;* That the former set them a *Praying*, and Us a *Cursing*. What I applaud them for, is their Discretion, in limiting their Devotions and their Deities to their several Districts, nor ever suffering the Liturgy of the *white* God, to cross or interfere with that of the *Black*. Not so with Us, who pretending by the Lines and Measures of our Reason, to extend the Dominion of one invisible Power, and contract that of the other, have discovered a gross Ignorance in the Natures of Good and Evil, and most horribly confounded the Frontiers of both. After Men have lifted up the Throne of their Divinity to the *Cælum Empyræum*, adorned with all such Qualities and Accomplishments, as themselves seem most to value and possess; After they have sunk their *Principle* of *Evil* to the lowest Center, bound him with Chains, loaded him with Curses, furnish'd him with viler Dispositions than any *Rake-hell* of the Town, accoutred him with Tail, and Horns, and huge Claws, and Sawcer Eyes; I laugh aloud, to see these Reasoners, at the same time, engaged in wise Dispute, about certain Walks and Purlieus, whether they are in the Verge of God or the Devil, seriously debating, whether such and such Influences come into Mens Minds, from above or below, whether certain Passions and Affections are guided by the Evil Spirit or the Good.

> *Dum fas atque nefas exiguo fine libidinum*
> *Discernunt avidi———.*

Thus do Men establish a Fellowship of *Christ* with *Belial,* and such is the Analogy they make between *cloven Tongues,* and *cloven Feet.* Of the like Nature is the Disquisition before us: It hath continued these hundred Years an even Debate, whether the Deportment and the Cant of our *English* enthusiastick Preachers, were *Possession,* or *Inspiration,* and a World of Argument has been drained on either side, perhaps, to little Purpose. For, I think, it is in *Life* as in *Tragedy,* where, it is held, a Conviction of great Defect, both in Order and Invention, to interpose the Assistance of preternatural Power, without an absolute and last Necessity. However, it is a Sketch of Human Vanity, for every Individual, to imagine the whole Universe is interess'd in his meanest Concern. If he hath got cleanly over a Kennel, some Angel, unseen, descended on purpose to help him by the Hand; if he hath knockt his Head against a Post, it was the Devil, for his Sins, let loose from Hell, on purpose to buffet him. Who, that sees a little paultry Mortal, droning, and dreaming, and drivelling to a Multitude, can think it agreeable to common good Sense, that either Heaven or Hell should be put to the Trouble of Influence or Inspection upon what he is about? Therefore, I am resolved immediately, to weed this Error out of Mankind, by making it clear, that this Mystery, of vending spiritual Gifts is nothing but a *Trade,* acquired by as much Instruction, and mastered by equal Practice and Application as others are. This will best appear, by describing and deducing the whole Process of the Operation, as variously as it hath fallen under my Knowledge or Experience.

*　*　*　*　*　*　*　*　*　*　*　*

Here the whole Scheme of spiritual Mechanism was deduced and explained, with an Appearance of great reading and observation; but it was thought neither safe nor Convenient to Print it.

*　*　*　*　*　*　*　*　*　*　*　*

Here it may not be amiss, to add a few Words upon the laudable Practice of wearing *quilted Caps;* which is not a Matter of meer Custom, Humor, or Fashion, as some would pretend, but an Institution of great Sagacity and Use; these, when moistned with Sweat, stop all Perspiration, and by reverberating the Heat, prevent the Spirit from evaporating any way, but at the Mouth; even as a skilful Housewife, that covers her Still with a wet Clout, for the same Reason, and finds the same Effect. For, it is the Opinion of Choice *Virtuosi,* that the Brain is only a Crowd of little Animals, but with Teeth and Claws extremely sharp, and therefore, cling together in the Contexture we behold, like the Picture of *Hobbes's Leviathan,* or like Bees in perpendicular swarm upon a Tree, or like a Carrion corrupted into Vermin, still preserving the Shape and Figure of the Mother Animal. That all invention is formed by the Morsure of two or more of these Animals, upon certain capillary Nerves, which proceed from thence, whereof three Branches spread into the Tongue, and two into the right Hand. They hold also, that these Animals are of a Constitution extremely cold; that their Food is the Air we attract, their Excrement Phlegm; and that what we vulgarly call Rheums, and Colds, and Distillations, is nothing else but an Epidemical Looseness, to which that little Commonwealth is very subject, from the Climate it lyes under. Farther, that nothing less than a violent Heat, can disentangle these

Creatures from their hamated Station of Life, or give them
Vigor and Humor, to imprint the Marks of their little Teeth.
That if the Morsure be Hexagonal, it produces Poetry; the
Circular gives Eloquence; If the Bite hath been Conical, the
Person, whose Nerve is so affected, shall be disposed to write
upon the Politicks; and so of the rest.

I shall now Discourse briefly, by what kind of Practices the
Voice is best governed, towards the Composition and Improvement of the *Spirit;* for, without a competent Skill in tuning
and toning each Word, and Syllable, and Letter, to their due
Cadence, the whole Operation is incompleat, misses entirely
of its effect on the Hearers, and puts the Workman himself to
continual Pains for new Supplies, without Success. For, it is
to be understood, that in the Language of the Spirit, *Cant* and
Droning supply the Place of *Sense* and *Reason,* in the Language
of Men: Because, in Spiritual Harangues, the Disposition of
the Words according to the Art of Grammar, hath not the
least Use, but the Skill and Influence wholly lye in the Choice
and Cadence of the Syllables; Even as a discreet *Composer,*
who in setting a Song, changes the Words and Order so often,
that he is forced to make it *Nonsense,* before he can make it
Musick. For this Reason, it hath been held by some, that the
Art of Canting is ever in greatest Perfection, when managed
by *Ignorance:* Which is thought to be enigmatically meant by
Plutarch, when he tells us, that the best Musical Instruments
were made from the Bones of an *Ass.* And the profounder
Criticks upon that Passage, are of Opinion, the Word in its
genuine Signification, means no other than a *Jaw-bone:* tho'
some rather think it to have been the *Os sacrum;* but in so nice
a Case, I shall not take upon me to decide: The Curious are
at Liberty, to *pick* from it whatever they please.

The first Ingredient, towards the Art of Canting, is a
competent Share of *Inward Light:* that is to say, a large
Memory, plentifully fraught with Theological Polysyllables,
and mysterious Texts from holy Writ, applied and digested by
those Methods, and Mechanical Operations already related:
The Bearers of this *Light,* resembling *Lanthorns,* compact of

Leaves from old *Geneva* Bibles; Which Invention, Sir *H——mphry Edw——n,* during his Mayoralty, of happy Memory, highly approved and advanced; affirming, the Scripture to be now fulfilled, where it says, *Thy Word is a Lanthorn to my Feet, and a Light to my Paths.*

Now, the Art of *Canting* consists in skilfully adapting the Voice, to whatever Words the Spirit delivers, that each may strike the Ears of the Audience, with its most significant Cadence. The Force, or Energy of this Eloquence, is not to be found, as among antient Orators, in the Disposition of Words to a Sentence, or the turning of long Periods; but agreeable to the Modern Refinements in Musick, is taken up wholly in dwelling, and dilating upon Syllables and Letters. Thus it is frequent for a single *Vowel* to draw Sighs from a Multitude; and for a whole Assembly of Saints to sob to the Musick of one solitary *Liquid.* But these are Trifles; when even Sounds inarticulate are observed to produce as forcible Effects. A Master Work-man shall *blow his Nose so powerfully,* as to pierce the Hearts of his People, who are disposed to receive the *Excrements* of his Brain with the same Reverence, as the *Issue* of it. Hawking, Spitting, and Belching, the Defects of other Mens Rhetorick, are the Flowers, and Figures, and Ornaments of his. For, the *Spirit* being the same in all, it is of no Import through what Vehicle it is convey'd.

It is a Point of too much Difficulty, to draw the Principles of this famous Art within the Compass of certain adequate Rules. However, perhaps, I may one day, oblige the World with my Critical Essay upon the Art of *Canting, Philosophically, Physically, and Musically considered.*

But, among all Improvements of the *Spirit,* wherein the Voice hath born a Part, there is none to be compared with That of *conveying the Sound thro' the Nose,* which under the Denomination of * *Snuffling,* hath passed with so great Applause in the World. The Originals of this Institution are

---

* *The Snuffling of Men, who have lost their Noses by lewd Courses, is said to have given Rise to that Tone, which our Dissenters did too much Affect.* W. Wotton.

very dark; but having been initiated into the Mystery of it, and Leave being given me to publish it to the World, I shall deliver as direct a Relation as I can.

This Art, like many other famous Inventions, owed its Birth, or at least, Improvement and Perfection, to an Effect of Chance, but was established upon solid Reasons, and hath flourished in this Island ever since, with great Lustre. All agree, that it first appeared upon the Decay and Discouragement of *Bag-pipes,* which having long suffered under the Mortal Hatred of the *Brethren,* tottered for a Time, and at last fell with *Monarchy.* The Story is thus related.

As yet, *Snuffling* was not; when the following Adventure happened to a *Banbury Saint.* Upon a certain Day, while he was far engaged among the Tabernacles of the *Wicked,* he felt the Outward Man put into odd Commotions, and strangely prick'd forward by the Inward: An Effect very usual among the Modern Inspired. For, some think, that the *Spirit* is apt to feed on the *Flesh,* like hungry Wines upon raw Beef. Others rather believe, there is a perpetual Game at *Leap-Frog* between both: and, sometimes, the *Flesh* is uppermost, and sometimes the *Spirit;* adding, that the former, while it is in the State of a *Rider,* wears huge *Rippon* Spurs, and when it comes to the Turn of being *Bearer,* is wonderfully headstrong, and hardmouth'd. However it came about, the *Saint* felt his *Vessel* full *extended* in every Part (a very natural effect of strong *Inspiration;*) and the Place and Time falling out so unluckily, that he could not have the Convenience of Evacuating upwards, by Repetition, Prayer, or Lecture; he was forced to open an inferior Vent. In short, he wrestled with the Flesh so long, that he at length subdued it, coming off with honourable Wounds, all *before.* The Surgeon had now cured the Parts, primarily affected; but the Disease driven from its Post, flew up into his Head; And, as a skilful General, valiantly attack'd in his Trenches, and beaten from the Field, by flying Marches withdraws to the Capital City, breaking down the Bridges to prevent Pursuit; So the Disease repell'd from its first Station, fled before the *Rod* of *Hermes,* to the upper Region, there fortifying it self; but, finding the Foe making Attacks at the *Nose,* broke down the *Bridge,* and retir'd to the *Head*-Quarters. Now, the Naturalists observe, that there is in human Noses, an *Idiosyncrasy,* by Virtue of which, the more the Passage is obstructed, the more our Speech delights to go through, as the Musick of a Flagelate is made by the *Stops.* By this Method, the Twang of the Nose, becomes perfectly to resemble the *Snuffle* of a Bag-pipe, and is found to be equally attractive of *British* Ears; whereof the Saint had sudden Experience, by practising his new Faculty with wonderful Success in the Operation of the *Spirit:* For, in a short Time, no Doctrine pass'd for Sound and Orthodox, unless it were delivered thro' the Nose. Strait, every Pastor copy'd after this Original; and those, who could not otherwise arrive to a Perfection, spirited by a noble Zeal, made use of the same Experiment to acquire it. So that, I think, it may be truly affirmed, the *Saints* owe their Empire to the *Snuffling* of one *Animal,* as *Darius* did his, to the *Neighing* of another; and both Stratagems were performed by the same Art; for we read, how the * *Persian Beast* acquired his Faculty, by *covering a Mare* the Day before.

I should now have done, if I were not convinced, that whatever I have yet advanced upon this Subject, is liable to great Exception. For, allowing all I have said to be true, it may still be justly objected, that there is in the Commonwealth of *artificial Enthusiasm,* some real Foundation for Art to work upon in the Temper and Complexion of Individuals, which other Mortals seem to want. Observe, but the Gesture, the Motion, and the Countenance, of some choice Professors, tho' in their most familiar Actions, you will find them of a different Race from the rest of human Creatures. Remark your commonest Pretender to a Light *within,* how dark, and dirty, and gloomy he is *without;* As Lanthorns, which the more Light they bear in their Bodies, cast out so much the more Soot, and Smoak, and fuliginous Matter to adhere to the Sides. Listen, but to

* *Herodot.*

their ordinary Talk, and look on the Mouth that delivers it; you will imagine you are hearing some antient Oracle, and your Understanding will be *equally* informed. Upon these, and the like Reasons, certain Objectors pretend to put it beyond all Doubt, that there must be a sort of preternatural *Spirit,* possessing the Heads of the Modern Saints; And some will have it to be the *Heat* of Zeal, working upon the *Dregs* of Ignorance, as other *Spirits* are produced from *Lees,* by the Force of Fire. Some again think, that when our earthly Tabernacles are disordered and desolate, shaken and out of Repair; the *Spirit* delights to dwell within them, as Houses are said to be haunted, when they are forsaken and gone to Decay.

To set this Matter in as fair a Light as possible; I shall here, very briefly, deduce the History of *Fanaticism,* from the most early Ages to the present. And if we are able to fix upon any one material or fundamental Point, wherein the chief Professors have universally agreed, I think we may reasonably lay hold on That, and assign it for the great Seed or Principle of the *Spirit.*

The most early Traces we meet with, of *Fanaticks,* in antient Story, are among the *Ægyptians,* who instituted those Rites, known in *Greece* by the Names of *Orgya, Panegyres,* and *Dionysia,* whether introduced there by *Orpheus* or *Melampus,* we shall not dispute at present, nor in all likelihood, at any time for the future. These feasts were celebrated to the Honor of *Osyris,** whom the *Grecians* called *Dionysius,* and is the same with *Bacchus:* Which has betray'd some superficial Readers to imagine, that the whole Business was nothing more than a Set of roaring, scouring Companions, over-charg'd with Wine; but this is a scandalous Mistake foisted on the World, by a sort of Modern Authors, who have too *literal* an Understanding; and, because Antiquity is to be traced *backwards,* do therefore, like *Jews,* begin their Books at the wrong End, as if Learning were a sort of *Conjuring.* These are the Men, who pretend to understand a Book, by scouting thro' the

---

* *Diod. Sic. L.* 1. *Plut. de Isside & Osyride.*

Index, as if a Traveller should go about to describe a *Palace,* when he had seen nothing but the *Privy:* or like certain Fortune-tellers in *Northern America,* who have a Way of reading a Man's Destiny, by peeping in his *Breech.* For, at the Time of instituting these Mysteries, * there was not one Vine in all *Egypt,* the Natives drinking nothing but *Ale;* which Liquor seems to have been far more antient than Wine, and has the Honor of owing its Invention and Progress, not only to the † *Egyptian Osyris,* but to the *Grecian Bacchus,* who in their famous Expedition, carried the Receipt of it along with them, and gave it to the Nations they visited or subdued. Besides, *Bacchus* himself, was very seldom, or never Drunk: For, it is recorded of him, that he was the first ‡ Inventor of the *Mitre,* which he wore continually on his Head (as the whole Company of *Bacchanals* did) to prevent Vapors and the Head-ach, after hard Drinking. And for this Reason (say some) the *Scarlet Whore,* when she makes the Kings of the Earth drunk with her Cup of Abomination, is always sober her self, tho' she never balks the Glass in her Turn, being, it seems, kept upon her Legs by the Virtue of her *Triple Mitre.* Now, these Feasts were instituted in imitation of the famous Expedition *Osyris* § made thro' the World, and of the Company that attended him, whereof the *Bacchanalian* Ceremonies were so many Types and Symbols. From which Account, it is manifest, that the Fanatick Rites of these *Bacchanals,* cannot be imputed to Intoxications by Wine, but must needs have had a deeper Foundation. What this was, we may gather large Hints from certain Circumstances in the Course of their Mysteries. For, in the first Place, there was in their Processions, an entire *Mixture and Confusion of Sexes;* they affected to ramble about Hills and Desarts: Their Garlands were of *Ivy* and *Vine,* Emblems of Cleaving and Clinging; or of *Fir,* the Parent of *Turpentine.* It is added, that they imitated *Satyrs,* were attended by *Goats,*

---

* *Herod.* L. 2.
† *Diod. Sic.* L. 1. & 3.
‡ *Id.* L. 4.
§ *See the Particulars in* Diod. Sic. L. 1 & 3.

and rode upon *Asses,* all Companions of great Skill and Practice in Affairs of Gallantry. They bore for their Ensigns, certain curious Figures, perch'd upon long Poles, made into the Shape and Size of the *Virga genitalis,* with its *Appurtenances,* which were so many Shadows and Emblems of the whole Mystery, as well as Trophies set up by the Female Conquerors. Lastly, in a certain Town of *Attica,* the whole Solemnity * stript of all its Types, was performed in *puris naturalibus,* the Votaries, not flying in Coveys, but sorted into Couples. The same may be farther conjectured from the Death of *Orpheus,* one of the Institutors of these Mysteries, who was torn in Pieces by Women, because he refused to † *communicate his Orgyes* to them; which others explained, by telling us, he has *castrated* himself upon Grief, for the Loss of his Wife.

Omitting many others of less Note, the next *Fanaticks* we meet with, of any Eminence, were the numerous Sects of *Hereticks* appearing in the five first Centuries of the *Christian Æra,* from *Simon Magus* and his Followers, to those of *Eutyches.* I have collected their Systems from infinite Reading, and comparing them with those of their Successors in the several Ages since, I find there are certain Bounds set even to the Irregularities of Human Thought, and those a great deal narrower than is commonly apprehended. For, as they all frequently interfere, even in their wildest Ravings; So there is one fundamental Point, wherein they are sure to meet, as Lines in a Center, and that is the *Community of Women:* Great were their Sollicitudes in this Matter, and they never fail'd of certain Articles in their Schemes of Worship, on purpose to establish it.

The last *Fanaticks* of Note, were those which started up in *Germany,* a little after the *Reformation* of *Luther;* Springing, as *Mushrooms* do at the *End of a Harvest;* Such were *John* of *Leyden, David George, Adam Neuster,* and many others; whose Visions and Revelations, always terminated in *leading about half a dozen Sisters, apiece,* and making That

* *Dionysia Brauronia.*
† *Vid. Photium in excerptis è Conone.*

Practice a fundamental Part of their System. For, Human Life is a continual Navigation, and, if we expect our *Vessels* to pass with Safety, thro' the Waves and Tempests of this fluctuating World, it is necessary to make a good Provision of the *Flesh*, as Sea-men lay in store of *Beef* for a long Voyage.

Now from this brief Survey of some Principal Sects, among the *Fanaticks*, in all Ages (having omitted the *Mahometans* and others, who might also help to confirm the Argument I am about) to which I might add several among our selves, such as the *Family of Love, Sweet Singers of Israel,* and the like: And from reflecting upon that fundamental Point in their Doctrines, about *Women,* wherein they have so unanimously agreed; I am apt to imagine, that the Seed or Principle, which has ever put Men upon *Visions* in Things *Invisible,* is of a Corporeal Nature: For the profounder Chymists inform us, that the Strongest *Spirits* may be extracted from *Human Flesh.* Besides, the Spinal Marrow, being nothing else but a Continuation of the Brain, must needs create a very free Communication between the Superior Faculties and those below: And thus the *Thorn in the Flesh* serves for a *Spur* to the *Spirit.* I think, it is agreed among Physicians, that nothing affects the Head so much, as a tentiginous Humor, repelled and elated to the upper Region, found by daily practice, to run frequently up into Madness. A very eminent Member of the Faculty, assured me, that when the *Quakers* first appeared, he seldom was without some Female Patients among them, for the *furor* ——— Persons of a visionary Devotion, either Men or Women, are in their Complexion, of all others, the most amorous: For, *Zeal* is frequently kindled from the same Spark with other Fires, and from inflaming Brotherly Love, will proceed to raise That of a Gallant. If we inspect into the usual Process of modern Courtship, we shall find it to consist in a devout Turn of the Eyes, called *Ogling;* an artificial Form of Canting and Whining by rote, every Interval, for want of other Matter, made up with a Shrug, or a Hum, a Sigh or a Groan; The Style compact of insignificant Words, Incoherences and Repetition. These, I take, to be the most accomplish'd Rules of

Address to a Mistress; and where are these performed with more Dexterity, than by the *Saints?* Nay, to bring this Argument yet closer, I have been informed by certain Sanguine Brethren of the first Class, that in the Height and *Orgasmus* of their Spiritual exercise it has been frequent with them * * * * * ; immediately after which, they found the *Spirit* to relax and flag of a sudden with the Nerves, and they were forced to hasten to a Conclusion. This may be farther Strengthened, by observing, with Wonder, how unaccountably all Females are attracted by Visionary or Enthusiastick Preachers, tho' never so contemptible in their *outward Men;* which is usually supposed to be done upon Considerations, purely Spiritual, without any carnal Regards at all. But I have Reason to think, the *Sex* hath certain Characteristicks, by which they form a truer Judgment of Human Abilities and Performings, than we our selves can possibly do of each other. Let That be as it will, thus much is certain, that however Spiritual Intrigues begin, they generally conclude like all others; they may branch upwards towards Heaven, but the Root is in the Earth. Too intense a Contemplation is not the Business of Flesh and Blood; it must by the necessary Course of Things, in a little Time, let go its Hold, and fall into *Matter.* Lovers, for the sake of Celestial Converse, are but another sort of *Platonicks,* who pretend to see Stars and Heaven in Ladies Eyes, and to look or think no lower; but the same *Pit* is provided for both; and they seem a perfect Moral to the Story of that Philosopher, who, while his Thoughts and Eyes were fixed upon the *Constellation,* found himself seduced by his *lower Parts* into a *Ditch.*

I had somewhat more to say upon this Part of the Subject; but the Post is just going, which forces me in great Haste to conclude,

                                                        SIR,

Pray, burn this Letter as soon   Yours, &c.
  as it comes to your Hands.

            F   I   N   I   S.

The Partridge-Bickerstaff Papers

Swift's literary persecution of the astrologer John Partridge constitutes one of the most hilarious and effective satiric campaigns in the history of our language. In creating and playing the role of Isaac Bickerstaff, Partridge's rival astrologer, and in the brilliant conceit involved in predicting and then reporting Partridge's death, Swift is at the height of his inventive powers. Beyond this, we see Swift here, as we do much later in the *Drapier's Letters*, flexibly conducting his satiric warfare with a superb exploitation of the enemy's counterattack; for Swift's final paper, *A Vindication of Isaac Bickerstaff, Esq.*, is a crowning blow which is made possible by Swift's alertness in seizing upon Partridge's absurd attempt to discredit Bickerstaff's report of his death.

In his time Swift courageously attacked a number of formidable antagonists, but Partridge cannot be numbered among them. By 1708, when Swift initiated his hoax, Partridge had already been lampooned by various fashionable wits. The folly of his reply to Swift further suggests that he was a foeman wretchedly unworthy of the elaborate attack directed against him by the most facile satirist of the age. There is, as well, some reason to wonder about Swift's gleeful assault upon a vulgar charlatan at a time when he was writing with great intensity upon religious problems and their implications for his nation's welfare. It should be remembered, however, that Partridge had at this time triumphantly survived the mockery of his enemies and was continuing to flourish as a leading practitioner of his dubious art. Originally a provincial cobbler, he had come to London many years earlier and, in the pursuit of his astrological calling, had profited not only from the credulity of the ignorant but from the patronage of King William himself.

Part of Swift's pleasure in attacking Partridge undoubtedly arose from the construction of a magnificently successful hoax. At the same time, there was a good deal about the astrologer to arouse Swift's genuine hatred. In *A Tale of a Tub* Swift's principal target is the false prophet who, whatever his vocation, "hath an Ambition to be Heard in a Crowd," and who, from his dubiously acquired eminence, dispenses bogus wisdom to a self-deluded public. Partridge fits the description well. To men of wit, he may have been merely a ludicrous spectacle; to a man of Swift's discernment, he may well have been a dangerous one. One source of Partridge's popularity, for example, lay in his virulent anti-Catholic bias, and from Swift's point of view this common prejudice had sinister implications. As Bickerstaff, Swift humorously lampoons Partridge's libels upon the Catholics, but in his more serious writings Swift repeatedly treats this same frightened hostility toward the Roman Church as an instrument upon which the enemies of the English Church and State can seize for purposes of impiety and subversion. For us today, Partridge survives chiefly as the outraged, impotent victim of Swift's devastating wit; but for Swift himself, who was ever the enemy of arrogance and hypocrisy, the destruction of Partridge may well have meant the removal of a genuinely malignant influence from the national scene.

Whatever Swift's motives, he created in Isaac Bickerstaff a famous figure. Fashionable London was delighted by Partridge's discomfiture, and the reigning wits joined in the fun by contributing their own obituary notices and elegies upon the death of Partridge. The Company of Stationers, on the assumption Partridge was dead, struck his name from their rolls and thus forced suspension of his almanac, *Merlinus Liberatus*. Richard Steele's first *Tatler*, in April, 1709, was attributed to Bickerstaff, and the Bickerstaff pseudonym appeared over contributions to that famous periodical even after Steele had relinquished the editorship. No jest of Swift's ever struck the public fancy more forcibly or more thoroughly served Swift's purpose. It is little wonder that, in later years, Alexander Pope linked Bickerstaff with Gulliver and the Drapier as the greatest of Swift's roles.

PREDICTIONS

for the Year 1708.

Wherein the Month, and Day of the Month, are
set down, the Persons named, and the great
Actions and Events of next Year particularly related as they will come to pass.

Written to prevent the People of England *from being
farther imposed on by vulgar Almanack-Makers.*

By ISAAC BICKERSTAFF, Esq;

HAVING long considered the gross Abuse of Astrology
in this Kingdom; upon debating the Matter with my self,
I could not possibly lay the Fault upon the Art, but upon
those gross Impostors, who set up to be the Artists. I know,
several learned Men have contended, that the whole is a Cheat;
that it is absurd and ridiculous to imagine, the Stars can have
any Influence at all upon human Actions, Thoughts, or Inclinations: And whoever hath not bent his Studies that Way,
may be excused for thinking so, when he sees in how wretched
a Manner this noble Art is treated, by a few mean illiterate
Traders between us and the Stars; who import a yearly Stock
of Nonsense, Lies, Folly, and Impertinence, which they offer to
the World as genuine from the Planets; although they descend
from no greater a Height than their own Brains.

I intend, in a short Time, to publish a large and rational
Defence of this Art; and, therefore, shall say no more in its
Justification at present, than that it hath been in all Ages de-

fended by many learned Men; and among the rest, by *Socrates* himself; whom I look upon as undoubtedly the wisest of uninspired Mortals: To which if we add, that those who have condemned this Art, although otherwise learned, having been such as either did not apply their Studies this Way; or at least did not succeed in their Applications; their Testimony will not be of much Weight to its Disadvantage, since they are liable to the common Objection of condemning what they did not understand.

Nor am I at all offended, or think it an Injury to the Art, when I see the common Dealers in it, the *Students in Astrology,* the *Philomaths,* and the rest of that Tribe, treated by wise Men with the utmost Scorn and Contempt: But I rather wonder, when I observe Gentlemen in the Country, rich enough to serve the Nation in Parliament, poring in *Partrige*'s Almanack, to find out the Events of the Year at Home and Abroad; not daring to propose a Hunting-Match, until *Gadbury,* or he, hath fixed the Weather.

I will allow either to the Two I have mentioned, or any other of the Fraternity, to be not only Astrologers, but Conjurers too; if I do not produce an Hundred Instances in all their Almanacks, to convince any reasonable Man, that they do not so much as understand Grammar and Syntax; that they are not able to spell any word out of the usual Road; nor even in their Prefaces to write common Sense, or intelligible *English*. Then, for their Observations and Predictions, they are such as will equally suit any Age, or Country in the World. *This Month a certain great Person will be threatened with Death, or Sickness.* This the News-Paper will tell them; for there we find at the End of the Year, that no Month passes without the Death of some Person of Note; and it would be hard, if it should be otherwise, when there are at least two Thousand Persons of Note in this Kingdom, many of them old; and the Almanack-maker has the Liberty of chusing the sickliest Season of the Year, where he may fix his Prediction. Again, *This Month an eminent Clergyman will be preferred;* of which there may be some Hundreds, Half of them with one

Foot in the Grave. Then, *Such a Planet in such a House shews great Machinations, Plots and Conspiracies, that may in Time be brought to Light:* After which, if we hear of any Discovery, the Astrologer gets the Honour; if not, his Prediction still stands good. And at last, *God preserve King* William *from all his open and secret Enemies, Amen.* When if the King should happen to have died, the Astrologer plainly foretold it; otherwise, it passeth but for the pious Ejaculation of a loyal Subject: Although it unluckily happened in some of their Almanacks, that poor King *William* was prayed for many Months after he was dead; because, it fell out that he died about the Beginning of the Year.

To mention no more of their impertinent Predictions: What have we to do with their Advertisements about *Pills, and Drinks for the Venereal Disease,* or their mutual Quarrels in Verse and Prose of *Whig* and *Tory?* wherewith the Stars have little to do.

Having long observed and lamented these, and a hundred other Abuses of this Art, too tedious to repeat; I resolved to proceed in a new Way; which I doubt not will be to the general Satisfaction of the Kingdom. I can this Year produce but a Specimen of what I design for the future; having employed most Part of my Time in adjusting and correcting the Calculations I made for some Years past; because I would offer nothing to the World of which I am not as fully satisfied, as that I am now alive. For these two last Years I have not failed in above one or two Particulars, and those of no very great Moment. I exactly foretold the Miscarriage at *Toulon,* with all its Particulars; and the Loss of Admiral *Shovel;* although I was mistaken as to the Day, placing that Accident about thirty six Hours sooner than it happened; but upon reviewing my Schemes, I quickly found the Cause of that Error. I likewise foretold the Battle at *Almanza* to the very Day and Hour, with the Loss on both Sides, and the Consequences thereof. All which I shewed to some Friends many Months before they happened; that is, I gave them Papers sealed up, to open at such a Time, after which they were at liberty to read them;

and there they found my Predictions true in every Article, except one or two, very minute.

As for the few following Predictions I now offer the World, I forebore to publish them, till I had perused the several Almanacks for the Year we are now entered upon: I found them all in the usual Strain, and I beg the Reader will compare their Manner with mine: And here I make bold to tell the World, that I lay the whole Credit of my Art upon the Truth of these Predictions; and I will be content that *Partrige,* and the rest of his Clan, may hoot me for a Cheat and Impostor, if I fail in any single Particular of Moment. I believe any Man, who reads this Paper, will look upon me to be at least a Person of as much Honesty and Understanding, as a common Maker of Almanacks. I do not lurk in the Dark; I am not wholly unknown in the World: I have set my Name at length, to be a Mark of Infamy to Mankind, if they shall find I deceive them.

In one Point I must desire to be forgiven; that I talk more sparingly of Home-Affairs. As it would be Imprudence to discover Secrets of State, so it might be dangerous to my Person: But in smaller Matters, and such as are not of publick Consequence, I shall be very free: And the Truth of my Conjectures will as much appear from these as the other. As for the most signal Events abroad in *France, Flanders, Italy* and *Spain,* I shall make no Scruple to predict them in plain Terms: Some of them are of Importance, and I hope, I shall seldom mistake the Day they will happen: Therefore, I think good to inform the Reader, that I all along make use of the *Old Stile* observed in *England;* which I desire he will compare with that of the News-Papers, at the Time they relate the Actions I mention.

I must add one Word more: I know it hath been the Opinion of several learned Persons, who think well enough of the true Art of Astrology, That the Stars do only *incline,* and not force the Actions or Wills of Men: And therefore, however I may proceed by right Rules, yet I cannot in Prudence so confidently assure that the Events will follow exactly as I predict them.

I hope, I have maturely considered this Objection, which in some Cases is of no little Weight. For Example: A Man may, by the Influence of an over-ruling Planet, be disposed or inclined to Lust, Rage, or Avarice; and yet by the Force of Reason overcome that evil Influence. And this was the Case of *Socrates:* But the great Events of the World usually depending upon Numbers of Men, it cannot be expected they should all unite to cross their Inclinations, from pursuing a general Design, wherein they unanimously agree. Besides, the Influence of the Stars reacheth to many Actions and Events, which are not any way in the Power of Reason; as Sickness, Death, and what we commonly call Accidents; with many more needless to repeat.

But now it is Time to proceed to my Predictions; which I have begun to calculate from the Time that the *Sun* enters into *Aries.* And this I take to be properly the Beginning of the natural Year. I pursue them to the Time that he enters *Libra,* or somewhat more, which is the busy Period of the Year. The Remainder I have not yet adjusted upon Account of several Impediments needless here to mention. Besides, I must remind the Reader again, that this is but a Specimen of what I design in succeeding Years to treat more at large, if I may have Liberty and Encouragement.

My first Prediction is but a Trifle; yet I will mention it, to shew how ignorant those sottish Pretenders to Astrology are in their own Concerns: It relates to *Partrige* the Almanack-Maker; I have consulted the Star of his Nativity by my own Rules, and find he will infallibly die upon the 29th of *March* next, about eleven at Night, of a raging Fever: Therefore I advise him to consider of it, and settle his Affairs in Time.

The Month of *APRIL* will be observable for the Death of many great Persons. On the 4th will die the Cardinal *de Noailles,* Archbishop of *Paris:* On the 11th the young Prince of *Asturias,* Son to the Duke of *Anjou:* On the 14th a great Peer of this Realm will die at his Country-House: On the 19th an old Layman of great Fame for Learning: And on the 23rd an eminent Goldsmith in *Lombard Street.* I could mention others, both at home and abroad, if I did not consider such Events of very little Use or Instruction to the Reader, or to the World.

As to publick Affairs: On the 7th of this Month, there will be an Insurrection in *Dauphine,* occasioned by the Oppressions of the People; which will not be quieted in some Months.

On the 15th will be a violent Storm on the South-East Coast of *France;* which will destroy many of their Ships, and some in the very Harbour.

The 19th will be famous for the Revolt of a whole Province or Kingdom, excepting one City; by which the Affairs of a certain Prince in the Alliance will take a better Face.

MAY, Against common Conjectures, will be no very busy Month in *Europe;* but very signal for the Death of the *Dauphine,* which will happen on the 7th, after a short Fit of Sickness, and grievous Torments with the Strangury. He dies less lamented by the Court than the Kingdom.

On the 9th a *Mareschal* of *France* will break his Leg by a Fall from his Horse. I have not been able to discover whether he will then die or not.

On the 11th will begin a most important Siege, which the Eyes of all *Europe* will be upon: I cannot be more particular; for in relating Affairs that so nearly concern the *Confederates,* and consequently this Kingdom; I am forced to confine my self, for several Reasons very obvious to the Reader.

On the 15th News will arrive of a very *surprizing Event,* than which nothing could be more unexpected.

On the 19th, three Noble Ladies of this Kingdom, will, against all Expectation, prove with Child, to the great Joy of their Husbands.

On the 23d, a famous Buffoon of the Play-House will die a ridiculous Death, suitable to his Vocation.

JUNE. This Month will be distinguished at home, by the utter dispersing of those ridiculous deluded Enthusiasts, commonly called the *Prophets;* occasioned chiefly by seeing the Time come, when many of their Prophecies were to be fulfilled; and then finding themselves deceived by contrary Events. It is indeed to be admired how any Deceiver can be so weak to foretel Things near at hand; when a very few Months must of Necessity discover the Imposture to all the World: In this Point less prudent than common Almanack-Makers, who are so wise to wander in Generals, talk dubiously, and leave to the Reader the Business of interpreting.

On the 1st of this Month a *French* General will be killed by a random Shot of a Cannon-Ball.

On the 6th a Fire will break out in the Suburbs of *Paris,* which will destroy above a thousand Houses; and seems to be the Foreboding of what will happen, to the Surprize of all *Europe,* about the end of the following Month.

On the 10th a great Battle will be fought, which will begin at four of the Clock in the Afternoon, and last till nine at Night with great Obstinacy, but no very decisive Event. I shall not name the Place, for the Reasons aforesaid; but the Commanders on each left Wing will be killed. ———— I see Bonfires and hear the Noise of Guns for a Victory.

On the 14th there will be a false Report of the *French* King's Death.

On the 20th Cardinal *Portocarero* will die of a Dissentery, with great Suspicion of Poison; but the Report of his Intention to revolt to King *Charles* will prove false.

JULY. The 6th of this Month a *certain General* will, by a glorious Action, recover the Reputation he lost by former Misfortunes.

On the 12th a *great Commander* will die a Prisoner in the Hands of his Enemies.

On the 14th a shameful Discovery will be made of a *French* Jesuit giving Poison to a great Foreign General; and when he is put to the Torture, will make wonderful Discoveries.

In short, this will prove a Month of great Action, if I might have Liberty to relate the Particulars.

At home, the Death of an old famous Senator will happen on the 15th at his Country-House, worn with Age and Diseases.

But that which will make this Month memorable to all Posterity, is the Death of the *French* King *Lewis* the Fourteenth, after a Week's Sickness at *Marli;* which will happen on the 29th, about six a-Clock in the Evening. It seems to be an Effect of the Gout in his Stomach, followed by a Flux. And in three Days after Monsieur *Chamillard* will follow his Master, dying suddenly of an Apoplexy.

In this Month likewise an *Ambassador* will die in *London;* but I cannot assign the Day.

AUGUST. The affairs of *France* will seem to suffer no Change for a while under the Duke of *Burgundy*'s Administration. But the Genius that animated the whole Machine being gone, will be the Cause of mighty Turns and Revolutions in the following Year. The new King makes yet little Change either in the Army or the Ministry; but the Libels against his Grandfather, that fly about his very Court, give him Uneasiness.

I see an Express in mighty Haste, with Joy and Wonder in his Looks, arriving by the Break of Day, on the 26th of this Month, having travelled in three Days a prodigious Journey by Land and Sea. In the Evening I hear Bells and Guns, and see the Blazing of a Thousand Bonfires.

A young Admiral, of noble Birth, does likewise this Month gain immortal Honour, by a great Atchievement.

The Affairs of *Poland* are this Month entirely settled: *Augustus* resigns his Pretensions, which he had again taken up for some Time: *Stanislaus* is peaceably possessed of the Throne; and the King of *Sweden* declares for the Emperor.

I cannot omit one particular Accident here at home; that near the End of this Month, much Mischief will be done at *Bartholomew* Fair, by the Fall of a Booth.

SEPTEMBER. This Month begins with a very surprizing Fit of frosty Weather, which will last near twelve Days.

The Pope having long languished last Month; the Swellings in his Legs breaking, and the Flesh mortifying, will die on the 11th Instant: And in three Weeks Time, after a mighty Contest, be succeeded by a Cardinal of the *Imperial* Faction, but Native of *Tuscany,* who is now about Sixty-One Years old.

The *French* Army acts now wholly on the Defensive, strongly fortified in their Trenches; and the young *French* King sends Overtures for a Treaty of Peace, by the Duke of *Mantua;* which, because it is a Matter of State that concerns us here at home, I shall speak no farther of it.

I shall add but one Prediction more, and that in mystical Terms, which shall be included in a Verse out of *Virgil.*

> *Alter erit jam Tethys, & altera quæ vehat Argo,*
> *Dilectos Heroas.*

Upon the 25th Day of this Month, the fulfilling of this Prediction will be manifest to every Body.

This is the farthest I have proceeded in my Calculations for the present Year. I do not pretend, that these are all the great Events which will happen in this Period; but that those I have set down will infallibly come to pass. It may, perhaps, still be objected, why I have not spoke more particularly of Affairs at home; or of the Success of our Armies abroad, which I might, and could very largely have done. But those in Power have wisely discouraged Men from meddling in publick Concerns; and I was resolved, by no Means, to give the least Offence. This I will venture to say; that it will be a glorious Campaign for the Allies; wherein the *English* Forces, both by Sea and Land, will have their full Share of Honour: That Her Majesty Queen Anne will continue in Health and Prosperity: And that no ill Accident will arrive to any in the chief Ministry.

As to the particular Events I have mentioned, the Readers may judge by the fulfilling of them, whether I am of the Level with common Astrologers; who, with an old paultry Cant, and a few Pot-hooks for Planets to amuse the Vulgar, have, in my Opinion, too long been suffered to abuse the World. But an honest Physician ought not to be despised, because there are such Things as Mountebanks. I hope, I have some Share of Reputation, which I would not willingly forfeit for a Frolick, or Humour: And I believe no Gentleman, who reads this Paper, will look upon it to be of the same Cast, or Mold, with the common Scribbles that are every Day hawked about. My Fortune hath placed me above the little Regard of writing for a few Pence, which I neither value nor want: Therefore, let not wise Men too hastily condemn this Essay, intended for a good Design, to cultivate and improve an antient Art, long in Disgrace by having fallen into mean unskilful Hands. A little Time will determine whether I have deceived others, or my self; and I think it is no very unreasonable Request, that Men would please to suspend their Judgments till then. I was once of the Opinion with those who despise all Predictions from the Stars, till in the Year 1686, a Man of Quality shewed me, written in his *Album,* that the most learned Astronomer Captain *Hally,* assured him, he would never believe any thing of the Stars Influence, if there were not a great Revolution in *England* in the Year 1688. Since that Time I began to have other Thoughts; and after Eighteen Years diligent Study and Application, I think I have no Reason to repent of my Pains. I shall detain the Reader no longer than to let him know, that the Account I design to give of next Year's Events, shall take in the principle Affairs that happen in *Europe:* And if I be denied the Liberty of offering it to my own Country, I shall appeal to the Learned World, by publishing it in *Latin,* and giving Order to have it printed in *Holland.*

THE

ACCOMPLISHMENT

OF THE FIRST OF

Mr. *Bickerstaff*'s PREDICTIONS.

BEING AN

ACCOUNT

OF THE

Death of Mr. *Partrige*, the Almanack-maker,
upon the 29th Inst.

In a Letter to a Person of Honour.

Written in the Year 1708.

My LORD,

IN Obedience to your Lordship's Commands, as well as to
satisfy my own Curiosity, I have for some Days past enquired
constantly after *Partrige* the Almanack-maker; of whom it was
foretold in Mr. *Bickerstaff*'s Predictions, published about a
Month ago, that he should die the 29th Instant, about Eleven
at Night, of a raging Fever. I had some Sort of Knowledge of
him when I was employed in the Revenue; because he used
every Year to present me with his Almanack, as he did other
Gentlemen upon the score of some little Gratuity we gave him.
I saw him accidentally once or twice about ten Days before

he died; and observed he began very much to droop and languish, although I hear his Friends did not seem to apprehend him in any Danger. About two or three Days ago he grew ill; was confined first to his Chamber, and in a few Hours after to his Bed; where Dr. *Case* and Mrs. *Kirleus** were sent for to visit, and to prescribe to him. Upon this Intelligence I sent thrice every Day one Servant or other to enquire after his Health; and Yesterday about four in the Afternoon, Word was brought me that he was past Hopes: Upon which I prevailed with my self to go and see him; partly out of Commiseration, and I confess, partly out of Curiosity. He knew me very well, seemed surprized at my Condescension, and made me Compliments upon it as well as he could in the Condition he was. The People about him said, he had been for some Hours delirious; but when I saw him, he had his Understanding as well as ever I knew, and spoke strong and hearty, without any seeming Uneasiness or Constraint. After I had told him I was sorry to see him in those melancholly Circumstances, and said some other Civilities, suitable to the Occasion; I desired him to tell me freely and ingenuously whether the Predictions Mr. *Bickerstaff* had published relating to his Death, had not too much affected and worked on his Imagination. He confessed he had often had it in his Head, but never with much Apprehension till about a Fortnight before; since which Time it had the perpetual Possession of his Mind and Thoughts; and he did verily believe was the true natural Cause of his present Distemper: For, said he, I am thoroughly persuaded, and I think I have very good Reasons, that Mr. *Bickerstaff* spoke altogether by guess, and knew no more what will happen this Year than I did my self. I told him his Discourse surprized me; and I would be glad he were in a State of Health to be able to tell me what Reason he had to be convinced of Mr. *Bickerstaff*'s Ignorance. He replied, I am a poor ignorant Fellow, bred to a mean Trade; yet I have Sense enough to know, that all Pretences of foretelling by

---

* *Two famous Quacks at that Time in* London.

Astrology are Deceits; for this manifest Reason, because the Wise and Learned, who can only judge whether there be any Truth in this Science, do all unanimously agree to laugh at and despise it; and none but the poor ignorant Vulgar give it any Credit, and that only upon the Word of such silly Wretches as I and my Fellows, who can hardly write or read. I then asked him, why he had not calculated his own Nativity, to see whether it agreed with *Bickerstaff*'s Predictions? At which he shook his Head, and said, O! Sir, this is no Time for jesting, but for repenting those Fooleries, as I do now from the very Bottom of my Heart. By what I can gather from you, said I, the Observations and Predictions you printed with your Almanacks were meer Impositions upon the People. He replied, if it were otherwise, I should have the less to answer for. We have a common Form for all those Things: As to foretelling the Weather, we never meddle with that, but leave it to the Printer, who takes it out of any old Almanack as he thinks fit: The rest was my own Invention to make my Almanack sell; having a Wife to maintain, and no other Way to get my Bread; for mending old Shoes is a poor Livelihood: And (added he, sighing) I wish I may not have done more Mischief by my Physick than my Astrology; although I had some good Receipts from my Grandmother, and my own Compositions were such, as I thought could at least do no Hurt.

I had some other Discourse with him, which now I cannot call to Mind; and I fear I have already tired your Lordship. I shall only add one Circumstance, That on his Death-Bed he declared himself a Nonconformist, and had a fanatick Preacher to be his spiritual Guide. After half an Hour's Conversation, I took my Leave, being almost stifled by the Closeness of the Room. I imagined he could not hold out long; and therefore withdrew to a little Coffee-House hard by, leaving a Servant at the House with Orders to come immediately, and tell me, as near as he could, the Minute when *Partrige* should expire, which was not above two Hours after; when looking upon my Watch, I found it to be above five Minutes after Seven: By which it is clear, that Mr. *Bickerstaff* was mistaken almost four Hours in his Calculation. In the other Circumstances he was exact enough. But whether he hath not been the Cause of this poor Man's Death, as well as the Predictor, may be very reasonably disputed. However, it must be confessed, the Matter is odd enough, whether we should endeavour to account for it by Chance or the Effect of Imagination: For my own Part, although I believe no Man hath less Faith in these Matters; yet I shall wait with some Impatience, and not without Expectation, the fulfilling of Mr. *Bickerstaff*'s second Prediction; that the Cardinal *de Noailles* is to die upon the 4th of *April;* and if that should be verified as exactly as this of poor *Partrige;* I must own, I should be wholly surprized, and at a Loss; and should infallibly expect the Accomplishment of all the rest.

'Squire BICKERSTAFF Detected:*

OR, THE

Astrological Impostor Convicted.

By JOHN PARTRIGE,
Student in PHYSICK and ASTROLOGY.

IT is hard, my dear Countrymen of these united Nations: It is very hard, that a *Briton* Born, a Protestant Astrologer, a Man of Revolution Principles, an Asserter of the Liberty and Property of the People, should cry out, in vain, for Justice against a *Frenchman,* a Papist, and an illiterate Pretender to Science; that would blast my Reputation, most inhumanly bury me alive, and defraud my Native Country of those Services, which in my †*double Capacity,* I daily offer the Publick.

What great Provocations I have received, let the impartial Reader judge, and how unwillingly, even in my own Defence, I now enter the Lists against Falshood, Ignorance, and Envy: But I am exasperated at length, to drag out this *Cacus* from the Den of Obscurity where he lurks, detect him by the Light

---

* The following Piece, under the Name of John Partrige, was written by that famous Poet Nicholas Row, Esq; and therefore being upon the same Subject, although not by the same Author, we have thought fit to publish it, that the Reader may have the whole Account together.

[This attribution is made by Faulkner in his 1735 edition of Swift's *Works,* which the present text follows. Swift allowed the piece to be published in the 1727 *Miscellanies,* but added a note in which he disavowed authorship. Whether or not it is by Swift, the work is generally viewed as an important Bickerstaffian document and, at the least, as a specimen of the high spirits with which others joined Swift in the sport of baiting Partridge.]

† Physician and Astrologer.

of those Stars he has so impudently traduced, and shew there is not a Monster in the Skies so pernicious and malevolent to Mankind, as an ignorant Pretender to Physick and Astrology, I shall not directly fall on the many gross Errors, nor expose the notorious Absurdities of this prostituted Libeller, till I have let the learned World fairly into the Controversy depending, and then leave the unprejudiced to judge of the Merits and Justice of my Cause.

It was towards the Conclusion of the Year 1707, when an impudent Pamphlet crept into the World, intituled, *Predictions,* &c. *by* Isaac Bickerstaff, *Esq;* Among the many arrogant Assertions laid down by that lying Spirit of Divination, he was pleased to pitch on the Cardinal *de Noailles,* and my self, among many other eminent and illustrious Persons, that were to die within the Compass of the ensuing Year; and peremptorily fixes the Month, Day, and Hour of our Deaths: This, I think, is sporting with great Men, and publick Spirits, to the Scandal of Religion, and Reproach of Power; and if sovereign Princes, and Astrologers, must make Diversion for the Vulgar; why then, farewel, say I, to all Governments, Ecclesiastical and Civil. But, I thank my better Stars, I am alive to confront this false and audacious Predictor, and to make him rue the Hour he ever affronted a Man of Science and Resentment. The Cardinal may take what Measures he pleases with him; as his Excellency is a Foreigner, and a Papist, he has no Reason to rely on me for his Justification; I shall only assure the World he is alive; but as he was bred to Letters, and is Master of a Pen, let him use it in his own Defence. In the mean Time, I shall present the Publick with a faithful Narrative of the ungenerous Treatment, and hard Usage, I have received from the virulent Papers, and malicious Practices of this pretended Astrologer.

A true and impartial Account of the Proceedings of *Isaac Bickerstaff*, Esq; against Me *John Partrige*, Student in Physick and Astrology.

THE 28th of *March, Anno Dom.* 1708, being the Night this sham Prophet had so impudently fixed for my last, which made little Impression on my self; but I cannot answer for my whole Family; for my Wife, with a Concern more than usual, prevailed on me to take somewhat to sweat for a Cold; and, between the Hours of Eight and Nine, to go to Bed: The Maid, as she was warming my Bed, with a Curiosity natural to young Wenches, runs to the Window, and asks of one passing the Street, who the Bell tolled for? Doctor *Partrige*, says he, the famous Almanack-maker, who died suddenly this Evening: The poor Girl provoked, told him, he lied like a Rascal; the other very sedately replied, the Sexton had so informed him, and if false, he was to blame for imposing upon a Stranger. She asked a Second, and a Third as they passed; and every one was in the same Tone. Now, I do not say these were Accomplices to a certain Astrological 'Squire, and that one *Bickerstaff* might be sauntring thereabouts; because I will assert nothing here, but what I dare attest, for plain Matter of Fact. My wife, at this, fell into a violent Disorder; and I must own, I was a little discomposed at the Oddness of the Accident. In the mean Time, one knocks at my Door; *Betty* runs down, and opening, finds a sober, grave Person; who modestly enquires, if this was Dr. *Partrige*'s? She taking him for some cautious City-Patient, that came at that Time for Privacy, shews him into the Dining-Room. As soon as I could compose my self, I went to him, and was surprized to find my Gentleman mounted on a Table, with a Two-foot Rule in his Hand, measuring my Walls, and taking the Dimensions of the Room. Pray, Sir, says I, not to interrupt you, have you any Business with me? Only, Sir, replies he, order the Girl to bring me a better Light, for this is but a very dim one. Sir, says I, my Name is *Partrige:* Oh! the Doctor's Brother, belike, cries he; the Stair-Case, I believe, and these two Apartments hung in close Mourning, will be sufficient, and only a Strip of Bays round the other Rooms. The Doctor must needs die rich, he had great Dealings in his Way for many Years; if he had no Family-Coat, you had as good use the Scutcheons of the Company; they are as showish, and will look as magnificent as if he was descended from the Blood-Royal. With that, I assumed a greater Air of Authority, and demanded who employed him, or how he came there? Why, I was sent, Sir, by the Company of Undertakers, says he, and they were employed by the honest Gentleman, who is Executor to the good Doctor departed; and our rascally Porter, I believe, is fallen fast asleep with the black Cloath, and Sconces; or he had been here, and we might have been tacking up by this Time. Sir, says I, pray be advised by a Friend, and make the best of your Speed out of my Doors, for I hear my Wife's Voice, (which, by the By, is pretty distinguishable) and in that Corner of the Room stands a good Cudgel, which some Body has felt before now; if that light in her Hands, and she know the Business you came about; without consulting the Stars, I can assure you it will be employed very much to the Detriment of your Person. Sir, cries he, bowing with great Civility, I perceive, extream Grief for the Loss of the Doctor disorders you a little at present; but early in the Morning I will wait on you, with all necessary Materials. Now I mention no Mr. *Bickerstaff;* nor do I say, that a certain Star-gazing 'Squire has been a playing my Executor before his Time; but I leave the World to judge, and if it puts Things and Things fairly together, it will not be much wide of the Mark.

Well, once more I get my Doors closed, and prepare for Bed, in Hopes of a little Repose, after so many ruffling Adventures; just as I was putting out my Light in order to it, another bounces as hard as he can knock; I open the Window, and ask **who** is there, and what he wants? I am *Ned,* the Sexton, replies

he, and come to know whether the Doctor left any Orders for
a Funeral Sermon; and where he is to be laid, and whether
his Grave is to be plain or bricked? Why, Sirrah, says I, you
know me well enough; you know I am not dead, and how dare
you affront me after this Manner? Alack-a-day, Sir, replies the
Fellow, why it is in Print, and the whole Town knows you are
dead; why, there is Mr. *White* the Joiner, is but fitting Screws
to your Coffin, he will be here with it in an Instant; he was
afraid you would have wanted it before this Time. Sirrah,
Sirrah, says I, you shall know To-morrow to your Cost that I
am alive, and alive like to be. Why, it is strange, Sir, says he,
you should make such a Secret of your Death, to us that are
your Neighbours; it looks as if you had a Design to defraud
the Church of its Dues; and let me tell you, for one that has
lived so long by the Heavens, that it is unhandsomely done.
Hist, hist, says another Rogue, that stood by him, away
Doctor into your Flanel Gear as fast as you can; for here is a
whole Pack of Dismals coming to you, with their black
Equipage; and how indecent will it look for you to stand
frightening Folks at your Window, when you should have been
in your Coffin this three Hours? In short, what with Undertakers, Embalmers, Joiners, Sextons, and your damned Elegy-
hawkers, upon a late Practitioner in Physick and Astrology, I
got not one Wink of Sleep that Night, nor scarce a Moment's
Rest ever since. Now, I doubt not but this villainous 'Squire
has the Impudence to assert, that these are entirely Strangers
to him; he, good Man, knows nothing of the Matter; and
honest *Isaac Bickerstaff,* I warrant you, is more a Man of
Honour, than to be an Accomplice with a Pack of Rascals,
that walk the Streets on Nights, and disturb good People in
their Beds. But he is out, if he thinks the whole World is
blind; for there is one *John Partrige* can smell a Knave as far
as *Grub-street;* although he lies in the most exalted Garret, and
writes himself 'Squire: But I will keep my Temper, and
proceed in the Narration.

I could not stir out of Doors for the Space of three Months
after this, but presently one comes up to me in the Street, Mr.

Partrige, that Coffin you was last buried in, I have not been yet paid for. Doctor, cries another Dog, how do you think People can live by making of Graves for nothing? Next Time you die, you may even toll out the Bell your self for *Ned.* A third Rogue tips me by the Elbow, and wonders how I have the Conscience to sneak abroad, without paying my Funeral Expences. Lord, says one, I durst have swore that was honest Dr. *Partrige,* my old Friend; but poor Man, he is gone. I beg your Pardon, says another, you look so like my old Acquaintance that I used to consult on some private Occasions; but alack, he is gone the Way of all Flesh. Look, look, look, cries a Third, after a competent Space of staring at me; would not one think our Neighbour the Almanack-maker, was crept out of his Grave, to take another Peep at the Stars in this World, and shew how much he is improved in Fortune-telling by having taken a Journey to the other?

Nay, the very Reader of our Parish, a good, sober, discreet Person, has sent two or three Times for me to come and be buried decently, or send him sufficient Reasons to the contrary; or, if I have been interred in any other Parish, to produce my Certificate as the Act requires. My poor Wife is almost run distracted with being called Widow *Partrige,* when she knows it is false; and once a Term she is cited into the Court, to take out Letters of Administration. But the greatest Grievance is, a paultry Quack, that takes up my Calling just under my Nose, and in his printed *Directions* with *N. B.* ☞ says he lives in the House of the late ingenious Mr. *Partrige,* an eminent Practitioner in Leather, Physick, and Astrology.

But to shew how far the wicked Spirit of Envy, Malice and Resentment can hurry some Men; my nameless old Persecutor had provided me a Monument at the Stone-Cutter's, and would have it erected in the Parish-Church; and this Piece of notorious and expensive Villainy had actually succeeded, if I had not used my utmost Interest with the Vestry, where it was carried at last but by two Voices, that I am still alive That Stratagem failing, out comes a long sable Elegy, bedecked with Hour-glasses, Mattocks, Sculls, Spades and Skeletons, with an Epitaph as confidently written to abuse me, and my Profession, as if I had been under Ground these twenty Years.

And after such barbarous Treatment as this, can the World blame me, when I ask, What is become of the Freedom of an *Englishman?* And where is the Liberty and Property, that my *old glorious* Friend came over to assert? We have drove Popery out of the Nation, and sent Slavery to foreign Climes. The Arts only remain in Bondage; when a Man of Science and Character shall be openly insulted in the Midst of the many useful Services he is daily paying the Publick. Was it ever heard, even in *Turky* or *Algiers,* that a State-Astrologer was bantered out of his Life by an ignorant Impostor, or bawled out of the World by a Pack of villainous deep-mouthed Hawkers? Though I print Almanacks, and publish Advertisements; although I produce Certificates under the Ministers and Church-Wardens Hands, I am alive, and attest the same on Oath at Quarter-Sessions; out comes *A full and true Relation of the Death and Interment of* JOHN PARTRIDGE; Truth is bore down, Attestations neglected, the Testimony of sober Persons despised, and a Man is looked upon by his Neighbours, as if he had been seven Years dead, and is buried alive in the Midst of his Friends and Acquaintance.

Now can any Man of common Sense think it consistent with the Honour of my Profession, and not much beneath the Dignity of a Philosopher, to stand bawling before his own Door ——— Alive! Alive! Ho! The famous Dr. *Partrige!* No Counterfeit, but all alive! ——— As if I had the twelve Celestial Monsters of the *Zodiack* to shew within, or was forced for a Livelihood to turn Retailer to *May* and *Bartholo-mew* Fairs. Therefore, if Her Majesty would but graciously be pleased to think a Hardship of this Nature worthy Her Royal Consideration; and the next Parliament, in their great Wisdom, cast but an Eye towards the deplorable Case of their old *Philomath,* that annually bestows his poetical good Wishes on them; I am sure there is one *Isaac Bickerstaff,* Esq; would soon be trussed up for his bloody Predictions, and putting good Subjects in Terror of their Lives: And that, henceforward, to murder a Man by Way of Prophecy, and bury him in a printed Letter, either to a Lord or Commoner, shall as legally entitle him to the present Possession of *Tyburn,* as if he robbed on the Highway, or cut your Throat in Bed.

I shall demonstrate to the Judicious, that *France* and *Rome,* are at the Bottom of this horrid Conspiracy against me; and that *Culprit* aforesaid, is a *Popish* Emissary, has paid his Visits to St. *Germains,* and is now in the Measures of *Lewis* XIV. That in attempting my Reputation, there is a general Massacre of Learning designed in these Realms: And through my Sides, there is a Wound given to all the Protestant Almanack-makers in the Universe.

Vinat Regina.

A

VINDICATION

O F

Isaac Bickerstaff, Esq;

A G A I N S T

What is objected to him by Mr. *Partrige,* is his
Almanack for the present Year 1709.

By the said ISAAC BICKERSTAFF, *Esq;*
Written in the YEAR 1709.

MR. *Partrige* hath been lately pleased to treat me after a
very rough Manner, in *that which is called,* His Almanack for
the present Year: Such Usage is very undecent from *one
Gentleman to another,* and doth not at all contribute to the
Discovery of Truth; which ought to be the great End in all
Disputes of the *Learned.* To call a Man *Fool* and *Villain,* and
impudent Fellow, only for differing from him in a Point
meerly speculative, is, in my humble Opinion, a very improper Stile for a Person of *his Education.* I appeal to the
learned World, whether in my last Year's Predictions, I gave
him the least Provocation for such unworthy Treatment.
Philosophers have differed in all Ages, but the discreetest
among them have always differed as became Philosophers.
Scurrility and Passion, in a Controversy among *Scholars,* is
just so much of nothing to the Purpose; and, at best, a tacit
Confession of a weak Cause: My Concern is not so much for
my own Reputation, as that of the *Republick of Letters,*
which Mr. *Partrige* hath endeavoured to wound through my

Sides. If Men of publick Spirit must be superciliously treated
for their ingenuous Attempts; how will true useful Knowledge
be ever advanced? I wish Mr. *Partrige* knew the Thoughts
which *foreign Universities* have conceived of his ungenerous
Proceedings with me; but I am too tender of his Reputation
to publish them to the World. That Spirit of Envy and Pride,
which blasts so many rising Genius's in our Nation, is yet
unknown among *Professors* abroad: The Necessity of justifying
my self, will excuse my Vanity, when I tell the Reader, that I
have near an Hundred *honorary* Letters from several Parts of
Europe, (some as far as *Muscovy*) in Praise of my Performance.
Besides several others, which, as I have been credibly informed,
were opened in the Post-Office, and never sent me.* It is true,
the *Inquisition* in *Portugal* was pleased to burn my Predictions,
and condemn the Author and Readers of them; but, I hope, at
the same Time, it will be considered in how deplorable a State
Learning lies at present in that Kingdom: And with the
profoundest Veneration for *crowned Heads*, I will presume to
add; that it a little concerned *his Majesty of Portugal*, to
interpose his Authority in Behalf of a *Scholar* and a *Gentleman*, the Subject of a Nation with which he is now in so
strict an Alliance. But, the other Kingdoms and States of
Europe have treated me with more Candour and Generosity.
If I had leave to print the *Latin* Letters transmitted to me
from foreign Parts, they would fill a Volume, and be a full
Defence against all that Mr. *Partrige*, or his Accomplices of the
Portugal Inquisition, will be ever able to object; who, by the
way, are the only Enemies my Predictions have ever met with
at home or abroad. But, I hope, I know better what is due to
the Honour of a *learned Correspondence*, in so tender a Point.
Yet, some of those illustrious Persons will, perhaps, excuse me
for transcribing a Passage or two in my own Vindication. The†
most learned Monsieur *Leibnitz* thus addresseth to me his third

---

* *This is Fact, as the Author was assured by Sir* Paul Methuen, *then
Ambassador to that Crown.*

† *The Quotations here inserted, are in Imitation of Dr.* Bentley, *in
some Part of the famous Controversy between him and* Charles Boyle,
Esq; afterwards Earl of Orrery.

Letter: *Illustrissimo Bickerstaffio Astrologiæ Instauratori,* &c. Monsieur *le Clerc* quoting my Predictions in a Treatise he published last Year, is pleased to say, *Ità nuperime Bicker-staffius magnum illud Angliæ sidus.* Another great Professor writing of me, has these Words: *Bickerstaffius, nobilis Anglus, Astrologorum hujusce Seculi facilè Princeps.* Signior *Maglia-becchi,* the *Great Duke*'s famous Library-keeper, spends almost his whole Letter in Compliments and Praises. It is true, the renowned *Professor* of Astronomy at *Utrecht,* seems to differ from me in one Article; but it is after the modern Manner that becomes a Philosopher; as, *Pace tanti viri dixerim:* And, *Page* 55, he seems to lay the Error upon the Printer, (as indeed it ought) and says, *vel forsan error Typographi, cum alioquin Bickerstaffius vir doctissimus,* &c.

If Mr. *Partrige* had followed these Examples in the Controversy between us, he might have spared me the Trouble of justifying my self in so publick a Manner. I believe few Men are readier to own their Errors than I, or more thankful to those who will please to inform him of them. But it seems this Gentleman, instead of encouraging the Progress of his own Art, is pleased to look upon all attempts of that Kind, as an Invasion of his Province. He hath been indeed so wise, to make no Objection against the Truth of my Predictions, except in one single Point, relating to himself: And to demonstrate how much Men are blinded by their own Partiality; I do solemnly assure the Reader, that he is the *only* Person from whom I ever heard that Objection offered; which Consideration alone, I think, will take off all its Weight.

With my utmost Endeavours, I have not been able to trace above two Objections ever made against the Truth of my last Year's Prophecies: The first is of a *French* Man, who was pleased to publish to the World, that *the Cardinal* de Noailles *was still alive, notwithstanding the pretended Prophecy of Monsieur* Biquerstaffe: But how far a *French* Man, *a Papist,* and an *Enemy* is to be believed, in his own Cause, against an *English Protestant,* who is *true to the Government,* I shall leave to the candid and impartial Reader.

The other Objection, is the unhappy Occasion of this Discourse; and relates to an Article in my Predictions, which foretold the Death of Mr. *Partrige* to happen on *March* 29, 1708. This he is pleased to contradict absolutely in the Almanack he hath published for the present Year; and in that ungentlemanly Manner, (pardon the Expression) as I have above related. In that Work, he very roundly asserts, That he *is not only now alive, but was likewise alive upon that very* 29*th of* March, *when I had foretold* he *should die*. This is the Subject of the present Controversy between us; which I design to handle with all Brevity, Perspicuity, and Calmness: In this Dispute, I am sensible, the Eyes not only of *England*, but of all *Europe*, will be upon us: And the *Learned* in every Country will, I doubt not, take Part on that Side where they find most Appearance of Reason and Truth.

Without entering into Criticisms of *Chronology* about the Hour of his Death; I shall only prove, that Mr. *Partrige* is not alive. And my first Argument is thus: Above a Thousand Gentlemen having bought his Almanacks for this Year, meerly to find what he said against me; at every Line they read, they would lift up their Eyes, and cry out, betwixt Rage and Laughter, *They were sure no Man* alive *ever writ such damned Stuff as this*. Neither did I hear that Opinion disputed: So that Mr. *Partrige* lies under a *Dilemma*, either of disowning his Almanack, or allowing himself to be *no Man alive*. But now, if an *uninformed* Carcass walks still about, and is pleased to call it self *Partrige*; Mr. *Bickerstaff* does not think himself any way answerable for that. Neither had the said Carcass any Right to beat the poor Boy, who happened to pass by it in the Street, crying, *A full and true Account of Dr.* Partrige's *Death*, &c. Secondly, Mr. *Partrige* pretends to tell Fortunes, and recover stolen Goods; which all the Parish says he must do by conversing with the Devil, and other evil Spirits: And no wise Man will ever allow he could converse personally with either, till after he was dead. Thirdly, I will plainly prove him to be dead, out of his own Almanack for this Year, and from the very Passage which he produceth to make us think him alive. He there says, *He is not only* now *alive, but was also alive upon that very* 29*th of* March, *which I foretold* he *should die on:* By this, he declares his Opinion, that a Man may be alive *now,* who was not alive a Twelve-month ago. And, indeed, there lies the Sophistry of his Argument. He dares not assert, he was alive ever since the 29th of *March,* but that he *is now alive, and was so on that Day:* I grant the latter, for he did not die till Night, as appears by the printed Account of his Death, in a *Letter to a Lord;* and whether he be since revived, I leave the World to judge. This, indeed, is perfect cavilling, and I am ashamed to dwell any longer upon it.

Fourthly, I will appeal to Mr. *Partrige* himself, whether it be probable I could have been so indiscreet, to begin my Predictions with the *only* Falshood that ever was pretended to be in them; and this is an Affair at Home, where I had so many Opportunities to be exact; and must have given such Advantages against me to a Person of Mr. *Partrige*'s Wit and Learning, who, if he could possibly have raised one single Objection more against the Truth of my Prophecies, would hardly have spared me.

And here I must take Occasion to reprove the above-mentioned Writer of the Relation of Mr. *Partrige*'s Death, in a *Letter to a Lord;* who was pleased to tax me with a Mistake of *four whole Hours* in my Calculation of that Event. I must confess, this Censure, pronounced with an Air of Certainty, in a Matter that so nearly concerned me, and by a *grave judicious Author,* moved me not a little. But although I was at that Time out of Town, yet several of my Friends, whose Curiosity had led them to be exactly informed, (for as to my Part, having no doubt at all in the Matter, I never once thought of it,) assured me I computed to something under half an Hour; which (I speak my private Opinion) is an Error of no very great Magnitude, that Men should raise Clamour about it. I shall only say, it would not be amiss, if that Author would henceforth be more tender of other Mens Reputation as well as his own. It is well there were no more

Mistakes of that Kind; if there had, I presume he would have told me of them with as little Ceremony.

There is one Objection against Mr. *Partrige*'s Death, which I have sometimes met with, although indeed very slightly offered; That he still continues to write Almanacks. But this is no more than what is common to all of that Profession; *Gadbury, Poor Robin, Dove, Wing,* and several others, do yearly publish their Almanacks, although several of them have been dead since before the *Revolution*. Now the natural Reason of this I take to be, that whereas it is the Privilege of Authors, *to live after their Death;* Almanack-makers are alone excluded; because their Dissertations treating only upon the Minutes as they pass, become useless as those go off. In consideration of which, *Time,* whose *Registers* they are, gives them a Lease in Reversion, to continue their Works after their Death.

I should not have given the Publick or my self the Trouble of this Vindication, if my Name had not been made use of by several Persons, to whom I never lent it; one of which, a few Days ago, was pleased to father on me a new Set of Predictions. But I think these are Things too serious to be trifled with. It grieved me to the Heart, when I saw my Labours, which had cost me so much Thought and Watching, bawled about by common Hawkers, which I only intended for the weighty Consideration of the gravest Persons. This prejudiced the World so much at first, that several of my Friends had the Assurance to ask me, Whether I were in jest? To which I only answered coldly, *That the Event will shew.* But it is the Talent of our Age and Nation, to turn Things of the greatest Importance into Ridicule. When the End of the Year had *verified all my Predictions;* out comes Mr. *Partrige*'s Almanack, disputing the Point of his Death; so that I am employed, like the General who was forced to kill his Enemies twice over, whom a *Necromancer* had raised to Life. If Mr. *Partrige* hath practised the same Experiment upon himself, and be again alive; long may he continue so; but that doth not in the least contradict my Veracity: For I think I have clearly proved, by *invincible Demonstration,* that he died at farthest within half an Hour of the Time I foretold; and not four Hours sooner, as the above-mentioned Author, in his Letter to a Lord, hath maliciously suggested, with Design to blast my Credit, by charging me with so gross a Mistake.

An Argument against
Abolishing Christianity

deism?

Swift tells us that the work which has come to be referred to, for the sake of convenience, as the *Argument against Abolishing Christianity* was written in 1708. If, as is likely, the date is correct, the *Argument* is only one of four pamphlets in which, within a period of one year, Swift is concerned with what he regards as the grave dangers threatening the Church of England. Swift's true views, which many readers tend to find obscured by the obliquity and sarcasm of the *Argument,* are set forth literally in other tracts he wrote at this time. These include *The Sentiments of a Church of England Man, A Project for the Advancement of Religion,* and *A Letter from a Member of the House of Commons in Ireland to a Member of the House of Commons in England concerning the Sacramental Test.* To these should be added Swift's *Remarks upon a Book Entitled "The Rights of the Christian Church,"* a series of critical strictures against the deist Tindal which was not published until after Swift's death but was written in 1707 or 1708.

For Swift, the threats to the established religion came from several sources, each reflected in one or more of the alleged advantages to the abolition of Christianity which the *Argument* considers. There were, in the first place, the opponents of the Test Act, largely members of the Whig party to which Swift still nominally adhered. In effect, the opponents of the Test sought to grant full rights of citizenship, including the right to hold public office, without requiring membership, real or professed, in the Church of England. In their appeals for toleration and liberty of conscience, which are mockingly distorted in the *Argument,* Swift found a sinister attempt to restore power to the hands of the Dissenting sects whom he regarded as the implacable enemies of the Church and the Monarchy. A second great danger to the Church came from the widely read writings of deistic thinkers, among whom were Toland, Tindal, and Asgill, who, while generally writing with such pious pretexts as the exposure of Catholic iniquities, managed to question matters so fundamental to Anglican faith that their implicit conclusions needed very little exaggeration to become the advantages offered in the *Argument.* A third source of Swift's distress lay in the very spirit of the times, in a climate of immorality and reverence so pervasive that it could be assigned to no single sect or faction. Blasphemy, anticlericalism, sabbath breaking, venery, and venality might all be variously traced to the influence of deists or Dissenters, but Swift clearly implies that, whatever their source, they had become the order of the day.

It is evident, then, that the *Argument* contains debasing distortions of a number of tendencies which, in Swift's opinion, seriously threaten the English Church and State. But, as the conflicting analyses of various scholars make abundantly clear, it is difficult to see what purpose is served by a series of patently feeble and discreditable arguments against the complete victory of these dangerous forces. What are we to make of the author's response to the views which are here extravagantly equated with the abolition of Christianity? Does Swift, as some students have maintained, actually adhere to a view substantially like that of his flabby, expediential spokesman? Is there some ironic device, apparent only to the initiate, by which wildly offensive proposals can be demolished by weak rejoinders? Has Swift created his spokesman only for the purpose of displaying a disdainful unwillingness seriously to counter the arguments of his enemies?

The problem cannot be met without clearly identifying Swift's principal satiric target. In the *Argument* this target is neither the deists nor the Dissenters, though of course their views suffer a merciless distortion: the target is the "nominal Christian" himself. Swift's chief concern is to show the shocking consequences of mere lip service to the Church of England at a time when much more is desperately needed. In his spokesman he displays a servile devotee of the *status quo,* a Christian only in his shaky and superficial loyalty to the name of his church. This fragile specimen is then brought face-to-face with the dangers that most immediately and drastically threaten his professed religion—the guile of deists and Dissenters as well as the widespread immorality of his countrymen. In the face of the forces which he himself recognizes as those of heresy, treason, and sin, the nominal Christian can produce only the weakest of materialistic arguments, destined to deliver him fatally into the hands of those who would destroy him. Ultimately, the entire *Argument* leads to one rhetorical question: When a man's Christianity lies only in a name, what better defenses than these can he produce against its destruction?

The present text, like that of Temple Scott, is based upon the Swift *Miscellanies* of 1711.

Swift – concerned w/religion
itself – not necessarily
dissent
concerned w/ lack of religion
agst nominal or quasi-religion
wants actual religion

writing
during a period of
the denial of the
doctrine of the
original sin

AN
ARGUMENT

Concerned w/diff. betw. nominal religion – theoretical religion &
actual religion

To prove that the Abolishing of CHRISTIANITY IN ENGLAND, may as Things now stand, be attended with some inconveniences, and perhaps not produce those many good Effects proposed thereby.

The speaker defends nominal religion

I AM very sensible what a Weakness and Presumption it is, to reason against the general Humour and Disposition of the World. I remember it was with great Justice, and a due Regard to the Freedom both of the Publick and the Press, forbidden upon several Penalties to write, or discourse, or lay wagers against the *Union* even before it was confirmed by Parliament; because that was look'd upon as a Design to oppose the Current of the People, which besides the Folly of it, is a manifest Breach of the fundamental Law, that makes this Majority of Opinions the Voice of God. In like manner, and for the very same reasons, it may perhaps be neither safe nor prudent to argue against the abolishing of Christianity, at a Juncture when all Parties seem so unanimously determined upon the Point, as we cannot but allow from their Actions, their Discourses, and their Writings. However, I know not how, whether from the Affectation of Singularity, or the Perverseness of human Nature, but so it unhappily falls out, that I cannot be entirely of this Opinion. Nay, though I were sure an Order were issued out for my immediate Prosecution by the Attorney-General, I should still confess, that in the present Posture of our Affairs at home or abroad, I do not yet see the absolute Necessity of extirpating the Christian Religion from among us.

This perhaps may appear too great a Paradox even for our wise and paradoxical Age to endure; therefore I shall handle it with all Tenderness, and with the utmost Deference to that great and profound Majority which is of another Sentiment.

And yet the Curious may please to observe, how much the Genius of a Nation is liable to alter in half an Age: I have heard it affirmed for certain by some very old People, that the contrary Opinion was even in their Memories as much in vogue as the other is now; and that a Project for the abolishing of Christianity would then have appeared as singular, and been thought as absurd, as it would be at this Time to write or discourse in its Defence.

Therefore I freely own, that all Appearances are against me. The System of the Gospel, after the Fate of other Systems, is generally antiquated and exploded; and the Mass or Body of the common People, among whom it seems to have had its latest Credit, are now grown as much ashamed of it as their Betters; Opinions, like Fashions, always, descending from those of Quality to the middle Sort, and thence to the Vulgar, where at length they are dropp'd and vanish.

But here I would not be mistaken, and must therefore be so bold as to borrow a Distinction from the Writers on the other Side, when they make a Difference betwixt nominal and real *Trinitarians*. I hope no Reader imagines me so weak to stand up in the Defence of real Christianity, such as used in primitive Times (if we may believe the Authors of those Ages) to have an Influence upon Men's Belief and Actions: To offer at the restoring of that, would indeed be a wild Project, it would be to dig up Foundations; to destroy at one Blow all the Wit, and half the Learning of the Kingdom; to break the entire Frame and Constitution of Things; to ruin Trade, extinguish Arts and Sciences, with the Professors of them; in short, to turn our Courts, Exchanges, and Shops into Desarts; and would be full as absurd as the Proposal of *Horace,* where he advises the *Romans,* all in a Body, to leave their City and seek a new Seat in some remote Part of the World, by way of a Cure for the Corruption of their Manners.

Therefore I think this Caution was in itself altogether un-necessary, (which I have inserted only to prevent all possibility of Cavilling) since every candid Reader will easily under-stand my Discourse to be intended only in Defence of nominal Christianity, the other having been for some time wholly laid aside by general Consent, as utterly inconsistent with all our present Schemes of Wealth and Power.

But why we should therefore cast off the Name and Title of Christians, although the general Opinion and Resolution be so violent for it, I confess I cannot (with Submission) ap-prehend the Consequence necessary. However, since the Undertakers propose such wonderful Advantages to the Nation by this Project, and advance many plausible Objec-tions against the System of Christianity, I shall briefly consider the Strength of both, fairly allow them their greatest Weight, and offer such Answers as I think most reasonable. After which I will beg leave to shew what Inconveniences may possibly happen by such an Innovation, in the present Posture of our Affairs.

First. One great Advantage proposed by the abolishing of Christianity is, That it would very much enlarge and establish Liberty of Conscience, that great Bulwark of our Nation, and of the Protestant Religion, which is still too much limited by Priest-craft, notwithstanding all the good Intentions of the Legislature, as we have lately found by a severe Instance. For it is confidently reported, that two young Gentlemen of real Hopes, bright Wit, and profound Judgment, who, upon a thorough Examination of Causes and Effects, and by the mere Force of natural Abilities, without the least Tincture of Learning, having made a Discovery, that there was no God, and generously communicating their Thoughts for the Good of the Publick, were some Time ago, by an unparallell'd Severity, and upon I know not what obsolete Law, broke for Blasphemy. And as it hath been wisely observed, if Persecution

This kind of religion in no way limits your thoughts

once begins, no Man alive knows how far it may reach, or where it will end.

In answer to all which, with Deference to wiser Judgments, I think this rather shews the Necessity of a nominal Religion among us. Great Wits love to be free with the highest Objects; and if they cannot be allowed a God to revile or renounce, they will speak evil of Dignities, abuse the Government, and reflect upon the Ministry, which I am sure few will deny to be of much more pernicious Consequence, according to the saying of *Tiberius, Deorum Offensa Diis curae*. As to the particular Fact related, I think it is not fair to argue from one Instance, perhaps another cannot be produced: yet (to the Comfort of all those who may be apprehensive of Persecution) Blasphemy we know is freely spoke a Million of Times in every Coffee-house and Tavern, or wherever else good Company meet. It must be allowed indeed, that to break an *English* Free-born Officer only for Blasphemy, was, to speak the gentlest of such an Action, a very high Strain of absolute Power. Little can be said in excuse for the General; perhaps he was afraid it might give Offence to the Allies, among whom, for ought we know, it may be the Custom of the Country to believe a God. But if he argued, as some have done, upon a mistaken Principle, that an Officer who is guilty of speaking Blasphemy, may some time or other proceed so far as to raise a Mutiny, the Consequence is by no means to be admitted: For, surely the Commander of an *English* Army is like to be but ill obey'd, whose Soldiers fear and reverence him as little as they do a Deity.

It is further objected against the Gospel System, that it obliges men to the Belief of Things too difficult for Free-Thinkers, and such who have shook off the Prejudices that usually cling to a confin'd Education. To which I answer, that Men should be cautious how they raise Objections which reflect upon the Wisdom of the Nation. Is not every Body freely allowed to believe whatever he pleases, and to publish his Belief to the World whenever he thinks fit, especially if it serves to strengthen the Party which is in the Right? Would any indifferent Foreigner, who should read the Trumpery lately written by *Asgill, Tindall, Toland, Coward,* and forty more, imagine the Gospel to be our Rule of Faith, and to be confirmed by Parliaments? Does any Man either believe, or say he believes, or desire to have it thought that he says he believes one Syllable of the Matter? and is any Man worse received upon that Score, or does he find his Want of nominal Faith a Disadvantage to him in the Pursuit of any Civil or Military Employment? What if there be an old dormant Statute or two against him, are they not now obsolete, to a Degree, that *Empson* and *Dudley* themselves, if they were now alive, would find it impossible to put them in execution?

It is likewise urged, that there are, by computation, in this Kingdom, above ten thousand Parsons, whose Revenues, added to those of my Lords the Bishops, would suffice to maintain at least two hundred young Gentlemen of Wit and Pleasure, and Free-thinking Enemies to Priest-craft, narrow Principles, Pedantry, and Prejudices, who might be an Ornament to the Court and Town: And then again, so great a Number of able [bodied] Divines might be a Recruit to our Fleet and Armies. This indeed appears to be a Consideration of some Weight: But then, on the other Side, several Things deserve to be considered likewise: As, First, Whether it may not be thought necessary that in certain Tracts of Country, like what we call Parishes, there should be one Man at least, of Abilities to read and write. Then it seems a wrong Computation, that the Revenues of the Church throughout this Island would be large enough to maintain two hundred young Gentlemen, or even half that Number, after the present refined Way of Living, that is, to allow each of them such a Rent, as in the modern Form of Speech, would make them easy. But still there is in this Project a greater Mischief behind; and we ought to beware of the Woman's Folly, who killed the Hen that every Morning laid her a golden Egg. For, pray what would become of the Race of Men in the next Age, if we had nothing to trust to besides the scrophulous consumptive Production furnished by our Men of Wit and Pleasure, when having squandered away their Vigour, Health, and Estates, they are forced, by some disagreeable Marriage, to piece up their broken Fortunes, and entail Rottenness and Politeness on their Posterity? Now, here are ten thousand Persons reduced, by the wise Regulations of *Henry* the Eighth, to the Necessity of a low Diet, and moderate Exercise, who are the only great Restorers of our Breed, without which the Nation would in an Age or two become one great Hospital.

Another Advantage proposed by the abolishing of Christianity, is the clear Gain of one Day in seven, which is now entirely lost, and consequently the Kingdom one seventh less considerable in Trade, Business, and Pleasure; beside the Loss to the Publick of so many stately Structures now in the Hands of the Clergy, which might be converted into Playhouses, Exchanges, Market-houses, common Dormitories, and other publick Edifices.

I hope I shall be forgiven a hard Word if I call this a perfect Cavil. I readily own there hath been an old Custom, Time out of mind, for People to assemble in the Churches every *Sunday,* and that Shops are still frequently shut, in order, as it is conceived, to preserve the Memory of that ancient Practice; but how this can prove a Hindrance to Business or Pleasure, is hard to imagine. What if the Men of Pleasure are forced, one Day in the Week, to game at Home instead of the *Chocolate-House?* Are not the *Taverns* and *Coffee-Houses* open? Can there be a more convenient Season for taking a Dose of Physick? Are fewer Claps got upon *Sundays* than other Days? Is not that the chief Day for Traders to sum up the Accounts of the Week, and for Lawyers to prepare their Briefs? But I would fain know how it can be pretended that the Churches are misapplied. Where are more Appointments and Rendezvouzes of Gallantry? Where more Care to appear in the foremost Box, with greater Advantage of Dress? Where more Meetings for Business? Where more Bargains driven of all Sorts? and where so many Conveniencies or Incitements to Sleep?

relation betw. religion & Factionalism (close to Defoe)
Nominalism not a cause of Factionalism — but a symptom
says Factionalism is rooted in the heart
248   AN ARGUMENT AGAINST ABOLISHING CHRISTIANITY

There is one Advantage greater than any of the foregoing,
proposed by the Abolishing of Christianity, that it will utterly
extinguish Parties among us, by removing those factious
Distinctions of High and Low Church, of *Whig* and *Tory,*
Presbyterian and *Church of England,* which are now so many
mutual Clogs upon Publick proceedings, and are apt to prefer
the gratifying themselves or depressing their Adversaries,
before the most important Interest of the State.

I Confess, if it were certain that so great an Advantage would
redound to the Nation by this Expedient, I would submit, and
be silent: But, will any man say, that if the Words *Whoring,*
Drinking, Cheating, Lying, Stealing, were by Act of Parliament
ejected out of the *English* Tongue and Dictionaries, we should
all awake next Morning chaste and temperate, honest and just,
and Lovers of Truth. Is this a fair Consequence? Or if the
Physicians would forbid us to pronounce the Words *Pox,*
Gout, Rheumatism, and *Stone,* would that Expedient serve
like so many *Talismans* to destroy the Diseases themselves?
Are Party and Faction rooted in Men's Hearts no deeper than
Phrases borrowed from Religion, or founded upon no firmer
Principles? And is our Language so poor, that we cannot find
other Terms to express them? Are Envy, Pride, Avarice and
Ambition such ill Nomenclators, that they cannot furnish
Appellations for their Owners? Will not *Heydukes* and *Mama-*
lukes, Mandarins, and *Patshaws,* or any other Words formed at
pleasure, serve to distinguish those who are in the Ministry
from others, who would be in it if they could? What, for
instance, is easier than to vary the Form of Speech, and
instead of the Word Church, make it a Question in Politicks,
Whether the Monument be in Danger? Because Religion was
nearest at hand to furnish a few convenient Phrases, is our
Invention so barren, we can find no other? Suppose, for
argument sake, that the *Tories* favoured *Margarita,* the *Whigs*
Mrs. *Tofts,* and the *Trimmers Valentini,* would not *Margari-*
tians, Toftians and *Valentinians* be very tolerable Marks of
Distinction? The *Prasini* and *Veneti,* two most virulent Factions in *Italy,* began (if I remember right) by a Distinction of

Colours in Ribbons, which we might do with as good a Grace about the Dignity of the *Blue* and the *Green,* and serve as properly to divide the Court, the Parliament, and the Kingdom between them, as any Terms of Art whatsoever, borrowed from Religion. And therefore I think there is little Force in this Objection against Christianity, or Prospect of so great an Advantage as is proposed in the abolishing of it.

'Tis again objected, as a very absurd ridiculous custom, that a Sett of Men should be suffered, much less employed and hired, to bawl one Day in Seven against the Lawfulness of those Methods most in Use towards the Pursuit of Greatness, Riches, and Pleasure, which are the constant Practice of all Men alive on the other six. But this Objection is, I think, a little unworthy so refined an Age as ours. Let us argue this Matter calmly; I appeal to the Breast of any polite Free-Thinker, whether, in the Pursuit of gratifying a predominant Passion, he hath not always felt a wonderful Incitement, by reflecting it was a Thing forbidden: And therefore we see, in order to cultivate this Taste, the Wisdom of the Nation hath taken special Care, that the Ladies should be furnished with prohibited Silks, and the Men with prohibited Wine: And indeed it were to be wished, that some other Prohibitions were promoted, in order to improve the Pleasures of the Town; which, for Want of such Expedients, begin already, as I am told, to flag and grow languid, giving way daily to cruel Inroads from the Spleen.

'Tis likewise proposed, as a great Advantage to the Publick, that if we once discard the System of the Gospel, all Religion will of course be banished for ever, and consequently along with it, those grievous Prejudices of Education, which, under the Names of Virtue, Conscience, Honour, Justice, and the like, are so apt to disturb the Peace of human Minds, and the Notions whereof are so hard to be eradicated by right Reason or Free-Thinking, sometimes during the whole Course of our Lives.

Here first I observe how difficult it is to get rid of a Phrase which the World is once grown fond of, tho' the Occasion that first produced it, be entirely taken away. For some Years past, if a Man had but an ill-favoured Nose, the deep Thinkers of the Age would some Way or other contrive to impute the Cause to the Prejudice of his Education. From this Fountain were said to be derived all our foolish Notions of Justice, Piety, Love of our Country; all our Opinions of God or a future State, Heaven, Hell, and the like: And there might formerly perhaps have been some Pretence for this Charge. But so effectual Care hath been since taken to remove those Prejudices, by an entire Change in the Methods of Education, that (with Honour I mention it to our polite Innovators) the young Gentlemen, who are now on the Scene, seem to have not the least Tincture left of those Infusions, or String of those Weeds, and by consequence the Reason for abolishing nominal Christianity upon that Pretext, is wholly ceas'd.

For the rest, it may perhaps admit a Controversy, whether the banishing all Notions of Religion whatsoever, would be convenient for the Vulgar. Not that I am in the least of opinion with those who hold Religion to have been the Invention of Politicians, to keep the lower Part of the World in Awe by the Fear of invisible Powers; unless Mankind were then very different from what it is now: For I look upon the Mass or Body of our People here in *England,* to be as Free-Thinkers, that is to say, as stanch Unbelievers, as any of the highest Rank. But I conceive some scattered Notions about a superior Power to be of singular Use for the common People, as furnishing excellent Materials to keep Children quiet when they grow peevish, and providing Topicks of Amusement in a tedious Winter Night.

Lastly, 'Tis proposed as a singular Advantage, that the abolishing of Christianity will very much contribute to the uniting of *Protestants,* by enlarging the Teams of Communion so as to take in all sorts of *Dissenters,* who are now shut out of the Pale upon Account of a few Ceremonies, which all Sides confess to be Things indifferent: That this alone will effectually answer the great Ends of a Scheme for Comprehension, by opening a large noble Gate, at which all Bodies may enter;

whereas the chaffering with *Dissenters,* and dodging about this or t'other Ceremony, is but like opening a few Wickets, and leaving them at Jar, by which no more than one can get in at a Time, and that not without stooping, and sideling, and squeezing his Body.

To all this I answer, That there is one darling Inclination of Mankind, which usually affects to be a Retainer to Religion, though she be neither its Parent, its Godmother, nor its Friend; I mean the Spirit of Opposition, that lived long before Christianity, and can easily subsist without it. Let us, for instance, examine wherein the Opposition of Sectaries among us consists; we shall find Christianity to have no share in it at all. Does the Gospel any where prescribe a starched squeezed Countenance, a stiff formal Gait, a Singularity of Manners and Habit, or any affected Forms and Modes of Speech different from the reasonable Part of Mankind? Yet, if Christianity did not lend its Name to stand in the Gap, and to employ or divert these Humours, they must of necessity be spent in Contraventions to the Laws of the Land, and Disturbance of the publick Peace. There is a Portion of Enthusiasm assigned to every Nation, which if it hath not proper Objects to work on, will burst out, and set all into a Flame. If the Quiet of a State can be bought by only flinging Men a few Ceremonies to devour, it is a Purchase no wise Man would refuse. Let the Mastiffs amuse themselves about a Sheep's Skin stuff'd with Hay, provided it will keep them from worrying the Flock. The Institution of Convents abroad, seems in one point a Strain of great Wisdom, there being few Irregularities in human Passions, which may not have recourse to vent themselves in some of those Orders, which are so many Retreats for the Speculative, the Melancholy, the Proud, the Silent, the Politick, and the Morose, to spend themselves, and evaporate the noxious Particles; for each of whom we in this Island are forced to provide a several Sect of Religion, to keep them quiet; and whenever Christianity shall be abolished, the Legislature must find some other Expedient to employ and entertain them. For what imports it how large a Gate you open, if there will be always left a Number who place a Pride and a Merit in not coming in?

Having thus consider'd the most important Objections against Christianity, and the chief Advantages proposed by the Abolishing thereof; I shall now with equal Deference and Submission to wiser Judgments, as before, proceed to mention a few Inconveniences that may happen, if the Gospel should be repealed; which perhaps the Projectors may not have sufficiently considered.

And first, I am sensible how much the Gentlemen of Wit and Pleasure are apt to murmur, and be shocked at the Sight of so many daggled-tail Parsons, that happen to fall in their Way, and offend their Eyes; but at the same time these wise Reformers do not consider what an Advantage and Felicity it is, for great Wits to be always provided with Objects of Scorn and Contempt, in order to exercise and improve their Talents, and divert their Spleen from falling on each other, or on themselves, especially when all this may be done without the least imaginable Danger to their Persons.

And to urge another Argument of a parallel Nature: If Christianity were once abolished, how could the Free-Thinkers, the strong Reasoners, and the Men of profound Learning, be able to find another Subject so calculated in all Points whereon to display their Abilities. What wonderful Productions of Wit should we be deprived of, from those whose Genius, by continual Practice, hath been wholly turn'd upon Raillery and Invectives against Religion, and would therefore never be able to shine or distinguish themselves upon any other Subject. We are daily complaining of the great Decline of Wit among us, and would we take away the greatest, perhaps the only Topick we have left? Who would ever have suspected *Asgill* for a Wit, or *Toland* for a Philosopher, if the inexhaustible Stock of Christianity had not been at hand to provide them with Materials? What other Subject through all Art or Nature could have produced *Tindall* for a profound Author, or furnished him with Readers? It is the wise Choice of the Subject that alone adorns and distinguishes the Writer. For had a Hundred such Pens as these been employed on the side of Religion, they would have immediately sunk into Silence and Oblivion.

Nor do I think it wholly groundless, or my Fears altogether imaginary, that the Abolishing of Christianity may perhaps bring the Church in Danger, or at least put the Senate to the Trouble of another securing Vote. I desire I may not be mistaken; I am far from presuming to affirm or think that the Church is in Danger at present, or as Things now stand; but we know not how soon it may be so, when the Christian Religion is repealed. As plausible as this Project seems, there may a dangerous Design lurk under it: Nothing can be more notorious, than that the *Atheists, Deists, Socinians, Anti-Trinitarians,* and other Subdivisions of Free-Thinkers, are Persons of little Zeal for the present ecclesiastical Establishment: Their declared Opinion is for repealing the sacramental Test; they are very indifferent with regard to Ceremonies; nor do they hold the *Jus Divinum* of Episcopacy: Therefore this may be intended as one politick Step towards altering the Constitution of the Church established, and setting up *Presbytery* in the Stead, which I leave to be further considered by those at the Helm.

In the last Place I think nothing can be more plain, than that by this Expedient, we shall run into the Evil we chiefly pretend to avoid; and that the Abolishment of the *Christian* Religion, will be the readiest Course we can take to introduce Popery. And I am the more inclined to this Opinion, because we know it has been the constant Practice of the *Jesuits* to send over Emissaries, with Instructions to personate themselves Members of the several prevailing Sects amongst us. So it is recorded, that they have at sundry times appeared in the Guise of *Presbyterians, Anabaptists, Independants,* and *Quakers,* according as any of these were most in Credit; so, since the Fashion hath been taken up of exploding Religion, the *Popish* Missionaries have not been wanting to mix with the Free-Thinkers; among whom *Toland,* the great Oracle of the *Anti-Christians,* is an *Irish* Priest, the Son of an *Irish*

Priest; and the most learned and ingenious Author of a Book called the *Rights of the Christian Church,* was in a proper Juncture reconciled to the *Romish* Faith, whose true Son, as appears by a hundred Passages in his Treatise, he still continues. Perhaps I could add some others to the Number; but the Fact is beyond Dispute, and the Reasoning they proceed by is right: For supposing Christianity to be extinguished, the People will never be at Ease till they find out some other Method of Worship; which will as infallibly produce Superstition, as this will end in *Popery*.

And therefore, if notwithstanding all I have said, it still be thought necessary to have a Bill brought in for repealing Christianity, I would humbly offer an Amendment, That instead of the Word Christianity, may be put Religion in general, which I conceive will much better answer all the good Ends proposed by the Projectors of it. For, as long as we leave in being, a God and his Providence, with all the necessary Consequences which curious and inquisitive Men will be apt to draw from such Premises, we do not strike at the Root of the Evil, though we should ever so effectually annihilate the present Scheme of the Gospel; For, of what Use is Freedom of Thought, if it will not produce Freedom of Action, which is the sole End, how remote soever in Appearance, of all Objections against Christianity; and therefore, the Free-Thinkers consider it as a Sort of Edifice, wherein all the Parts have such a mutual Dependance on each other, that if you happen to pull out one single Nail, the whole Fabrick must fall to the Ground. This was happily exprest by him who had heard of a Text brought for proof of the Trinity, which in an ancient Manuscript was differently read; he thereupon immediately took the Hint, and by a sudden Deduction of a long Sorites, most Logically concluded: Why, if it be as you say, I may safely whore and drink on, and defy the Parson. From which, and many the like Instances easy to be produced, I think nothing can be more manifest, than that the Quarrel is not against any particular Points of hard Digestion in the Christian System, but against Religion in general, which, by laying Restraints on human Nature, is supposed the great Enemy to the Freedom of Thought and Action.

Upon the whole, if it shall still be thought for the Benefit of Church and State, that Christianity be abolished, I conceive however, it may be more convenient to defer the Execution to a Time of Peace, and not venture in this Conjuncture to disoblige our Allies, who, as it falls out, are all Christians, and many of them, by the Prejudices of their Education, so bigotted, as to place a sort of Pride in the Appellation. If upon being rejected by them, we are to trust to an Alliance with the *Turk,* we shall find our selves much deceived: For, as he is too remote, and generally engaged in War with the *Persian* Emperor, so his People would be more scandalized at our Infidelity, than our Christian Neighbours. For they are not only strict Observers of religious Worship, but, what is worse, believe a God; which is more than is required of us, even while we preserve the Name of Christians.

To conclude: Whatever some may think of the great Advantages to Trade by this favourite Scheme, I do very much apprehend, that in six Months Time after the Act is past for the Extirpation of the Gospel, the Bank and *East-India* Stock, may fall at least One *per Cent*. And since that is fifty Times more than ever the Wisdom of our Age thought fit to venture for the Preservation of Christianity, there is no Reason we should be at so great a Loss, merely for the sake of destroying it.

A Modest Proposal

The most famous of Swift's short tracts, *A Modest Proposal,* was first published in Dublin in the autumn of 1729. Two years earlier, Swift had returned from what proved to be his final visit to England in a mood of disgust toward politics of any sort; Stella had died the following year; Swift complained increasingly of his own wretched health. Yet *A Modest Proposal* is only one, albeit the most striking, of a number of pamphlets in which, over a period of five years, Swift addressed himself to the political and economic plight of Ireland and reaffirmed his position as the great spokesman of Irish patriotism.

As is so often true of Swift's satire, *A Modest Proposal* strikes out in several directions. In his jaunty advocacy of nationwide cannibalism, the putative author of the piece can be taken as a devastating symbol of politicians and absentee landlords, English and Anglo-Irish, whose smoothly rationalized inhumanity, Swift suggests, needs be stretched very little to encompass such a scheme as this. The tract may also be read as a parody of various plans for the relief of Irish problems advanced by economists and political projectors whom Swift attacks elsewhere. Swift's professedly modest but calmly systematic development of his shocking theme closely follows the manner of such proposals, while the substance of the project strikes at the impracticality of the proposals and the indifference of the projectors to the reality of human needs. More particularly, the document may, as Professor Louis Landa has pointed out, be taken as a grimly literal application of the widely accepted economic theory that people constitute the real wealth of a nation.

But the audience—in fact, in an important sense, the chief satiric target of *A Modest Proposal*—is the Irish people themselves. Swift's attitude toward his countrymen is, throughout, complex and, for some students of the subject, paradoxical. It is, on the one hand, a feeling of compassionate understanding of the misery of the Irish and of cold hatred toward their oppressors. On the other hand, the self-indulgent complacency of the fortunate Irish minority, the apathetic suffering of the cruelly underprivileged majority, and the universal acceptance of perfidious leaders and false principles in the conduct of Irish affairs aroused in Swift a desperate contempt. His frequently expressed sentiments on the subject are tersely expressed in a letter which he wrote to Pope in 1728. "I do profess," he says, "without affectation, that your kind opinion of me as a patriot, since you call it so, is what I do not deserve; because what I do is owing to perfect rage and resentment, and the mortifying sight of slavery, folly, and baseness about me, among which I am forced to live."

The slavery, to be sure, was imposed from without Ireland, but, as Swift repeatedly points out in letters, pamphlets, and poems, it was perpetuated by the dumb resignation of the Irish populace and the venal servility of their leaders. The "paradox" of Swift's Irish patriotism is perhaps its greatest glory, for in his long, lonely fight, his greatest enemy was the mulish indifference of the nation he sought to restore to self-respect.

Swift's italics are not needed to enforce the climactic intensity of that passage in *A Modest Proposal* in which "other Expedients," the urgent, sensible courses which Swift continually urged, are rejected as impossible for "this one individual Kingdom of Ireland." Each of these alternative courses lies within the power of the Irish, and the Irish alone; in rejecting them and accepting, by default, the premises of their enemies, the Irish have left the door open to just such a ghastly solution to their difficulties as the present proposal. Some readers have found in this document an urgent call-to-arms, still hopefully designed to arouse the Irish nation from its lethargy. Others find in it only the expression of a black despair. Whatever the ultimate motives of its composition, it clearly confronts a people who would "think it a great Happiness to have been sold for food at a Year old" with a shocking assessment of their own condition.

diff from Defoe

A
MODEST
PROPOSAL

For Preventing the Children of Ireland

FROM

Being a Burden to their Parents

OR

COUNTRY;

AND

For Making them Beneficial to the

PUBLICK

IT is a melancholly Object to those, who walk through this great Town or travel in the Country; when they see the *Streets,* the *Roads* and *Cabbin-doors* crowded with *Beggars* of the Female Sex, followed by three, four, or six Children, *all in Rags,* and importuning every Passenger for an Alms. These *Mothers,* instead of being able to work for their honest Lively-hood, are forced to employ all their Time in stroling to beg Sustenance for their *helpless Infants;* who, as they grow up, either turn *Thieves* for want of Work; or leave their *dear Native Country, to* fight for the *Pretender* in Spain, or sell themselves to the *Barbadoes.*

I think it is agreed by all Parties, that this prodigious number of Children in the Arms, or on the Backs, or at the *Heels* of their *Mothers,* and frequently of their *Fathers, is in the present deplorable state of the Kingdom,* a very great additional Grievance; and therefore, whoever could find out a fair, cheap, and easy Method of making these Children sound and useful Members of the Commonwealth, would deserve so well of the Publick, as to have his Statue set up for a Preserver of the Nation.

But my Intention is very far from being confined to provide only for the Children of *professed Beggars:* It is of a much greater Extent, and shall take in the whole Number of Infants at a certain Age, who are born of Parents in effect as little able to support them, as those who demand our Charity in the Streets.

As to my own Part, having turned my Thoughts, for many Years, upon this important Subject, and maturely weighed the several *Schemes of other Projectors,* I have always found them grossly mistaken in their Computation. It is true, a Child, *just dropt from its Dam,* may be supported by her Milk, for a Solar Year with little other Nourishment; at most not above the Value of two Shillings; which the Mother may certainly get, or the Value in *Scraps,* by her lawful Occupation of *Begging:* and it is exactly at one Year old that I propose to provide for them in such a manner, as, instead of being a Charge upon their *Parents,* or the *Parish,* or *wanting Food and Raiment* for the rest of their Lives; they shall, on the contrary, contribute to the Feeding and partly to the Cloathing, of many Thousands.

There is likewise another great Advantage in my *Scheme,* that it will prevent those *voluntary Abortions,* and that horrid practice of *Women murdering their Bastard Children,* alas! too frequent among us; Sacrificing the *poor innocent Babes,* I doubt, more to avoid the Expence than the Shame; which would move Tears and Pity in the most Savage and inhuman breast.

The number of Souls in *Ireland* being usually reckoned one

Million and a half; of these I calculate there may be about Two hundred Thousand Couple whose Wives are Breeders; from which number I subtract thirty Thousand Couples, who are able to maintain their own Children, although I apprehend there cannot be so many under the *present Distresses of the Kingdom;* but this being granted, there will remain an Hundred and Seventy Thousand Breeders. I again Subtract Fifty Thousand, for those Women who miscarry, or whose Children die by Accident, or Disease, within the Year. There only remain an Hundred and Twenty Thousand Children of poor Parents, annually born: The Question therefore is, How this Number shall be reared, and provided for? Which, as I have already said, under the present Situation of Affairs, is utterly impossible, by all the Methods hitherto proposed: For we can *neither employ them in Handicraft* or *Agriculture;* we neither build Houses, (I mean in the Country) nor cultivate Land: They can very seldom pick up a Livelyhood *by Stealing* until they arrive at six Years old; except where they are of towardly Parts; although, I confess, they learn the Rudiments much earlier; during which Time, they can, however be properly looked upon only as *Probationers;* as I have been informed by a principal Gentleman in the County of *Cavan,* who protested to me, that he never knew above one or two Instances under the Age of six, even in a part of the Kingdom *so renowned for the quickest Proficiency in that Art.*

I am assured by our Merchants, that a Boy or a Girl before twelve Years old, is no saleable Commodity; and even when they come to this Age, they will not yield above Three Pounds, or Three Pounds and half a Crown at most, on the Exchange; which cannot turn to Account either to the Parents or the Kingdom; the Charge of Nutriment and Rags, having been at least four Times that Value.

I shall now therefore humbly propose my own Thoughts; which I hope will not be liable to the least Objection.

I have been assured by a very knowing *American* of my Acquaintance in *London,* that a young healthy Child, well nursed is, at a Year old, a most delicious, nourishing and wholesome Food, whether *Stewed, Roasted, Baked,* or *Boiled;* and I make no doubt that it will equally serve in a *Fricasie,* or *Ragoust.*

I do therefore humbly offer it to *publick Consideration,* that of the Hundred and Twenty Thousand Children, already computed, Twenty thousand may be reserved for Breed; whereof only one Fourth Part to be Males; which is more than we allow to *Sheep, black Cattle,* or *Swine;* and my Reason is, that these Children are seldom the Fruits of Marriage, *a Circumstance not much regarded by our Savages;* therefore, *one Male* will be sufficient to serve *four Females.* That the remaining Hundred thousand, may, at a Year old be offered in Sale to the *Persons of Quality* and *Fortune,* through the Kingdom; always advising the Mother to let them suck plentifully in the last Month, so as to render them plump, and fat for a good Table. A Child will make two Dishes at an Entertainment for Friends; and when the Family dines alone, the fore or hind Quarter will make a reasonable Dish; and seasoned with a little Pepper or Salt, will be very good Boiled on the fourth Day, especially in *Winter.*

I have reckoned upon a Medium, that a Child just born will weigh Twelve Pounds; and in a solar Year, if tolerably nursed, increaseth to 28 Pounds.

I grant this Food will be somewhat dear, and therefore very *proper for Landlords;* who, as they have already devoured most of the Parents, seem to have the best Title to the Children.

Infant's Flesh will be in Season throughout the Year; but more plentiful in *March,* and a little before and after; for we are told by a grave *Author an eminent *French* Physician, that *Fish being a prolifick Dyet,* there are more Children born in *Roman Catholick Countries* about Nine Months after *Lent,* than at any other Season: Therefore reckoning a Year after *Lent,* the Markets will be more glutted than usual; because the Number of *Popish Infants,* is, at least, three to one in this Kingdom; and therefore it will have one other Collat-

* Rabelais.

eral advantage; by lessening the Number of *Papists* among us.

I have already computed the Charge of nursing a Beggar's Child (in which List I reckon all *Cottagers, Labourers,* and Four fifths of the *Farmers*) to be about two Shillings *per Annum,* Rags included; and I believe no Gentleman would repine to give Ten Shillings for the *Carcase of a good fat Child;* which, as I have said, will make four Dishes of excellent nutritive meat, when he hath only some particular Friend, or his own Family, to dine with him. Thus the Squire will learn to be a good Landlord, and grow popular among his Tenants; the Mother will have Eight Shillings net Profit, and be fit for Work till she produceth another Child.

Those who are more thrifty (as *I must confess the Times require*) may flay the Carcase; the Skin of which, artificially dressed, will make admirable *Gloves for Ladies,* and *Summer Boots for fine Gentlemen.*

As to our City of *Dublin;* Shambles may be appointed for this Purpose, in the most convenient Parts of it, and Butchers we may be assured will not be wanting; although I rather recommend buying the Children alive, and dressing them hot from the Knife, as we do *roasting Pigs.*

A very worthy Person, *a true Lover of his Country,* and whose Virtues I highly esteem, was lately pleased, in discoursing on this Matter, to offer a Refinement upon my Scheme. He said, that many Gentlemen of this Kingdom, having of late destroyed their Deer; he conceived that the Want of Venison might be well supplied by the Bodies of young Lads and Maidens, not exceeding fourteen Years of Age, nor under twelve; so great a Number of both Sexes in every County being ready to Starve, for want of Work and Service: And these to be disposed of by their Parents, if alive, or otherwise by their nearest Relations. But with due Deference to so excellent a Friend, and so deserving a Patriot, I cannot be altogether in his Sentiments. For as to the Males, my *American* Acquaintance assured me from frequent Experience, that their Flesh was generally tough and lean, like that of our School-boys, by continual Exercise, and their Taste disagreeable; and to fatten them would not answer the Charge. Then, as to the Females, it would, I think, with humble Submission, *be a Loss to the Publick,* because they soon would become Breeders themselves: And besides it is not improbable, that some scrupulous People might be apt to censure such a Practice, (although indeed very unjustly) as a little bordering upon Cruelty; which, I confess, hath always been with me the strongest Objection against any Project, how well soever intended.

But in order to justify my Friend; he confessed, that this Expedient was put into his Head by the famous *Salmanaazor,* a Native of the Island *Formosa,* who came from thence to *London,* above twenty Years ago, and in Conversation told my Friend, that in his Country, when any young Person happened to be put to Death, the Executioner sold the Carcase to *Persons of Quality,* as a prime Dainty, and that, in his Time, the Body of a plump Girl of fifteen, who was crucified for an Attempt to poison the Emperor, was sold to his Imperial *Majesty's prime Minister of State,* and other great *Mandarins* of the Court, *in Joints from the Gibbet,* at Four hundred Crowns. Neither indeed can I deny, that if the same Use were made of several plump young girls in this Town, who, without one single Groat to their Fortunes, cannot stir Abroad without a Chair, and appear at the *Play-house,* and *Assemblies* in foreign fineries, which they never will pay for; the Kingdom would not be the worse.

Some Persons of a desponding Spirit are in great Concern about that vast Number of poor People, who are Aged, Diseased, or Maimed; and I have been desired to imploy my Thoughts what Course may be taken, to ease the Nation of so grievous an Incumbrance. But I am not in the least Pain upon that Matter; because it is very well known, that they are every Day *dying,* and *rotting,* by *Cold* and *Famine,* and *Filth,* and *Vermin,* as fast as can be reasonably expected. And as to the younger Labourers, they are now in almost as hopeful a Condition: They cannot get Work, and consequently pine away for Want of Nourishment, to a Degree, that if at any Time they are accidentally hired to common Labour, they have not Strength to perform it; and thus the Country, and themselves, are in a fair Way of being delivered from the Evils to come.

I have too long digressed; and therefore shall return to my Subject. I think the Advantages by the Proposal which I have made are obvious, and many, as well as of the highest Importance. ADVANTAGES OF PROPOSAL

For *First,* as I have already observed, it would greatly lessen the *Number of Papists,* with whom we are Yearly over-run; being the principal Breeders of the Nation, as well as our most dangerous Enemies; and who stay at home on Purpose, with a Design to *deliver the Kingdom to the Pretender;* hoping to take their Advantage by the Absence of *so many good Protestants,* who have chosen rather to leave their Country, than stay at home, and pay Tithes against their Conscience, to an idolatrous *Episcopal Curate.*

Secondly, The poorer Tenants will have something valuable of their own, which, by Law, may be made liable to Distress, and help to pay their Landlord's Rent; their Corn and Cattle being already seized, and *Money a Thing unknown.*

Thirdly, Whereas the Maintenance of an Hundred Thousand Children, from two Years old, and upwards, cannot be computed at less than ten Shillings a Piece *per Annum,* the Nation's Stock will be thereby encreased Fifty Thousand Pounds *per Annum;* besides the Profit of a new Dish, introduced to the Tables of all *Gentlemen of Fortune* in the Kingdom, who have any Refinement in Taste; and the Money will circulate among ourselves, the Goods being entirely of our own Growth and Manufacture.

Fourthly, The constant Breeders, besides the Gain of Eight Shillings *Sterling per Annum,* by the Sale of their Children, will be rid of the Charge of maintaining them after the first Year.

Fifthly, This Food would likewise bring great *Custom to Taverns,* where the Vintners will certainly be so prudent, as to procure the best Receipts for dressing it to Perfection; and consequently, have their Houses frequented by all the *fine*

Gentlemen, who justly value themselves upon their Knowledge in good Eating; and a skilful Cook, who understands how to oblige his Guests, will contrive to make it as expensive as they please.

Sixthly, This would be a great Inducement to Marriage, which all wise Nations have either encouraged by Rewards, or enforced by Laws and Penalties. It would encrease the Care and Tenderness of Mothers towards their Children, when they were sure of a Settlement for Life, to the poor Babes, provided in some Sort by the Publick, to their annual Profit instead of Expence. We should soon see an honest Emulation among the married Women, *which of them could bring the fattest Child to the Market.* Men would become as *fond* of their Wives, during the Time of their Pregnancy, as they are now of their *Mares* in Foal, their *Cows* in Calf, or *Sows* when they are ready to farrow; nor offer to beat or kick them, (as is too *frequent* a Practice) for fear of a Miscarriage.

Many other Advantages might be enumerated. For instance, the Addition of some Thousand Carcases in our Exportation of barrel'd Beef: The Propagation of *Swine's Flesh,* and Improvement in the Art of making good *Bacon;* so much wanted among us by the great Destruction of *Pigs,* too frequent at our Tables, and are no way comparable in Taste, or Magnificence, to a well-grown, fat yearling Child; which, roasted whole, will make a considerable Figure at a *Lord Mayor's Feast,* or any other publick Entertainment. But this, and many others, I omit; being studious of Brevity.

Supposing that one Thousand Families in this City, would be constant Customers for Infants Flesh, besides others who might have it at *merry Meetings,* particularly *Weddings* and *Christenings;* I compute that *Dublin* would take off, annually, about Twenty Thousand Carcasses; and the rest of the Kingdom (where probably they will be sold somewhat cheaper) the remaining Eighty Thousand.

I can think of no one Objection, that will possibly be raised against this Proposal; unless it should be urged, that the Number of People will be thereby much lessened in the Kingdom.

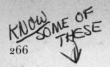

This I freely own; and it was indeed one principal Design in offering it to the World. I desire the Reader will observe, that I calculate my Remedy *for this one individual Kingdom of IRELAND, and for no other that ever was, is, or, I think, ever can be upon Earth.* Therefore, let no man talk to me of other Expedients: *Of taxing our Absentees at five Shillings a Pound: Of using neither Cloaths, nor Household Furniture, except what is of our own Growth and Manufacture: Of utterly rejecting the Materials and Instruments that promote foreign Luxury: Of curing the Expensiveness of Pride, Vanity, Idleness, and Gaming in our Women: Of introducing a Vein of Parsimony, Prudence and Temperance: Of learning to love our Country, wherein we differ even from LAPLANDERS, and the Inhabitants of TOPINAMBOO: Of quitting our Animosities, and Factions; nor act any longer like the* Jews, *who were murdering one another at the very Moment their City was taken: Of being a little cautious not to sell our Country and Consciences for nothing: Of teaching* Landlords *to have, at least, one Degree of Mercy towards their Tenants.* Lastly, *of Putting a Spirit of Honesty, Industry, and Skill into our* Shopkeepers; *who, if a Resolution could now be taken to buy only our native Goods, would immediately unite to cheat and exact upon us in the Price, the Measure, and the Goodness; nor could ever yet be brought to make one fair Proposal of just Dealing, though often and earnestly invited to it.*

landlords

Therefore I repeat, let no Man talk to me of these and the like Expedients; till he hath, at least, a Glimpse of Hope, that there will ever be some hearty and sincere Attempt to put them in Practice.

SWIFT'S PURPOSE

But, as to my self; having been wearied out for many Years with offering vain, idle, visionary Thoughts; and at length utterly despairing of Success, I fortunately fell upon this Proposal; which, as it is wholly new, so it hath something *solid* and *real*, of no Expence and little Trouble, full in our own Power; and whereby we can incur no Danger in *disobliging* ENGLAND: For this Kind of Commodity will not bear Exportation; the Flesh being of too tender a Consistence, to admit a long Continuance in Salt; *although, perhaps, I could name a Country, which would be glad to eat up our whole Nation without it.*

After all, I am not so violently bent upon my own Opinion, as to reject any Offer, proposed by wise Men, which shall be found equally innocent, cheap, easy, and effectual. But before something of that Kind shall be advanced in Contradiction to my Scheme, and offering a better; I desire the Author, or Authors, will be pleased maturely to consider two Points. *First,* As Things now stand, how they will be able to find Food and Raiment, for a Hundred Thousand useless Mouths and Backs? And *Secondly,* There being a round Million of Creatures in human Figure, throughout this Kingdom; whose whole Subsistence, put into a common Stock, would leave them in Debt two Millions of Pounds *Sterling;* adding those, who are Beggars by Profession, to the Bulk of Farmers, Cottagers and Labourers, with their Wives and Children, who are Beggars in Effect; I desire those Politicians, who dislike my Overture, and may perhaps be so bold to attempt an Answer, that they will first ask the Parents of these Mortals, Whether they would not at this Day think it a great Happiness to have been sold for Food at a Year old, in the Manner I prescribe; and thereby have avoided such a perpetual Scene of Misfortunes, as they have since gone through; by the *Oppression of Landlords;* the Impossibility of paying Rent, without Money or Trade; the Want of common Sustenance, with neither House nor Cloaths, to cover them from the Inclemencies of the Weather; and the most inevitable Prospect of intailing the like, or greater Miseries upon their Breed for ever.

I profess, in the Sincerity of my Heart, that I have not the least personal Interest, in endeavouring to promote this necessary Work, having no other Motive than the *publick Good of my Country, by advancing our Trade, providing for Infants, relieving the Poor, and giving some Pleasure to the Rich.* I have no Children, by which I can propose to get a single Penny; the youngest being nine Years Old and my Wife past Child-bearing.

The Drapier's Letters

In July of 1722, an obscure English manufacturer named William Wood was granted a royal patent to coin, for use in Ireland, a large amount of copper money. In the patent and the subsequent importation of Wood's coinage into Ireland there was much to enrage the patriotic Irishman. The patent had been granted without consulting representatives of Ireland; it appeared to authorize a far greater amount of coinage than was needed; it contravened the wishes of the Irish for a guaranteed legal coinage to be produced in their own country. Wood was, moreover, widely believed to have secured his patent by bribing the King's mistress, in anticipation of realizing inordinate profits by producing coins of debased intrinsic value.

For eighteen months the English administration appeared indifferent to the public clamor and official remonstrances of the Irish. It was clear, early in 1724, that the repeal of the patent could be achieved only by stronger steps. It was at this point that Swift entered the affair, assuming for the purpose one of his greatest roles, that of "M.B.," the humble draper, whose voice was triumphantly to speak to and for the entire Irish nation.

Swift's principal task in the *Drapier's Letters* was to initiate a general boycott of Wood's coinage and to sustain this boycott in the fact of English efforts at suppression. This mission was substantially achieved in the first four letters, of which only the fourth is reprinted in this volume. A fifth letter, to the Irish Whig, Lord Middleton, is essentially a rather humorous summary and defense of the Drapier's previous activities, while two other letters to which Swift appended the Drapier's name remained unpublished until years after the controversy was over. The first four letters reflect the main current of events surrounding the coinage: the initial Irish case against the patent; the belated and unsatisfactory report of a Committee of the Privy Council charged with investigating the matter; the arrival of Swift's friend, Lord Carteret, as new Lord Lieutenant of Ireland, with obvious instructions to push Irish acceptance of the coinage; the growing but impotent wrath of the English, including the Prime Minister, Robert Walpole. And, as the letters proceed, they make clear, too, that Swift had achieved—although, as he bitterly realized, only temporarily—a Kingdom "firmly united . . . against that detestable Fraud."

There were, however, at least three important occurrences which followed the fourth letter and which should be noted here. The first was a proclamation by the Lord Lieutenant, calling for the identification and arrest of the Drapier—a hollow and entirely ineffectual proceeding on the part of Carteret, who was as aware of the Drapier's identity as he was of the folly of prosecuting him. The second was the arrest of Swift's printer, Harding. Despite the manipulations of a hostile Chief Justice, the Grand Jury refused to prosecute Harding and, urged on by a pamphlet of Swift's, actually made a bold declaration against Wood's coinage. The final, triumphant event was the arrival in Dublin, in August, 1725, of the news that Wood's patent had been canceled. "The work is done," wrote Swift a few days later, "and there is no more need of the Drapier."

The outstanding qualities of the *Drapier's Letters* are not so much those of satire as of powerful tractarian rhetoric. In adopting the role of the Drapier, Swift is not seeking to convince by artifice or indirection; the Drapier's convictions are literally Swift's own, and where the language or experience of a humble tradesman is employed, it is only for reasons of increased clarity. Even the distortions of facts, and more especially of figures, are the headlong exaggerations of angry argument. Only in the closing paragraphs of the fourth letter, where Swift seizes upon Walpole's alleged threats with a kind of fierce playfulness, does mockery supplant the tone of honest, outraged logic which is otherwise sustained throughout.

It is worth remembering that the *Drapier's Letters* were produced at a time when Swift had made considerable progress in the writing of *Gulliver's Travels*. There is no greater measure of his genius than his pausing, in the creation of one of the world's greatest books, to win, almost single-handedly, a resounding victory for the cause of Irish nationalism.

LETTER

To The Whole People of

IRELAND

My Dear COUNTRYMEN,

HAVING already written three *Letters,* upon so dis-agreeable a Subject as Mr. *Wood* and his *Half-pence;* I con-ceived my Task was at an End: But, I find that Cordials must be frequently applied to weak Constitutions, *Political* as well as *Natural.* A People long used to Hardships, lose by Degrees the very Notions of *Liberty;* they look upon themselves as Creatures at Mercy; and that all Impositions laid on them by a stronger Hand, are, in the Phrase of the *Report, legal* and *obligatory.* Hence proceed that *Poverty* and *Lowness of Spirit,* to which a *Kingdom* may be subject, as well as a *particular Person.* And when *Esau* came fainting from the Field, at the Point to die, it is no wonder that he sold his *Birth-Right for a Mess of Pottage.*

I thought I had sufficiently shewn to all who could want Instruction, by what Methods they might safely proceed, when-ever this *Coin* should be offered to them: And, I believe, there hath not been, for many Ages, an Example of any Kingdom so firmly united in a Point of great Importance, as this of ours is at present, against that detestable Fraud. But, however, it so happens, that some weak People begin to be alarmed a-new, by Rumours industriously spread. *Wood* prescribes to the News-Mongers in *London* what they are to write. In one of their

Papers published here by some obscure Printer, (and certainly with a bad Design) we are told, that the *Papists in* Ireland *have entered into an Association against his Coin;* although it be notoriously known, that they never once offered to stir in the Matter: So, that the two Houses of Parliament, the Privy-Council, the great Numbers of Corporations, the Lord-Mayor, and Aldermen of *Dublin,* the Grand-Juries, and principal Gentlemen of several Counties, are stigmatized in a Lump, under the Name of *Papists.*

This Impostor and his Crew, do likewise give out, that, by refusing to receive his Dross for Sterling, we *dispute the King's Prerogative; are grown ripe for Rebellion, and ready to shake off the Dependency of* Ireland *upon the Crown of* England. To Countenance which Reports, he hath published a Paragraph in another News-Paper, to let us know, that *the Lord Lieutenant is ordered to come over immediately, to settle his Half-pence.*

I intreat you, my dear Countrymen, not to be under the least Concern, upon these and the like Rumours; which are no more than the last Howls of a Dog dissected alive, as I hope he hath sufficiently been. These Calumnies are the only Reserve that is left him. For surely, our continued and (almost) unexampled Loyalty, will never be called in Question, for not suffering our selves to be robbed of all that we have, by one obscure *Ironmonger.*

As to disputing the King's *Prerogative,* give me leave to explain to those who are ignorant, what the Meaning of that Word *Prerogative* is.

The Kings of these Realms enjoy several Powers, wherein the Laws have not interposed: So they can make War and Peace without the Consent of Parliament; and this is a very great *Prerogative.* But if the Parliament doth not approve of the War, the King must bear the Charge of it out of his own Purse; and this is a great Check on the Crown, So the King hath a *Prerogative* to coin Money, without Consent of Parliament: But he cannot compel the Subject to take that Money, except it be Sterling, Gold or Silver; because, herein he is limited by Law. Some Princes have, indeed, extended their *Prerogative* further than the Law allowed them: Wherein, however, the Lawyers of succeeding Ages, as fond as they are of *Precedents,* have never dared to justify them. But, to say the Truth, it is only of late Times that *Prerogative* hath been fixed and ascertained. For, whoever reads the Histories of *England,* will find that some former Kings, and those none of the worst, have, upon several Occasions, ventured to controul the Laws, with very little Ceremony or Scruple, even later than the Days of Queen *Elizabeth.* In her Reign, that pernicious Counsel of sending *base Money* hither, very narrowly failed of losing the Kingdom; being complained of by the Lord Deputy, the Council, and the whole Body of the *English* here: So that soon after her Death, it was recalled by her Successor, and lawful Money paid in Exchange.

Having thus given you some Notion of what is meant by the King's *Prerogative,* as far as a *Tradesman* can be thought capable of explaining it, I will only add the Opinion of the great Lord *Bacon;* that, *as God governs the World by the settled Laws of Nature, which he hath made, and never transcends those Laws, but upon high important Occasions: So, among earthly Princes, those are the Wisest and the Best, who govern by the known Laws of the Country, and seldomest make use of their* Prerogative.

Now, here you may see that the vile Accusation of Wood and his Accomplices, charging us with *disputing the King's Prerogative,* by refusing his Brass, can have no Place; because compelling the Subject to take any Coin, which is not Sterling, is no Part of the King's *Prerogative;* and I am very confident, if it were so, we should be the last of his People to dispute it; as well from that inviolable Loyalty we have always paid to his Majesty, as from the Treatment we might in such a Case justly expect from some, who seem to think, we have neither *common Sense,* nor *common Senses.* But, God be thanked, the best of them are only our *Fellow-Subjects,* and not our *Masters.* One great Merit I am sure we have, which those of *English* Birth can have no Pretence to; that our Ancestors reduced this Kingdom to the Obedience of England; for which we have been rewarded with a worse Climate, the Privilege of being governed by Laws to which we do not consent; a ruined Trade, a House of *Peers* without *Jurisdiction;* almost an Incapacity for all Employments, and the Dread of *Wood's* Half-pence.

But we are so far from disputing the King's *Prerogative* in coining, that we own he hath Power to give a Patent to any Man, for setting his Royal Image and Superscription upon whatever Materials he pleaseth; and Liberty to the Patentee to offer them in any Country from *England* to *Japan,* only attended with one small Limitation, that *no body alive is obliged to take them.*

Upon these Considerations, I was ever against all Recourse to *England* for a Remedy against the present impending Evil; especially, when I observed, that the Addresses of both Houses, after long Expectance, produced nothing but a Report altogether in Favour of *Wood;* upon which, I made some Observations in a former Letter; and might at least have made as many more: For, it is a Paper of as singular a Nature, as I ever beheld.

But I mistake; for before this *Report* was made, his Majesty's *most gracious Answer* to the House of Lords was sent over, and printed; wherein there are these Words, *granting the Patent for coining Half-pence and Farthings,* AGREEABLE TO THE PRACTICE OF HIS ROYAL PREDECESSORS, &c. That King *Charles II,* and King *James II,* (and they only) did grant Patents for this Purpose, is indisputable, and I have shewn it at large. Their Patents were passed under the great Seal of *Ireland,* by References to *Ireland;* the Copper to be coined in *Ireland,* the Patentee was bound, on Demand, to receive his Coin back in *Ireland,* and pay Silver and Gold in Return. *Wood's* Patent was made under the Great Seal of *England,* the Brass coined in *England,* not the least Reference made to *Ireland;* the Sum immense, and the Patentee under no Obligation to receive it again, and give good Money for it: This I only mention, because, in my private Thoughts, I have sometimes made a Query, whether the *Penner* of those Words in his Majesty's most *gracious Answer,* AGREEABLE TO THE PRACTICE OF HIS ROYAL PREDECESSORS, had maturely considered the several Circumstances; which, in my poor Opinion, seem to make a Difference.

Let me now say something concerning the other great Cause of some People's Fear; as *Wood* has taught the *London* News-Writer to express it: That *his Excellency the Lord Lieutenant is coming over to settle* Wood's *Half-pence.*

We know very well, that the Lords Lieutenants for several Years past, have not thought this Kingdom *worthy the Honour of their Residence,* longer than was absolutely necessary for the King's Business; which consequently *wanted no Speed in the Dispatch.* And therefore, it naturally fell into most Mens Thoughts, that a new Governor coming at an *unusual* Time, must portend some *unusual* Business to be done; especially, if the common Report be true; that the Parliament prorogued to I know not when, is, by a new Summons (revoking that Prorogation) to assemble soon after his Arrival: For which extraordinary Proceeding, the Lawyers, on t'other Side the Water, have, by great good Fortune, found two *Precedents.*

All this being granted, it can never enter into my Head, that so *little a Creature as Wood* could find Credit enough with the King and his Ministers, to have the Lord Lieutenant of *Ireland* sent hither in a Hurry, upon his Errand.

For, let us take the whole Matter nakedly, as it lies before us, without the Refinements of some People, with which we have nothing to do. Here is a Patent granted under the great Seal of *England,* upon false Suggestions, to one *William Wood,* for coining Copper Half-pence for *Ireland:* The Parliament here, upon Apprehensions of the worst Consequences from the said Patent, address the King to have it recalled: This is refused, and a Committee of the Privy-Council *report* to his Majesty, that *Wood* has performed the Conditions of his Patent. He then is left to do the best he can with his Half-pence; no Man being obliged to receive them; the People here, being likewise left to themselves, unite as one Man; resolving they will have nothing to do with his Ware. By this plain Account of the Fact, it is manifest, that the King and his Ministry are wholly out of the Case; and the Matter is left to be disputed between him and us. Will any Man therefore attempt to persuade me, that a Lord Lieutenant is to be dispatched over in great Haste, before the ordinary Time, and a Parliament summoned, by anticipating a Prorogation; merely to put an Hundred Thousand Pounds into the Pocket of a *Sharper,* by the Ruin of a most loyal Kingdom?

But supposing all this to be true. By what Arguments could a Lord Lieutenant prevail on the same Parliament, which addressed with so much Zeal and Earnestness against this Evil; to pass it into a Law? I am sure their Opinion of *Wood* and his Project is not mended since their last Prorogation: And supposing those *Methods* should be used, which, *Detractors* tell us, have been sometimes put in Practice for *gaining Votes;* it is well known, that in this Kingdom there are few Employments to be given; and if there were more; it is *as well known* to whose Share they must fall.

But, because great Numbers of you are altogether ignorant in the Affairs of your Country, I will tell you some Reasons, why there are so few Employments to be disposed of in this Kingdom. All considerable Offices for Life here, are possessed by those, to whom the Reversions were granted; and these have been generally Followers of the Chief Governors, or Persons who had Interest in the Court of *England.* So the Lord *Berkely* of *Stratton,* holds that great Office of *Master of the Rolls;* the Lord *Palmerstown* is *First Remembrancer,* worth near 2,000*l. per Ann.* One *Dodington,* Secretary to the Earl of *Pembroke,* begged the Reversion of *Clerk of the Pells,* worth 2,500*l.* a Year, which he now enjoys by the Death of the Lord *Newtown.* Mr. *Southwell* is Secretary of State, and the Earl of *Burlington* Lord High Treasurer of *Ireland* by Inheritance. These are only a few among many others, which I have been told of, but cannot remember. Nay the Reversion of several Employments during Pleasure are granted the same way. This among many others, is a Circumstance whereby the Kingdom of *Ireland* is distinguished from all other Nations upon Earth; and makes it so difficult an Affair to get into a Civil Employ, that Mr. *Addison* was forced to purchase an old obscure Place, called *Keeper of the Records* in Bermingham's *Tower,* of Ten Pounds a Year, and to get a Salary of 400*l.* annexed to it, though all the Records there are not worth half a Crown, either for Curiosity or Use. And we lately saw a *Favourite Secretary,** descend to be *Master of the Revels,* which by his *Credit and Extortion* he hath made *Pretty Considerable.* I say nothing of the Under-Treasurership worth about 9000*l.* a Year; nor the Commissioners of the Revenue, Four of whom generally live in *England:* For I think none of these are granted in Reversion. But the Jest is, that I have known upon Occasion, some of these absent Officers as *Keen* against the Interest of *Ireland,* as if they had never been indebted to her for a *Single Groat.*

I confess, I have been sometimes tempted to wish that this Project of *Wood* might succeed; because I reflected with some Pleasure what a *Jolly Crew* it would bring over among us of *Lords* and *Squires,* and *Pensioners* of *Both Sexes,* and Officers *Civil* and *Military;* where we should live together as merry and sociable as Beggars; only with this one Abatement, that we should neither have *Meat* to feed nor *Manufactures* to cloath us; unless we could be content to *Prance* about in *Coats of Mail;* or eat Brass as Ostritches do Iron.

I return from this Digression, to that which gave me the Occasion of making it: And, I believe you are now convinced, that if the Parliament of *Ireland* were as *Temptable* as any *other* Assembly *within a Mile of* Christendom (which God forbid) yet the *Managers* must of Necessity fail for want of *Tools* to work with. But I will yet go one Step further, by supposing that a Hundred new Employments were erected on Purpose to gratify *Compliers:* Yet still an insuperable Difficulty would remain. For it happens, I know not how, that *Money* is neither *Whig* nor *Tory,* neither of *Town* nor *Coun-*

---

* Mr. Hopkins, Secretary to the Duke of Grafton.

try Party; and it is not improbable, that a Gentleman would rather chuse to live upon his *own Estate,* which brings him *Gold* and *Silver,* than with the Addition of any *Employment;* when his *Rents* and *Sallary* must both be paid in *Wood's* Brass, at above Eighty *per Cent.* Discount.

For these, and many other Reasons, I am confident you need not be under the least Apprehensions, from the sudden Expectation of the *Lord Lieutenant,* while we continue in our present hearty Disposition; to alter which there is no suitable Temptation can possibly be offered: And if, as I have often asserted from the best Authority, the *Law* hath not left a *Power* in the *Crown* to force any Money, except Sterling, upon the Subject; much less can the Crown *devolve* such a *Power* upon *another.*

This I speak with the utmost Respect to the *Person* and *Dignity* of his Excellency the Lord *Carteret;* whose Character was lately given me, by a Gentleman that hath known him from his first Appearance in the World: That Gentleman describes him as a young Man of great Accomplishments, excellent Learning, Regular in his Life, and of much Spirit and Vivacity. He hath since, as I have heard, been employed abroad; was Principal Secretary of State; and is now about the 37th Year of his Age appointed Lord Lieutenant of *Ireland.* From such a Governour this Kingdom may reasonably hope for as much Prosperity, as *under so many Discouragements* it can be capable of receiving.

It is true indeed, that within the Memory of Man, there have been Governors of so much Dexterity, as to carry Points of terrible Consequence to this Kingdom, by their Power with *those who were in Office;* and by their Arts in managing or deluding others with *Oaths, Affability,* and even with *Dinners.* If *Wood's* Brass had, in those Times, been upon the *Anvil,* it is obvious enough to conceive what Methods would have been taken. *Depending* Persons would have been told in plain Terms, that it was a *Service expected from them, under Pain of the publick Business being put into more complying Hands.* Others would be allured by *Promises.* To the *Country Gentle-*

men, besides *good Words, Burgundy* and *Closeting;* it might, perhaps, have been hinted, how *kindly it would be taken to comply with a Royal Patent although it were not compulsory.* That if any Inconveniencies ensued, it might be made up with other *Graces or Favours hereafter:* That *Gentlemen ought to consider, whether it were prudent or safe to disgust* England: They would be desired to *think of some good Bills for encouraging of Trade, and setting the Poor to work: Some further Acts against Popery, and for uniting Protestants.* There would be solemn Engagements, that we should *never be troubled with above Forty Thousand Pounds in his Coin, and all of the best and weightiest Sort; for which we should only give our Manufactures in Exchange, and keep our Gold and Silver at home.* Perhaps, *a seasonable Report of some Invasion would have been spread in the most proper Juncture;* which is a great Smoother of Rubs in publick Proceedings: And we should have been told, that *this was no Time to create Differences, when the Kingdom was in Danger.*

These, I say, and the like Methods, would, in corrupt Times, have been taken to let in this Deluge of Brass among us: And, I am confident, would even then have not succeeded; much less under the Administration of so excellent a Person as the Lord *Carteret;* and in a Country, where the People of all Ranks, Parties, and Denominations, are convinced to a Man, that the utter undoing of themselves and their Posterity for ever, will be dated from the Admission of that execrable Coin: That if it once enters, it can be no more confined to a small or moderate Quantity, than the *Plague* can be confined to a few Families; and that no *Equivalent* can be given by any earthly Power, any more than a dead Carcase can be recovered to Life by a Cordial.

There is one comfortable Circumstance in this universal Opposition to Mr. *Wood,* that the People sent over hither from *England,* to *fill up our Vacancies, Ecclesiastical, Civil, and Military,* are all on our Side: *Money,* the great *Divider* of the World, hath, by a strange Revolution, been the great *Uniter* of a most *divided* People. Who would leave a Hundred

Pounds a Year in *England,* (*a Country of Freedom*) to be paid a Thousand in *Ireland* out of *Wood's* Exchequer? The *Gentleman they* have lately made *Primate,* would never quit his Seat in an *English* House of Lords, and his Preferments at *Oxford* and *Bristol,* worth Twelve Hundred Pounds a Year, for four times the Denomination here, but not half the Value: Therefore, I expect to hear he will be as good an *Irishman,* at least, upon *this one Article,* as any of his Brethren; or even of *Us,* who have had the *Misfortune* to be born in this Island. For those, who in the common Phrase, do not *come hither to learn the Language,* would never change a better Country for a worse, to receive *Brass* instead of *Gold.*

Another Slander spread by *Wood* and his Emissaries is, that, by opposing him, we discover an Inclination to *shake off our Dependance upon the Crown of* England. Pray observe, how important a Person is this same *William Wood;* and how the publick Weal of two Kingdoms, is involved in his private Interest. First, all those who refuse to take his Coin *are Papists;* for he tells us, that *none but Papists are associated against him.* Secondly, they *dispute the King's Prerogative.* Thirdly, they *are ripe for Rebellion.* And Fourthly, they are going to *shake off their Dependance upon the Crown of* England; that is to say, *they are going to chuse another King:* For there can be no other Meaning in this Expression, however some may pretend to strain it.

And this gives me an Opportunity of explaining, to those who are ignorant, another Point, which hath often *swelled in my Breast.* Those who come over hither to us from *England,* and some *weak* People among ourselves, whenever, in Discourse, we make mention of *Liberty* and *Property* shake their Heads, and tell us, that *Ireland* is a *depending Kingdom;* as if they would seem, by this Phrase, to intend, that the People of *Ireland* is in some State of Slavery or Dependance, different from those of *England:* Whereas, a *depending Kingdom* is a *modern Term of Art;* unknown, as I have heard, to all antient *Civilians,* and *Writers upon Government;* and *Ireland* is, on the contrary, called in some Statutes an *Imperial Crown,* as held only from God; which is as high a Style, as any Kingdom is capable of receiving. Therefore by this Expression, a *depending Kingdom,* there is no more understood, than that by a Statute made here, in the 33d Year of *Henry* VIII, *The King and his Successors, are to be Kings Imperial of this Realm, as united and knit to the Imperial Crown of* England. I have looked over all the *English* and *Irish* Statutes, without finding any Law that makes *Ireland* depend upon *England;* any more than *England* doth upon *Ireland.* We have, indeed, obliged ourselves to have *the same King with them;* and consequently they are obliged to have the *same King with us.* For the Law was made by *our own Parliament;* and our Ancestors then were not such *Fools (whatever they were in the preceding Reign)* to bring themselves under I know not what *Dependance,* which is now talked of, without any Ground of *Law, Reason,* or *common Sense.*

Let whoever think otherwise, I *M. B. Drapier,* desire to be excepted. For I declare, next under God, I *depend* only on the King my Sovereign, and on the Laws of my own Country, And I am so far from *depending* upon the People of *England,* that, if they should ever *rebel* against my Sovereign, (which God forbid) I would be ready at the first Command from his Majesty to take Arms against them; as some of *my* Countrymen did against *theirs* at *Preston.* And, if such a Rebellion should prove so successful as to fix the *Pretender* on the Throne of *England;* I would venture to transgress that *Statute* so far, as to lose every Drop of my Blood, to hinder him from being *King* of *Ireland.*

It is true, indeed, that within the Memory of Man, the Parliaments of *England,* have *sometimes* assumed the Power of binding this Kingdom, by Laws enacted there; wherein they were, at first, openly opposed (as far as *Truth, Reason,* and *Justice* are capable of *opposing*) by the famous Mr. *Molineaux,* an *English* Gentleman born here; as well as by several of the greatest Patriots, and *best Whigs* in *England;* but the *Love and Torrent* of Power prevailed. Indeed, the Arguments on both Sides were invincible. For in *Reason,* all *Government* without the Consent of the *Governed,* is the *very Definition of Slavery:* But in *Fact, eleven Men well armed, will certainly subdue one single Man in his Shirt.* But I have done. For those who have used *Power* to cramp *Liberty,* have gone so far as to resent even the *Liberty* of *Complaining;* although a Man upon the Rack, was never known to be refused the Liberty of *roaring* as loud as he thought fit.

And, as we are apt to *sink* too much under *unreasonable* Fears, so we are too soon inclined to be *raised* by groundless Hopes, (according to the Nature of all *consumptive* Bodies like ours.) Thus, it hath been given about for several Days past, that *Somebody in England,* empowered a second *Somebody* to write to a third *Somebody* here, to assure us, that we *should no more be troubled with those Half-pence.* And this is reported to have been done by the *same Person,** who was said to have sworn some Months ago, that he would *ram them down our Throats,* (though I doubt they would *stick in our Stomachs*). But which ever of these Reports is true or false, it is no Concern of ours. For, *in this Point,* we have nothing to do with *English Ministers:* And I should be sorry to leave it in their Power to *redress* this Grievance, or to *enforce* it: For the *Report of the Committee* hath given me a *Surfeit.* The Remedy is wholly in your own Hands; and therefore I have digressed a little, in order to refresh and continue that *Spirit* so seasonably raised amongst you; and to let you see, that by the Laws of GOD, of Nature, of Nations, and of your own Country, you ARE and OUGHT to be as FREE a People as your Brethren in *England.*

If the Pamphlets published at *London* by *Wood* and his *Journeymen,* in Defence of his Cause, were Re-printed here, and that our Countrymen could be persuaded to read them, they would convince you of his wicked Design, more than all I shall ever be able to say. In short, I make him a perfect *Saint,* in Comparison of what he appears to be, from the writings of those whom he *Hires,* to justify his *Project.* But

---

* *Mr.* Walpole, *now Sir* Robert.

he is so far *Master of the Field* (*let others guess the Reason*) that no *London* Printer dare publish any Paper written in Favour of *Ireland:* And here no Body hath yet been so *bold,* as to publish any Thing in *Favour* of *him.*

There was a few Days ago a Pamphlet sent me of near 50 Pages, written in Favour of Mr. *Wood* and his Coinage; printed in *London:* It is not worth answering, because probably it will never be published here: But it gave me an Occasion, to reflect upon an Unhappiness we lie under, that the People of *England* are utterly ignorant of our Case; Which, however, is no Wonder; since it is a Point they do not in the least concern themselves about; farther than, perhaps, as a Subject of Discourse in a Coffee-house, when they have nothing else to talk of. For I have Reason to believe, that no Minister ever gave himself the Trouble of reading any Papers written in our Defence; because, I suppose, *their Opinions are already determined,* and are formed wholly upon the Reports of *Wood* and his Accomplices; else it would be impossible, that any Man could have the Impudence, to write such a Pamphlet, as I have mentioned.

Our *Neighbours, whose Understandings are just upon a Level with Ours* (which perhaps are none of the *Brightest*) have a strong Contempt for most Nations, but especially for *Ireland:* They look upon us as a Sort of *Savage Irish,* whom our Ancestors conquered several Hundred Years ago: And, if I should describe the *Britons* to you, as they were in *Cæsar's* Time, when they *painted their Bodies, or cloathed themselves with the Skins of Beasts,* I should act full as reasonably as they do. However, they are so far to be excused, in Relation to the present Subject, that, hearing *only one Side of the Cause,* and having neither Opportunity nor Curiosity to examine the *other,* they *believe a Lye,* meerly for their Ease; and conclude, because Mr. *Wood* pretends to have *Power,* he hath also *Reason* on his Side.

Therefore, to let you see how this Case is represented in *England* by *Wood* and his Adherents, I have thought it proper to extract out of that Pamphlet, a few of those notorious

Falshoods, in Point of *Fact* and *Reasoning,* contained therein; the Knowledge whereof, will confirm my Countrymen in their *Own* Right Sentiments, when they will see by comparing both, how much their *Enemies are in the Wrong*.

First, The Writer positively asserts, *That* Wood's *Half-pence were current among us for several Months, with the universal Approbation of all People, without one single Gain-sayer; and we all to a Man thought our selves Happy in having them.*

Secondly, He affirms, *That we were drawn into a Dislike of them, only by some Cunning Evil-designing Men among us, who opposed this Patent of Wood, to get another for themselves.*

Thirdly, That *those who most declared at first against* WOOD's *Patent, were the very Men who intend to get another for their own Advantage.*

Fourthly, That *our Parliament and Privy-Council, the Lord Mayor and Alderman of* Dublin, *the Grand Juries and Merchants, and in short the whole Kingdom; nay, the very Dogs,* (as he expresseth it) *were fond of these Half-pence, till they were inflamed by those few designing Persons aforesaid.*

Fifthly, He says directly, That *all those who opposed the Half-pence, were Papists, and Enemies to King George.*

Thus far I am confident, the most ignorant among you can safely swear from your own Knowledge, that the Author is a most notorious Lyar in every Article; the direct contrary being so manifest to the whole Kingdom, that if occasion required, we might get it confirmed *under Five Hundred Thousand Hands.*

Sixthly, He would perswade us, That *if we sell Five Shillings worth of our Goods or Manufactures for Two Shillings and Four-pence worth of Copper, although the Copper were melted down, and that we could get Five Shillings in Gold and Silver for the said Goods; yet to take the said Two Shillings and Four-pence in Copper, would be greatly for our Advantage.*

And, Lastly, He makes us a very fair Offer, as empowered by *Wood,* That *if we will take off Two hundred thousand Pounds in his Half-pence for our Goods, and likewise pay him*

Three per Cent. *Interest for Thirty Years, for an hundred and Twenty thousand Pounds* (*at which he computes the Coinage above the intrinsick Value of the Copper*) *for the Loan of his Coin, he will after that Time give us good Money for what Half-pence will be then left.*

Let me place this Offer in as clear a Light as I can, to shew the insupportable Villainy and Impudence of that incorrigible Wretch. First, (says he) *I will send Two hundred thousand Pounds of my Coin into your Country: The Copper I compute to be in real Value Eighty thousand Pounds, and I charge you with an hundred and twenty thousand Pounds for the Coinage; so that you see, I lend you an Hundred and twenty thousand Pounds for Thirty Years; for which you shall pay me Three* per Cent. *That is to say, Three thousand Six hundred Pounds* per Ann., *which in Thirty Years, will amount to an Hundred and eight thousand Pounds.* And *when these Thirty Years are expired, return me my Copper, and I will give you good Money for it.*

This is the Proposal made to us by *Wood,* in that Pamphlet, written by one of his *Commissioners:* And the Author is supposed to be the same infamous *Coleby,* one of his *Under-Swearers* at the *Committee of Council,* who was tryed for *Robbing the Treasury here,* where he was an Under-Clerk.

By this Proposal he will first receive Two hundred thousand Pounds, in Goods or Sterling, for as much Copper as he values at Eighty thousand Pounds; but in Reality not worth Thirty thousand Pounds. Secondly, He will receive for Interest an Hundred and Eight thousand Pounds: And when our Children come Thirty Years hence, to return his Half-pence upon his Executors, (for before that Time he will be probably gone *to his own Place*) those Executors will very reasonably reject them as Raps and Counterfeits; which they will be, and Millions of them of his own Coinage.

Methinks, I am fond of such a *Dealer* as this, who mends every Day upon our Hands, like a *Dutch* Reckoning; where, if you dispute the Unreasonableness and Exorbitancy of the

Bill, the Landlord shall bring it up every Time with new Additions.

Although these and the like Pamphlets, published by *Wood* in *London,* be altogether unknown here, where no Body could read them, without as much *Indignation* as *Contempt* would allow; yet I thought it proper to give you a Specimen how this *Man* employs his Time; where he Rides alone without any Creature to contradict him; while OUR FEW FRIENDS there, wonder at our Silence: And the *English* in general, if they think of this Matter at all, impute our Refusal to *Wilfulness* or *Disaffection,* just as *Wood* and his *Hirelings* are pleased to represent.

But, although our Arguments are not suffered to be printed in *England,* yet the Consequence will be of little Moment. Let *Wood* endeavour to *persuade* the People *There,* that we ought to *Receive* his Coin; and let Me *Convince* our People *Here,* that they ought to *Reject it,* under Pain of our utter Undoing. And then let him do his *Best* and his *Worst.*

Before I conclude, I must beg Leave in all Humility to tell Mr. *Wood,* that he is guilty of great *Indiscretion,* by causing so Honourable a Name as that of Mr. *Walpole* to be mentioned so often, and in such a Manner, upon this Occasion. A short Paper, printed at *Bristol,* and reprinted here, reports Mr. *Wood* to say, that he *wonders at the Impudence and Insolence of the* Irish, *in refusing his Coin,* and *what he will do when Mr.* Walpole *comes* to *Town.* Where, by the Way, he is mistaken; for it is the *True English People* of *Ireland,* who refuse it; although we take it for granted, that the Irish will do so too, whenever they are asked. In another printed Paper of his contriving, it is roundly expressed, that Mr. *Walpole will cram his Brass down our Throats.* Sometimes it is given out, that we must *either take these Half-pence or eat our Brogues.* And, in another News-Letter, but of Yesterday, we read, that the same great Man *hath sworn to make us swallow his Coin in Fire-Balls.*

This brings to my Mind the known Story of a *Scotch* Man, who receiving Sentence of Death, with all the Circumstances of

Hanging, Beheading, Quartering, Embowelling, and the like; cried out, *What need all this COOKERY?* And, I think, we have Reason to ask the same Question: For, if we believe *Wood,* here is a *Dinner* getting ready for us, and you see the *Bill of Fare;* and I am sorry the *Drink* was forgot, which might easily be supplied with *Melted Lead* and *Flaming Pitch.*

What vile Words are these to put into the Mouth of a great Counsellor, in high Trust with his Majesty, and looked upon as a Prime Minister? If Mr. *Wood* hath no better a Manner of representing his Patrons; when I come to be a *Great Man,* he shall never be suffered to attend at my *Levee.* This is not the Style of a Great Minister; it savours too much of the *Kettle* and the *Furnace;* and came entirely out of *Wood's Forge.*

As for the Threat of making us *eat our Brogues,* we need not be in Pain; for if his Coin should pass, that *un-Polite Covering for the Feet,* would no longer be a *National Reproach;* because then, we should have neither *Shoe* nor *Brogue* left in the Kingdom. But here the Falshood of Mr. *Wood* is fairly detected; for I am confident, Mr. *Walpole* never heard of a *Brogue* in his whole Life.

As to *Swallowing these Half-pence in Fire-Balls,* it is a Story equally improbable. For, to execute this *Operation,* the whole Stock of Mr. *Wood's* Coin and Metal must be melted down, and molded into hollow *Balls,* with *Wild-Fire,* no bigger than a *reasonable* Throat can be able to swallow. Now, the Metal he hath prepared, and already coined, will amount to at least Fifty Millions of Half-pence, to be *Swallowed* by a Million and a Half of People; so, that allowing Two Half-pence to each *Ball,* there will be about Seventeen *Balls* of *Wild-Fire* a-piece, to be swallowed by every Person in the Kingdom: And to administer this Dose, there cannot be conveniently fewer than Fifty Thousand *Operators,* allowing one *Operator* to every Thirty; which, considering the *Squeamishness* of some Stomachs, and the *Peevishness* of *Young Children,* is but reasonable. Now, under Correction of better Judgments, I think the Trouble and Charge of such an Experiment, would exceed the Profit; and therefore I take this

Report to be *spurious;* or at least, only a new *Scheme* of Mr. *Wood* himself; which, to make it pass the better in *Ireland,* he would father upon a *Minister of State.*

But I will now demonstrate, beyond all Contradiction, that Mr. *Walpole* is against this Project of Mr. *Wood,* and is an entire Friend to *Ireland,* only by this one invincible Argument, That he has the Universal Opinion of being a wise Man, an able Minister, and, in all his Proceedings, pursuing the *True Interest* of the *King his Master:* And, that as his *Integrity* is above all *Corruption,* so is his *Fortune* above all *Temptation.* I reckon therefore, we are perfectly safe from that *Corner;* and shall never be under the Necessity of contending with so *Formidable a Power;* but be left to possess our *Brogues* and *Potatoes* in *Peace,* as *Remote from Thunder, as we are from Jupiter.**

> *I am, my dear Countrymen,*
> *Your Loving Fellow-Subject,*
> *Fellow-Sufferer, and*
> *Humble Servant,*

Oct. 13.   M. B.
1724.

---

* *Procul à Jove, procul à fulmine.*

A Meditation upon a Broomstick

A Meditation upon a Broomstick is a happy example of Swift's willingness to turn his powers to the purposes of amusement and the gentlest of raillery within the circle of those whom he loved. Swift's great friend, Thomas Sheridan, reports that the work was composed in 1704 when Swift, serving as chaplain to Lord Berkeley, was living on the most congenial terms with the members of that nobleman's household. Among his social duties was to read aloud to Lady Berkeley from the pages of Robert Boyle's *Meditations,* a work for which he could not share her ladyship's enthusiasm. Accordingly, says Sheridan, Swift "took an opportunity of conveying away the book, and dexterously inserted a leaf, on which he had written his own 'Meditation on a Broomstick.'" When, in the next session with Boyle's work, Swift, "with an inflexible gravity of countenance . . . in the same solemn tone," read his own composition, Lady Berkeley was loud in her praises. On learning of the hoax, Sheridan tells us, she joined in the laughter at her own expense, saying, "What a vile trick that rogue played me. But it is his way, he never balks his humour in any thing."

Though written as a good-natured jest, the *Meditation* displays to excellent advantage Swift's gift for parody. Despite its droll extravagance, its manner is remarkably similar to that of Boyle.

The earliest surviving edition of the work is dated 1710 and provides the text reproduced here. If, as is believed in some quarters, earlier editions were published, no copies are known to be in existence.

A

MEDITATION

UPON A BROOMSTICK

THIS single Stick, which you now behold ingloriously lying in that neglected Corner, I once knew in a flourishing State in a Forest: It was full of Sap, full of Leaves, and full of Boughs: But now, in vain does the busy Art of Man pretend to vye with Nature, by tying that wither'd Bundle of Twigs to its sapless Trunk: 'Tis now as best but the Reverse of what it was, a Tree turned upside down, the Branches on the Earth, and the Root in the Air: 'Tis now handled by every dirty Wench, condemned to do her Drudgery, and, by a capricious kind of Fate, destin'd to make other Things Clean, and be Nasty itself: At length, worn to the Stumps in the Service of the Maids, 'tis either thrown out of Doors, or condemned to the last Use of kindling a Fire. When I beheld this, I sigh'd, and said within my self, Surely mortal Man is a Broom-stick; Nature sent him into the World strong and lusty in a thriving Condition, wearing his own Hair on his Head, the proper Branches of this Reasoning Vegetable, till the Axe of Intemperance has lopp'd off his green Boughs, and left him a wither'd Trunk: He then flies to Art, and puts on a Periwig, valuing himself upon an unnatural Bundle of Hairs, all covered with Powder that never grew on his Head; but now should this our Broom-stick pretend to enter the Scene, proud of those Birchen Spoils it never bore, and all covered with Dust, though the Sweepings of the finest Lady's Chamber, we should be apt to ridicule and despise its Vanity. Partial Judges that we are of our own Excellencies, and other Men's Defaults!

But a Broom-stick, perhaps you will say, is an Emblem of a Tree standing on its Head; and pray what is Man, but a topsy-turvy Creature, his Animal Faculties perpetually mounted on his Rational, his Head where his Heels should be, groveling on the Earth! And yet, with all his Faults, he sets up to be an universal Reformer and Corrector of Abuses, a Remover of Grievances, rakes into every Slut's Corner of Nature, bringing hidden Corruptions to the Light, and raises a mighty Dust where there was none before, sharing deeply all the while in the very same Pollutions he pretends to sweep away: His last Days are spent in Slavery to Women, and generally the least deserving; till worn to the Stumps, like his Brother Bezom, he is either kick'd out of Doors, or made use of to kindle Flames, for others to warm themselves by.

Selected Poems

The full importance of Swift's poems has been recognized only very recently—largely as the result of Sir Harold Williams's superb edition, *The Poems of Jonathan Swift* (3 vols., Oxford, 1937). In the Williams edition the poems Swift wrote have been freed from an accumulation of false attributions and corrupt texts, have received precise and indispensable annotation, and, not least, have been dated with the greatest possible degree of accuracy. What has emerged may or may not be a distinguished body of English verse; there are those for whom Swift's indifference to the traditional notions of beauty bar him forever from the ranks of the great poets. No one can deny, however, that properly ordered and annotated, the poems constitute a biographical resource of the first importance.

Swift constantly wrote verses, not as a professional poet seeking themes of universal significance, but as a nimble versifier for whom the writing of a poem could express the anger or admiration or glee produced by a particular situation. Not all of Swift's poems, to be sure, are the spontaneous products of leisure moments; the longer pieces in particular are clearly the result of artful deliberation and often of careful revision. Yet virtually all the poetic works must be seen as, in a sense, personal communications. Whether Swift writes teasingly for Lady Betty Germain, tenderly for Stella, or fiercely for a corrupt world, he writes from motives that are immediate, transparent, and genuine.

Even Swift's earliest poems, the undistinguished efforts to produce Pindaric odes in the manner of Cowley, are sincere expressions of admiration for King William, the Athenian Society, Sir William Temple, and Archbishop Sancroft. Swift never again attempted the sustained sober formality of these early pieces, and there is good reason to rejoice in his judgment. There remained at his disposal a wealth of poetic forms, which he exploited to good advantage. In the terse epigram, the ballad, the poetic dialogue, the verse fable, and many other forms, he is able to give full play to his temperament and talent. There is hardly a poem which is not a direct expression of the bitterness or gaiety, the fierce political hatreds or warm personal attachments, the gleeful jesting or cold realism which, in turn, dominated his mind. And, although the quality of the poems is exceedingly unequal, there is in even the least of them that arresting clarity which, in verse as in prose, is the outstanding feature of Swift's style.

In the limits of the present volume it is impossible to produce even a representative sampling of the two hundred and fifty complete poems now known to be Swift's. Although there are many pieces which, because of their obvious triviality or indecency, the editor is not tempted to reprint, several important works must be omitted for reasons of space alone. Among these none is more interesting than the extraordinary "Cadenus and Vanessa," Swift's long poetic attempt to place into proper perspective the passionate and ultimately tragic love he had inspired in Esther Vanhomrigh, the "Vanessa" of the poem. By the omission of this and several other lengthy poems, however, the editor has been able to include, in addition to various short verses, "On Poetry: A Rhapsody" and "Verses on the Death of Dr. Swift," both of which deserve, above all other poems of Swift's, to be read in their entirety.

VERSES WROTE IN A LADY'S IVORY TABLE-BOOK

[On its first publication, in the *Miscellanies* of 1711, this poem bore
the date 1698. Various editors have conjectured that it was written
—or at least revised—as late as 1706.]

PERUSE my Leaves thro' ev'ry Part,
And think thou seest my owners Heart,
Scrawl'd o'er with Trifles thus, and quite
As hard, as sensless, and as light:
Expos'd to every Coxcomb's Eyes,
But hid with Caution from the Wise.
Here you may read (*Dear Charming Saint*)
Beneath (*A new Receit for Paint*)
Here in Beau-spelling (*tru tel deth*)
There in her own (*far an el breth*)   10
Here (*lovely Nymph pronounce my doom*)
There (*A safe way to use Perfume*)
Here, a Page fill'd with Billet Doux;
On t'other side (*laid out for Shoes*)
(*Madam, I dye without your Grace*)
(*Item, for half a Yard of Lace.*)
Who that had Wit would place it here,
For every peeping Fop to Jear.
To think that your Brains Issue is
Expos'd to th' Excrement of his,   20
In power of Spittle and a Clout
When e'er he please to blot it out;
And then to heighten the Disgrace
Clap his own Nonsence in the place.
Whoe're expects to hold his part
In such a Book and such a Heart,
If he be Wealthy and a Fool
Is in all Points the fittest Tool,
Of whom it may be justly said,
He's a Gold Pencil tipt with Lead.   30

A DESCRIPTION OF THE MORNING

[This poem first appeared in Steele's *Tatler,* No. 9, in April, 1709. It was reprinted in the *Miscellanies* of 1711, from which, following the Williams edition, this text is taken.]

NOW hardly here and there an Hackney-Coach
Appearing, show'd the Ruddy Morns Approach.
Now *Betty* from her Masters Bed had flown,
And softly stole to discompose her own.
The Slipshod Prentice from his Masters Door,
Had par'd the Dirt, and Sprinkled round the Floor.
Now *Moll* had whirl'd her Mop with dext'rous Airs,
Prepar'd to Scrub the Entry and the Stairs.
The Youth with Broomy Stumps began to trace
The Kennel-Edge, where Wheels had worn the Place.   10
The Smallcoal-Man was heard with Cadence deep,
'Till drown'd in Shriller Notes of Chimney-Sweep,
Duns at his Lordships Gate began to meet,
And Brickdust *Moll* had Scream'd through half the Street.
The Turnkey now his Flock returning sees,
Duly let out a Nights to Steal for Fees.
The watchful Bailiffs take their silent Stands,
And School-Boys lag with Satchels in their Hands.

A DESCRIPTION OF A CITY SHOWER

[*Tatler,* No. 238, which appeared on October 17, 1710, contained this poem, which met with an immediate, highly enthusiastic public response. It was reprinted in the *Miscellanies* of 1711, from which the present text is taken.]

CAREFUL Observers may fortel the Hour
(By sure Prognosticks) when to dread a Show'r:
While Rain depends, the pensive Cat gives o'er
Her Frolicks, and pursues her Tail no more.

Returning Home at Night, you'll find the Sink
Strike your offended Sense with double Stink.
If you be wise, then go not far to Dine,
You'll spend in Coach-hire more than save in Wine.
A Coming Show'r your shooting Corns presage,
Old Arches throb, your hollow Tooth will rage. 10
Sauntring in Coffee-house is *Dulman* seen;
He damns the Climate, and complains of Spleen.

    Mean while the South rising with dabbled Wings,
A Sable Cloud a-thwart the Welkin flings,
That swill'd more Liquor than it could contain,
And like a Drunkard gives it up again.
Brisk *Susan* whips her Linen from the Rope,
While the first drizzling Show'r is born aslope,
Such is that Sprinkling which some careless Quean
Flirts on you from her Mop, but not so clean. 20
You fly, invoke the Gods; then turning, stop
To rail; she singing, still whirls on her Mop.
Not yet, the Dust had shun'd th' unequal Strife,
But aided by the Wind, fought still for Life;
And wafted with its Foe by violent Gust,
'Twas doubtful which was Rain, and which was Dust.
Ah! where must needy Poet seek for Aid,
When Dust and Rain at once his Coat invade;
His only Coat, where Dust confus'd with Rain,
Roughen the Nap, and leave a mingled Stain. 30

    Now in contiguous Drops the Flood comes down,
Threat'ning with Deluge this *Devoted* Town.
To Shops in Crouds the dagged Females fly,
Pretend to cheapen Goods, but nothing buy.
The Templer spruce, while ev'ry Spout's a-broach,
Stays till 'tis fair, yet seems to call a Coach.
The tuck'up Sempstress walks with hasty Strides,
While Streams run down her oil'd Umbrella's Sides.
Here various Kinds by various Fortunes led,
Commence Acquaintance underneath a Shed. 40
Triumphant Tories, and desponding Whigs,

Forget their Fewds, and join to save their Wigs.
Box'd in a Chair the Beau impatient sits,
While Spouts run clatt'ring o'er the Roof by Fits;
And ever and anon with frightful Din
The Leather sounds, he trembles from within.
So when *Troy* Chair-men bore the Wooden Steed,
Pregnant with *Greeks,* impatient to be freed,
(Those Bully *Greeks,* who, as the Moderns do,
Instead of paying Chair-men, run them thro'.)   50
Laoco'n struck the Outside with his Spear,
And each imprison'd Hero quak'd for Fear.
   Now from all Parts the swelling Kennels flow,
And bear their Trophies with them as they go:
Filth of all Hues and Odours seem to tell
What Street they sail'd from, by their Sight and Smell.
They, as each Torrent drives, with rapid Force
From *Smithfield,* or St. *Pulchre*'s shape their Course,
And in huge Confluent join at *Snow-Hill* Ridge,
Fall from the *Conduit* prone to *Holborn-Bridge.*   60
Sweepings from Butchers Stalls, Dung, Guts, and Blood,
Drown'd Puppies, stinking Sprats, all drench'd in Mud,
Dead Cats and Turnip-Tops come tumbling down the Flood.

THE AUTHOR UPON HIMSELF

[These revealing verses were written in the summer of 1714, when Swift, convinced that there was little hope of making peace between Oxford and Bolingbroke and hence preserving the toppling Tory administration, had left London for Letcombe in Berkshire. Swift's worst fears were soon realized. The Tory ministry, fatally weakened by internal hostilities, did not survive the death of Queen Anne on August 1; within a few weeks from that date; Swift had returned to his Dublin deanery, his career in English politics permanently finished. The poem mentions several of Swift's most prominent political enemies, including Sir Robert Walpole (referred to by the initial letter in line 41) and Daniel Finch, the Earl of Nottingham, who, under the name of "Dismal," had been bitterly satirized by

Swift. The verses contain, as well, one of the few references Swift ever made to *A Tale of a Tub*, which, he believed, had been unfavorably called to the Queen's attention by John Sharp, Archbishop of York (the "crazy prelate" of the second line). On the poem's first printed appearance, in Faulkner's edition of 1735, the spaces in lines 1 and 53 were left blank. Lord Orrery, in a manuscript note to his own *Remarks,* asserts that, in both instances, Swift intended a reference to the Duchess of Somerset, the influential, red-haired intimate of the Queen whom Swift, by a viciously satiric poem, had thoroughly antagonized. Orrery indicates that the first line should read "By an old, redhaired, murder'ring Hag pursued," and that the Duchess is referred to in line 53 as "Madame Coningsmark," in malicious allusion to a suitor of hers who had been tried for the murder of her former husband.]

BY an ——— ——— ——— pursu'd,
A Crazy Prelate, and a Royal Prude.
By dull Divines, who look with envious Eyes,
On ev'ry Genius that attempts to rise;
And pausing o'er a Pipe, with doubtful Nod,
Give Hints, that Poets ne'er believe in God.
So, Clowns on Scholars as on Wizards look,
And take a Folio for a conj'ring Book.

   S—— had the Sin of Wit no venial Crime;
Nay, 'twas affirm'd, he sometimes dealt in Rhime: 10
Humour, and Mirth, had Place in all he writ:
He reconcil'd Divinity and Wit.
He mov'd, and bow'd, and talk't with too much Grace;
Nor shew'd the Parson in his Gait or Face;
Despis'd luxurious Wines, and costly Meat;
Yet, still was at the Tables of the Great.
Frequented Lords; *saw those that saw the Queen;*
At *Child*'s or *Truby*'s never once had been;
Where Town and Country Vicars flock in Tribes,
Secur'd by Numbers from the Lay-men's Gibes;   20
And deal in Vices of the graver Sort,
Tobacco, Censure, Coffee, Pride, and Port.

But, after sage Monitions from his Friends,
His Talents to employ for nobler Ends;
To better Judgments willing to submit,
He turns to Pol[it]icks his dang'rous Wit,

And now, the publick Int'rest to support,
By *Harley S*—— invited comes to Court.
In Favour grows with Ministers of State;
Admitted private, when Superiors wait: 30
And, *Harley,* not asham'd his Choice to own,
Takes him to *Windsor* in his Coach, alone
At *Windsor S*—— no sooner can appear,
But, *St. John* comes and whispers in his Ear;
The Waiters stand in Ranks; the Yeomen cry,
Make Room; as if a Duke were passing by.

Now *Finch* alarms the Lords; he hears for certain,
This dang'rous Priest is got behind the Curtain:
Finch, fam'd for tedious Elocution, proves
That *S*—— oils many a Spring which *Harley* moves.   40
W—— and *Ayslaby,* to clear the Doubt,
Inform the Commons, that the Secret's out:
"A *certain* Doctor is observ'd of late,
"To haunt a *certain* Minister of State:
"From whence, with half an Eye we may discover,
"The Peace is made, and *Perkin* must come over.
York is from *Lambeth* sent, to shew the Queen
A dang'rous Treatise writ against the Spleen;
Which by the Style, the Matter, and the Drift,
'Tis thought could be the Work of none but *S*——   50
Poor *York!* the harmless Tool of others Hate;
He sues for Pardon, and repents too late.

Now, —— —— —— her Vengeance vows
On *S*——'s Reproaches for her —— ——
From her red Locks her Mouth with Venom fills:
And thence into the Royal Ear instills.
The *Qu*—— incens'd, his Services forgot,
Leaves him a Victim to the vengeful *Scot;*

Now, through the Realm a Proclamation spread,
To fix a Price on his devoted Head.   60
While innocent, he scorns ignoble Flight;
His watchful Friends preserve him by a Sleight.

   By *Harley*'s Favour once again he shines;
Is now caress't by Candidate Divines;
Who change Opinions with the changing Scene:
Lord! how were they mistaken in the Dean!
Now, *Delawere* again familiar grows;
And, in S – – – – *t*'s Ear thrusts half his powder'd Nose.
The *Scottish* Nation, whom he durst offend,
Again apply that S—— would be their Friend.   70

   By Faction tir'd, with Grief he waits a while,
His great contending Friends to reconcile.
Performs what Friendship, Justice, Truth require:
What could he more, but decently retire?

PHILLIS, OR THE PROGRESS OF LOVE

[This poem first appeared in the third (self-styled "last") volume of
the Pope-Swift *Miscellanies* in January, 1728. It is one of a number
of works, written by Swift at some unknown previous date, which
were collected and transcribed by Stella for submission to Pope, who
completely directed the publication of the *Miscellanies*. Stella's manuscript, which survives, employs the spelling "Phillis"; it is followed
in this and all other particulars by the present text.]

D ESPONDING Phillis was endu'd
With ev'ry Talent of a Prude,
She trembled when a Man drew near;
Salute her, and she turn'd her Ear:
If o'er against her you were plac't
She durst not look above your Wast;
She'd rather take you to her Bed
Then let you see her dress her Head;
In Church you heard her thrô the Crowd

Repeat the Absolution loud;   10
In Church, secure behind her Fan
She durst behold that Monster, Man:
There practic'd how to place her Head,
And bit her Lips to make them red:
Or on the Matt devoutly kneeling
Would lift her Eyes up to the Ceeling,
And heave her Bosom unaware
For neighb'ring Beaux to see it bare.
　　At length a lucky Lover came,
And found Admittance from the Dame,   20
Suppose all Partyes now agreed,
The Writings drawn, the Lawyer fee'd,
The Vicar and the Ring bespoke:
Guess how could such a Match be broke.
See then what Mortals place their Bliss in!
Next morn betimes the Bride was missing,
The Mother scream'd, the Father chid,
Where can this idle Wench be hid?
No news of Phil. The Bridegroom came,
And thought his Bride had sculk't for shame,   30
Because her Father us'd to say
The Girl had such a Bashfull way.
　　Now, John the Butler must be sent
To learn the Way that Phillis went;
The Groom was wisht to saddle Crop,
For John must neither light nor stop;
But find her where so'er she fled,
And bring her back, alive or dead.
See here again the Dev'l to do;
For truly John was missing too: 40
The Horse and Pillion both were gone
Phillis, it seems, was fled with John.
Old Madam who went up to find
What Papers Phil had left behind,
A Letter on the Toylet sees
To my much honor'd Father; These:

('Tis always done, Romances tell us,
When Daughters run away with Fellows)
Fill'd with the choicest common-places,
By others us'd in the like Cases.   50
That, long ago a Fortune-teller
Exactly said what now befell her,
And in a Glass had made her see
A serving-Man of low Degree:
It was her Fate; must be forgiven;
For Marriages are made in Heaven:
His Pardon begg'd, but to be plain,
She'd do't if 'twere to do again.
Thank God, 'twas neither Shame nor Sin,
For John was come of honest Kin: 60
Love never thinks of Rich and Poor,
She'd beg with John from Door to Door:
Forgive her, if it be a Crime,
She'll never do't another Time,
She ne'r before in all her Life
Once disobey'd him, Maid nor Wife.
One Argument she summ'd up all in,
The Thing was done and past recalling:
And therefore hop'd she would recover
His Favor, when his Passion's over.   70
She valued not what others thought her;
And was—His most obedient Daughter.
    Fair Maidens all attend the Muse
Who now the wandring Pair pursues:
Away they rode in homely Sort
Their Journy long, their Money short;
The loving Couple well bemir'd,
The Horse and both the Riders tir'd:
Their Vittells bad, their Lodging worse,
Phil cry'd, and John began to curse;   80
Phil wish't, that she had strained a Limb
When first she ventur'd out with him.
John wish't, that he had broke a Leg

When first for her he quitted Peg.
  But what Adventures more befell 'um
The Muse has now not time to tell 'um.
How Jonny wheadled, threatned, fawnd,
Till Phillis all her Trinkets pawn'd:
How oft she broke her marriage Vows
In kindness to maintain her Spouse;   90
Till Swains unwholsome spoyld the Trade,
For now the Surgeon must be paid;
To whom those Perquisites are gone
In Christian Justice due to John.
  When Food and Rayment now grew scarce
Fate put a Period to the Farce;
And with exact Poetick Justice:
For John is Landlord, Phillis Hostess;
They keep at Stains the old blue Boar,
Are Cat and Dog, and Rogue and Whore.   100

A SATIRICAL ELEGY

ON THE DEATH OF A LATE FAMOUS GENERAL

[As the idol of the prowar faction during Queen Anne's reign, the Duke of Marlborough was a prime target for Tory attacks—including those of Swift. To his partisan malice, Swift seems to have added considerable personal aversion, based largely on Marlborough's alleged venality. Although presumably written upon Swift's hearing of the death of the Duke, this poem did not appear in print until 1764. The text is that printed by Deane Swift in 1765.]

HIS Grace! impossible! what dead!
Of old age too, and in his bed!
And could that Mighty Warrior fall?
And so inglorious, after all!
Well, since he's gone, no matter how,
The last loud trump must wake him now:
And, trust me, as the noise grows stronger,

He'd wish to sleep a little longer.
And could he be indeed so old
As by the news-papers we're told?   10
Threescore, I think, is pretty high;
'Twas time in conscience he should die.
This world he cumber'd long enough;
He burnt his candle to the snuff;
And that's the reason, some folks think,
He left behind *so great a s — — — k.*
Behold his funeral appears,
Nor widow's sighs, nor orphan's tears,
Wont at such times each heart to pierce,
Attend the progress of his herse.   20
But what of that, his friends may say,
He had those honours in his day.
True to his profit and his pride,
He made them weep before he dy'd.

  Come hither, all ye empty things,
Ye bubbles rais'd by breath of Kings;
Who float upon the tide of state,
Come hither, and behold your fate.
Let pride be taught by this rebuke,
How very mean a thing's a Duke;   30
From all his ill-got honours flung,
Turn'd to that dirt from whence he sprung.

ADVICE TO THE GRUB-STREET VERSE WRITERS

[Pope's well-known habit of writing upon every available scrap of
blank paper is hardly exaggerated in these jocular verses, which were
first printed by Faulkner in 1735. The shabby reputation of Edmund
Curll the bookseller survives chiefly because of the attacks made on
him by both Swift and Pope, whose works were among those he
published in pirated editions.]

Y E Poets ragged and forlorn,
   Down from your Garrets haste,

Ye Rhimers, dead as soon as born,
   Not yet consign'd to Paste;

I know a Trick to make you thrive;
   O, 'tis a quaint Device:
Your still-born Poems shall revive,
   And scorn to wrap up Spice.

Get all your Verses printed fair,
   Then, let them well be dry'd;   10
And, *Curl* must have a special Care
   To leave the Margin wide.

Lend these to Paper-sparing *Pope;*
   And, when he sits to write,
No Letter with an *Envelope*
   Could give him more Delight.

When *Pope* has fill'd the Margins round,
   Why, then recal your Loan;
Sell them to *Curl* for Fifty Pound,
   And swear they are your own.   20

DR. SWIFT TO MR. POPE

WHILE HE WAS WRITING THE *DUNCIAD*

[This poem is of biographical interest as a record of Swift's last visit to England in 1727, during which he stayed for some time with Pope at Twickenham. During this period Swift was afflicted with one of his recurring attacks of deafness. The poem was first published in the Pope-Swift *Miscellanies* of 1732; the title in that edition refers to the two men as "Dr. Sw—— and Mr. P—e."]

*P*OPE has the Talent well to speak,
   But not to reach the Ear;
His loudest Voice is low and weak,
   The *Dean* too deaf to hear.

A while they on each other look,
   Then diff'rent Studies chuse,
The *Dean* sits plodding on a Book,
   Pope walks, and courts the Muse.

Now Backs of Letters, though design'd
   For those who more will need 'em,   10
Are fill'd with Hints, and interlin'd,
   Himself can hardly read 'em.

Each Atom by some other struck,
   All Turns and Motion tries;
Till in a Lump together stuck,
   Behold a *Poem* rise!

Yet to the *Dean* his Share allot;
   He claims it by a Canon;
That, without which a Thing is not
   Is, causa sina quâ non.   20

Thus, *Pope,* in vain you boast your Wit;
   For, had our deaf Divine
Been for your Conversation fit,
   You had not writ a Line.

Of Prelate thus, for preaching fam'd,
   The Sexton reason'd well,
And justly half the Merit claim'd
   Because he *rang the Bell.*

THE FURNITURE OF A WOMAN'S MIND

[In Faulker's edition of Swift's *Works* (1735), which is the earliest surviving printed appearance of this poem, the date of its composition is given as 1727. The Mrs. Harding referred to is the widow of the Harding who was prosecuted for publishing the *Drapier's Letters;* following her husband's death, she did some publishing for Swift.]

A SET of Phrases learn't by Rote;
A Passion for a Scarlet-Coat;
When at a Play to laugh, or cry,
Yet cannot tell the Reason why:
Never to hold her Tongue a Minute;
While all she prates has nothing in it.
Whole Hours can with a Coxcomb sit,
And take his Nonsense all for Wit:
Her Learning mounts to read a Song,
But, half the Words pronouncing wrong;   10
Has ev'ry Repartee in Store,
She spoke ten Thousand Times before.
Can ready Compliments supply
On all Occasions, cut and dry.
Such Hatred to a Parson's Gown,
The Sight will put her in a Swown.
For Conversation well endu'd;
She calls it witty to be rude;
And, placing Raillery in Railing,
Will tell aloud your greatest Failing;   20
Nor makes a Scruple to expose
Your bandy Leg, or crooked Nose.
Can, at her Morning Tea, run o'er
The Scandal of the Day before.
Improving hourly in her Skill,
To cheat and wrangle at Quadrille.

   In chusing Lace a Critick nice,
Knows to a Groat the lowest Price;
Can in her Female Clubs dispute
What Lining best the Silk will suit;   30
What Colours each Complexion match:
And where with Art to place a Patch.

   If chance a Mouse creeps in her Sight,
Can finely counterfeit a Fright;
So, sweetly screams if it comes near her,

She ravishes all Hearts to hear her.
Can dext'rously her Husband teize,
By taking Fits whene'er she please:
By frequent Practice learns the Trick
At proper Seasons to be sick;   40
Thinks nothing gives one Airs so pretty;
At once creating Love and Pity.
If *Molly* happens to be careless,
And but neglects to warm her Hair-Lace,
She gets a Cold as sure as Death;
And vows she scarce can fetch her Breath.
Admires how modest Women can
Be so *robustious* like a Man.

In Party, furious to her Power;
A bitter Whig, or Tory sow'r;   50
Her Arguments directly tend
Against the Side she would defend:
Will prove herself a Tory plain,
From Principles the Whigs maintain;
And, to defend the Whiggish Cause,
Her Topicks from the Tories draws.

O yes! If any Man can find
More virtues in a Woman's Mind,
Let them be sent to Mrs. *Harding;*
She'll pay the Charges to a Farthing: 60
Take Notice, she has my Commission
To add them in the next Edition;
They may out-sell a better Thing;
So, Holla Boys; God save the King.

ON STEPHEN DUCK, THE THRESHER, AND

FAVORITE POET, A QUIBBLING EPIGRAM

[Stephen Duck, now a virtually forgotten figure, was an erstwhile
farm laborer, whose indifferent poetry enjoyed a fashionable vogue

and won him, in 1730, the patronage of the Queen. Swift's con-
temptuous lines first appeared in the 1735 edition of the *Works* but
were probably written in 1730, as that edition indicates.]

T HE Thresher *Duck,* could o'er the *Q*—— prevail.
The Proverb says; *No Fence against a Flayl.*
From *threshing* Corn, he turns to *thresh his Brains;*
For which Her *M*——*y* allows him *Grains.*
Though 'tis confess't that those who ever saw
His Poems, think them all not worth a *Straw.*
Thrice happy *Duck,* employ'd in threshing *Stubble!*
Thy Toil is lessen'd, and thy Profits double.

THE CHARACTER OF SIR ROBERT WALPOLE

[These lines, written in imitation of some French verses attacking
Cardinal Fleury, seem to have accompanied a letter which Swift
wrote to the Countess of Suffolk in 1731. They are reprinted by
Sir Harold Williams from a manuscript in the British Museum.
Swift's dislike for Walpole, which began with the political con-
flicts of Queen Anne's reign, was intensified during Walpole's
period of unique power under Hanoverian rule.]

W I T H favour & fortune fastidiously blest
he's loud in his laugh & he's coarse in his Jest
of favour & fortune unmerited vain
a sharper in trifles a dupe in the main
atchieving of nothing Still promising wonders
by dint of experience improving in Blunders
oppressing true merit exalting the base
and selling his Country to purchase his peace
a Jobber of Stocks by retailing false news
a prater at Court in the Stile of the Stews   10
of Virtue & worth by profession a giber
of Juries & senates the bully & briber
Tho I name not the wretch you know who I mean
T'is the Cur dog of Brittain & spaniel of Spain.

VERSES ON THE DEATH
OF DR. SWIFT, D.S.P.D.

[These famous verses, "occasioned by reading a maxim in Roche-foucault," were written in the winter of 1731-1732 but were not published until 1739, when a London edition was supervised by Swift's friend, Dr. William King. The editorial history of the "Verses" has been a complicated and, until recently, unfortunate one. King, acting on the advice of Pope, not only made many deletions before the publication of the original manuscript but attempted to compensate for this abridgement by introducing lines from an earlier poem of Swift's on the same subject. A subsequent Dublin edition did much to restore the original manuscript text but left a good deal to be supplied and corrected. There still survive, however, certain manuscript annotations, in a contemporary hand, which can be taken to represent Swift's own corrections to the printed text. By relying upon the Dublin edition as well as these manuscript additions, Sir Harold Williams, in his edition of the *Poems,* has produced the first authoritative attempt to reproduce in full the original text as well as Swift's own notes. The text and Swift's notes, as printed in the present volume, follow the Williams recension, for which the present editor, together with all students of Swift, has occasion to be most grateful.]

As *Rochefoucault* his Maxims drew
From Nature, I believe 'em true:
They argue no corrupted Mind
In him; the Fault is in Mankind.

This Maxim more than all the rest
Is thought too base for human Breast;
"In all Distresses of our Friends
"We first consult our private Ends,
"While Nature kindly bent to ease us,
"Points out some Circumstance to please us.   10

If this perhaps your Patience move
Let Reason and Experience prove.

We all behold with envious Eyes,
Our *Equal* rais'd above our *Size;*

Who wou'd not at a crowded Show,
Stand high himself, keep others low?
I love my Friend as well as you,
But would not have him stop my View;
Then let him have the higher Post;
I ask but for an Inch at most.   20

    If in a Battle you should find,
One, whom you love of all Mankind,
Had some heroick Action done,
A Champion kill'd, or Trophy won;
Rather than thus be over-topt,
Would you not wish his Lawrels cropt?

    Dear honest *Ned* is in the Gout,
Lies rackt with Pain, and you without:
How patiently you hear him groan!
How glad the Case is not your own!   30

    What Poet would not grieve to see,
His Brethren write as well as he?
But rather than they should excel,
He'd wish his Rivals all in Hell.

    Her End when Emulation misses,
She turns to Envy, Stings and Hisses:
The strongest Friendship yields to Pride,
Unless the Odds be on our Side.

    Vain human Kind! Fantastick Race!
Thy various Follies, who can trace?   40
Self-love, Ambition, Envy, Pride,
Their Empire in our Hearts divide:
Give others Riches, Power, and Station,
'Tis all on me an Usurpation.
I have no Title to aspire;
Yet, when you sink, I seem the higher.
In Pope, I cannot read a Line,
But with a Sigh, I wish it mine:

When he can in one Couplet fix
More Sense than I can do in Six: 50
It gives me such a jealous Fit,
I cry, Pox take him, and his Wit.

    Why must I be outdone by GAY,
In my own hum'rous biting Way?

    ARBUTHNOT is no more my Friend,
Who dares to Irony pretend;
Which I was born to introduce,
Refin'd it first, and shew'd its Use.

    ST. JOHN, as well as PULTNEY knows,
That I had some repute for Prose;   60
And till they drove me out of Date,
Could maul a Minister of State:
If they have mortify'd my Pride,
And made me throw my Pen aside;
If with such Talents Heav'n hath blest 'em
Have I not Reason to detest 'em?

    To all my Foes, dear Fortune, send
Thy Gifts, but never to my Friend:
I tamely can endure the first,
But, this with Envy makes me burst.   70

    Thus much may serve by way of Proem,
Proceed we therefore to our Poem.

    The Time is not remote, when I
Must by the Course of Nature dye:
When I foresee my special Friends,
Will try to find their private Ends:
Tho' it is hardly understood,
Which way my Death can do them good;
Yet, thus methinks, I hear 'em speak;
See, how the Dean begins to break: 80
Poor Gentleman, he droops apace,
You plainly find it in his Face:

That old Vertigo in his Head,
Will never leave him, till he's dead:
Besides, his Memory decays,
He recollects not what he says;
He cannot call his Friends to Mind;
Forgets the Place where last he din'd:
Plyes you with Stories o'er and o'er,
He told them fifty Times before.   90
How does he fancy we can sit,
To hear his out-of-fashion'd Wit?
But he takes up with younger Fokes,
Who for his Wine will bear his Jokes:
Faith, he must make his Stories shorter,
Or change his Comrades once a Quarter:
In half the Time, he talks them round;
There must another Sett be found.

For Poetry, he's past his Prime,
He takes an Hour to find a Rhime: 100
His Fire is out, his Wit decay'd,
His Fancy sunk, his Muse a Jade.
I'd have him throw away his Pen;
But there's no talking to some Men.

And, then their Tenderness appears,
By adding largely to my Years:
"He's older than he would be reckon'd,
"And well remembers *Charles* the Second.

"He hardly drinks a Pint of Wine;
"And that, I doubt, is no good Sign.   110
"His Stomach too begins to fail:
"Last Year we thought him strong and hale;
"But now, he's quite another Thing;
"I wish he may hold out till Spring.

Then hug themselves, and reason thus;
"It is not yet so bad with us."

In such a Case they talk in Tropes,
And, by their Fears express their Hopes:
Some great Misfortune to portend,
No Enemy can match a Friend;   120
With all the Kindness they profess,
The Merit of a lucky Guess,
(When daily Howd'y's come of Course,
And Servants answer; *Worse and Worse*)
Wou'd please 'em better than to tell,
That, GOD be prais'd, the Dean is well.
Then he who prophecy'd the best,
Approves his Foresight to the rest:
"You know, I always fear'd the worst,
"And often told you so at first:"   130
He'd rather chuse that I should dye,
Than his Prediction prove a Lye.
Not one foretels I shall recover;
But, all agree, to give me over.

Yet shou'd some Neighbour feel a Pain,
Just in the Parts, where I complain;
How many a Message would he send?
What hearty Prayers that I should mend?
Enquire what Regimen I kept;
What gave me Ease, and how I slept?   140
And more lament, when I was dead,
Than all the Sniv'llers round my Bed.

My good Companions, never fear,
For though you may mistake a Year;
Though your Prognosticks run too fast,
They must be verify'd at last.

"Behold the fatal Day arrive!
"How is the Dean? He's just alive.
"Now the departing Prayer is read:
"He hardly breathes. The Dean is dead.   150
"Before the Passing-Bell begun,

"The News thro' half the Town has run.
"O, may we all for Death prepare!
"What has he left? And who's his Heir?
"I know no more than what the News is,
" 'Tis all bequeath'd to publick Uses.
"To publick Use! A perfect Whim!
"What had the Publick done for him!
"Meer Envy, Avarice, and Pride!
"He gave it all:—But first he dy'd.   160
"And had the Dean, in all the Nation,
"No worthy Friend, no poor Relation?
"So ready to do Strangers good,
"Forgetting his own Flesh and Blood?

    Now Grub-Street Wits are all employ'd;
With Elegies, the Town is cloy'd:
Some Paragraph in ev'ry Paper,
[1] To *curse* the *Dean,* or *bless* the *Drapier.*

    The Doctors tender of their Fame,
Wisely on me lay all the Blame: 170
"We must confess his Case was nice;
"But he would never take Advice:
"Had he been rul'd, for ought appears,
"He might have liv'd these Twenty Years:
"For when we open'd him we found,
"That all his vital Parts were sound.

    From *Dublin* soon to *London* spread,
[2] 'Tis told at Court, the Dean is dead.

---

[1] *The Author imagines, that the Scriblers of the prevailing Party, which he always opposed, will libel him after his Death; but that others will remember him with Gratitude, who consider the Service he had done to* Ireland, *under the Name of* M. B. *Drapier, by utterly defeating the destructive Project of* Wood's *Half-pence, in five Letters to the People of* Ireland, *at that Time read universally, and convincing every Reader.*

[2] *The Dean supposeth himself to dye in* Ireland.

³ Kind Lady *Suffolk* in the Spleen,
Runs laughing up to tell the Queen.   180
The Queen, so Gracious, Mild, and Good,
Cries, "Is he gone? 'Tis time he shou'd.
"He's dead you say; why let him rot;
⁴ "I'm glad the Medals were forgot.
"I promis'd them, I own; but when?
"I only was the Princess then;
"But now as Consort of the King,
"You know 'tis quite a different Thing.

⁵ Now, *Chartres* at Sir *Robert*'s Levee,
Tells, with a Sneer, the Tidings heavy: 190
"Why, is he dead without his Shoes?
⁶ (Cries *Bob*) "I'm Sorry for the News;

---

³ *Mrs.* Howard, *afterwards Countess of* Suffolk, *then of the Bed-chamber to the Queen, professed much Friendship for the Dean. The Queen then Princess, sent a dozen times to the Dean (then in* London*) with her Command to attend her; which at last he did, by Advice of all his Friends. She often sent for him afterwards, and always treated him very Graciously. He taxed her with a Present worth Ten Pounds, which she promised before he should return to* Ireland, *but on his taking Leave, the Medals were not ready.*

⁴ *The Medals were to be sent to the Dean in four Months, but she forgot them, or thought them too dear. The Dean, being in* Ireland, *sent Mrs.* Howard *a Piece of* Indian *Plad made in that Kingdom: which the Queen seeing took from her, and wore it herself, and sent to the Dean for as much as would cloath herself and Children, desiring he would send the Charge of it. He did the former. It cost thirty-five Pounds, but he said he would have nothing except the Medals. He was the Summer following in* England, *was treated as usual, and she being then Queen, the Dean was promised a Settlement in* England, *but returned as he went, and, instead of Favour or Medals, hath been ever since under her Majesty's Displeasure.*

⁵ Chartres, *is a most infamous, vile Scoundrel, grown from a Foot-Boy, or worse, to a prodigious Fortune both in* England *and* Scotland: *He had a Way of insinuating himself into all Ministers under every Change, either as Pimp, Flatterer, or Informer. He was Tryed at Seventy for a Rape, and came off by sacrificing a great Part of his Fortune (he is since dead, but this Poem still preserves the Scene and Time it was writ in.)*

⁶ *Sir* Robert Walpole, *Chief Minister of State, treated the* Dean *in* 1726, *with great Distinction, invited him to Dinner at* Chelsea, *with the* Dean's

Oh, were the Wretch but living still,
7 And in his Place my good Friend *Will;*
Or, had a Mitre on his Head
8 Provided *Bolingbroke* were dead.

9 Now *Curl* his Shop from Rubbish drains;
Three genuine Tomes of *Swift*'s Remains.
And then to make them pass the glibber,
10 Revis'd by *Tibbalds, Moore, and Cibber.*   200
He'll treat me as he does my Betters.
11 Publish my Will, my Life, my Letters.

Friends chosen on Purpose; appointed an Hour to talk with him of Ireland, *to which* Kingdom *and* People *the* Dean *found him no great Friend; for he defended* Wood's *Project of Half-pence, &c. The* Dean *would see him no more; and upon his next Year's return to* England, Sir Robert *on an accidental Meeting, only made a civil Compliment, and never invited him again*

7 *Mr.* William Pultney, *from being Mr.* Walpole's *intimate Friend, detesting his Administration, opposed his Measures, and joined with my* Lord Bolingbroke, *to represent his Conduct in an excellent Paper, called the* Craftsman, *which is still continued.*

8 Henry St. John, *Lord Viscount* Bolingbroke, *Secretary of State to* Queen Anne *of blessed Memory. He is reckoned the most Universal Genius in* Europe; Walpole *dreading his Abilities, treated him most injuriously, working with King* George, *who forgot his Promise of restoring the said Lord, upon the restless Importunity of* Walpole.

9 Curl *hath been the most infamous Bookseller of any Age or Country: His Character in Part may be found in Mr.* POPE's *Dunciad. He published three Volumes all charged on the Dean, who never writ three Pages of them: He hath used many of the Dean's Friends in almost as vile a Manner.*

10 *Three stupid Verse Writers in* London, *the last to the Shame of the Court, and the highest Disgrace to Wit and Learning, was made Laureat.* Moore, *commonly called* Jemmy Moore, *Son of* Arthur Moore, *whose Father was Jaylor of* Monaghan *in* Ireland. *See the Character of* Jemmy Moore, *and* Tibbalds, Theobald *in the Dunciad.*

11 Curl *is notoriously infamous for publishing the Lives, Letters, and last Wills and Testaments of the Nobility and Ministers of State, as well as of all the Rogues, who are hanged at* Tyburn. *He hath been in Custody of the House of Lords for publishing or forging the Letters of many Peers; which made the Lords enter a Resolution in their Journal Book, that no Life or Writings of any Lord should be published without the Consent of the next Heir at Law, or Licence from their House.*

Revive the Libels born to dye;
Which POPE must bear, as well as I.

Here shift the Scene, to represent
How those I love, my Death lament.
Poor POPE will grieve a Month; and GAY
A Week; and ARBUTHNOTT a Day.

ST. JOHN himself will scarce forbear,
To bite his Pen, and drop a Tear.   210
The rest will give a Shrug and cry,
I'm sorry; but we all must dye.
Indifference clad in Wisdom's Guise,
All Fortitude of Mind supplies:
For how can stony Bowels melt,
In those who never Pity felt;
When *We* are lash'd, *They* kiss the Rod;
Resigning to the Will of God.

The Fools, my Juniors by a Year,
Are tortur'd with Suspence and Fear.   220
Who wisely thought my Age a Screen,
When Death approach'd, to stand between:
The Screen remov'd, their Hearts are trembling,
They mourn for me without dissembling.

My female Friends, whose tender Hearts
Have better learn'd to act their Parts.
Receive the News in *doleful Dumps*,
"The Dean is dead, (*and what is Trumps?*)
"Then Lord have Mercy on his Soul.
"(Ladies I'll venture for the *Vole.*)   230
"Six Deans they say must bear the Pall.
"(I wish I knew what *King* to call.)
"Madam, your Husband will attend
"The Funeral of so good a Friend.
"No Madam, 'tis a shocking Sight,
"And he's engag'd To-morrow Night!
"My Lady *Club* wou'd take it ill,
"If he shou'd fail her at *Quadrill.*

"He lov'd the Dean. (*I lead a Heart.*)
"But dearest Friends, they say, must part.   240
"His Time was come, he ran his Race;
"We hope he's in a better Place.

    Why do we grieve that Friends should dye?
No Loss more easy to supply.
One Year is past; a different Scene;
No further mention of the Dean;
Who now, alas, no more is mist,
Than if he never did exist.
Where's now this Fav'rite of *Apollo?*
Departed; *and his Works must follow:*   250
Must undergo the common Fate;
His Kind of Wit is out of Date.
Some Country Squire to [12] *Lintot* goes,
Enquires for SWIFT in Verse and Prose:
Says *Lintot,* "I have heard the Name:
"He dy'd a Year ago." The same.
He searcheth all his Shop in vain;
"Sir you may find them in [13] *Duck-lane:*
"I sent them with a Lord of Books,
"Last *Monday* to the Pastry-cooks.   260
"To fancy they cou'd live a Year!
"I find you're but a Stranger here.
"The Dean was famous in his Time;
"And had a Kind of Knack at Rhyme:
"His way of Writing now is past;
"The Town hath got a better Taste:
"I keep no antiquated Stuff;
"But, spick and span I have enough.
"Pray, do but give me leave to shew 'em;
"Here's *Colley Cibber's* Birth-day Poem.   270
"This Ode you never yet have seen,
"By *Stephen Duck,* upon the Queen.

---

[12] Bernard Lintot, *a Bookseller in* London. *Vide Mr.* Pope's *Dunciad.*
[13] *A Place in* London *where old Books are sold.*

"Then, here's a Letter finely penn'd
"Against the *Craftsman* and his Friend;
"It clearly shews that all Reflection
"On Ministers, is disaffection.
[14] "Next, here's Sir *Robert*'s Vindication,
[15] "And Mr. *Henly*'s last Oration:
"The Hawkers have not got 'em yet,
"Your Honour please to buy a Set?   280

[16] "Here's *Wolston*'s Tracts, the twelfth Edition;
" 'Tis read by ev'ry Politician:
"The Country Members, when in Town,
"To all their Boroughs send them down:
"You never met a Thing so smart;
"The Courtiers have them all by Heart:
"Those Maids of Honour (who can read)
"Are taught to use them for their Creed.
"The Rev'rend Author's good Intention,
"Hath been rewarded with a Pension: 290
"He doth an Honour to his Gown,
"By bravely running *Priest-craft* down:
"He shews, as sure as GOD's in *Gloc'ster,*
"That *Jesus* was a Grand Impostor:
"That all his Miracles were Cheats,
"Perform'd as Juglers do their Feats:

---

[14] Walpole *hires a Set of Party Scriblers, who do nothing else but write in his Defence.*

[15] Henly *is a Clergyman who, wanting both Merit and Luck to get Preferment, or even to keep his Curacy in the Established Church, formed a new Conventicle, which he calls an Oratory. There, at set Times, he delivereth strange Speeches compiled by himself and his Associates, who share the Profit with him: Every Hearer pays a Shilling each Day for Admittance. He is an absolute Dunce, but generally reputed crazy.*

[16] Wolston *was a Clergyman, but for want of Bread, hath in several Treatises, in the most blasphemous Manner, attempted to turn* Our Saviour *and his Miracles into Ridicule. He is much caressed by many great Courtiers, and by all the Infidels, and his Books read generally by the Court Ladies.*

"The Church had never such a Writer:
"A Shame, he hath not got a Mitre!

Suppose me dead; and then suppose
A Club assembled at the *Rose;*   300
Where from Discourse of this and that,
I grow the Subject of their Chat:
And, while they toss my Name about,
With Favour some, and some without;
One quite indiff'rent in the Cause,
My Character impartial draws:

"The Dean, if we believe Report,
"Was never ill receiv'd at Court:
"As for his Works in Verse and Prose,
"I own my self no Judge of those: 310
"Nor, can I tell what Criticks thought 'em;
"But, this I know, all People bought 'em;
"As with a moral View design'd
"To cure the Vices of Mankind:
"His Vein, ironically grave,
"Expos'd the Fool, and lash'd the Knave:
"To steal a Hint was never known,
"But what he writ was all his own.

"He never thought an Honour done him,
"Because a Duke was proud to own him: 320
"Would rather slip aside, and chuse
"To talk with Wits in dirty Shoes:
"Despis'd the Fools with Stars and Garters,
"So often seen caressing [17] *Chartres:*
"He never courted Men in Station,
"*Nor Persons had in Admiration;*
"Of no Man's Greatness was afraid,
"Because he sought for no Man's Aid.
"Though trusted long in great Affairs,
"He gave himself no haughty Airs: 330

---

[17] *See the Notes before on* Chartres.

"Without regarding private Ends,
"Spent all his Credit for his Friends:
"And only chose the Wise and Good;
"No Flatt'rers; no Allies in Blood;
"But succour'd Virtue in Distress,
"And seldom fail'd of good Success;
"As Numbers in their Hearts must own,
"Who, but for him, had been unknown.

   "With Princes kept a due Decorum,
"But never stood in Awe before 'em: 340
"He follow'd *David*'s Lesson just,
"*In Princes never put thy Trust.*
"And, would you make him truly sower;
"Provoke him with *a slave in Power:*
"The *Irish* Senate, if you nam'd,
"With what Impatience he declaim'd!
"Fair LIBERTY was all his Cry;
"For her he stood prepar'd to die;
"For her he boldly stood alone;
"For her he oft expos'd his own.   350
18 "Two Kingdoms, just as Faction led,
"Had set a Price upon his Head;
"But, not a Traytor cou'd be found,
"To sell him for Six Hundred Pound.

   "Had he but spar'd his Tongue and Pen,
"He might have rose like other Men:
"But, Power was never in his Thought;

---

18 *In the Year* 1713, *the late Queen was prevailed with by an Address of the House of Lords in* England, *to publish a Proclamation, promising Three Hundred Pounds to whatever Person would discover the Author of a Pamphlet called,* The Publick Spirit of the Whiggs; *and in* Ireland, *in the Year* 1724, *my Lord* Carteret *at his first coming into the Government, was prevailed on to issue a Proclamation for promising the like Reward of Three Hundred Pounds, to any Person who could discover the Author of a Pamphlet called,* The Drapier's Fourth Letter, &c. *writ against that destructive Project of coining Half-pence for* Ireland; *but in neither Kingdoms was the Dean discovered*

"And, Wealth he valu'd not a Groat:
"Ingratitude he often found,
"And pity'd those who meant the Wound: 360
"But, kept the Tenor of his Mind,
"To merit well of human Kind:
"Nor made a Sacrifice of those
"Who still were true, to please his Foes.
[19] "He labour'd many a fruitless Hour
"To reconcile his Friends in Power;
"Saw Mischief by a Faction brewing,
"While they pursu'd each others Ruin.
"But, finding vain was all his Care,
"He left the Court in meer Despair.   370

"And, oh! how short are human Schemes!
"Here ended all our golden Dreams.
"What St. John's Skill in State Affairs,
"What Ormond's *Valour*, Oxford's Cares,
"To save their sinking Country lent,
"Was all destroy'd by one Event.
[20] "Too soon that precious Life was ended,
"On which alone, our Weal depended.
[21] "When up a dangerous Faction starts,

[19] *Queen* ANNE's *Ministry fell to Variance from the first Year after their Ministry began:* Harcourt *the Chancellor, and Lord* Bolingbroke *the Secretary, were discontented with the Treasurer* Oxford, *for his too much Mildness to the Whig Party; this Quarrel grew higher every Day till the Queen's Death: The Dean, who was the only Person that endeavoured to reconcile them, found it impossible; and thereupon retired to the Country about ten Weeks before that fatal Event: Upon which he returned to his Deanry in* Dublin, *where for many Years he was worryed by the new People in Power, and had Hundreds of Libels writ against him in* England.

[20] *In the Height of the Quarrel between the Ministers, the Queen died.*

[21] *Upon Queen* ANNE's *Death the Whig Faction was restored to Power, which they exercised with the utmost Rage and Revenge; impeached and banished the Chief Leaders of the Church Party, and stripped all their Adherents of what Employments they had, after which* England *was never known to make so mean a Figure in* Europe. *The greatest Preferments in the Church in both Kingdoms were given to the most ignorant*

"With Wrath and Vengeance in their Hearts: 380
"*By solemn League and Cov'nant bound,*
"To ruin, slaughter, and confound;
"To turn Religion to a Fable,
"And make the Government a *Babel:*
"Pervert the Law, disgrace the Gown,
"Corrupt the Senate, rob the Crown;
"To sacrifice old *England's* Glory,
"And make her infamous in Story.
"When such a Tempest shook the Land,
"How could unguarded Virtue stand?   390

 "With Horror, Grief, Despair the Dean
"Behold the dire destructive Scene:
"His Friends in Exile, or the Tower,
22 "Himself within the Frown of Power;
"Pursu'd by base envenom'd Pens,
23 "Far to the Land of Slaves and Fens;
"A servile Race in Folly nurs'd,
"Who truckle most, when treated worst.

 "By Innocence and Resolution,
"He bore continual Persecution;   400
"While Numbers to Preferment rose;
"Whose Merits were, to be his Foes.
"When, *ev'n his own familiar Friends*
"Intent upon their private Ends;
"Like Renegadoes now he feels,
"*Against him lifting up their Heels.*

Men, Fanaticks were publickly caressed, Ireland *utterly ruined and en-slaved, only great Ministers heaping up Millions, and so Affairs continue until this present third Day of May, 1732, and are likely to go on in the same Manner.*

22 *Upon the Queen's Death, the Dean returned to live in* Dublin, *at his Deanry-House: Numberless Libels were writ against him in* England, *as a Jacobite; he was insulted in the Street, and at Nights was forced to be attended by his Servants armed.*

23 *The Land of Slaves and Fens, is* Ireland.

"The Dean did by his Pen defeat
24 "An infamous destructive Cheat.
"Taught Fools their Int'rest how to know;
"And gave them Arms to ward the Blow.   410
"Envy hath own'd it was his doing,
"To save that helpless Land from Ruin,
"While they who at the Steerage stood,
"And reapt the Profit, sought his Blood.

   "To save them from their evil Fate,
"In him was held a Crime of State.
25 "A wicked Monster on the Bench,
"Whose Fury Blood could never quench;
"As vile and profligate a Villain,
"As modern 26 Scroggs, or old Tressilian;   420
"Who long all Justice had discarded,
"Nor fear'd he GOD, nor Man regarded;
"Vow'd on the Dean his Rage to vent,
"And make him of his Zeal repent;
"But Heav'n his Innocence defends,
"The grateful People stand his Friends:

---

24 One Wood, a Hardware-man from England, had a Patent for coining Copper Half-pence in Ireland, to the Sum of 108,000 l. which in the Consequence, must leave that Kingdom without Gold or Silver (See Drapier's Letters.)

25 One Whitshed was then Chief Justice: He had some Years before prosecuted a Printer for a Pamphlet writ by the Dean, to perswade the people of Ireland to wear their own Manufactures. Whitshed sent the Jury down eleven Times, and kept them nine Hours, until they were forced to bring in a special Verdict. He sat as Judge afterwards on the Tryal of the Printer of the Drapier's Fourth Letter; but the Jury, against all he could say or swear, threw out the Bill: All the Kingdom took the Drapier's Part, except the Courtiers, or those who expected Places. The Drapier was celebrated in many Poems and Pamphlets: His Sign was set up in most Streets of Dublin (where many of them still continue) and in several Country Towns.

26 Scroggs was Chief Justice under King Charles the Second: His Judgment always varied in State Tryals, according to Directions from Court. Tressilian was a wicked Judge, hanged above three hundred Years ago.

"Not Strains of Law, nor Judges Frown,
"Nor Topicks brought to please the Crown,
"Nor Witness hir'd, nor Jury pick'd,
"Prevail to bring him in convict.   43(?)

27 "In Exile with a steady Heart,
"He spent his Life's declining Part;
"Where, Folly, Pride, and Faction sway,
28 "Remote from St. John, Pope, and Gay.

29 "His Friendship there to few confin'd,
"Were always of the midling Kind:
"No Fools of Rank, a mungril Breed,
"Who fain would pass for Lords indeed:
30 "Where Titles give no Right or Power,
"And Peerage is a wither'd Flower,   440
"He would have held it a Disgrace,
"If such a Wretch had known his Face.
"On Rural Squires, that Kingdom's Bane,
"He vented oft his Wrath in vain:
31 "Biennial Squires, to Market brought;
"Who sell their Souls and Votes for Naught;
"The Nation stript go joyful back,
"To rob the Church, their Tenants rack,

---

27 *In* Ireland, *which he had Reason to call a Place of Exile;* *to which Country nothing could have driven him, but the Queen's Death, who had determined to fix him in* England, *in Spight of the Dutchess of Somerset, &c.*

28 Henry St. John, *Lord Viscount* Bolingbroke, *mentioned before.*

29 *In* Ireland *the Dean was not acquainted with one single Lord Spiritual or Temporal. He only conversed with private Gentlemen of the Clergy or Laity, and but a small Number of either.*

30 *The Peers of* Ireland *lost a great Part of their Jurisdiction by one single Act, and tamely submitted to this infamous Mark of Slavery without the least Resentment, or Remonstrance.*

31 *The Parliament (as they call it) in* Ireland *meet but once in two Years; and, after giving five Times more than they can afford, return Home to reimburse themselves by all Country Jobs and Oppressions, of which some few only are here mentioned.*

"Go Snacks with Thieves and [32] Rapparees,
"And, keep the Peace, to pick up Fees: 450
"In every Jobb to have a Share,
"A Jayl or [33] Barrack to repair;
"And turn the Tax for publick Roads
"Commodious to their own Abodes.

"Perhaps I may allow, the Dean
"Had too much Satyr in his Vein;
"And seem'd determin'd not to starve it,
"Because no Age could more deserve it.
"Yet, Malice never was his Aim;
"He lash'd the Vice but spar'd the Name.   460
"No Individual could resent,
"Where Thousands equally were meant.
"His Satyr points at no Defect,
"But what all Mortals may correct;
"For he abhorr'd that senseless Tribe,
"Who call it Humour when they jibe:
"He spar'd a Hump or crooked Nose,
"Whose Owners set not up for Beaux.
"True genuine Dulness mov'd his Pity,
"Unless it offer'd to be witty.   470
"Those, who their Ignorance confess'd,
"He ne'er offended with a Jest;
"But laugh'd to hear an Idiot quote,
"A Verse from *Horace,* learn'd by Rote.

"He knew an hundred pleasant Stories,
"With all the Turns of *Whigs* and *Tories:*
"Was chearful to his dying Day,
"And Friends would let him have his Way.

---

[32] *The Highway-Men in* Ireland *are, since the late Wars there, usually called Rapparees, which was a Name given to those* Irish *Soldiers who in small Parties used, at that Time, to plunder the Protestants.*

[33] *The Army in* Ireland *is lodged in Barracks, the building and repairing whereof, and other Charges, have cost a prodigious Sum to that unhappy Kingdom.*

  "He gave the little Wealth he had,
"To build a House for Fools and Mad: 480
"And shew'd by one satyric Touch,
"No Nation wanted it so much:
[34] "That Kingdom he hath left his Debtor,
"I wish it soon may have a Better.

---

[34] *Meaning* Ireland, *where he now lives, and probably may dye.*

THE BEASTS CONFESSION TO THE PRIEST
ON OBSERVING HOW MOST MEN MISTAKE
THEIR OWN TALENTS

[This poem, here reprinted, as traditionally, with Swift's lively Preface and Advertisement, was first published in Dublin in 1736. Although professing to be written in 1732, it refers to Walpole's unpopular and ultimately futile attempt to collect revenue from bonded warehouses by an Excise Bill, which was introduced in 1733.]

The Preface.

I HAVE been long of Opinion, that there is not a more general and greater Mistake, or of worse Consequences through the Commerce of Mankind, than the wrong Judgments they are apt to entertain of their own Talents: I knew a stuttering Alderman in London, a great Frequenter of Coffee-Houses; who, when a fresh News-Paper was brought in, constantly seized it first, and read it aloud to his Brother Citizens; but in a Manner, as little intelligible to the Standers-by as to himself. How many Pretenders to Learning expose themselves by chusing to discourse on those very Parts of Science wherewith they are least acquainted? It is the same case in every other Qualification. By the Multitude of those who deal in Rhimes from Half a Sheet to Twenty, which come out every Minute, there must be at least five hundred Poets in the City and Suburbs of London; half as many Coffee-House Orators, exclusive of the Clergy; forty thousand Politicians; and four thousand five hundred profound Scholars: Not to mention the Wits, the Railliers, the Smart Fellows, and Criticks; all as illiterate and impudent as a Suburb Whore. What are we to think of the fine dressed Sparks, proud of their own Personal Deformities, which appear the more hideous by the Contrast *of wearing Scarlet and Gold, with what they call Toupees on their Heads, and all the Frippery of a modern Beau, to make a Figure before*

Women; some of them with Hump-Backs, others hardly five Foot high, and every Feature of their Faces distorted; I have seen many of these insipid Pretenders entering into Conversation with Persons of Learning, constantly making the grossest Blunders in every Sentence, without conveying one single Idea fit for a rational Creature to spend a Thought on; perpetually confounding all Chronology and Geography even of present Times. I compute, that London *hath eleven native Fools of the Beau and Puppy-Kind, for one among us in* Dublin; *besides two thirds of ours transplanted thither, who are now naturalized; whereby that overgrown Capital exceeds ours in the Article of Dunces by forty to one; and what is more to our further Mortification, there is not one distinguished Fool of* Irish *Birth or Education, who makes any Noise in that famous Metropolis, unless the* London *Prints be very partial or defective; whereas* London *is seldom without a Dozen of their own educating, who engross the Vogue for half a Winter together, and are never heard of more, but give Place to a new Sett. This hath been the constant Progress of at least thirty Years past, only allowing for the Change of Breed and Fashion.*

Advertisement.

The following Poem is grounded upon the universal Folly in Mankind of mistaking their Talents; by which the Author doth a great Honour to his own Species, almost equalling them with certain Brutes; wherein, indeed, he is too partial, as he freely confesseth: And yet he hath gone as low as he well could, by specifying four Animals; the Wolf, the Ass, the Swine and the Ape; all equally mischievous, except the last, who outdoes them in the Article of Cunning: So great is the Pride of Man.

THE

Beasts Confession

TO THE

PRIEST, &c.

WHEN Beasts could speak, (the Learned say
They still can do so every Day)
It seems, they had Religion then,
As much as now we find in Men.
It happen'd when a Plague broke out,
(Which therefore made them more devout)
The King of Brutes (to make it plain,
Of Quadrupeds I only mean)
By Proclamation gave Command,
That ev'ry Subject in the Land   10
Should to the Priest confess their Sins;
And, thus the pious Wolf begins:

  Good Father I must own with Shame,
That, often I have been to blame:
I must confess, on *Friday* last,
Wretch that I was, I broke my Fast:
But, I defy the basest Tongue
To prove I did my Neighbour wrong;
Or ever went to seek my Food
By Rapine, Theft, or Thirst of Blood.   20

  The Ass approaching next, confess'd,
That in his Heart he lov'd a Jest:
A Wag he was, he needs must own,
And could not let a Dunce alone:
Sometimes his Friend he would not spare,
And might perhaps be too severe:
But yet, the worst that could be said,

He was a *Wit* both born and bred;
And if it be a Sin or Shame,
Nature alone must bear the Blame: 30
One Fault he hath, is sorry for't,
His Ears are half a Foot too short;
Which could he to the Standard bring,
He'd shew his Face before the K——:
Then, for his Voice, there's none disputes
That he's the Nightingal of Brutes.

    The Swine with contrite Heart allow'd,
His Shape and Beauty made him proud:
In Dyet was perhaps too nice,
But Gluttony was ne'er his Vice: 40
In ev'ry Turn of Life content,
And meekly took what Fortune sent:
Inquire through all the Parish round
A better Neighbour ne'er was found:
His Vigilance might some displease;
'Tis true, he hated Sloth like Pease.

    The Mimick Ape began his Chatter,
How evil Tongues his Life bespatter:
Much of the cens'ring World complain'd,
Who said, his Gravity was feign'd: 50
Indeed, the Strictness of his Morals
Engag'd him in a hundred Quarrels:
He saw, and he was griev'd to see't,
His Zeal was sometimes indiscreet:
He found, his Virtues too severe
For our corrupted Times to bear;
Yet, such a lewd licentious Age
Might well excuse a Stoick's Rage.

    The Goat advanc'd with decent Pace;
And, first excus'd his youthful Face;
Forgiveness begg'd, that he appear'd   60
('Twas Nature's Fault) without a Beard.

'Tis true, he was not much inclin'd
To Fondness for the Female Kind;
Not, as his Enemies object,
From Chance, or natural Defect
Not by his frigid Constitution;
But, through a pious Resolution;
For, he had made a holy Vow
Of Chastity, as Monks do now;
Which he resolv'd to keep for ever hence,   70
As strictly too; as doth * his Reverence.

    Apply the Tale, and you shall find
How just it suits with human Kind.
Some Faults we own: But, can you guess?
Why?—Virtues carry'd to Excess;
Wherewith our Vanity endows us,
Through neither Foe nor Friend allows us.

    The Lawyer swears, you may rely on't,
He never squeez'd a needy Clyent:
And, this he makes his constant Rule;   80
For which his Brethren call him Fool:
His Conscience always was so nice,
He freely gave the Poor Advice;
By which he lost, he may affirm,
A hundred Fees last *Easter* Term.
While others of the learned Robe
Would break the Patience of a *Job,*
No Pleader at the Bar could match
His Diligence and quick Dispatch;
Ne'er kept a Cause, he well may boast,   90
Above a Term or two at most.

    The cringing Knave who seeks a Place
Without Success; thus tells his Case:
Why should he longer mince the Matter?
He fail'd, because he could not flatter:

---

* *The Priest his Confessor.*

He had not learn'd to turn his Coat,
Nor for a Party give his Vote:
His Crime he quickly understood;
Too zealous for the Nation's Good:
He found, the Ministers resent it,   100
Yet could not for his Heart repent it.

　　The Chaplain vows, he cannot fawn,
Though it would raise him to the Lawn:
He pass'd his Hours among his Books;
You find it in his meagre Looks:
He might, if he were worldly-wise,
Preferment get, and spare his Eyes:
But own'd, he had a stubborn Spirit
That made him trust alone in Merit:
Would rise by Merit to Promotion;   110
Alas! a meer Chymerick Notion.

　　The Doctor, if you will believe him,
Confess'd a Sin, and God forgive him:
Call'd up at Mid-night, ran to save
A blind old Beggar from the Grave:
But, see how *Satan* spreads his Snares;
He quite forgot to say his Pray'rs.
He cannot help it for his Heart
Sometimes to act the Parson's Part:
Quotes from the Bible many a Sentence   120
That moves his Patients to Repentance:
And, when his Med'cines do no good,
Supports their Minds with heav'nly Food.
At which, however well intended,
He hears the Clergy are offended;
And grown so bold behind his Back
To call him Hypocrite and Quack.
In his own Church he keeps a Seat;
Says Grace before, and after Meat;
And calls, without affecting Airs,   130
His Houshold twice a Day to Pray'rs.

He shuns Apothecary's Shops;
And hates to cram the Sick with Slops:
He scorns to make his Art a Trade;
Nor bribes my Lady's fav'rite Maid.
Old Nurse-keepers would never hire
To recommend him to the Squire;
Which others, whom he will not name,
Have often practis'd to their Shame.

    The Statesman tells you with a *Sneer,*   140
His Fault is to be too *Sincere;*
And, having no sinister Ends,
Is apt to disoblige his Friends.
The Nation's Good, his Master's Glory,
Without Regard to *Whig* or *Tory,*
Were all the Schemes he had in View;
Yet he was seconded by few:
Though some had spread a thousand Lyes;
'Twas *He* defeated the EXCISE.
'Twas known, tho' he had born Aspersion;   150
That, *Standing Troops* were his Aversion:
His Practice was, in ev'ry Station
To serve the King, and please the Nation.
Though hard to find in ev'ry Case
The fittest Man to fill a Place:
His Promises he ne'er forgot,
But took Memorials on the Spot:
His Enemies, for want of Charity,
Said, he affected Popularity:
'Tis true, the People understood,   160
That all he did was for their Good;
Their kind Affections he has try'd;
No Love is lost on either Side.
He came to Court with Fortune clear,
Which now he runs out every Year;
Must, at the Rate that he goes on,
Inevitably be undone.
Oh! if his Majesty would please

To give him but a Writ of Ease,
Would grant him Licence to retire,   170
As it hath long been his Desire,
By fair Accounts it would be found
He's poorer by ten thousand Pound.
He owns, and hopes it is no Sin,
He ne'er was partial to his Kin;
He thought it base for Men in Stations,
To crowd the Court with their Relations:
His Country was his dearest Mother,
And ev'ry virtuous Man his Brother:
Through Modesty, or aukward Shame,   180
(For which he owns himself to blame)
He found the wisest Men he could,
Without Respect to Friends, or Blood,
Nor ever acts on private Views,
When he hath Liberty to chuse.

    The Sharper swore he hated Play,
Except to pass an Hour away:
And, well he might; for to his Cost,
By want of Skill, he always lost:
He heard, there was a Club of Cheats   190
Who had contriv'd a thousand Feats;
Could change the Stock, or cog a Dye,
And thus deceive the sharpest Eye:
No Wonder how his Fortune sunk,
His Brothers fleece him when he's drunk.

    I own, the Moral not exact;
Besides, the Tale is false in Fact;
And, so absurd, that could I raise up
From Fields *Elyzian,* fabling *Esop;*
I would accuse him to his Face   200
For libelling the *Four-foot* Race.
Creatures of ev'ry Kind but ours
Well comprehend their nat'ral Powers;
While We, whom *Reason* ought to sway,

Mistake our Talents ev'ry Day:
The Ass was never known so stupid
To act the Part of *Tray,* or *Cupid;*
Nor leaps upon his Master's Lap,
There to be stroak'd and fed with Pap;
As *Esop* would the World perswade;   210
He better understands his Trade:
Nor comes whene'er his Lady whistles;
But, carries Loads, and feeds on Thistles;
Our Author's Meaning, I presume, is
A Creature † *bipes et implumis;*
Wherein the Moralist design'd
A Compliment on Human-Kind:
For, here he owns, that now and then
‡ Beasts may *degen'rate* into Men.

ON POETRY: A RHAPSODY

[This famous satire deals with several broad aspects of contemporary poetry, but its fiercest attack is upon the poets who flattered England's political leaders at a time which called, in Swift's opinion, for very different treatment. In the conduct of the general argument, the strictures against individual figures are perhaps of secondary importance. The critics and writers, living and dead, whose names are mentioned are for the most part men whom wits of the time could safely employ for symbols of literary mediocrity. The list includes Colley Cibber, ultimately to become immortal as the mock hero of Pope's revised *Dunciad;* Richard Flecknoe, the poet-priest whose shabby reputation had years before prompted Dryden to stigmatize Shadwell as Flecknoe's true son; the undistinguished playwright, Sir Robert Howard; Sir Richard Blackmore, the physician whose attempts at epic verse were so inept as to be ludicrous; Viscount Grimston who, early in his essentially political career, had written a wretched play called *The Lawyer's Fortune or Love*

---

  † *A Definition of Man, disapproved by all Logicians. Homo est Animal bipes, implume, erecto vultu.*

  ‡ *Vide* Gulliver *in his Account of the Houyhnhnms.*

in a Hollow Tree; Leonard Welsted, Matthew Concanen, and James Moore Smyth ("Jemmy Moor"), all writers of indifferent talent and questionable motives who are treated harshly by Pope as well as by Swift. The name of Dryden appears among the critics, of whom at least one, John Dennis, was regarded with contempt by Swift and Pope. Dryden is also represented by the figure of Battus, who pontificates at Will's coffeehouse, headquarters for writers and wits. The sarcastic hymn of praise deals in order with King George II; Frederick Lewis, Prince of Wales; his brother, the Duke of Cumberland, and, finally, Sir Robert Walpole. Thomas Woolston, referred to in the final line, was notorious for his deistic writings.

The first edition of the poem, published in London in 1733, contains a number of blank spaces, with or without a telltale initial letter. It is possible to supply these blanks with considerable certainty as well as to correct several palpable errors in the first edition. In the present text, these changes have been made for the reader's convenience, such additions or alterations being indicated by brackets. The notes, presumably Swift's own, are those found in the first edition.]

ALL Human Race wou'd fain be *Wits,*
And Millions miss, for one that hits.
Young's universal Passion, *Pride,*
Was never known to spread so wide.
Say *Britain,* cou'd you ever boast,—
Three *Poets* in an Age at most?
Our chilling Climate hardly bears
A *Sprig* of Bays in Fifty Years:
While ev'ry Fool his Claim alledges,
As if it grew in common Hedges.   10
What Reason can there be assign'd
For this Perverseness in the Mind?
Brutes find out where their Talents lie:
A *Bear* will not attempt to fly:
A founder'd *Horse* will oft debate,
Before he tries a five-barr'd Gate:
A *Dog* by Instinct turns aside,
Who sees the Ditch too deep and wide.

But *Man* we find the only Creature,
Who, led by *Folly,* fights with *Nature;*   20
Who, when *she* loudly cries, *Forbear,*
With Obstinacy fixes there;
And, where his *Genius* least inclines,
Absurdly bends his whole Designs.

    Not *Empire* to the Rising-Sun,
By Valour, Conduct, Fortune won;
Nor highest *Wisdom* in Debates
For framing Laws to govern States;
Nor Skill in Sciences profound,
So large to grasp the Circle round;   30
Such heavenly Influence require,
As how to strike the *Muses Lyre.*

    Not Beggar's Brat, on Bulk begot;
Nor Bastard of a Pedlar *Scot;*
Nor Boy brought up to cleaning Shoes,
The Spawn of *Bridewell,* or the Stews;
Nor Infants dropt, the spurious Pledges
Of *Gipsies* littering under Hedges,
Are so disqualified by Fate
To rise in *Church,* or *Law,* or *State,*   40
As he, whom *Phebus* in his Ire
Hath *blasted* with poetick Fire.

    What hope of Custom in the *Fair,*
While not a Soul demands your Ware?
Where you have nothing to produce
For private Life, or publick Use?
Court, City, Country want you not;
You cannot bribe, betray, or plot.
For Poets, Law makes no Provision:
The Wealthy have you in Derision.   50
Of State-Affairs you cannot smatter,
Are awkward when you try to flatter.
Your Portion, taking *Britain* round,

* Was just one annual Hundred Pound.
Now not so much as in Remainder
Since *Cibber* brought in an Attainder;
For ever fixt by Right Divine,
(A Monarch's Right) on *Grubstreet* Line.
Poor starv'ling Bard, how small thy Gains!
How unproportion'd to thy Pains!   60

And here a *Simile* comes Pat in:
Tho' *Chickens* take a Month to fatten,
The Guests in less than half an Hour
Will more than half a Score devour.
So, after toiling twenty Days,
To earn a Stock of Pence and Praise,
Thy Labours, grown the Critick's Prey,
Are swallow'd o'er a Dish of Tea;
Gone, to be never heard of more,
Gone, where the *Chickens* went before.   70

How shall a new Attempter learn
Of diff'rent Spirits to discern,
And how distinguish, which is which,
The Poet's Vein, or scribling Itch?
Then hear an old experienc'd Sinner
Instructing thus a young Beginner.

Consult yourself, and if you find
A powerful Impulse urge your Mind,
Impartial judge within your Breast
What Subject you can manage best;   80
Whether your Genius most inclines
To Satire, Praise, or hum'rous Lines;
To Elegies in mournful Tone,
Or Prologue sent from Hand unknown.
Then rising with *Aurora*'s Light,
The Muse invok'd, sit down to write;

---

* Paid to the Poet Laureat, which Place was given to one *Cibber,* a
Player.

Blot out, correct, insert, refine,
Enlarge, diminish, interline;
Be mindful, when Invention fails,
To scratch your Head, and bite your Nails.   90

     Your Poem finish'd, next your Care
Is needful, to transcribe it fair.
In modern Wit all printed Trash, is
Set off with num'rous *Breaks*————and *Dashes*—

     To Statesmen wou'd you give a Wipe,
You print it in *Italick Type*.
When Letters are in vulgar Shapes,
'Tis ten to one the Wit escapes;
But when in *Capitals* exprest,
The dullest Reader smoaks the Jest: 100
Or else perhaps he may invent
A better than the Poet meant,
As learned Commentators view
In *Homer* more than *Homer* knew.

     Your Poem in its modish Dress,
Correctly fitted for the Press,
Convey by Penny-Post to *Lintot*,
But let no Friend alive look into't.
If *Lintot* thinks 'twill quit the Cost,
You need not fear your Labour lost: 110
And, how agreeably surpriz'd
Are you to see it advertiz'd!
The Hawker shews you one in Print,
As fresh as Farthings from the Mint:
The Product of your Toil and Sweating;
A Bastard of your own begetting.

     Be sure at *Will*'s the following Day,
Lie Snug, and hear what Criticks say.
And if you find the general Vogue
Pronounces you a stupid Rogue;   120
Damns all your Thoughts as low and little,

Sit still, and swallow down your Spittle.
Be silent as a Politician,
For talking may beget Suspicion:
Or praise the Judgment of the Town,
And help yourself to run it down.
Give up your fond paternal Pride,
Nor argue on the weaker Side;
For Poems read without a Name
We justly praise, or justly blame: 130
And Criticks have no partial Views,
Except they know whom they abuse.
And since you ne'er provok'd their Spight,
Depend upon't their Judgment's right:
But if you blab, you are undone;
Consider what a Risk you run.
You lose your Credit all at once;
The Town will mark you for a Dunce:
The vilest Doggrel *Grubstreet* sends,
Will pass for yours with Foes and Friends.   140
And you must bear the whole Disgrace,
'Till some fresh Blockhead takes your Place.

   Your Secret kept, your Poem sunk,
And sent in Quires to line a Trunk;
If still you be dispos'd to rhime,
Go try your Hand a second Time.
Again you fail, yet Safe's the Word,
Take Courage, and attempt a Third.
But first with Care imploy your Thoughts,
Where Criticks mark'd your former Faults.   150
The trivial Turns, the borrow'd Wit,
The *Similes* that nothing fit;
The *Cant* which ev'ry Fool repeats,
Town-Jests, and Coffee-house Conceits;
Descriptions tedious, flat and dry,
And introduc'd the Lord knows why;
Or where we find your Fury set

Against the harmless Alphabet;
On A's and B's your Malice vent,
While Readers wonder whom you meant.   160
A publick, or a private *Robber;*
A *Statesman,* or a South-Sea *Jobber;*
A *Prelate* who no God believes;
A ———, or Den of Thieves.
A Pick-purse at the Bar, or Bench;
A Duchess, or a Suburb-Wench.
Or oft when Epithets you link,
In gaping Lines to fill a Chink;
Like stepping Stones to save a Stride,
In Streets where Kennels are too wide: 170
Or like a Heel-piece to support
A Cripple with one Foot too short:
Or like a Bridge that joins a Marish
To Moorlands of a diff'rent Parish.
So have I seen ill-coupled Hounds,
Drag diff'rent Ways in miry Grounds.
So Geographers in *Afric*-Maps
With Savage-Pictures fill their Gaps;
And o'er unhabitable Downs
Place Elephants for want of Towns.   18(

   But tho' you miss your third Essay,
You need not throw your Pen away.
Lay now aside all Thoughts of Fame,
To spring more profitable Game.
From Party-Merit seek Support;
The vilest Verse thrives best at Court.
A Pamphlet in Sir *Rob*'s Defence
Will never fail to bring in Pence;
Nor be concern'd about the Sale,
He pays his Workmen on the Nail.   190

   A Prince the Moment he is crown'd,
Inherits ev'ry Virtue round,
As Emblems of the sov'reign Pow'r,

Like other Bawbles of the Tow'r.
Is gen'rous, valiant, just and wise,
And so continues 'till he dies.
His humble *Senate* this professes,
In all their *Speeches, Votes, Addresses.*
But once you fix him in a Tomb,
His Virtues fade, his Vices bloom;   200
And each Perfection wrong imputed
Is Folly, at his Death confuted.
The Loads of Poems in his Praise,
Ascending make one Funeral-Blaze.
As soon as you can hear his Knell,
This God on Earth turns *Devil* in Hell.
And lo, his Ministers of State,
Transform'd to Imps, his Levee wait.
Where, in this Scene of endless Woe,
They ply their former Arts below.   210
And as they sail in *Charon*'s Boat,
Contrive to bribe the Judge's Vote.
To *Cerberus* they give a Sop,
His triple-barking Mouth to Stop:
Or in the Iv'ry Gate of Dreams,
Project [Excise] and [South Sea Schemes]:
Or hire their Party-Pamphleteers,
To set *Elysium* by the Ears.

  Then *Poet,* if you mean to thrive,
Employ your Muse on Kings alive;   220
With Prudence gath'ring up a Cluster
Of all the Virtues you can muster:
Which form'd into a Garland sweet,
Lay humbly at your Monarch's Feet;
Who, as the Odours reach his Throne,
Will smile, and think 'em all his own:
For *Law* and *Gospel* both determine
All Virtues lodge in royal Ermine.
(I mean the Oracles of Both,

Who shall depose it upon Oath.)   230
Your Garland in the following Reign,
Change but their Names will do again.

    But if you think this Trade too base,
(Which seldom is the Dunce's Case)
Put on the Critick's Brow, and sit
At *Wills* the puny Judge of Wit.
A Nod, a Shrug, a scornful Smile,
With Caution us'd, may serve a-while.
Proceed no further in your Part,
Before you learn the Terms of Art: 240
(For you may easy be too far gone,
In all our modern Criticks Jargon.)
Then talk with more authentick Face,
Of *Unities, in Time and Place.*
Get Scraps of *Horace* from your Friends,
And have them at your Fingers Ends.
Learn *Aristotle*'s Rules by Rote,
And at all Hazards boldly quote:
Judicious *Rymer* oft review:
Wise *Dennis,* and profound *Bossu.*   250
Read all the *Prefaces* of *Dryden,*
For these our Criticks much confide in,
(Tho' meerly writ at first for filling
To raise the Volume's Price, a Shilling.)

    A forward Critick often dupes us
With sham Quotations† *Peri Hupsous:*
And if we have not read *Longinus,*
Will magisterially out-shine us.
Then, lest with *Greek* he over-run ye,
Procure the Book for Love or Money,   260
Translated from *Boileau*'s Translation,‡
And quote *Quotation* on *Quotation.*

---

† A famous Treatise of *Longinus.*
‡ By Mr. *Welsted.*

At *Wills* you hear a Poem read,
Where *Battus* from the Table-head,
Reclining on his Elbow-chair,
Gives Judgment with decisive Air.
To whom the Tribe of circling Wits,
As to an Oracle submits.
He gives Directions to the Town,
To cry it up, or run it down.   270
(Like *Courtiers*, when they send a Note,
Instructing *Members* how to Vote.)
He sets the Stamp of Bad and Good,
Tho' not a Word be understood.
Your Lesson learnt, you'll be secure
To get the Name of *Conoisseur*.
And when your Merits once are known,
Procure Disciples of your own.

  Our Poets (you can never want 'em,
Spread thro' *Augusta Trinobantum*)   280
Computing by their Pecks of Coals,
Amount to just Nine thousand Souls.
These o'er their proper Districts govern,
Of Wit and Humour, Judges sov'reign.
In ev'ry Street a City-bard
Rules, like an Alderman his Ward.
His indisputed Rights extend
Thro' all the Lane, from End to End.
The Neighbours round admire his *Shrewdness*,
For songs of *Loyalty* and *Lewdness*.   290
Out-done by none in Rhyming well,
Altho' he never learnt to spell.

  Two bordering Wits contend for Glory;
And one is *Whig*, and one is *Tory*.
And this, for Epicks claims the Bays,
And that, for Elegiack Lays.
Some famed for Numbers soft and smooth,
By Lovers spoke in *Punch*'s Booth.

And some as justly Fame extols
For lofty Lines in *Smithfield* Drols.   300
Bavius in *Wapping* gains Renown,
And *Mævius* reigns o'er *Kentish-Town:*
Tigellius plac'd in *Phœbus'* Car,
From *Ludgate* shines to *Temple-bar.*
Harmonius *Cibber* entertains
The Court with annual Birth-day Strains;
Whence *Gay* was banish'd in Disgrace,
Where *Pope* will never show his Face;
Where Y[*oung*] must torture his Invention,
To flatter *Knaves,* or lose his *Pension.*   310

But these are not a thousandth Part
Of Jobbers in the Poets Art,
Attending each his proper Station,
And all in due Subordination;
Thro' ev'ry Alley to be found,
In Garrets high, or under Ground:
And when they join their *Pericranies,*
Out skips a *Book of Miscellanies.*
Hobbes clearly proves that ev'ry Creature
Lives in a State of War by Nature.   320
The Greater for the Smallest watch,
But meddle seldom with their Match.
A Whale of moderate Size will draw
A Shole of Herrings down his Maw.
A Fox with Geese his Belly crams;
A Wolf destroys a thousand Lambs.
But search among the rhiming Race,
The Brave are worried by the Base.
If, on *Parnassus'* Top you sit,
You rarely bite, are always bit: 330
Each Poet of inferior Size
On you shall rail and criticize;
And strive to tear you Limb from Limb,
While others do as much for him.

The Vermin only teaze and pinch
Their Foes superior by an Inch.
So, Nat'ralists observe, a Flea
Hath smaller Fleas that on him prey,
And these have smaller Fleas to bite 'em,
And so proceed *ad infinitum:*   340
Thus ev'ry Poet in his Kind,
Is bit by him that comes behind;
Who, tho' too little to be seen,
Can teaze, and gall, and give the Spleen;
Call Dunces, Fools, and Sons of Whores,
Lay *Grubstreet* at each others Doors:
Extol the *Greek* and *Roman* Masters,
And curse our modern Poetasters.
Complain, as many an ancient Bard did,
How Genius is no more rewarded;   350
How wrong a Taste prevails among us;
How much our Ancestors out-sung us;
Can personate an awkward Scorn
For those who are not Poets born:
And all their Brother Dunces lash,
Who crowd the Press with hourly Trash.

O, *Grubstreet!* how do I bemoan thee,
Whose graceless Children scorn to own thee!
Their filial Piety forgot,
Deny their Country like a SCOT: 360
Tho' by their Idiom and Grimace
They soon betray their native Place:
Yet *thou* hast greater Cause to be
Asham'd of them, than they of thee.
Degenerate from their ancient Brood,
Since first the Court allow'd them Food.

Remains a Difficulty still,
To purchase Fame by writing ill:
From *Flecknoe* down to *Howard*'s Time,
How few have reach'd the *low Sublime?*   370

For when our high-born *Howard* dy'd,
Blackmore alone his Place supply'd:
And least a Chasm should intervene,
When Death had finish'd *Blackmore*'s Reign,
The *leaden Crown* devolv'd to thee,
Great § Poet of the *Hollow-Tree*.
But, oh, how unsecure thy Throne!
A thousand Bards thy Right disown:
They plot to turn in factious Zeal,
Duncenia to a Common-weal;   380
And with rebellious Arms pretend
An equal Priv'lege to *descend*.

    In Bulk there are not more Degrees,
From *Elephants* to *Mites* in Cheese,
Than what a curious Eye may trace
In Creatures of the rhiming Race.
From bad to worse, and worse they fall,
But, who can reach the Worst of all?
For, tho' in Nature Depth and Height
Are equally held infinite,   390
In Poetry the Height we know;
'Tis only infinite below.
For Instance: When you rashly || think,
No Rhymer can like *Welsted* sink.
His Merits ballanc'd you shall find,
That *Feilding* leaves him far behind.
Concannen, more aspiring Bard,
Climbs downwards, deeper by a Yard:
Smart JEMMY MOOR with Vigor drops,
The Rest pursue as thick as Hops: 400
With Heads to Points the Gulph they enter,
Linkt perpendicular to the Centre:
And as their Heels elated rise,
Their Heads attempt the nether Skies.

---

§ Lord G[rimston].
|| *Vide* The Treatise on the *Profound,* and Mr. *Pope's Dunciad.*

O, what Indignity and Shame
To prostitute the Muse's Name,
By flatt'ring—whom Heaven design'd
The Plagues and Scourges of Mankind.
Bred up in Ignorance and Sloth,
And ev'ry Vice that nurses both.   410

Fair *Britain* in thy Monarch blest,
Whose Virtues bear the strictest Test;
Whom never *Faction* cou'd bespatter,
Nor *Minister,* nor *Poet* flatter.
What Justice in rewarding Merit?
What Magnanimity of Spirit?
What Lineaments divine we trace
Thro' all the Features of his Face;
Tho' Peace with Olive bind his Hands,
Confest the conqu'ring Hero stands.   420
Hydaspes, Indus, and the *Ganges,*
Dread from his Hand impending Changes.
From him the *Tartar,* and *Chinese,*
Short by the Knees intreat for Peace.
The *Consort* of his Throne and Bed,
A perfect Goddess born and bred.
Appointed sov'reign Judge to sit
On Learning, Eloquence and Wit.
Our eldest Hope, divine *Iülus,*
(Late, very late, O, may he rule us.)   430
What early Manhood has he shown,
Before his downy Beard was grown!
Then think, what Wonders will be done
By going on as he begun;
An Heir for *Britain* to secure
As long as Sun and Moon endure.

The Remnant of the royal Blood,
Comes pouring on me like a Flood.
Bright Goddesses, in Number five;
Duke *William,* sweetest Prince alive.   440

Now sing the *Minister* of *State*,
Who shines alone, without a Mate.
Observe with what majestick Port
This *Atlas* stands to prop the Court:
Intent the Publick Debts to pay,
Like prudent ** *Fabius* by *Delay*.
Thou great Vicegerent of the King,
Thy Praises ev'ry Muse shall sing.
In all Affairs thou sole Director,
Of Wit and Learning chief Protector;   450
Tho' small the Time thou hast to spare,
The Church is thy peculiar Care.
Of pious Prelates what a Stock
You chuse to rule the Sable-flock.
You raise the Honour of the Peerage,
Proud to attend you at the Steerage.
You dignify the noble Race,
Content yourself with humbler Place.
Now Learning, Valour, Virtue, Sense,
To Titles give the sole Pretence.   460
St. George beheld thee with Delight,
Vouchsafe to be an azure Knight,
When on thy Breast and Sides *Herculean,*
He fixt the *Star* and *String Cerulean*.

Say, Poet, in what other Nation,
Shone ever such a Constellation.
Attend ye *Popes,* and *Youngs,* and *Gays,*
And tune your Harps, and strow your Bays.
Your Panegyricks here provide,
You cannot err on Flatt'ry's Side.   470
Above the Stars exalt your Stile,
You still are low ten thousand Mile.
On *Lewis* all his Bards bestow'd,
Of Incense many a thousand Load;
But *Europe* mortify'd his Pride,

** *Unus Homo nobis* Cunctando *restituit rem.*

And swore the fawning Rascals ly'd:
Yet what the World refus'd to *Lewis,*
Apply'd to [George] exactly true is:
Exactly true! Invidious Poet!
'Tis fifty thousand Times below it.   480

 Translate me now some Lines, if you can,
From *Virgil, Martial, Ovid, Lucan;*
They could all Pow'r in Heaven divide,
And do no Wrong to either Side:
They'll teach you how to split a Hair,
†† Give [George] and *Jove* an equal Share.
Yet, why should we be lac'd so straight;
I'll give my [Monarch] Butter-weight.
And Reason good; for many a Year
[Christ] never intermeddl'd here: 490
Nor, tho' his Priests be duly paid,
Did ever we *desire* his Aid:
We now can better do without him,
Since *Woolston* gave us Arms to rout him.
* * * * * *Cætera desiderantur* * * * * *

THE DAY OF JUDGEMENT

[In a letter to Voltaire, the famous Lord Chesterfield asserts that
Swift's own manuscript of a poem on the Day of Judgment is in his
possession. Chesterfield's letter was published in a posthumous edition
of his correspondence in April, 1774, and within a few days the
poem reproduced below appeared in print for the first time in a
London periodical. There is little reason to doubt that it is Swift's
work, but it cannot be assigned a precise date of composition.]

WITH a Whirl of Thought oppress'd,
I sink from Reverie to Rest.
An horrid Vision seiz'd my Head,
I saw the Graves give up their Dead.

†† *Divisum Imperium cum* Jove Cæsar *habet.*

Jove, arm'd with Terrors, burst the Skies,
And Thunder roars, and Light'ning flies!
Amaz'd, confus'd, its Fate unknown,
The World stands trembling at his Throne.
While each pale Sinner hangs his Head,
Jove, nodding, shook the Heav'ns, and said,   10
"Offending Race of Human Kind,
By Nature, Reason, Learning, blind;
You who thro' Frailty step'd aside,
And you who never fell—*thro' Pride;*
You who in different Sects have shamm'd,
And come to see each other damn'd;
(So some Folks told you, but they knew
No more of Jove's Designs than you)
The World's mad Business now is o'er,
And I resent these Pranks no more.   20
I to such Blockheads set my Wit!
I damn such Fools!—Go, go, you're bit."

ON STELLA'S BIRTHDAY (1718-1719)

[Specimens of Swift's poetry to Stella are here grouped together in
the only deliberate violation of chronology among these selections
from Swift's verse. This is the earliest of the verses with which
Swift marked, with two exceptions, each of Stella's birthdays until
her death in 1728. Swift's references to Stella's age are seldom
accurate: this poem was actually written for her thirty-eighth birth-
day, and she was probably closer to eight than to sixteen upon
Swift's first seeing her. The poem is among those which Stella
copied into her manuscript book, and the present text follows her
transcription.]

STELLA this Day is thirty four,
(We won't dispute a Year or more)
However Stella, be not troubled,
Although thy Size and Years are doubled,
Since first I saw Thee at Sixteen

The brightest Virgin of the Green,
So little is thy Form declin'd
Made up so largely in thy Mind.
Oh, would it please the Gods to split
Thy Beauty, Size, and Years, and Wit,   10
No Age could furnish out a Pair
Of Nymphs so gracefull, Wise and fair
With half the Lustre of Your Eyes,
With half thy Wit, thy Years and Size:
And then before it grew too late,
How should I beg of gentle Fate,
(That either Nymph might have her Swain,)
To split my Worship too in twain.

Stella, don't worry about your size; your beauty remains the same

TO STELLA

WHO COLLECTED AND TRANSCRIBED HIS POEMS

[The third (self-styled "last") volume of the Pope-Swift *Miscellanies* (January, 1728), in which these verses first appeared, contained a number of Swift's verses that had been collected and copied by Stella. The text is that of the *Miscellanies*.]

As when a lofty Pile is rais'd,
We never hear the Workmen prais'd,
Who bring the Lime, or place the Stones;
But all admire *Inigo Jones*: *an architect*
So if this Pile of scatter'd Rhymes
Should be approv'd in After-times,
If it both pleases and endures,
The Merit and the Praise are yours.

  Thou *Stella,* wert no longer young,
When first for thee my Harp I strung: 10
Without one Word of *Cupid*'s Darts,
Of killing Eyes, or bleeding Hearts:
With Friendship and Esteem possesst,
I ne'er admitted Love a Guest.

354 TO STELLA

In all the Habitudes of Life,
The Friend, the Mistress, and the Wife,
Variety we still Pursue,
In Pleasure seek for something new:
Or else, comparing with the rest,
Take Comfort, that our own is best: 20
(The best we value by the worst,
As Tradesmen shew their Trash at first:)
But his Pursuits are at an End,
Whom *Stella* chuses for a *Friend*.

A Poet, starving in a Garret,
Conning old Topicks like a Parrot,
Invokes his Mistress and his Muse,
And stays at home for want of Shoes:
Should but his Muse descending drop
A Slice of Bread, and Mutton-Chop,   30
Or kindly when his Credit's out,
Surprize him with a Pint of Stout,
Or patch his broken Stocking Soals,
Or send him in a Peck of Coals;
Exalted in his mighty Mind
He flies, and leaves the Stars behind,
Counts all his Labours amply paid,
Adores her for the timely Aid.

Or should a Porter make Enquiries
For *Chloe, Sylvia, Phillis, Iris;*   40
Be told the Lodging, Lane, and Sign,
The Bow'rs that hold those Nymphs divine;
Fair *Chloe* would perhaps be found
With Footmen tippling under Ground, *In some cellar*
The charming *Silvia* beating Flax,
Her Shoulders mark'd with bloody Tracks;
Bright *Phillis* mending ragged Smocks,
And radiant *Iris* in the Pox. - *Venereal disease*

These are the Goddesses enroll'd
In *Curll's* Collections, new and old,   50

↓ scandalous publisher

Whose Scoundrel Fathers would not know 'em,
If they should meet 'em in a Poem.

True Poets can depress and raise;
Are Lords of Infamy and Praise:
They are not scurrilous in Satire,
Nor will in Panygyrick flatter.
Unjustly Poets we asperse;
Truth shines the brighter, clad in Verse;
And all the Fictions they pursue
Do but insinuate what is true.   60

Now should my Praises owe their Truth
To Beauty, Dress, or Paint, or Youth,
What Stoicks call *without our Power*,
They could not be insur'd an Hour;
'Twere grafting on an annual Stock
That must our Expectation mock,
And making one luxuriant Shoot
Die the next Year for want of Root:
Before I could my Verses bring,
Perhaps you're quite another Thing.   70

So *Mævius,* when he drain'd his Skull
To celebrate some Suburb Trull;
His Similes in Order set,
And ev'ry Crambo he could get;
Had gone through all the Common-Places
Worn out by Wits who rhyme on Faces;
Before he could his Poem close,
The lovely Nymph had lost her Nose.

Your Virtues safely I commend,
They on no Accidents depend: 80
Let Malice look with all her Eyes,
She dares not say the Poet lyes.

Stella, when you these Lines transcribe,
Lest you should take them for a Bribe,

Resolv'd to mortify your Pride,
I'll here expose your weaker Side.

Your Spirits kindle to a Flame,
Mov'd with the lightest Touch of Blame,
And when a Friend in Kindness tries
To shew you where your Error lies,   90
Conviction does but more incense;
Perverseness is your whole Defence:
Truth, Judgment, Wit, give Place to Spite,
Regardless both of Wrong and Right.
Your Virtues, all suspended, wait
Till Time hath open'd Reason's Gate:
And what is worse, your Passion bends
Its Force against your nearest Friends;
Which Manners, Decency, and Pride,
Have taught you from the World to hide;   100
In vain; for see, your Friend hath brought
To publick Light your only Fau't;
And yet a Fault we often find
Mix'd in a noble generous Mind;
And may compare to Ætna's Fire,
Which, tho' with Trembling, all admire;
The Heat that makes the Summit glow,
Enriching all the Vales below.
Those who in warmer Climes complain
From Phœbus Rays they suffer Pain,   110
Must own, that Pain is largely paid
By gen'rous Wines beneath a Shade.

Yet when I find your Passions rise,
And Anger sparkling in your Eyes,
I grieve those Spirits should be spent,
For nobler Ends by Nature meant.
One Passion, with a diff'rent Turn,
Makes Wit inflame, or Anger burn;
So the Sun's Heat, with different Powers,
Ripens the Grape, the Liquor sours,   120

Thus *Ajax,* when with Rage possesst
By *Pallas* breath'd into his Breast,
His Valour would no more employ;
Which might alone have conquer'd *Troy;*
But blinded by Resentment, seeks
For Vengeance on his Friends the *Greeks.*

You think this Turbulence of Blood
From stagnating preserves the Flood;
Which thus fermenting, by Degrees
Exalts the Spirits, sinks the Lees.   130

Stella, for once you reason wrong;
For should this Ferment last too long,
By Time subsiding, you may find
Nothing but Acid left behind.
From Passion you may then be freed,
When Peevishness and Spleen succeed.

Say, *Stella,* when you copy next,
Will you keep strictly to the Text?
Dare you let these Reproaches stand,
And to your Failing set your Hand?   140
Or if these Lines your Anger fire,
Shall they in baser Flames expire?
Whene'er they burn, if burn they must,
They'll prove my Accusation just.

STELLA'S BIRTHDAY (1724-1725)

[The text of this poem follows that of the third volume of the
Swift-Pope *Miscellanies,* in which it was first published. The initial
letters stand for the names of Swift's good friends, Thomas Sheridan
and Patrick Delany.]

As when a beauteous Nymph decays
We say, she's past her Dancing Days;
So, Poets lose their Feet by Time,

And can no longer dance in Rhyme.
Your Annual Bard had rather chose
To celebrate your Birth in Prose;
Yet, merry Folks who want by chance
A Pair to make a Country Dance,
Call the Old Housekeeper, and get her
To fill a Place, for want of better;　　　10
While *S — — — n* is off the hooks,
And Friend *D — — — y* at his Books,
That *Stella* may avoid Disgrace
Once more the *D — — n* supplies their Place.

Beauty and Wit, too sad a Truth,
Have always been confin'd to Youth;
The God of Wit, and Beauty's Queen,
He Twenty one, and She Fifteen:
No Poet ever sweetly sung,
Unless he were like *Phœbus,* young;　　　20
Nor ever Nymph inspir'd to Rhyme,
Unless, like *Venus,* in her Prime.
At Fifty six, if this be true,
Am I a Poet fit for you?
Or at the Age of Forty three,
Are you a Subject fit for me?
Adieu bright Wit, and radiant Eyes;
You must be grave, and I be wise.
Our Fate in vain we would oppose,
But I'll be still your Friend in Prose:　　　30
Esteem and Friendship to express,
Will not require Poetick Dress;
And if the Muse deny her Aid
To have them *sung,* they may be *said.*

But, *Stella* say, what evil Tongue
Reports you are no longer young?
That *Time* sits with his Scythe to mow
Where erst sate *Cupid* with his Bow;
That half your Locks are turn'd to Grey;

I'll ne'er believe a Word they say.   40
'Tis true, but let it not be known,
My Eyes are somewhat dimmish grown;
For Nature, always in the Right,
To your Decays adapts my Sight,
And Wrinkles undistinguish'd pass,
For I'm asham'd to use a Glass;
And till I see them with these Eyes,
Whoever says you have them, lyes.

    No Length of Time can make you quit
Honour and Virtue, Sense and Wit,   50
Thus you may still be young to me,
While I can better *hear* than *see;*
Oh, ne'er may Fortune shew her Spight,
To make me *deaf,* and mend my *Sight.*

STELLA'S BIRTHDAY (1726-1727)

[These Verses were written for Stella's last birthday. She died in
January, 1728, shortly before the appearance of the third volume of
the *Miscellanies,* in which the poem was first printed and from which
the present text is taken.]

THIS Day, whate'er the Fates decree,
Shall still be kept with Joy by me:
This Day then, let us not be told,
That you are sick, and I grown old,
Nor think on our approaching Ills,
And talk of Spectacles and Pills;
To morrow will be Time enough
To hear such mortifying Stuff.
Yet, since from Reason may be brought
A better and more pleasing Thought,   10
Which can in spite of all Decays,
Support a few remaining Days:

From not the gravest of Divines,
Accept for once some serious Lines.

Although we now can form no more
Long Schemes of Life, as heretofore;
Yet you, while Time is running fast,
Can look with Joy on what is past.

Were future Happiness and Pain,
A mere Contrivance of the Brain,   20
As Atheists argue, to entice,
And fit their Proselytes for Vice;
(The only Comfort they propose,
To have Companions in their Woes.)
Grant this the Case, yet sure 'tis hard,
That Virtue, stil'd its own Reward,
And by all Sages understood
To be the chief of human Good,
Should acting, die, nor leave behind
Some lasting Pleasure in the Mind,   30
Which by Remembrance will assuage,
Grief, Sickness, Poverty, and Age;
And strongly shoot a radiant Dart,
To shine through Life's declining Part.

Say, *Stella,* feel you no Content,
Reflecting on a Life well spent?
Your skilful Hand employ'd to save
Despairing Wretches from the Grave;
And then supporting with your Store,
Those whom you dragg'd from Death before: 40
(So Providence on Mortals waits,
Preserving what it first creates)
Your gen'rous Boldness to defend
An innocent and absent Friend;
That Courage which can make you just,
To Merit humbled in the Dust:
The Detestation you express
For Vice in all its glitt'ring Dress:

That Patience under tort'ring Pain,
Where stubborn Stoicks would complain.   50

    Must these like empty Shadows pass,
Or Forms reflected from a Glass?
Or mere Chimæra's in the Mind,
That fly and leave no Marks behind?
Does not the Body thrive and grow
By Food of twenty Years ago?
And, had it not been still supply'd,
It must a thousand Times have dy'd.
Then, who with Reason can maintain,
That no Effects of Food remain?   60
And, is not Virtue in Mankind
The Nutriment that feeds the Mind?
Upheld by each good Action past,
And still continued by the last:
Then, who with Reason can pretend,
That all Effects of Virtue end?

    Believe me *Stella,* when you show
That true Contempt for Things below,
Nor prize your Life for other Ends
Than merely to oblige your Friends;   70
Your former Actions claim their Part,
And join to fortify your Heart.
For Virtue in her daily Race,
Like *Janus,* bears a double Face;
Looks back with Joy where she has gone,
And therefore goes with Courage on.
She at your sickly Couch will wait,
And guide you to a better State.

    O then, whatever Heav'n intends,
Take Pity on your pitying Friends;   80
Nor let your Ills affect your Mind,
To fancy they can be unkind.
Me, surely me, you ought to spare,
Who gladly would your Suff'rings share;

Or give my Scrap of Life to you,
And think it far beneath your Due;
You, to whose Care so oft I owe,
That I'm alive to tell you so.

The Journal to Stella

There are two principal reasons why an introduction to Swift should include at least a slight acquaintance with *The Journal to Stella*. These letters are, in the first place, the chief surviving record of a relation which was probably the closest Swift ever enjoyed with another human being. In the second place, they contain an intimate account of his daily life during the period, between 1710 and 1713, when he was vitally associated with the Tory administration and its conduct of the affairs of England.

Stella, whose real name was Esther Johnson, was brought up in the household of Sir William Temple. It was here that Swift first met her, quite possibly on his originally joining the establishment in 1689, when Stella was a child of eight. During his years with Temple, Swift served as Stella's tutor, "directing," he tells us, "what books she should read, and perpetually instructing her in the principles of honour and virtue." About two years after Temple's death, Stella, together with an older companion named Rebecca Dingley, was induced by Swift to move to Ireland. Here she lived the rest of her life, always, wherever Swift moved, his close neighbor, yet never sharing his roof. Not only the *Journal* but Swift's other correspondence and poems reveal that there existed between Swift and Stella a deep affection, a relation that was warm and informal, yet in which all overt signs of physical passion were meticulously avoided. Stella's death in 1728 tragically affected Swift's life, for it removed the one person who, in all likelihood, could elicit from him the confidence, the sentiment, and the childlike humor which is uniquely evident in the *Journal*.

Beyond these few facts, Swift's relation with Stella is surrounded by a mystery which the most earnest efforts of scholars have done little to diminish. From various quarters have come speculations that Stella was the natural child of Sir William Temple; that Swift, too, was a natural child of Temple and hence her half brother; that, the two preceding facts being true, Swift was unable to marry Stella; that, the same facts being true but only belatedly learned by Swift, the two were married but the marriage was never consummated; that, though no legal bar to marriage existed, Swift was destined, by one sort of abnormality or another, to remain a celibate throughout his life.

Today most serious scholars are agreed that such questions should be shelved in favor of more hopeful and profitable inquiries. Certainly we have no right to expect a closer scrutiny of a private relation than that afforded by *The Journal to Stella*. Never, of course, intended for other eyes than those of Stella and Rebecca Dingley, it brings us astonishingly near to Swift in his rare moments of candor and warmth. The *Journal is* filled with "little language," the childish distortions of certain words to create the same kind of baby talk countless other adults have used in moments of playful affection. The same childlike quality appears in Swift's use of initials and abbreviations to convey special meanings. Among these are "MD," probably meaning "My Dear" or "My Dears," which is used for Stella or for Stella and Mrs. Dingley; "Ppt," perhaps for "Poppet," to refer to Stella; "Pdfr," referring to Swift himself and agreeably conjectured to stand for Poor Dear Foolish Rogue; and "FW," which can mean either "Farewell" or "Foolish Wenches." In this connection, it should be noted that the name Stella is never actually employed in the *Journal* but was applied by Swift to Esther Johnson in later years; its appearance in the printed text is accounted for by the *Journal*'s first editors, who inserted it in place of some of the more cryptic terms of endearment.

Whimsical, teasing, highly personal though it is, the *Journal* contains the record of an increasingly influential man, closely connected with political affairs of the greatest importance. In September, 1710, Swift arrived in London as an emissary of the Irish clergy, sent to aid in securing for his brethren the remission of the "first fruits," an ancient levy by the Crown upon the first year's profits from clerical livings. But the Whig administration, with which Swift had previously negotiated on this matter, was on the brink of total collapse. This was the moment of Swift's disaffection from his former friends among the Whigs—a process clearly recorded in the *Journal.* In part it may have derived from the hard bargain the Whigs had sought to drive in the matter of the "first fruits"; in part, too, it may have been a matter of Swift's inveterate High Church beliefs, vigorously espoused by the Tories in the face of Whig demands for the extension of toleration. Certainly the warm and appreciative welcome he found among the new Tory leaders had much to do with Swift's change of allegiance. Whatever the cause, within a few months Swift found himself closely allied with the new Tory cabinet, headed by Robert Harley and Henry St. John. Swift's new Tory friends were able speedily to arrange the matter of the "first fruits," but Swift stayed on in London to assume a leading role in the publication of the Tory *Examiner* and to produce a number of tracts in the Tory interest. In the pages of the *Journal* are the details of this period of Tory supremacy, when Swift aided his friends in the defense of the Established Church, the advocacy of the peace with France that came in 1713, and the continuing effort to retain for Harley the confidence of the Queen and the people. In the *Journal*, too, is the account of growing discord within the Tory party—the discord which, within a few short years, would bring about the permanent collapse of Harley's brand of Toryism and, with it, the end of Swift's power in English politics.

There are sixty-five letters in the *Journal*, each composed of a series of daily entries, usually written as Swift sat in bed in the evening or early morning. A good number of these letters—although unfortunately a minor portion—have been preserved in manuscript in the British Museum. For letters II through XL, which have long been lost, we must depend on Deane Swift who, after printing some extracts in his biography of his uncle (1755), contributed the letters to an edition of Swift's *Works*, published in London in 1768. For letter LIV we are dependent on the publisher Hawkesworth who, in 1766, brought out the first and the twenty-five last letters in an edition of Swift's correspondence. The survival of original manuscripts is a matter of some importance for the modern reader. Where the manuscripts exist, they can be faithfully reproduced; where early editions must be relied on, the *Journal* comes to today's reader from the hands of an editor for whom questions of decorum, regularity, and convenience often outweighed the desire to preserve Swift's original words.

SELECTIONS FROM

THE

JOURNAL TO STELLA

LETTER II

London, *Sept.* 9, 1710.

[Saturday]

I GOT here last Thursday after five days travelling, weary
the first, almost dead the second, tolerable the third, and well
enough the rest; and am now glad of the fatigue, which has
served for exercise; and I am at present well enough. The
Whigs were ravished to see me, and would lay hold on me as
a twig while they are drowning, and the great men making me
their clumsy apologies, &c. But my lord treasurer received me
with a great deal of coldness, which has enraged me so, I am
almost vowing revenge. I have not yet gone half my circle;
but I find all my acquaintance just as I left them. I hear my
lady Giffard is much at Court, and lady Wharton was ridiculing it t'other day; so I have lost a friend there. I have not
yet seen her, nor intend it; but I will contrive to see Stella's
mother some other way. I writ to the bishop of Clogher from
Chester; and I now write to the archbishop of Dublin. Every
thing is turning upside down; every Whig in great office will, to
a man, be infallibly put out; and we shall have such a winter
as hath not been seen in England. Every body asks me, how
I came to be so long in Ireland, as naturally as if here were
my *Being;* but no soul offers to make it so: and I protest I
shall return to Dublin, and the Canal at Laracor, with more
satisfaction than ever I did in my life. The Tatler expects
every day to be turned out of his employment; and the duke

of Ormond, they say, will be lieutenant of Ireland. I hope you are now peaceably in Presto's lodgings; but I resolve to turn you out by Christmas; in which time I shall either do my business, or find it not to be done. Pray be at Trim by the time this letter comes to you, and ride little Johnson, who must needs be now in good case. I have begun this letter unusually, on the post-night, and have already written to the archbishop; and cannot lengthen this. Henceforth I will write something every day to MD, and make it a sort of journal; and when it is full, I will send it whether MD writes or no; and so that will be pretty: and I shall always be in conversation with MD, and MD with Presto. Pray make Parvisol pay you the ten pounds immediately; so I ordered him. They tell me I am grown fatter, and look better; and, on Monday, Jervas is to retouch my picture, I thought I saw Jack Temple and his wife pass by me to-day in their coach; but I took no notice of them. I am glad I have wholly shaken off that family. Tell the provost I have obeyed his commands to the duke of Ormond; or let it alone, if you please. I saw Jemmey Leigh just now at the Coffee-house, who asked after you with great kindness: he talks of going in a fortnight to Ireland. My service to the dean, and Mrs. Walls and her archdeacon. Will Frankland's wife is near bringing to-bed, and I have promised to christen the child. I fancy you had my Chester letter the Tuesday after I writ. I presented Dr. Raymond to lord Wharton at Chester. Pray let me know when Joe gets his money. It is near ten, and I hate to send by the bell-man. MD shall have a longer letter in a week, but I send this only to tell I am safe in London; and so farewell, &c.

LETTER IV

London, *Sept.* 21, 1710.

[Thursday]

HERE must I begin another letter, on a whole sheet, for fear sawcy little MD should be angry, and think *much* that the paper is too *little*. I had your letter this night, as I told you just and no more in my last; for this must be taken up in answering yours, saucebox. I believe I told you where I dined to-day; and to-morrow I go out of town for two days to dine with the same company on Sunday; Molesworth the Florence envoy, Stratford, and some others. I heard to-day that a gentlewoman from lady Giffard's house had been at the Coffee-house to enquire for me. It was Stella's mother, I suppose. I shall send her a penny-post letter to-morrow, and contrive to see her without hazarding seeing lady Giffard, which I will not do until she begs my pardon.

22. I dined to-day at Hampstead with lady Lucy, &c. and when I got home found a letter from Joe, with one inclosed to lord Wharton, which I will send to his excellency, and second it as well as I can; but to talk of getting the queen's order, is a jest. Things are in such a combustion here, that I am advised not to meddle yet in the affair I am upon, which concerns the clergy of a whole kingdom; and does he think any body will trouble the queen about Joe? We shall, I hope, get a recommendation from the lord lieutenant to the trustees for the linen business, and I hope that will do; and so I will write to him in a few days, and he must have patience. This is an answer to part of your letter as well as his. I lied, it is to-morrow I go to the country, and I won't answer a bit more of your letter yet.

23. Here is such a stir and bustle with this little MD of ours; I must be writing every night; I can't go to-bed without a word to them; I can't put out my candle till I have bid

them good night: O Lord, O Lord! Well, I dined the first time, to-day, with Will Frankland and his Fortune: she is not very handsome. Did I not say I would go out of town to-day; I hate lying abroad and clutter; I go to-morrow in Frankland's chariot, and come back at night. Lady Berkeley has invited me to Berkeley-castle, and lady Betty Germain to Drayton in Northamptonshire, and I'll go to neither. Let me alone, I must finish my pamphlet. I have sent a long letter to Bickerstaff: let the bishop of Clogher smoak it if he can. Well, I'll write to the bishop of Killala, but you might have told him how sudden and unexpected my journey was though. Deuce take lady S——; and if I know D——y, he is a rawboned-faced fellow, not handsome, nor visibly so young as you say: she sacrifices two thousand pounds a year, and keeps only six hundred. Well, you have had all my land journey in my second letter, and so much for that. So you have got into Presto's lodgings; very fine, truly! We have had a fortnight of the most glorious weather on earth, and still continues: I hope you have made the best of it. Ballygall will be a pure good place for air, if Mrs. Ashe makes good her promise. Stella writes like an emperor: I am afraid it hurts your eyes; take care of that pray, pray Mrs. Stella. Can't you do what you will with your own horse? Pray don't let that puppy Parvisol sell him. Patrick is drunk about three times a week, and I bear it, and he has got the better of me; but one of these days I will positively turn him off to the wide world, when none of you are by to inter-cede for him.—Stuff—how can I get her husband into the Charter-house? get, a ——— into the Charter-house.—Write constantly! Why, sirrah, don't I write every day, and some-times twice a day to MD? Now I have answered all your letter, and the rest must be as it can be: send me my bill. Tell Mrs. Brent what I say of the Charter-house. I think this enough for one night; and so farewel till this time to-morrow.

24. To-day I dined six miles out of town at Will Pate's, with Stratford, Frankland, and the Molesworth's, and came home at night, and was weary and lazy. I can say no more now, but good night.

25. I was so lazy to-day that I dined at next door, and have sat at home since six, writing to the bishop of Clogher, dean Stern, and Mr. Manley: the last, because I am in fear for him about his place, and have sent him my opinion, what I and his other friends here think he ought to do. I hope he will take it well. My advice was, To keep as much in favour as possible with sir Thomas Frankland, his master here.

26. Smoak how I widen the margin by lying in bed when I write. My bed lies on the wrong side for me, so that I am forced often to write when I am up. Manley you must know has had people putting in for his place already; and has been complained of for opening letters. Remember that last Sunday, September 24, 1710, was as hot as Midsummer. This was written in the morning; 'tis now night, and Presto in bed. Here's a clutter, I have gotten MD's second letter, and I must answer it here. I gave the bill to Tooke, and so———Well, I dined to-day with sir John Holland the comptroller, and sat with him till eight; then came home and sent my letters, and writ a part of a lampoon, which goes on very slow, and now I am writing to sawcy MD; no wonder, indeed, good boys must write to naughty girls. I han't seen your mother yet; my penny-post letter, I suppose, miscarried: I will write another. Mr. S—— came to see me; and said M—— was going to the country next morning with her husband (who I find is a surly brute) so I could only desire my service to her.

27. To-day all our company dined at Will Frankland's, with Steele and Addison too. This is the first rainy day since I came to town; I can't afford to answer your letter yet. Morgan, the puppy, writ me a long letter to desire I would recommend him for purse-bearer or secretary to the next lord-chancellor that would come with the next governor. I will not answer him; but beg you will say these words to his father Raymond, or any body that will tell him: That Dr. Swift has received his letter, and would be very ready to serve him, but cannot do it in what he desires, because he has no sort of interest in the persons to be applied to. These words you may write, and let Joe, or Mr. Warburton, give them to him: a pox on him!

However, 'tis by these sort of ways that fools get preferment. I must not end yet, because I can't say good night without losing a line, and then MD would scold; but now, good night.

28. I have the finest piece of Brazil tobacco for Dingley that ever was born. You talk of Leigh; why he won't be in Dublin these two months: he goes to the country, then returns to London, to see how the world goes here in Parliament. Good night, sirrahs; no, no, not night; I writ this in the morning, and looking carelessly I thought it had been of last night. I dined to day with Mrs. Barton alone at her lodgings, where she told me for certain that lady S—— was with child when she was last in England, and pretended a tympany, and saw every body; then disappeared for three weeks, her tympany was gone, and she looked like a ghost, &c. No wonder she married when she was so ill at containing. Conolly is out, and Mr. Roberts in his place, who loses a better here, but was formerly a commissioner in Ireland. That employment cost Conolly three thousand pounds to lord Wharton; so he has made one ill bargain in his life.

29. I wish MD a merry Michaelmas. I dined with Mr. Addison, and Jervas the painter, at Addison's country place; and then came home, and writ more to my lampoon. I made a *Tatler* since I came: guess which it is and whether the bishop of Clogher smoaks it. I saw Mr. Sterne to-day: he will do as you order, and I will give him chocolate for Stella's health. He goes not these three weeks. I wish I could send it some other way. So now to your letter, brave boys. I don't like your way of saving shillings: nothing vexes me but that it does not make Stella a coward in a coach. I don't think any lady's advice about my ear signifies two-pence: However I will, in compliance to you, ask Dr. Cockburn. Radcliffe I know not, and Bernard I never see. Walls will certainly be stingier for seven years, upon pretence of his robbery. So Stella puns again; why, 'tis well enough; but I'll not second it, though I could make a dozen: I never thought of a pun since I left Ireland.— Bishop of Clogher's bill? Why, he paid it me; do you think I was such a fool to go without it? As for the four shillings, I

will give you a bill on Parvisol for it on t'other side of this paper; and pray tear off the two letters I shall write to him and Joe, or let Dingley transcribe and send them; though that to Parvisol, I believe, he must have my hand for. No, no, I'll eat no grapes; I ate about six t'other day at sir John Holland's; but would not give six-pence for a thousand, they are so bad this year. Yes, faith, I hope in God Presto and MD will be together this time twelvemonth: What then? Last year I suppose I was at Laracor; but next I hope to eat my Michaelmas goose at my two little gooses' lodgings. I drink no *aile* (I suppose you mean *ale*) but yet good wine every day, of five and six shillings a bottle. O Lord, how much Stella writes: pray don't carry that too far, young women, but be temperate to hold out. To-morrow I go to Mr. Harley. Why; small hopes from the duke of Ormond: he loves me very well, I believe, and would, in my turn, give me something to make me easy; and I have good interest among his best friends. But I don't think of any thing further than the business I am upon: you see I writ to Manley before I had your letter, and I fear he will be out. Yes, Mrs. Owl, Blighe's corpse came to Chester when I was there, and I told you so in my letter, or forgot it. I lodge in Burystreet, where I removed a week ago. I have the first floor, a dining-room, and bed-chamber, at eight shillings a week; plaguy deep, but I spend nothing for eating, never go to a tavern, and very seldom in a coach; yet after all it will be expensive. Why do you trouble yourself, Mistress Stella, about my *instrument*? I have the same the archbishop gave me; and it is as good now the bishops are away. The dean friendly; the dean be poxt: a great piece of friendship indeed, what you heard him tell the bishop of Clogher; I wonder he had the face to talk so: but he lent me money, and that's enough. Faith I would not send this these four days, only for writing to Joe and Parvisol. Tell the dean, that when the bishops send me any pacquets, they must not write to me at Mr. Steele's; but direct for Mr. Steele, at his office at the Cockpit; and let the inclosed be directed for me: that mistake cost me eighteen-pence t'other day.

30. I dined with Stratford to-day, but am not to see Mr. Harley till Wednesday: 'tis late, and I send this before there is occasion for the bell; because I would have Joe have his letter, and Parvisol too; which you must so contrive as not to cost them doublé postage. I can say no more, but that I am, etc.

LETTER XVII

London, *Feb.* 24, 1710-11.

[Saturday]

NOW, young women, I gave in my sixteenth this evening. I dined with Ford, it was his Opera-day as usual; it is very convenient to me to do so, for coming home early after a walk in the Park, which now the days will allow. I called on the secretary at his office, and he had forgot to give the memorial about Bernage to the duke of Argyle; but two days ago I met the duke, who desired I would give it him myself, which should have more power with him than all the ministry together, as he protested solemnly, repeated it two or three times, and bid me count upon it. So that I verily believe Bernage will be in a very good way to establish himself. I think I can do no more for him at present, and there's an end of that; and so get you gone to bed, for it is late.

25. The three weeks are out yesterday since I had your last, and so now I will be expecting every day a pretty dear letter from my own MD, and hope to hear that Stella has been much better in her head and eyes; my head continues as it was, no fits, but a little disorder every day, which I can easily bear, if it will not grow worse. I dined to-day with Mr. secretary St. John, on condition I might chuse my company, which were lord Rivers, lord Cataret, Sir Thomas Mansel, and Mr. Lewis; I invited Masham, Hill, Sir John Stanley, and George Granville, but they were engaged; and I did it in revenge of his having such bad company when I dined with him before; so we

laughed, &c. And I ventured to go to church to-day, which I have not done this month before. Can you send me such a good account of Stella's health, pray now? Yes, I hope, and better too. We dined (says you) at the dean's, and played at cards till twelve, and there came in Mr. French, and Dr. Travors, and Dr. Whittingham, and Mr. (I forget his name, that I always tell Mrs. Walls of) the banker's son, a pox on him. And we were so merry; I vow they are pure good company. But I lost a crown; for you must know I had always hands tempting me to go out, but never took in any thing, and often two black aces without a manilio; was not that hard, Presto? Hold your tongue, &c.

26. I was this morning with Mr. secretary about some business, and he tells me, that colonel Fielding is now going to make Bernage his captain-lieutenant, that is, a captain by commission, and the perquisites of the company, but not captain's pay, only the first step to it. I suppose he will like it, and the recommendation to the duke of Argyle goes on. And so trouble me no more about your Bernage; the jackanapes understands what fair solicitors he has got, I warrant you. Sir Andrew Fountain and I dined, by invitation, with Mrs. Vanhomrigh. You say they are of no consequence: why, they keep as good female company as I do male; I see all the drabs of quality at this end of the town with them; I saw two lady Bettys there this afternoon, the beauty of one, the good breeding and nature of t'other, and the wit of neither, would have made a fine woman. Rare walking in the Park now: why don't you walk in the Green of St. Stephen? The walks there are finer gravelled than the Mall. What beasts the Irish women are, never to walk!

27. Darteneuf and I and little Harrison, the new *Tatler,* and Jervas the painter, dined to-day with James, I know not his other name, but it is one of Darteneuf's dining places, who is a true epicure. James is clerk of the kitchen to the queen, and has a little snug house at St. James's, and we had the queen's wine, and such very fine victuals, that I could not eat it.—Three weeks and three days since my last letter from MD,

rare doings; why truly we were so busy with poor Mrs. Walls, that indeed, Presto, we could not write, we were afraid the poor woman would have died; and it pitied us to see the arch-deacon, how concerned he was. The dean never came to see her but once; but now she is up again, and we go and sit with her in the evenings. The child died the next day after it was born, and I believe, between friends, she is not very sorry for it.—Indeed, Presto, you are plaguy silly to-night, and han't guest one word right; for she and the child are both well, and it is a fine girl, likely to live; and the dean was godfather, and Mrs. Catherine and I were godmothers; I was going to say Stoite, but I think I have heard they don't put maids and married women to-gether; though I know not why I think so, nor I don't care; what care I? but I must prate, &c.

28. I walked to-day into the city for my health, and there dined, which I always do when the weather is fair, and busi-ness permits, that I may be under a necessity of taking a good walk, which is the best thing I can do at present for my health. Some bookseller has raked up every thing I writ, and published it t'other day in one volume; but I know nothing of it, 'twas without my knowledge or consent: it makes a four shilling book, and is called *Miscellanies in Prose and Verse*. Took pre-tends he knows nothing of it, but I doubt he is at the bottom. One must have patience with these things; the best of it is, I shall be plagued no more. However, I'll bring a couple of them over with me for MD, perhaps you may desire to see them. I hear they sell mightily.

March 1. Morning. I have been calling to Patrick to look in his Almanack for the day of the month; I did not know but it might be Leap-year. The Almanack says 'tis The third after Leap-year, and I always thought till now, that every third year was Leap-year. I'm glad they come so seldom; but I'm sure 'twas otherwise when I was a young man; I see times are mightily changed since then.—Write to me, sirrahs, be sure do by the time this side is done, and I'll keep t'other side for the answer: so I'll go write to the bishop of Clogher; good morrow, sirrahs.—Night. I dined to-day at Mrs. Vanhomrigh's, being a rainy day, and lady Betty Butler knowing it, sent to let me know she expected my company in the evening where the *Vans* (so we call them) were to be. The duchess and she do not go over this summer with the duke; so I go to bed.

2. This rainy weather undoes me in coaches and chairs. I was traipsing to-day with your Mr. Sterne, to go along with them to Moor, and recommend his business to the treasury. Sterne tells me his dependence is wholly on me; but I have absolutely refused to recommend it to Mr. Harley, because I troubled him lately so much with other folks affairs; and besides, to tell the truth, Mr. Harley told me he did not like Sterne's business; however, I will serve him, because I suppose MD would have me. But in saying his dependence lies wholly on me, he lies, and is a fool. I dined with lord Abercorn, whose son Peasley will be married at Easter to ten thousand pounds.

3. I forgot to tell you that yesterday morning I was at Mr. Harley's levee: he swore I came in spight, to see him among a parcel of fools. My business was to desire I might let the duke of Ormond know how the affair stood of the First-Fruits. He promised to let him know it, and engaged me to dine with him to-day. Every Saturday lord keeper, secretary St. John, and I dine with him, and sometimes lord Rivers, and they let in none else. Patrick brought me some letters into the Park; among which was one from Walls, and t'other, yes faith, t'other was from our little MD, N. 11. I read the rest in the Park, and MD's in a chair as I went from St. James's to Mr. Harley, and glad enough I was faith to read it, and see all right: Oh, but I won't answer it these three or four days, at least, or may be sooner. An't I silly; Faith your letters would make a dog silly, if I had a dog to be silly, but it must be a little dog.—I staid with Mr. Harley till past nine, where we had much discourse together after the rest were gone; and I gave him very truly my opinion where he desired it. He complained he was not very well, and has engaged me to dine with him again on Monday. So I came home afoot, like a fine gentleman, to tell you all this.

4. I dined to-day with Mr. secretary St. John; and after

dinner he had a note from Mr. Harley, that he was much out of order; pray God preserve his health, every thing depends upon it. The Parliament at present cannot go a step without him, nor the queen neither. I long to be in Ireland; but the ministry beg me to stay: however, when this parliament lurry is over, I will endeavour to steal away; by which time I hope the First-Fruit business will be done. This kingdom is certainly ruined as much as was ever any bankrupt merchant. We must have *Peace,* let it be a bad or a good one, though no-body dares talk of it. The nearer I look upon things, the worse I like them. I believe the confederacy will soon break to pieces; and our factions at home increase. The ministry is upon a very narrow bottom, and stand like an Isthmus between the Whigs on one side, and violent Tories on the other. They are able seamen, but the tempest is too great, the ship too rotten, and the crew all against them. Lord Somers had been twice in the queen's closet, once very lately; and your duchess of Somerset, who now has the key, is a most insinuating woman, and I believe they will endeavour to play the same game that has been played against them.—I have told them of all this, which they know already, but they cannot help it. They have cautioned the queen so much against being governed, that she observes it too much. I could talk till to-morrow upon these things, but they make me melancholy. I could not but observe that lately, after much conversation with Mr. Hartley, though he is the most fearless man alive, and the least apt to despond, he confessed to me, that uttering his mind to me gave him ease.

5. Mr. Harley continues out of order, yet his affairs force him abroad: he is subject to a sore throat, and was cupped last night: I sent and called two or three times. I hear he is better this evening. I dined to-day in the city with Dr. Freind at a third body's house, where I was to pass for some body else, and there was a plaguy silly jest carried on, that made me sick of it. Our weather grows fine, and I will walk like camomile. And pray walk you to your dean's, or your Stoyte's, or your Manley's, or your Walls'. But your new lodgings make

you so proud, you'll walk less than ever. Come, let me go to bed, sirrahs.

6. Mr. Harley's going out yesterday has put him a little backwards. I called twice, and sent, for I am in pain for him. Ford caught me, and made me dine with him on his Opera-day; so I brought Mr. Lewis with me, and sat with him till six. I have not seen Mr. Addison these three weeks; all our friendship is over. I go to no Coffee-house. I presented a parson of the bishop of Clogher's, one Richardson, to the duke of Ormond to-day: he is translating prayers and sermons into Irish, and has a project about instructing the Irish in the protestant religion.

7. Morning. Faith, a little would make me, I could find in my heart, if it were not for one thing, I have a good mind, if I had not something else to do, I would answer your dear saucy letter. O Lord, I am going awry with writing in bed. O faith, but I must answer it, or I shan't have room, for it must go on Saturday; and don't think I'll fill the third side, I an't come to that yet, young women. Well, then, as for your Bernage, I have said enough: I writ to him last week.—Turn over that leaf. Now, what says MD to the world to come? I tell you, madam Stella, my head is a great deal better, and I hope will keep so. How came yours to be fifteen days coming, and you had my fifteenth in seven? Answer me that, rogues. Your being with goody Walls is excuse enough: I find I was mistaken in the sex, 'tis a boy. Yes, I understand your cypher, and Stella guesses right, as she always does. He gave me al bsadnuk lboinlpl dfaonr ufainfbtoy dpionufnad,[1] which I sent him again by Mr. Lewis, to whom I writ a very complaining letter that was shewed him; and so the matter ended. He told me he had a quarrel with me; I said I had another with him, and we returned to our friendship, and I should think he loves

---

[1] [The present editor's decision to omit footnotes (since only voluminous annotation can even begin to comment adequately on the *Journal*) is here briefly suspended in justice to the compositor. Swift is here responding to Stella's Cipher, and his meaning can be extracted by reading the alternate letters.]

me as well as a great minister can love a man in so short a
time. Did I not do right? I am glad at heart you have got your
palsey-water; pray God Almighty it may do my dearest little
Stella good. I suppose Mrs. Edgworth set out last Monday
se'nnight. Yes, I do read the *Examiners,* and they are written
very finely, as you judge. I do not think they are too severe on
the duke; they only tax him of avarice, and his avarice has
ruined us. You may count upon all things in them to be
true. The author has said, It is not Prior; but perhaps it may
be Atterbury.—Now, madam Dingley, says she, 'tis fine weather,
says she: yes, says she, and we have got to our new lodgings. I
compute you ought to save eight pounds by being in the others
five months; and you have no more done it than eight
thousand. I am glad you are rid of that squinting, blinking
Frenchman. I will give you a bill on Parvisol for five pound
for the half year. And must I go on at four shillings a week,
and neither eat nor drink for it? Who the D—— said Atterbury and your dean were alike? I never saw your chancellor,
nor his chaplain. The latter has a good deal of learning, and
is a well-wisher to be an author: your chancellor is an excellent
man. As for Patrick's bird, he bought him for his tameness,
and is grown the wildest I ever saw. His wings have been quilled
thrice, and are now up again: he will be able to fly after us to
Ireland, if he be willing.—Yes, Mrs. Stella, Dingley writes
more like Presto than you; for all you superscribed the letter,
as who should say, Why should I not write like our Presto as
well as Dingley? You with your aukward SS s; cannot you write
them thus, SS? No, but always SSS. Spiteful sluts, to affront
Presto's writing; as that when you shut your eyes you write
most like Presto. I know the time when I did not write to
you half so plain as I do now; but I take pity on you both.
I am very much concerned for Mrs. Walls's eyes. Walls says
nothing of it to me in his letter dated after yours. You say, If
she recovers she may lose her sight. I hope she is in no danger
of her life. Yes, Ford is as sober as I please: I use him to walk
with me as an easy companion, always ready for what I please,
when I am weary of business and ministers. I don't go to a

Coffee-house twice a month. I am very regular in going to sleep before eleven.—And so you say that Stella's a pretty girl; and so she be, and methinks I see her just now as handsome as the day's long. Do you know what? when I am writing in our language I make up my mouth just as if I was speaking it. I caught myself at it just now. And I suppose Dingley is so fair and so fresh as a lass in May, and has her health, and no spleen.—In your account you sent do you reckon as usual from the 1st of November was twelvemonth? Poor Stella, won't Dingley leave her a little day-light to write to Presto? Well, well, we'll have day-light shortly, spight of her teeth; and zoo must cly Lele and Hele, and Hele aden. Must loo mimitate pdfr, pay? Iss, and so la shall. And so leles fol ee rettle. Dood mollow.—At night. Mrs. Barton sent this morning to invite me to dinner; and there I dined, just in that genteel manner that MD used when they would treat some better sort of body than usual.

8. O dear MD, my heart is almost broken. You will hear the thing before this comes to you. I writ a full account of it this night to the archbishop of Dublin; and the dean may tell you the particulars from the archbishop. I was in a sorry way to write, but thought it might be proper to send a true account of the fact; for you will hear a thousand lying circumstances. 'Tis of Mr. Harley's being stabbed this afternoon at three o'clock at a committee of the council. I was playing lady Catherine Morris's cards, where I dined, when young Arundel came in with the story. I ran away immediately to the secretary, which was in my way: no one was at home. I met Mrs. St. John in her chair; she had heard it imperfectly. I took a chair to Mr. Harley, who was asleep, and they hope in no danger; but he has been out of order, and was so when he came abroad to-day, and it may put him in a fever: I am in mortal pain for him. That desperate French villain, Marquis de Guiscard, stabbed Mr. Harley. Guiscard was taken up by Mr. secretary St. John's warrant for high treason, and brought before the lords to be examined; there he stabbed Mr. Harley. I have told all the particulars already to the archbishop. I have

now at nine sent again, and they tell me he is in a fair way. Pray pardon my distraction; I now think of all his kindness to me.—The poor creature now lies stabbed in his bed by a desperate French popish villain. Good night, and God preserve you both, and pity me; I want it.

9. Morning; seven, in bed. Patrick is just come from Mr. Harley's. He slept well till four; the surgeon sat up with him: he is asleep again: he felt a pain in his wound when he waked: they apprehend him in no danger. This account the surgeon left with the porter, to tell people that send. Pray God preserve him. I am rising and going to Mr. secretary St. John. They say Guiscard will die with the wounds Mr. St. John and the rest gave him. I shall tell you more at night.— Night. Mr. Harley still continues on the mending hand; but he rested ill last night, and felt pain. I was early with the secretary this morning, and I dined with him, and he told me several particularities of this accident, too long to relate now. Mr. Harley is still mending this evening, but not at all out of danger; and till then I can have no peace. Good night, &c. and pity Presto.

10. Mr. Harley was restless last night; but he has no fever, and the hopes of his mending increase. I had a letter from Mr. Walls, and one from Mr. Bernage. I will answer them here, not having time to write. Mr. Walls writes about three things. First, about a hundred pounds from Dr. Raymond, of which I hear nothing, and 'tis now too late. Secondly, about Mr. Clements: I can do nothing in it, because I am not to mention Mr. Pratt; and I cannot recommend without knowing Mr. Pratt's objections, whose relation Clements is, and who brought him into the place. The third is about my being godfather to the child: that is in my power, and (since there is no remedy) will submit. I wish you could hinder it; but if it can't be helped, pay what you think proper, and get the provost to stand for me, and let his christian name be Harley, in honour of my friend, now lying stabbed and doubtful of his life. As for Bernage, he writes me word, that his colonel has offered to make him captain-lieutenant for a hundred pounds. He was

such a fool to offer him money without writing to me till it was done, though I have had a dozen letters from him; and then he desires I would say nothing of this, for fear his colonel should be angry. People are mad. What can I do? I engaged colonel Disney, who was one of his solicitors to the secretary, and then told him the story. He assured me, that Fielding (Bernage's colonel) said he might have got that sum; but on account of those great recommendations he had, would give it him for nothing: and I would have Bernage write him a letter of thanks, as of a thing given him for nothing, upon recommendations, &c. Disney tells me he will again speak to Fielding, and clear up this matter; and then I will write to Bernage. A pox on him for promising money till I had it promised to me, and then making it such a ticklish point, that one cannot expostulate with the colonel upon it: but let him do as I say, and there's an end. I engaged the secretary of state in it; and am sure it was meant a kindness to me, and that no money should be given, and a hundred pounds is too much in a Smithfield bargain, as a major general told me, whose opinion I asked. I am now hurried, and can say no more. Farewel, &c. &c.

How shall I superscribe to your new lodgings, pray madams? Tell me but that, impudence and saucy-face.

An't you sauceboxes to write lele like Presto?

O poor Presto!

Mr. Harley is better to-night, that makes me so pert, you saucy Gog and Magog.

LETTER XLIV

London, *Mar.* 22d. 1711-12

44 [Saturday]

UGLY nasty Weather. I was in the City to day with Mrs Wesly & Mr Percivll to get money from a Banker for Mrs

Wesly, who goes to the Bath on Thursday. . I left them there, & dined with a friend, & went to see Ld Treasr: but he had People with him I did not know, so I went to Ldy Mashams, and lost a Crown with her at Picquet, and then sate with Ld Masham, & Ld Treasr &c there till past one. But I had my Man with me to come hom; I gave in my 43d and one for the Bp. of Cl. to the Post office as I came from the City, and so oo know tis late now, and I have nothing to say for this day, Our Mohocks are all vanisht; however I shall take care of my Person. Nite my own two deelest nuntyes Md.

23. I was this morning before Church with the Secrty about Ld Abercorn's Business, & some others. My Solliciting Season is come, and will last as long as the Sessions. . I went late to Court, and the Company was almost gone. The Court serves me for a Coffee-house, once a week I meet acquaintance there that I should not otherwise see in a quarter. There is a flying Report that the French have offered a Cessation of Arms, and to give us Dunkerk, & the Dutch Namur for security till the Peace is made. The D. of Ormd thy say goes in a week. Abundance of his Equipage is already gone. Is Friends are afraid the Expence of this Employmt will ruin him, since he must lose the Governmt of Ireld. I dined privately with a Friend, and refused all Dinners offerd me at Court, wch however were but two, and I did not like eithr Did I tell you of a Scoundrel about the Court, that sells Employnts to ignorant People, and cheats them of their Money. he lately made a Bargain for the Vice-chamberlns Place for 7000ll, and had received some Guinneas Earnest, but the whole Thing was discoverd tothr day, and Examination taken of it by Ld. Dartmouth, & I hope he will be swingd. The Vicechambrln told me sevrll Particulars of it last night at Ld Mashams. Can dd play at Ombre yet? enough hod te Cards while ppt steps into next Room—Nite deelest sollahs.

24. This morning I recommended Newcomb agn to the D. of Ormd, and left Dick Stewart to [do] it furthr; then I went to visit the Dutchess of Hamilton who was not awake: so I went to the Dutchess of Shrewsbury and sate an hour at her

Toilet. I [spoke] to her about the Dukes being Ld Lt; she sayd she knew nothig of it, but I rallyd her out of that, and she resolves not to stay behind the Duke. I intend to recommd the Bp of Cl—— to her for an Acquaintance. He will like her very well. She is indeed a most agreeable woman, & a great Favorite of mine. I know not whethr the Ladyes in Ireld will like her. I was at the Court of Requests to get some Lds to be at a Commttee to morrow about a Friends Bill; & there the Duke of Beaufort gave me a Poem finely bound in Folio, printed at Stamford, & writt by a Country Squire. Ld Exetr desired the Duke to give it the Qu—— because the Authr is his Friend: but the Duke desird I would let him know whethr it was good for any thing; I brought it home & will return it to morrow, as the dullest thing I ever read; & advise the Duke not to present it. I dind with Domvile at his Lodgings by Invitation, for he goes in a few days for Ireld. Nite dee Md.

25. There is a mighty Feast at a Tory Sheriffs to day in the City, 12 hundred dishes of meat, about 5 Lds, and sevll hundrd Gentlemen will be there, and give 4 or 5 Guinneas a Piece, according to Custom. Dr. Coghill & I dined by Invitation at Mrs. Van's. It has raind or mizzled all day as my Pockets feel. There are two new Answers come out to the Conduct of the Allyes The last years Examiners printd togethr in a small Volume, go off but slowly. The Printer overprintd himself by at least a thousand, so soon out of Fashion are Party papers however so well writt. The Medlys are coming out in the same Volume, & perhaps may sell better. Our news about a Cessation of Arms begins to flag; and I have not these two days since [seen] any body in Business, to ask them about it. We had a terrible Fire last night in Drury lane, or thereabouts, and 3 or 4 People destroyd. One of the Maids of Honr has the Small-pox, but the best is, she can lose no beauty, & we have one new handsom Md of Honr. Nite Md.

26. I forgot to tell you that on Sunday last about 7 at night, it lightend above 50 times as I walkt the Mall, wch I think is extdy at this at this time of the Year. & the Weather was very hot. Had you any thing of this in Dublin? I intended to dine

with Ld Treasr today: but Ld Mansel & Mr Lewis made me dine with them at Kit Musgrave's. Now you don't know who Kit Musgrave is. I sate the Evening with Mrs Wesley who goes to morrow to the Bath. She is much better than she was. The News of the French desiring a Cessation of Arms &c was but Town talk. . We shall know in a few days as I am told, whethr there will be a Peace or no. The D. or Ormd will go in a Week for Flanders, they say: Our Mohawks go on still, & cut Peoples faces evry night; fais they shan't cut mine, I like it better as it is, the Dogs will cost me at least a Crown a Wcck in Chairs. I believe the souls of your Houghers of Cattle have got into them, and now they don't distinguish between a Cow and a Christian. I forgot to wish you yesterday a happy new Year, you know the 25 of March is the first day of the Year, And now you must leave of Cards, and put out your fire: I'll put out mine the 1st of April, cold or not cold. I believe I shall lose Credit with you by not coming over at the Beginning of April: but I hoped the Session would be ended, and I must stay till then, & yet I would fain be at the Beginning of my Willows growing. Percivll tells me that the Quick-setts upon the flatt in the Garden, do not grow so well as those famous ones on the Ditch. They want digging about them; The Cherry trees by the River side my Heart is sett upon; Nite Md.

27. Society day. You know that I suppose. Dr. Arthburnett was Presidt. His dinner was dresst in the Qu——s Kitchin, and was mighty fine; & we eat it at Ozinda's Chocolate house just by St. James's. We were never merryer nor bettr company, and did not part till after 11 I did not summon Ld Lansdown: He and I are fallen out. There was something in an Ex-aminr a fortnight ago that he thought reflected on the Abuses in his Office, (he is Secrtry at War) & he writt to the Secty that he heard I had inserted that Paragraph. This I resented highly, that he should complain of me before he spoke to me; and I sent him a peppering Letter, and would not summon him by a Note as I do the rest; nor ever will have anything to say to him till he begs my Pardon. I mett Ld Treasr to day at

Ldy Masham's he would have fain carryed me home to dinner, but I begged his Pardon; what? upon a Society day? No, no. Tis rate Sollahs; I ant dlunk. Nite Md.

28. I was with my Friend Lewis to day getting Materials for a little Mischief; and I dined with Ld Treasr, and 3 or 4 fellows I never saw before: I left them at 7, and came home, and have been writing to the A.Bp Dubln, and Cozn Dean in answer to one of his 4 months old, that I spied by chance routing among my Papers. I have a Pain these 2 days exactly upon the Top of my left Shouldr, I fear it is something Rheumatick, it winches now and then. Shall I putt Flannell to it? Domvile is going to Ireld; he came here this morning to take leave of me; but I shall dine with him to-morrow. Does the Bp of Cl talk of coming for Engd this Summer? I think Ld Molesworth told me so about 2 Months ago. The weathr is bad again, rainy and very cold this Evening. Do you know what the Longitude is? a Projector has been applying himself to me to recommend him to the Ministry, because he pretends to have found out the Longitude. I believe He has no more found it out, than he found out mine. . . . However I will gravely hear what he says, and discover him a Knave or Fool. Nite Md.

29. I am plagued with these Pains in my Shouldr; I believe it is Rheumatick: I will do something for it to Night. Mr Lewis & I dined with Mr Domvile to take our Leave of him: I drunk 3 or 4 Glasses of Champigne by perfect teazing; thô it is bad for my Pain; but if it continues I will not drink any wine without Water till I am well. The Weathr is abominably cold and wet.—I am got into bed and have put some old Flannel for want of new to my Shouldr, and rubbd it with Hungary water.—Tis plaguy hard; I never would drink any Wine, if it were not for my Head, and drinking has given me this Pain. I will try Abstemiousness for a while. How does Md do now? how does Dd & ppt? You must know I hate Pain, as the old woman sd—But I'll try to go seep; My Flesh sucks up Hungary water rarely. My Man's an awkward Rascal, and

makes me peevish. Do you know that tother day he was
to beg my Pardon that he could not shave my Head, his h
shook so. He is drunk every day & I design to turn him off soo.
as ever I get to Ireld. I ll write no more now, but go to Sleep,
and see whether Sleep & Flannell will cure my Shouldr. Nite
deelest Md.

30. I was not able to go to Church or Court to day, for my
Shouldr; the Pain has left my Shouldr and crept to my neck
and Collar bone. It makes me think of poopt's bladebone.
Urge urge urge, dogs gnawing. . I went in a Chair at 2 and
dined with Mrs Van, where I could be easy; & came back at
7. My Hungary water is gone, & to night I use Spirits of wine,
wch my Landlady tells me is very good. It has raind terribly
all day long; & is extreamly cold: I am very uneasy, and such
cruell Twinges every moment. Nite deelest Md.

31. Ap. 1, 2, 3, 4, 5, 6, 7,-8. All these days I have been extreamly ill, tho I twice crawld out a week ago; but am now
recovering, thô very weak. The violence of my Pain abated the
night before last; I will just tell you how I was & then send
away this lettr wch ought to have gone Saterday last. The
Pain encreasd with mighty Violence in my left Shouldr &
Collar bone & that side my Neck. On Thursday morning appeared great Red Spots in all those Places where my Pain was,
& the violence of the Pain was confined to my Neck behind
a little on the left side; which was so violent that I not a
minutes ease nor hardly a minutes sleep in 3 days & nights. the
Spots encreasd every day & had little Pimples which are now
grown white & full of corruption [tho] small. the Red still continues too, and most prodigious hott & inflamed. The Disease
is the Shingles. I eat nothing but Water gruell; I am very weak
but out of all violent Pain. The Doctrs say it would have
ended in some violent Disease if had not come out thus. I
shall now recover fast. I have been in no danger of Life, but
miserable Torture. I must not write too much—so adieu
deelest Md Md Md FW FW Me Me Me Lele I can say lele
yet oo see—Fais I dont conceal a bitt. as hope savd.

[Note written on fold of cover]

I must prge & clystr after this; and my next Lettr will not be in the old order of Journall till I have done with Physick. An't oo surprised to see the Lettr want half a side.

Selected Letters

In a letter to Alexander Pope, written in 1735, Swift says, "I believe my letters have escaped being published, because I writ nothing but nature and friendship, and particular incidents which could make no figure in writing." Though the assertion does not apply with uniform accuracy to all of Swift's correspondence, it indicates clearly what can be expected from the great bulk of his letters. Unlike Pope, who wrote in transparent anticipation of seeing many of his letters in print, Swift seems invariably to have in mind only his immediate correspondent and the particular occasion, whether serious or frivolous, which has prompted him to write. In consequence, there are in the letters very few specimens of the kind of sustained intellectual exposition which is intended for a general audience. The occasional profession of purpose or belief—such as the famous expression of hatred for "that animal called man" in the letter to Pope of September 29, 1725—is all the more to be cherished.

But if Swift's letters are not notable as works of art or as the vehicle for basic ideas, they nonetheless powerfully illuminate many aspects of his life—and in particular his friendships. Swift's correspondents are a widely diversified group. There are those illustrious contemporaries who are still remembered for their own achievements: Robert Harley, Earl of Oxford; Henry St. John, Viscount Bolingbroke; Alexander Pope; John Arbuthnot, the amiable wit, writer, and court physician; John Gay, of *Beggar's Opera* fame, and others who, though of lesser stature, like Ambrose Philips, the pastoral poet, occupy some place in the history of art or of ideas. There are men and women of nobility and fashion like Lord Carteret and Lord Bathurst, Lady Betty Germain and the Duchess of Ormond. There are ecclesiastical associates like Archbishop King of Dublin and businessmen like the printer Benjamin Motte. And there are Charles Ford and Thomas Sheridan, to whom Swift wrote with the easy, confiding informality of long and close friendship.

In the correspondence we see not only the unusual range of Swift's friendships but his willingness to adjust the style and substance of each letter to the character of the recipient and the occasion. Thus the many letters to Archbishop King which have been preserved are astute and tactful documents. They reveal Swift's agile conduct of his own ecclesiastical career as well as a certain coolness which existed between Swift and King, despite their close professional association. At the opposite extreme are Swift's letters to Thomas Sheridan, the gifted but perennially unsuccessful schoolmaster and cleric who was for many years one of Swift's genuinely intimate friends. These letters are replete with jokes, extravagant puns in English and Latin, and a kind of schoolboy humor which, in its frequent bawdiness, has distressed more than one Victorian commentator. In its diversity, the entire correspondence reveals most of the characteristics we have come to associate with Swift: the wit, wisdom, and moral strength on the one hand; the petulance, impatience, and dogmatism on the other.

Many of Swift's letters have been in print—although with varying degrees of accuracy—since the earliest eighteenth-century collections of his works. It remained, however, for the late F. Elrington Ball to provide a reliable scholarly edition of all letters then available for reproduction in his *Correspondence of Jonathan Swift* (6 vols., London, 1910-1914). This collection has been invaluably augmented by *The Letters of Jonathan Swift to Charles Ford,* edited by D. Nichol Smith (Oxford, 1935). The most casual browsing in these collections has its rewards. One cannot read for long without encountering the stamp of Swift's wit or temper or a detail of intrinsic historic importance. If, however, as in the present volume, a choice must be made, it is natural to turn chiefly to the letters which Swift wrote to men like Bolingbroke, Pope, Arbuthnot, and Gay. For it is here we find Swift in open, natural communication with his peers—with men equipped by their own intellectual gifts to respond to Swift with affectionate understanding.

To John Gay

I WONDER how you could have the impudence to know where I am. I have this post writ to Mr. Harley, who is just come from Hanover, to desire he would give you a letter. I have described you to him, and told him I would write to you to wait on him, which will do you no hurt neither about your affair in the Treasury. You begin to be an able courtier, which I know from two instances: first for giving me thanks for your preferment, to which I only contributed by saying to Dr. Arbuthnot and Mr. Lewis that I wished it; secondly for wheedling my Lord Treasurer with an epigram, which I like very well, and so I am sure will he, and I reckon you will succeed. But pray learn to be a manager, and pick up language as fast as you can, and get Aristotle upon politics, and read other books upon government, Grotius de Jure Belli et Pacis, and accounts of negotiations and treaties, etc.; and be a perfect master of the Latin, and be able to learn everything of the Court where you go; and keep correspondence with Mr. Lewis, who if you write letters worth showing, will make them serviceable to you with Lord Treasurer; and take Mr. Lewis's advice in all things, and do not despise mine, and so God bless you, and make you able to make my fortunes. I am glad Mr. Pope has made so much despatch. My service to him and the Parnellian.

To John Arbuthnot

Dear BROTHER,

MY stomach is prouder than you imagine, and I scorned to write till I was writ to. I have already half lost the ideas of Courts and Ministers. I dine between twelve and one, and the whole house is abed by ten and up at six. I drink no wine, and see but one dish of meat. I pay a guinea a week for dieting and lodging myself and man with an honest clergyman of my old acquaintance, and my paying is forced, for he has long invited me. I did not know till last night that the Princess Sophia was dead, when my landlord and I chanced to pay a visit to a farmer in a neighbouring village, and was told so over a mug of ale, by a brisk young fellow just come from London, who talked big and looked on us with great contempt. I thank you for your kindness to poor Gay. Was the money paid, or put off till the day after he went? I reckon by what you tell me that it is now a high season to be very merry in Lady Fair's lodgings. I heartily pity you in particular. Look after your mistress and yourself, grow rich, and since nothing better can be done, let the world *vadere*.

I have a mind to live in Yorkshire for a year, in order to put myself out of memory and debt. The fashion of this world passeth away: however, I am angry at those who disperse us sooner than there was need. I have a mind to be very angry, and to let my anger break out in some manner that will not please them at the end of a pen. I wish you could get Lady M[asham] to give you those hints we have often spoke of, and to muster up your own; for the Dragon, I despair he will do that any more than anything else, and indeed you are all of you Dragons more or less, for I am sure it is above three years since I have spoke to Lady M[asham] and you about this. My humble service to my Lord and her, whom I love as much as you do, though I have greater obligations to them, and my humble services and thanks to the Qu[een] of Prudes for remembering me.

You are a set of people drawn almost to the dregs; you must try another game; this is at an end. Your Ministry is fourscore and ten years old, and all you can endeavour at is an euthanasia, or rather it is in a deep consumption at five-and-twenty. I approve Lady M[asham]'s conduct, and think all she can now do in relation to the Dragon is to be passive; for the rest to cultivate her own credit to the utmost. Writing to you much would make me stark mad; judge his condition who has nothing to keep him from being miserable but endeavouring to forget those for whom he has the greatest value, love, and friendship. But you are a philosopher and a physician, and can overcome by your wisdom and your faculty those weaknesses which other men are forced to reduce by not thinking on them. Adieu, and love me half so well as I do you.

To the Earl of Oxford

July 3, 1714.

WHEN I was with you, I have said more than once, that I would never allow quality or station made any real difference between men. Being now absent and forgotten, I have changed my mind. You have a thousand people who can pretend they love you, with as much appearance of sincerity as I, so that according to common justice I can have but a thousandth part in return of what I give. And this difference is wholly owing to your station. And the misfortune is still the greater, because I always loved you just so much the worse for your station. For in your public capacity you have often angered me to the heart, but as a private man, never once. So that if I only looked towards myself, I could wish you a private man to-morrow. For I have nothing to ask, at least nothing that you will give, which is the same thing, and then you would see whether I should not with much more willingness attend you in a retirement, whenever you pleased to give me leave, than ever I did at London or Windsor. From these sentiments I will never write to you, if I can help it, otherwise than as to a private person, nor allow myself to have been obliged by you in any other capacity.

The memory of one great instance of your candour and justice, I will carry to my grave, that having been in a manner domestic with you for almost four years, it was never in the power of any public or concealed enemy, to make you think ill of me, though malice and envy were often employed to that end. If I live, posterity shall know that and more, which, though you, and somebody that shall be nameless, seem to value less than I could wish, is all the return I can make you. Will you give me leave to say how I would desire to stand in your memory; as one, who was truly sensible of the honour you did him, though he was too proud to be vain upon it; as one, who was neither assuming, officious, nor teasing, who never wilfully misrepresented persons or facts to you, nor consulted his passions when he gave a character; and lastly, as one whose indiscretions proceeded altogether from a weak head, and not an ill heart? I will add one thing more, which is the highest compliment I can make, that I never was afraid of offending you, nor am now in any pain for the manner I write to you in. I have said enough; and, like one at your levee, having made my bow, I shrink back into the crowd.

To John Arbuthnot

July 3, 1714.

I RECKONED you would have held up for one letter and so have given over; this is the usual way I treat my best absent friends when I am in London. Did I describe myself in a happy state here? Upon my faith you read wrong: I have no happiness but being so far out of the way of the Dragon and the rest. Lewis reproaches me as one who has still an itch to the Court, only because I asked him how the *summa rerum* went. Was not that unjust? And quotes upon me, *quae lucis miseris tam dira cupido.* I do assert that living near a Court with some circumstances is a most happy life, and would be so still if the Dragon did not spoil it. I find the triumvirate of honest counsellors is at an end; I am gone, Lewis says he lives in ignorance in his castle, and you meddle as little as you can. One thing still lies upon you, which is to be a constant adviser to Lady Masham. The game will of course be played into her hand. She has very good sense, but may be imposed upon. And I had a whisper, that the Squire plies there again. It is as you say, if the Dragon speaks kindly of Parnell, he is gone. It is the Ossorys that get the Derrys and the Chesters the Yorks.

To talk of Martin in any hands but yours, is a folly. You every day give better hints than all of us together could do in a twelvemonth; and to say the truth, Pope who first thought of the hint has no genius at all to it, in my mind. Gay is too young; Parnell has some ideas of it, but is idle; I could put together, and lard, and strike out well enough, but all that relates to the sciences must be from you. I am a vexed un-settled vagabond, and my thoughts are turned towards some papers I have, and some other things I would fain get from you and Lady Masham and would have had from the Dragon, but that is impossible till he is out and then I will go to him to Herefordshire and make him give me hints. I have got my History from Secretary Bromley; and they shall never have it again; and it shall be an altered thing if I live.

The hints you mention relating to medicine are admirable; I wonder how you can have a mind so *degagé* in a Court where there is so many million of things to vex you. You must under-stand, I have writ this post to the Dragon, but you must not take notice of it, nor I fancy will he; for what I writ is very odd and serious. I think to go and ramble for a month about Herefordshire and those parts. Ask the Dragon whether he will order his people at his castle to receive me. Why do you not send your Parliament a grazing? What do you mean by your proclamation and five thousand pounds? Till I hear reasons I dislike your politics. Why do I talk of it say you? Why did that puppy Barber write it to me? But the Commons offer a hundred thousand pounds. If I was the Pretender, I would come over myself and take the money to help to pay my troops. They had better put out a proclamation that whoever discovers the Pretender or the longitude shall have a hundred thousand pounds. This strain is a sacrifice to Hanover, the Whigs, and the Queen's state of health. It will neither satisfy Hanover, silence the Whigs, nor cure the gout. Give him a pension, and oblige him to live beyond the Alps. What is become of your project to make it high treason to bring over foreign troops? I wish a little care was taken for securing the kingdom as well as the succession.

But country politics are doubly insupportable, and so I have done, and retire to lament with my neighbours the want of rain, and dryness of hay. Farmer Tyler says, the white mead at Chawdry has not been so bad in the memory of man, and the summer barley is quite dried up; but we hope to have a pretty good crop of wheat. Parson Hunsdon it is thought must stick to his bargain, but all the neighbours say the attorney was an arrant rogue. We cannot get a bit of good butter for love or money. I could tell you more of the state of our affairs, but doubt your taste is not refined enough for it.

To Viscount Bolingbroke

May, 1719.

My LORD,

I FORGET whether I formerly mentioned to you what I have observed in Cicero, that in some of his letters, while he was in exile, there is a sort of melancholy pleasure, which is wonderfully affecting. I believe the reason must be, that in those circumstances of life there is more leisure for friendship to operate, without any mixture of envy, interest, or ambition. But, I am afraid, this was chiefly when Cicero writ to his brethren in exile, or they to him, because common distress is a great promoter both of friendship and speculation; for, I doubt, prosperity and adversity are too much at variance, ever to suffer a near alliance between their owners.

Friendship, we say, is created by a resemblance of humours. You allow that adversity both taught you to think and reason much otherwise than you did; whereas, I can assure you, that those who contrived to stay at home, and keep what they had, are not changed at all, and if they sometimes drink an absent friend's health, they have fully discharged their duty. I have been, for some time, nursing up an observation, which, perhaps, may be a just one, that no men are used so ill, upon a change of times, as those who acted upon a public view, without regard to themselves. I do not mean from the circumstance of saving more or less money, but because I take it, that the same grain of caution which disposes a man to fill his coffers, will teach him how to preserve them upon all events. And I dare hold a wager that the Duke of Marlborough, in all his campaigns, was never known to lose his baggage. I am heartily glad to hear of that unconditional offer you mention; because I have been taught to believe there is little good-nature to be had from that quarter; and if the offer were sincere I know not why it has not succeeded, since everything is granted that can be asked for, unless there be an exception only for generous and good-natured actions. When I think of you with a relation to Sir Roger, I imagine a youth of sixteen marrying a woman of thirty for love; she decays every year, while he grows up to his prime, and when it is too late, he wonders how he could think of so unequal a match, or what is become of the beauty he was so fond of. I am told, he outdoes himself in every quality for which we used to quarrel with him.

I do not think, that leisure of life, and tranquillity of mind, which fortune and your own wisdom has given you, could be better employed than in drawing up very exact memoirs of those affairs, wherein, to my knowledge, you had the most difficult and weighty part; and I have often thought, in comparing periods of time, there never was a more important one in England than that which made up the four last years of the late Queen. Neither do I think anything could be more entertaining, or useful, than the story of it fully and exactly told, with such observations, in such a spirit, style, and method, as you alone are capable of performing it. One reason why we have so few memoirs written by principal actors, is, because much familiarity with great affairs makes men value them too little; yet such persons will read Tacitus and Commines with wonderful delight. Therefore I must beg two things; first, that you will not omit any passage because you think it of little moment; and secondly, that you will write to an ignorant world, and not suppose your reader to be only of the present age, or to live within ten miles of London. There is nothing more vexes me in old historians, than when they leave me in the dark in some passages which they suppose every one to know. It is this laziness, pride, or incapacity of great men, that has given way to the impertinents of the nation where you are, to pester us with memoirs full of trifling and romance. Let a Frenchman talk twice with a Minister of State, he desires no more to furnish out a volume; and I, who am no Frenchman, despairing ever to see anything of what you tell me, have been some time providing materials for such a work, only upon the strength of having been always amongst you, and used with more kindness and confidence than it often happens to men of my trade and level. But I am heartily glad of so good a reason to think no farther that way, although I could say many things which you would never allow yourself to write. I have already drawn your character at length in one tract, and a sketch of it in another. But I am sensible that when Caesar describes one of his own battles we conceive a greater idea of him from thence, than from all the praises any other writer can give him.

I read your paraphrase with great pleasure; and the goodness of the poetry convinces me of the truth of your philosophy. I agree, that a great part of our wants is imaginary, yet there is a different proportion, even in real want, between one man and another. A King deprived of his kingdom would be allowed to live in real want, although he had ten thousand a year; and the case is parallel in every degree of life. When I reason thus on the case of some absent friends, it frequently takes away all the quiet of my mind. I think it indecent to be merry, or take satisfaction in anything, while those who presided in councils or armies, and by whom I had the honour to be beloved, are either in humble solicitude, or attending, like Hannibal, in foreign Courts, *donec Bithyno libeat vigilare tyranno*. My health, a thing of no moment, is somewhat mended; but, at best, I have an ill head and an aching heart.

Pray God send you soon back to your country in peace and honour, that I may once more see him *cum quo morantem saepe diem fregi, etc.*

To Charles Ford

Dublin. *Decbr.* 8th. 1719

I HAD yours of above six weeks ago, and your last yesterday. I do not think that Men who want their Health, are answerable for Lazyness and Indolence. If they keep the same Affection for their Friends, no more in justice ought to be required. Indeed I fear, when Life grows indifferent every Thing grows so too. I was somewhat recovered from a long Disorder when a pitifull broken shin, which I skillfully cookt up into a sore of Importance, confined me above a Month, and is not yet well, and my want of Exercise under it, has been of ill use to my Head; Thus in Excuse for my Silence, I am forced to entertain you like an old Woman with my Aylments. But your Complaint is not dans les formes. You live in the midst of the World, I wholly out of it, and therefore ought to be the Writer and complain of you. I am very confident, that in the whole year I do not speak to above a dozen Persons, and make choice onely of such with whom it is of no manner of Consequence what I say to them, or what they say to me. When it happens otherwise I am not at my Ease, and that is the true Reason why I cannot think of a Journy to England till I get more Health and Spirits. I will tell you a grievous unhappyness under the Sun, that when Time brings a man to be hard to please, he finds the World less carefull to please him. Which however is less to be wondered at because it is what every man finds in himself. When his Invention decays, his Judgment grows nicer, and thus he is left in the state of those who ruin their Fortunes, and enlarge their Appetites. Take this Philosophy in return of your Apology for writing a word of Politicks. But as the World is now turned, no Cloyster is retired enough to keep Politicks out, and I will own they raise my Passions whenever they come in my way, perhaps more than yours who live amongst them, as a great noise is likelyer to disturb a Hermit than a Citizen.

I began this a week ago, and between disorder and Interruption was not able to finish it. I am heartily glad Mr Dopping has found Benefit by his Journy. It is impossible to describe to you how I have been hindred from accompanying or following him. This silly station I am in engages me in more trifling Business than a high Treasurer, and besides the publick wind is full in my Teeth. But however I will try next Spring what can be done, thô I foresee a foolish Impediment already: But the Truth is, the fear of returning in ten times worse humor than I should go, has been my strongest discouragement, as a prudent Prisoner would not chuse to be a day out of Jayl, if he must certainly go back at night. I here inclose a Letter to Monsr ——— and hope it will not miscarry like the former. I saw a very foolish Pamphlet of Steele's to Lord Oxford without Method Argument or Style, for my own Part I wish the Bill has passt upon Sr James Forbes's Reason: And I remember to have agreed many years ago with some very great men, who thought a Bill for limiting the Prerogative in making Peers would mend the Constitution, but as much as I know of this it was wholly naught, and there is one invincible obvious Argument which Steel lightly touches; That the Lords degenerate by Luxury Idleness &c and the Crown is always forced to govern by new Men. I think Titles should fall with Estates. The ABD (who is half a Tory) seems to be at a Loss what the Bill was intended for, and will not allow the common Reason. I should not be sorry to know what is said on that Subject. If you see Mr. Charleton pray tell him I had his Letter, but have not seen the Doctor he mentions. I hear My Sister O—— has very ill Health, which is an Affliction she does not want. I desire you will present my most humble Service to her and L^d A—— when you see them, and particularly to Mr. L—— D^r. A—— &c, and to M^r. Pope and

Gay.—I write nothing but Verses of late, and they are all Panegyricks.—I like Mr. L——s manner of Life, strolling thro the Kingdom, better than any amongst you.

To Viscount Bolingbroke

December 19, 1719.

My LORD,

I FIRST congratulate with you upon growing rich; for I hope our friend's information is true, *Omne solum diti patria.* Euripides makes the Queen Jocasta ask her exiled son, how he got his victuals. But who ever expected to see you a trader or dealer in stocks? I thought to have seen you where you are, or perhaps nearer; but *diis aliter visum.* It may be with one's country as with a lady; if she be cruel and ill-natured, and will not receive us, we ought to consider that we are better without her. But, in this case, we may add, she has neither virtue, honour, nor justice. I have gotten a mezzotinto, for want of a better, of Aristippus, in my drawing-room. The motto at the top is, *Omnis Aristipum, etc.,* and at the bottom, *Tanta foedus cum gente ferire, commissum juveni.* But, since what I heard of Mississippi, I am grown fonder of the former motto. You have heard that Plato followed merchandise three years, to show he knew how to grow rich, as well as to be a philosopher; and I guess, Plato was then about forty, the period which the Italians prescribe for being wise, in order to be rich at fifty. *Senes ut in otia tuta recedant.*

I have known something of Courts and Ministers longer than you, who knew them so many thousand times better, but I do not remember to have ever heard of, or seen, one great genius, who had long success in the Ministry; and recollecting a great many, in my memory and acquaintance, those who had the smoothest time, were, at best, men of middling degree in understanding. But, if I were to frame a romance of a great

minister's life, he should begin it as Aristippus has done; then
be sent into exile, and employ his leisure in writing the
memoirs of his own administration; then be recalled, invited
to resume his share of power, act as far as was decent; at last
retire to the country, and be a pattern of hospitality, politeness,
wisdom, and virtue. Have you not observed, that there is a
lower kind of discretion and regularity, which seldom fails of
raising men to the highest stations, in the Court, the Church,
and the law? It must be so; for Providence, which designed
the world should be governed by many heads, made it a
business within the reach of common understandings; while
one great genius is hardly found among ten millions. Did you
never observe one of your clerks cutting his paper with a
blunt ivory knife? Did you ever know the knife to fail going
the true way? Whereas, if he had used a razor, or a penknife, he
had odds against him of spoiling a whole sheet. I have twenty
times compared the motion of that ivory implement, to those
talents that thrive best at court. Think upon Lord Bacon,
Williams, Strafford, Laud, Clarendon, Shaftesbury, the last
Duke of Buckingham; and of my own acquaintance, the Earl
of Oxford and yourself, all great geniuses in their several
ways, and, if they had not been so great, would have been less
unfortunate. I remember but one exception, and that was Lord
Somers, whose timorous nature, joined with the trade of a
common lawyer, and the consciousness of a mean extraction,
had taught him the regularity of an alderman, or a gentleman-
usher. But of late years I have been refining upon this thought;
for I plainly see, that fellows of low intellectuals, when they are
gotten at the head of affairs, can sally into the highest ex-
orbitances, with much more safety, than a man of great talents
can make the least step out of the way. Perhaps it is for the
same reason, that men are more afraid of attacking a vicious
than a mettlesome horse; but I rather think it owing to that
incessant envy, wherewith the common rate of mankind pursues
all superior natures to their own. And I conceive, if it were
left to the choice of an ass, he would rather be kicked by
one of his own species, than a better.

If you will recollect that I am towards six years older than when I saw you last, and twenty years duller, you will not wonder to find me abound in empty speculations. I can now express in a hundred words, what would formerly have cost me ten. I can write epigrams of fifty distichs, which might be squeezed into one. I have gone the round of all my stories three or four times with the younger people, and begin them again. I give hints how significant a person I have been, and nobody believes me. I pretend to pity them, but am inwardly angry. I lay traps for people to desire I would show them some things I have written, but cannot succeed; and wreak my spite, in condemning the taste of the people and company where I am. But it is with place, as it is with time. If I boast of having been valued three hundred miles off, it is of no more use than if I told how handsome I was when I was young. The worst of it is, that lying is of no use; for the people here will not believe one half of what is true. If I can prevail on anyone to personate a hearer and admirer, you would wonder what a favourite he grows. He is sure to have the first glass out of the bottle, and the best bit I can carve. Nothing has convinced me so much that I am of a little subaltern spirit, *inopis, atque pusilli animi,* as to reflect how I am forced into the most trifling amusements, to divert the vexation of former thoughts, and present objects. Why cannot you lend me a shred of your mantle, or why did not you leave a shred of it with me when you were snatched from me? You see I speak in my trade, although it is growing fast a trade to be ashamed of.

I cannot but wish that you would make it possible for me to see a copy of the papers you are about; and I do protest it necessary that such a thing should be in some person's hands besides your own, and I scorn to say how safe they would be in mine. Neither would you dislike my censures, as far as they might relate to circumstantials. I tax you with two minutes a-day, until you have read this letter, although I am sensible you have not half so much from business more useful and entertaining.

My letter which miscarried was, I believe, much as edifying as this, only thanking and congratulating with you for the delightful verses you sent me. And I ought to have expressed my vexation, as seeing you so much better a philosopher than myself; a trade you were neither born nor bred to. But I think it is observed that gentlemen often dance better than those that live by the art. You may thank fortune that my paper is no longer, etc.

To Alexander Pope

Dublin, *September* 20, 1723.

SIR,

RETURNING from a summer expedition of four months on account of my health, I found a letter from you, with an appendix longer than yours from Lord Bolingbroke. I believe there is not a more miserable malady than an unwillingness to write letters to our best friends, and a man might be philosopher enough in finding out reasons for it. One thing is clear, that it shows a mighty difference betwixt friendship and love, for a lover, as I have heard, is always scribbling to his mistress. If I could permit myself to believe what your civility makes you say, that I am still remembered by my friends in England, I am in the right to keep myself here. *Non sum qualis eram.* I left you in a period of life when one year does more execution than three at yours, to which if you add the dulness of the air, and of the people, it will make a terrible sum. I have often made the same remark with you of my infelicity in being so strangely attached to traitors, as they call them, and exiles and state criminals. I hope Lord Peterborough, with whom you live at present, is in no danger of any among those characters. I always loved him well; but of late years the few I converse with have not known well how

to describe him. I have no very strong faith in you pretenders
to retirement. You are not of an age for it, nor have gone
through either good or bad fortune enough to go into a corner,
and form conclusions *de contemptu mundi et fuga saeculi,*
unless a poet grows weary of too much applause, as ministers
do of too much weight of business.

Your happiness is greater than your merit, in choosing your
favourites so indifferently among either party. This you owe
partly to your education, and partly to your genius employing
you in an art in which faction has nothing to do, for I suppose
Virgil and Horace are equally read by Whigs and Tories. You
have no more to do with the constitution of Church and
State, than a Christian at Constantinople; and you are so
much the wiser and happier, because both parties will approve
your poetry as long as you are known to be of neither. But
I who am sunk under the prejudices of another education, and
am every day persuading myself that a dagger is at my throat,
a halter about my neck, or chains about my feet, all prepared
by those in power, can never arrive at the serenity of mind you
possess.

Your notions of friendship are new to me; I believe every
man is born with his *quantum,* and he cannot give to one
without robbing another. I very well know to whom I would
give the first places in my friendship, but they are not in the
way. I am condemned to another scene, and therefore I
distribute it in pennyworths to those about me, and who displease me least, and should do the same to my fellow prisoners,
if I were condemned to jail. I can likewise tolerate knaves much
better than fools, because their knavery does me no hurt in
the commerce I have with them, which however I own is more
dangerous, though not so troublesome, as that of fools. I have
often endeavoured to establish a friendship among all men of
genius, and would fain have it done. They are seldom above
three or four contemporaries, and if they could be united,
would drive the world before them. I think it was so among
the poets in the time of Augustus; but envy, and party, and
pride, have hindered it among us. I do not include the

subalterns, of which you are seldom without a large tribe. Under the name of poets and scribblers I suppose you mean the fools you are content to see sometimes, when they happen to be modest, which was not frequent among them while I was in the world.

I would describe to you my way of living, if any method could be called so in this country. I choose my companions among those of least consequence and most compliance. I read the most trifling books I can find, and whenever I write, it is upon the most trifling subjects; but riding, walking, and sleeping take up eighteen of the twenty-four hours. I procrastinate more than I did twenty years ago, and have several things to finish which I put off to twenty years hence.

> *Haec est*
> *Vita solutorum misera ambitione gravique.*

I send you the compliments of a friend of yours, who has passed four months this summer with two grave acquaintance at his country house, without ever once going to Dublin, which is but eight miles distant. Yet when he returns to London, I will engage you shall find him as deep in the Court of Requests, the park, the operas, and the coffee-house, as any man there. I am now with him for a few days.

I am going to write to the person who joined in your letter. We are made to fear that he may not succeed in what will be attempted for him in Parliament, which would leave him in a worse situation than he was before. You must remember me with great affection to Dr. Arbuthnot, Mr. Congreve, and Gay. I think there are no more *eodem tertios* between you and me, except Mr. Jervas, to whose house I address this for want of knowing where you live; for it was not clear from your last whether you lodge with Lord Peterborough, or he with you. I am ever,

                            Your most faithful humble servant.

   I never subscribe my name *et pour cause.*

To Charles Ford

I HAVE been resolving for some time past to go to England about the End of this month, and have lately communicated my Intention to five or six Friends, who are all dissuading me with the greatest Violence, and desire that I would at least defer it till next Year. Their Reasons I do not all approve; because I know very well how apt the People of Ireland are to think that their little Affairs are regarded in England. They would have it that what has been lately written about the Drapier has given great Offence on your side, that the private Malice of the Projector and those who were examined in his Behalf might tempt them to some violent Action of Revenge, and that M^r W—— thinks himself personally offended, and that somebody for whose Advantage that Project was contrived would use all means to prosecute whoever has opposed it, which may end in Messengers heads, Accusations, Imprisonments &c. Now in my own Mind I am quite of another Opinion. I do not think the thing is of Weight enough for a Ministry to trouble themselves about, and as for the Malice of mean paltry Rascals it may be avoyded by common Care. There was a Time when in England some great Friends looked on me as in Danger, and used to warn me against Night walking &c.; but I thought it was a shame to be afraid of such Accidents and looked as if a man affected to be thought of Importance. Neither do I find that Assassinations are things in fashion at present; and in my Opinion a Secretary of State is a much more terrible animal, when he has a mind to be malicious. Our Friend in Grafton Street swears it is a Fatality upon me. In order to their Satisfaction I desire to know your Opinion, whether I may be in any Danger of being teazed at Whitehall, or have Searches for Papers &c. for as to private malice, I very little apprehend it. Pray write me your Thoughts as soon as you can, that I may take my Measures.

Our Friend with the weak Stomach eats less than ever, and
I am in pain about her, and would fain persuade her to go
for England, but she will not. Your People are well, I dined
with them very lately—

Y^r—

To Alexander Pope

September 29, 1725.

SIR,

I CANNOT guess the reason of Mr. Stopford's management, but impute it at a venture to either haste or bashfulness,
in the latter of which he is excessive to a fault, although he
had already gone the tour of Italy and France to harden himself. Perhaps this second journey, and for a longer time, may
amend him. He treated you just as he did Lord Carteret, to
whom I recommended him.

My letter you saw to Lord Bolingbroke has shown you the
situation I am in, and the company I keep, if I do not forget
some of its contents, but I am now returning to the noble
scene of Dublin, into the *grand monde,* for fear of burying my
parts, to signalise myself among curates and vicars, and correct
all corruptions crept in relating to the weight of bread and
butter, through those dominions where I govern. I have
employed my time, besides ditching, in finishing, correcting,
amending, and transcribing my Travels, in four parts complete,
newly augmented, and intended for the press, when the world
shall deserve them, or rather when a printer shall be found
brave enough to venture his ears. I like the scheme of our
meeting after distresses and dispersions; but the chief end I
propose to myself in all my labours is to vex the world rather
than divert it; and if I could compass that design, without
hurting my own person or fortune, I would be the most indefatigable writer you have ever seen, without reading. I am
exceedingly pleased that you have done with translations.

Lord Treasurer Oxford often lamented that a rascally world should lay you under a necessity of misemploying your genius for so long a time. But since you will now be so much better employed, when you think of the world give it one lash the more at my request. I have ever hated all nations, professions, and communities, and all my love is toward individuals: for instance, I hate the tribe of lawyers, but I love Counsellor Such-a-one, and Judge Such-a-one: so with physicians—I will not speak of my own trade—soldiers, English, Scotch, French, and the rest. But principally I hate and detest that animal called man, although I heartily love John, Peter, Thomas, and so forth. This is the system upon which I have governed myself many years, but do not tell, and so I shall go on till I have done with them. I have got materials toward a treatise, proving the falsity of that definition *animal rationale,* and to show it would be only *rationis capax.* Upon this great foundation of misanthropy, though not in Timon's manner, the whole building of my Travels is erected; and I never will have peace of mind till all honest men are of my opinion. By consequence you are to embrace it immediately, and procure that all who deserve my esteem may do so too. The matter is so clear that it will admit of no dispute; nay, I will hold a hundred pounds that you and I agree in the point.

I did not know your Odyssey was finished, being yet in the country, which I shall leave in three days. I shall thank you kindly for the present, but shall like it three-fourths the less, from the mixture you mention of another hand; however, I am glad you saved yourself so much drudgery. I have been long told by Mr. Ford of your great achievements in building and planting, and especially of your subterranean passage to your garden, whereby you turned a blunder into a beauty, which is a piece of *ars poetica.*

I have almost done with harridans, and shall soon become old enough to fall in love with girls of fourteen. The lady whom you describe to live at court, to be deaf, and no party woman, I take to be mythology, but know not how to moralise it. She cannot be Mercy, for Mercy is neither deaf, nor lives at Court. Justice is blind, and perhaps deaf, but neither is she a Court lady. Fortune is both blind and deaf, and a Court lady, but then she is a most damnable party woman, and will never make me easy, as you promise. It must be Riches, which answers all your description. I am glad she visits you, but my voice is so weak that I doubt she will never hear me.

Mr. Lewis sent me an account of Dr. Arbuthnot's illness, which is a very sensible affliction to me, who, by living so long out of the world, have lost that hardness of heart contracted by years and general conversation. I am daily losing friends, and neither seeking nor getting others. Oh! if the world had but a dozen Arbuthnots in it, I would burn my Travels. But, however, he is not without fault. There is a passage in Bede highly commending the piety and learning of the Irish in that age, where, after abundance of praises he overthrows them all, by lamenting that, alas! they kept Easter at a wrong time of the year. So our Doctor has every quality and virtue that can make a man amiable or useful; but, alas! he has a sort of slouch in his walk. I pray God protect him, for he is an excellent Christian, though not a Catholic, and as fit a man either to live or die as ever I knew.

I hear nothing of our friend Gay, but I find the Court keeps him at hard meat. I advised him to come over here with a Lord Lieutenant. Mr. Tickell is in a very good office. I have not seen Philips, though formerly we were so intimate. He has got nothing and by what I find will get nothing, though he writes little flams, as Lord Leicester called those sorts of verses, on Miss Carteret. It is remarkable, and deserves recording that a Dublin blacksmith, a great poet, has imitated his manner in a poem to the same Miss. Philips is a complainer, and on this occasion I told Lord Carteret that complainers never succeed at Court, though railers do.

Are you altogether a country gentleman, that I must address to you out of London, to the hazard of your losing this precious letter, which I will now conclude, although so much paper is left. I have an ill name, and therefore shall not subscribe it, but you will guess it comes from one who esteems and loves you about half as much as you deserve, I mean as much as he can.

I am in great concern, at what I am just told is in some of the newspapers, that Lord Bolingbroke is much hurt by a fall in hunting. I am glad he has so much youth and vigour left, of which he has not been thrifty, but I wonder he has no more discretion.

To Alexander Pope

February 7, 1735-6.

IT is some time since I dined at the Bishop of Derry's, where Mr. Secretary Carey told me, with great concern, that you were taken very ill. I have heard nothing since, only I have continued in great pain of mind, yet for my own sake and the world's more than for yours; because I well know how little you value life, both as a philosopher, and a Christian, particularly the latter, wherein hardly one in a million of us heretics can equal you. If you are well recovered, you ought to be reproached for not putting me especially out of pain, who could not bear the loss of you; although we must be for ever distant as much as if I were in the grave, for which my years and continual indisposition are preparing me every season. I have stayed too long from pressing you to give me some ease by an account of your health. Pray do not use me so ill any more. I look upon you as an estate from which I receive my best annual rents, although I am never to see it. Mr. Tickell was at the same meeting under the same real concern, and so were a hundred others of this town who had never seen you.

I read to the Bishop of Derry the paragraph in your letter which concerned him, and his Lordship expressed his thankfulness in a manner that became him. He is esteemed here as a person of learning, and conversation, and humanity; but he is beloved by all people. He is a most excessive Whig, but without any appearing rancour, and his idol is King William; besides three thousand a year is an invincible sweetener.

I have nobody now left but you. Pray to be so kind as to outlive me, and then die as soon as you please, but without pain; and let us meet in a better place, if my religion will permit, but rather my virtue, although much unequal to yours. Pray let my Lord Bathurst know how much I love him. I still insist on his remembering me, although he is too much in the world to honour an absent friend with his letters. My state of health is not to boast of; my giddiness is more or less too constant; I have not an ounce of flesh between skin and bone; I sleep ill, and have a poor appetite. I can as easily write a poem in the Chinese language as my own. I am as fit for matrimony as invention; and yet I have daily schemes for innumerable essays in prose, and proceed sometimes to no less than half a dozen lines, which the next morning become waste paper. What vexes me most is, that my female friends, who could bear me very well a dozen years ago, have now forsaken me, although I am not so old in proportion to them, as I formerly was, which I can prove by arithmetic, for then I was double their age, which now I am not.

Pray put me out of fear as soon as you can, about that ugly report of your illness; and let me know who this Cheselden is, that has so lately sprung up in your favour. Give me also some account of your neighbour who writ to me from Bath. I hear he resolves to be strenuous for taking off the Test, which grieves me extremely, from all the unprejudiced reasons I ever was able to form, and against the maxims of all wise Christian governments, which always had some established religion, leaving at best a toleration to others. Farewell, my dearest friend, ever, and upon every account that can create friendship and esteem.

Rinehart Editions